SAUDI ARABIA AND INDONESIAN NETWORKS

SAUDI ARABIA AND INDONESIAN NETWORKS

Migration, Education, and Islam

Sumanto Al Qurtuby

I.B. TAURIS
LONDON • NEW YORK • OXFORD • NEW DELHI • SYDNEY

I.B. TAURIS
Bloomsbury Publishing Plc
50 Bedford Square, London, WC1B 3DP, UK
1385 Broadway, New York, NY 10018, USA
29 Earlsfort Terrace, Dublin 2, Ireland

BLOOMSBURY, I.B. TAURIS and the Diana logo are trademarks of
Bloomsbury Publishing Plc

First published in Great Britain 2020
Paperback edition published 2021

Copyright © Sumanto Al Qurtuby 2020

Sumanto Al Qurtuby has asserted his right under the Copyright, Designs and Patents Act, 1988, to be identified as Editor of this work.

For legal purposes the Acknowledgments on p. viii constitute an extension of this copyright page.

Cover design: Adriana Brioso

Cover image: King of Saudi Arabia Salman bin Abdulaziz Al Saud (L) with Indonesian President Joko Widodo (R) at the Presidential Palace in Bogor, Indonesia on March 1, 2017. (© Bandar Algaloud / Saudi Kingdom Council / Handout/Anadolu Agency/Getty Images)

All rights reserved. No part of this publication may be reproduced or transmitted in any form or by any means, electronic or mechanical, including photocopying, recording, or any information storage or retrieval system, without prior permission in writing from the publishers.

Bloomsbury Publishing Plc does not have any control over, or responsibility for, any third-party websites referred to or in this book. All internet addresses given in this book were correct at the time of going to press. The author and publisher regret any inconvenience caused if addresses have changed or sites have ceased to exist, but can accept no responsibility for any such changes.

A catalogue record for this book is available from the British Library.

A catalog record for this book is available from the Library of Congress.

ISBN HB: 978-1-8386-0220-8
       PB: 978-0-7556-4502-2
       eISBN: 978-1-8386-0223-9
       ePDF: 978-1-8386-0222-2

Typeset by Integra Software Services Pvt. Ltd.

To find out more about our authors and books visit www.bloomsbury.com and sign up for our newsletters.

To the loving memory of my father, to my mentor, Professor Augustus Richard Norton, and to Professor Peter Sluglett

CONTENTS

Acknowledgments	viii
INTRODUCTION	1
Chapter 1 SAUDI ARABIAN–INDONESIAN RELATIONS	25
Chapter 2 SAUDI INFLUENCES ON INDONESIAN ISLAM AND SOCIETY	53
Chapter 3 SAUDI ARABIA AS A CENTER OF LEARNING AND EDUCATION FOR INDONESIANS	87
Chapter 4 INDONESIAN ISLAMIC SCHOLARS, TEACHERS, AND SCIENTISTS IN SAUDI ARABIA	111
Chapter 5 INDONESIAN STUDENTS IN CONTEMPORARY SAUDI ARABIA	137
Chapter 6 SAUDI ARABIA-TRAINED INDONESIAN ISLAMIC SCHOLARS AND ACTIVISTS: CONSERVATIVE AND PROGRESSIVE	161
CONCLUSION	191
Glossary	197
Notes	204
Bibliography	214
Index	226

ACKNOWLEDGMENTS

The birth of this book, at first, was driven by my "intellectual anxiety" at the extreme lack of academic work and publications that discuss the history and contemporary developments of intellectual, educational connections between Saudi Arabia and Indonesia. This lack of scholarships for sure is an "irony" and unpleasant news in part because people in the Arabian Peninsula and the Indonesian archipelago have a long established connection and, in fact, each has made significant contributions to the other related to culture, religion, education, and Islamic learning in particular.

To my knowledge, Azyumardi Azra, an eminent Indonesian historian of Islam, is perhaps the first scholar to have written an academic work on this topic, titled *The Origins of Islamic Reformism in Southeast Asia: Networks of Malay-Indonesian and Middle Eastern Ulama in the Seventeenth and Eighteenth Centuries* (2004), which seems to be a revised version of his 1992 doctoral thesis at Columbia University, United States. Due to this lack of scholarly works, I was keen to conduct research and write a book on this subject. This book benefited greatly from the invaluable input of the anonymous reviewers whose detailed comments, suggestions, and criticism were enormously useful when it came to making the final round of revisions.

In the years that it has taken for this book to come to fruition, I have owed a great many debts to some people and academic institutions. First of all, it has been a great privilege to have had the opportunity to be a faculty member in the Department of Global and Social Studies (formerly General Studies Department) at King Fahd University of Petroleum and Minerals (KFUPM) at Dhahran, Saudi Arabia, so that I could spend years teaching Arab (mostly Saudi) students, conducting field research across the kingdom, and writing academic work on multiple topics. This book possibly would not have come into being if I did not teach at KFUPM. Accordingly, I owe my debt of gratitude to this university. The initial research project, which has contributed some of the findings used in this book, was also funded by the Deanship of Scientific Research at KFUPM through the Junior Faculty Research Grant.

I also owe a very special thanks to the Middle East Institute, National University of Singapore, which provided me with generous support during the writing stage of this manuscript. The Institute granted me a Visiting Senior Research Fellowship in the summers of 2016 and 2017 so that I could complete this monograph. Special gratitude, in particular, goes to the late Professor Peter Sluglett (1943–2017), a very humble scholar of Islam and a specialist of the Middle East studies who was the institute's director at the time. He showed me a short cut to get to the cheap markets and to take a bus from and to the university's faculty housing compound.

I had been fortunate to have met and discussed many issues related to the Middle East with him. Accordingly, I was truly shocked to hear of his sudden death during my stay at the institute. Due to this reason, this book will be dedicated, among others, to his loving memory.

Moreover, I want to express my deepest thanks to Professor Engseng Ho, the current Director of the Middle East Institute and Muhammad Alagil Distinguished Visiting Professor of Arabia Asia Studies at the Asia Research Institute, National University of Singapore, as well as Professor of Anthropology and History at Duke University, for his support and encouragement. Professor Ho has been instrumental in shaping the academic foundations and arguments of this book, as well as in co-sponsoring its publication. At the Middle East Institute, he organized two events (a mini-workshop and a public lecture) to discuss the book manuscript in order to get feedback from colleagues and audience. He also provided me with helpful comments and suggestions on an earlier draft of this manuscript.

I would also like to express my gratitude to Michelle Teo, the institute's deputy director, who was also heartening and supportive on the project. Thanks also to my former vibrant colleagues at the institute who shared their knowledge, experience, ideas, and joy: Madawi Al-Rasheed, Toby Dodge, Jeremy Kingsley, Zoltan Pall, Nisha Mathew, Mattia Tomba, Victor Kattan, Shuang Wen, and Fannar Haddad. At the institute, I am also thankful to Rozita Bte Ahmad, Helen Yeo, and Rommel Hernando for providing the organizational and technical support during my fellowship year. At the National University of Singapore, I also would like to thank colleagues at the Asia Research Institute, particularly Michelle Ann Miller, Amelia Fauzia, and Tay Minghua, who organized a public lecture on Indonesian students in the Arab Middle East so that I received helpful comments from a wider audience.

At I.B. Tauris/Bloomsbury Publishing, I would like to express my special thanks to Sophie Rudland, editor of the Middle East Studies and Islamic Studies, who has been in contact with me since the initial book proposal, for her fine counsel, support, and feedback. In the Department of Global and Social Studies, furthermore, I would like to thank my energetic colleagues for their intellectual support, cheers, and collegiality, particularly Shafi Aldamer (the department's chair), Mark C. Thompson, Simeon Magliveras, Tarik Abdlrheem, Muhammad Mughal, and Gregory Bonn. Mark Thompson, in particular, has been instrumental in introducing me to I.B. Tauris. As an expert of Saudi Arabia, Mark Thompson has also been a good partner of discussions on issues related to the kingdom's cultures, politics, and societies.

I am also indebted to my research assistants, especially Aditia Rifai (King Fahd University of Petroleum and Minerals), Zia ul Haramein (Islamic University of Medina), and Azwar Hakiem (Imam Muhammad Ibn Saud Islamic University), for their assistance during the fieldwork and data gathering in Saudi Arabia. Thanks also to numerous Indonesian students in Saudi Arabia whom I cannot mention all here (my apologies) for their willingness to participate in the questionnaire survey as well as to share and talk with me about their ideas, knowledge, and experiences.

Last but not least, I, as always, would like to express my profound appreciation to Professor Robert Hefner at Boston University, my great *guru* (teacher), mentor, and friend, who has become a never-ending source of intellectual inspiration. Thanks also to other intellectual mentors, teachers, friends, and supporters of mine: Professors Augustus Richard Norton, Scott Appleby, Houchang Chehabi, Robert Weller, Thomas Barfield, Nancy Smith-Hefner, Jenny White, Charles Lindholm, David Cortright, John Paul Lederach, Lawrence Yoder, Lisa Schirch, Dave Brubaker, R. Michael Feener, and Ariel Heryanto, among others. My apologies for any misspelling and for those not mentioned in this brief list.

Greatest of all, my debt of appreciation goes to my strongest supporters: my wife and my parents (especially my mother who, since the death of my father, has been living alone in a small village in the highland of Central Java, Indonesia), in whom I could always find consolation in the disparate times and the inspiration to keep on working. I would not have made it this far without them. My lovely wife Asri N. Wahyuningsih and my beautiful daughter Victoria Astra Nawa have always encouraged and supported my journey, career, study, research, and writing. Many thanks for your patience, devotion, and love.

Jabal Dhahran, Arabian Peninsula

INTRODUCTION

Since September 2001's terrorist attacks on the Pentagon and the World Trade Center in the United States, many international observers, political analysts, religious scholars and pundits, and mass media have dubbed Saudi Arabia, while neglecting contributions of other countries, a major source of global terrorism, militancy, and radicalism (see, e.g., Abuza 2002, 2003; Gunaratna 2002; Gold 2003; Lewis 2003, 2004; Schwartz 2003; Spencer 2004). As one of the world's primary, if not the world's primary, centers of Islam, views on Saudi Arabia will certainly affect those on other Muslim-majority nations across the globe. In effect, many people throughout the world erroneously see "the house of Islam" via the "room of Saudi." While it may be accurate to observe Saudi's role in producing militancy in the past, it is misleading to see contemporary Saudi as a home of intolerance, extremism, radicalism, and terrorism.

In contrast to the negative images portrayed by foreign observers, commentators, and the media, this book discusses how Saudi Arabia has served as a vital, vigorous center for learning and schooling and a major source for knowledge, sciences, and wisdom for Muslims across the world; thereby it will undoubtedly help create a constructive portrayal about Islam, Saudi, and Muslim societies more generally. In fact, Saudi is the world's fifth favorite travel and transnational migrant destination, and people come for various reasons, ranging from occupation to education, even though many political observers, religious scholars, think-tank institutions, and international media outlets have routinely characterized the kingdom as being "the most religiously fanatical, socially conservative, and politically oppressive" (Johnson 2010: 2).

How can a social scientist, observer, or a researcher explain such a paradox?

What is the book about?

This book, in general, is about Muslim travel, an unexpectedly complex subject. In particular, the book is about *rihla*, here defined as a sojourn in the pursuit of knowledge (science and wisdom) within the Islamic tradition. It is imperative to note that Muslim migration for study and education is not a new phenomenon. It has taken place since the early phases of Islamic formation in the seventh century.

Accordingly, the journey for learning and pursuing sciences (*thalab al-ilm*) has become the norm and tradition within Muslim societies across the globe, including Indonesia, the world's largest Muslim-majority country with some 89 percent of its nearly 260 million people professing Islam.

For centuries, many Muslims in this archipelagic country have traveled in search of knowledge, science, and wisdom at multiple centers of Islamic learning from place to place, from region to region within the archipelago, or even sojourned overseas—from the Middle East and North/West Africa to the Western and Asian regions, a tradition that still continues today. In Islam, as Shalabi (1954: 182–83) aptly puts it, travel is untrammeled. Although Indonesian Muslim students have conducted *rihla* to many different parts of the world, Saudi Arabia, in addition to Egypt, has been a particularly important niche for them. The two countries have long been sources of learning, knowledge, spirituality, and religious wisdom for many Muslims in the world.

Throughout history, many Indonesian Muslims have also studied Islamic sciences in these two countries. However, in recent decades, a sizable number of Indonesian Muslims have learned Islam from multiple perspectives and disciplines at universities outside Egypt and Saudi such as Malaysia, Turkey, Sudan, Morocco, the United States, Australia, and several countries in Europe. Some study Islam in various universities in Singapore, Japan, China, or even Taiwan and Russia. Study has become possible in these places due to generous support from the Indonesian government, and international governments and institutions that have provided multiple types of scholarships, ranging from undergraduate to master and doctoral students. For instance, via the "5,000 Doctors" program the government, through the Indonesian Ministry of Religious Affairs, provided scholarships to Muslim lecturers of Islamic universities and colleges throughout Indonesia for further study overseas in any discipline, not limited to the Islamic sciences, at graduate levels, especially doctorate studies.

The "conventional wisdom" of Muslim travel in search of knowledge is that particular Islamic doctrines and teachings prescribe certain kinds of travel and that the ritual movement of Muslims leads to a heightened identification with Islam and with fellow Muslims. In reality, however, as this book shows, Muslim travel for learning is not simply about learning and it is not solely motivated by the Islamic doctrine of learning and education. There are indeed multiple factors and motives for a Muslim who sojourns in search of knowledge from past to present. In other words, travel in search of knowledge is not merely about pursuing knowledge and the sciences but also about other things, such as social status, privilege, position, amulets, networks, relationships, trade, leisure, and pilgrimage, among others.

This book tries to understand the complexity of travel, particularly *rihla*, among Indonesian[1] Muslims. It studies the links between Islam, migration, and education through the lens of Indonesian Muslims who have studied or taught in Saudi Arabia, including Hijaz in the past.[2] More generally, the book focuses on the study of the origins, history, and contemporary development of Saudi–Indonesian contact and analyzes factors that have contributed to the shifting nature of relations. More specifically, this work examines Indonesian Muslim educational travelers and intellectual migrants—for example, students, teachers, researchers, and scholars of both Islamic and secular sciences—in Saudi Arabia, highlighting their motives and the purposes of their study, teaching, or search of knowledge and (religious or secular) sciences, activities during their study or teaching at madrasah, schools, and universities as well as intellectual and institutional networks.

The book does not only examine the activities of these educational travelers during their stay or life in Saudi, it also investigates their impacts, activities, influences, and contributions in Indonesia in shaping the country's Islamic knowledge, discourses, and understandings. The research findings suggest that Saudi universities, colleges, and other Islamic learning institutes, where Indonesian Muslims have studied, have produced multiple types of graduates, ranging from conservative and radical to moderate and liberal. While many, if not most, scholars tend to overemphasize the role of Saudi clerics, teachers, and learning institutions in transforming Indonesian students into conservative and radical graduates, this study suggests that Indonesian conservative and radical alumni are not necessarily shaped by Saudi teachers, clerics, and educational centers, in part because many of the students had been radical and conservative before starting to study in Saudi Arabia.

Also, as this book suggests, many Indonesian students in Saudi actually have been radicalized by the Indonesian Muslim community in the kingdom. Some Indonesian conservative communities have Islamic study clubs and groups in various cities in the kingdom that regularly run social gatherings, religious sermons (Indonesian: *pengajian*), and Qur'anic studies. Indonesian students, besides workers and expats along with their families, have been devout participants of these religious events. Equally important, many Indonesian graduates have been moderate and liberal before departing Saudi for further study in the Islamic sciences or have been formed by Indonesian moderate Muslim groups in the kingdom. There is a tendency to believe that Indonesian Muslim students will form groups with those of similar ideological and organizational backgrounds; accordingly, conservatives will tend to group with conservatives, moderates with moderates, and so forth. Students with membership of Indonesia's puritanical (or traditional, modernist, moderate, and others) Muslim organizations will tend to gather and make a club with those of a similar background. It is also vital to underline that even though Indonesian students study in Saudi Arabia, this does not mean that they learn Islam under the guidance of Saudi teachers and clerics. They might study Islam in Saudi Arabia with scholars or teachers from Egypt, Sudan, Yemen, India, Pakistan, Jordan, Turkey, and other countries, who teach at Saudi educational institutions. This is to say that Saudi influences on Indonesians who study in Saudi learning institutions are not as dramatically transformative as is often assumed.

Moreover, the alumni do not only pursue jobs in Islamic schools and universities, becoming school teachers or university lecturers (or owners of educational institutions), or in mosques, becoming Islamic preachers or imams, but also in political parties, parliaments, governments, business enterprises, social organizations, and many others. In fact, many alumni of Saudi institutions have become bureaucrats, ministers, politicians, social activists, or businessmen.

It is imperative to note that, historically, the role of Saudi alumni (in addition to Egyptian graduates) has been influential in the formation and development of Indonesia's Muslim politics and cultures, including in the field of education, and their vital role continues today. Examining the shifting dynamics and transformation of the idea of Islamic education and cultures through the lens of those students' and alumni's thoughts and activities is fundamental since they have served as the carriers, transformers, and transmitters who have functioned as the agents of knowledge and the vehicles of change for the notions of science and knowledge. As discussed in this book, in the past, Indonesian disciples pursued merely Islamic knowledge and sciences, whereas contemporary Indonesian students are more diverse, not only studying the Islamic sciences but also science, engineering, and technology.

By examining their complex thoughts and activities, we will know how the process of knowledge production and cultural reproduction of Islamic education and cultures takes place in different times and social settings. Anthropologist Dale Eickelman (1992) calls this approach social biography. It allows a researcher to explore the themes of their study in contextual detail without losing sight of more general issues of historical and social thought.

In brief, this book studies the following main issues and themes:

- The bilateral relationship between Saudi Arabia and Indonesia, placing the contemporary development of their mutual relationships and cooperation into historical context, with religion, education, and occupation in addition to politics and business as the central motives for driving people of both nations to make contact and establish productive mutual relations. In this regard, the book depicts not only formal political economic relationships but also informal cultural, educational, and religious relations between the two countries. The book argues that although socioreligious and people-to-people interactions are vital to these relationships, these are not the only factors in the inherently pragmatic contemporary relationship between Saudi Arabia and Indonesia, which is built increasingly on the basis of national interests.
- The complex role of Saudi's Islamic educational institutions (formal or informal) in shaping thoughts and practices of Indonesian students and alumni. The book shows that, in contrast with popular opinion and assumption, Saudi Islamic centers of learning do not always produce conservatism, fanaticism, and extremism among their graduates since there is a great deal of Indonesian alumni of Saudi institutions that have been the vanguard of moderation, tolerance, and democracy. There are indeed multiple factors that contribute to the shape of conservatism or moderation among Indonesian students; thereby, putting too much emphasis on the role of Saudi institution is a true oversimplification. In fact, many Indonesians have become conservative, following particular forms of strict Salafism and Islamism, long before their departure to Saudi Arabia. Indonesian organizational and educational institutions, such as DDII (Dewan Dakwah Islam Indonesia), al-Irshad, Persis (Persatuan Islam), al-Wahdah, Pesantren

Gontor, Islamic Center Bin Baz, Darun Najah, Al-Birr, among others, have contributed to the shape of conservatism among Indonesian students. Also, Indonesian Salafi groups and networks in Saudi have played a central role in changing and transforming some students to conservatism, fanaticism, and militantism. Equally important, the book examines Saudi contributions and influences in the modern history of Indonesian Islam and Islamic education, and discusses Indonesian responses toward these influences and dynamics.

- The intellectual trajectory of Indonesian scholars, scientists, teachers, and students (educational travelers and migrants) in Saudi Arabia from past to present. The book shows the ups and downs of Indonesian travelers and migrants traveling to Saudi for learning and education. While in the past there was a large number of Indonesian Muslim students and Islamic scholars in Saudi Arabia, which reached its peak in the nineteenth and early twentieth centuries, there has been a decline in their presence in the kingdom since the 1970s and 1980s for multiple reasons. However, in the last two decades or so, there has been a new wave of Indonesians who study or teach in the kingdom, namely those who study or teach non-Islamic studies and sciences such as hard sciences, engineering, computer science, medicine, geosciences, and other subjects. Equally important, this book examines the emergence (and re-emergence), development, and collapse of Indonesian schools in Mecca, or Hijaz more broadly. Plus, it identifies learning centers or educational institutions (madrasah, mosques, or informal learning places such as *halaqah* and *ribat*, and formal universities) for Indonesians in the past and in the contemporary era.

Scholarship shortcomings on rihla

Themes studied in this book are undoubtedly significant. However, scholarship on these topics is still rare. Eickelman and Piscatori state: "The role of travel in Muslim societies and in Islamic doctrine is not a topic which has been systematically explored by historians and social scientists" (1990: xvi). Although there are some studies of Muslim pilgrimage or migration and transnationalism, only a few are devoted to the study of *rihla* in Islamic doctrine and Muslim history (e.g., Abaza 1994; Touati 2010).

Equally important, there is no single study so far that exhaustively examines Indonesian Muslim educational travelers and intellectual migrants in Saudi Arabia and their impact and influences in Indonesia upon finishing their studies. There is also no single study available in English that documents the social biographies of Indonesian alumni of Saudi educational institutions and their contributions to Indonesian society. Most studies on Indonesian migrants in Saudi (and other Gulf countries) are more interested in the investigation of menial workers such as laborers, drivers, housemaids, and shopkeepers, who live and work in harsh informal economic sectors. Moreover, given the overwhelming influx of and issues on menial workers, especially women migrants abroad, it is unsurprising if researchers, scholars, and social scientists of Indonesia have given more emphasis to examining and analyzing domestic female workers than educational-intellectual migrant groups.

Until now, Indonesian educational travelers (teachers, scholars, researchers, and students) are a largely unreported and under-researched diaspora in Arab countries and the Middle East, despite the fact that this group has played a vital role in shaping the country's Islamic education, cultures, and public discourses. A narrow emphasis on "unskilled" menial laborers and domestic female workers hence neglects the vitality of Saudi Arabia or the Middle East more generally as a strategic target for realizing Islamic educational dreams, religious purposes, entrepreneurial ambitions, and middle-class aspirations.

Some scholars and researchers of Indonesians in Saudi Arabia, with a few notable exceptions, are more interested in studying and conducting research on this unskilled migrant group than educational travelers. As well, most academic studies and analyses tend to focus on—and overemphasize—the destructive issues of the former group while neglecting the constructive contributions of the latter. The negative perceptions on Indonesia and Saudi Arabia today concerning issues of Indonesian migrant workers are due to the changing nature of Indonesian migrants and transnationals—from educational travelers to menial laborers— and the lack of scholarships and reportages on the constructive contact between the two countries and on the productive contributions of Indonesian teachers, scholars, and students.

Scholars usually discuss issues such as transnational connection of migration, domestication of laborers, gendered work, the workers' economic contributions for their families, and the exploitation of workers, among others (see, for instance, Silvey 2004a, 2004b, 2006, 2007). More specifically, research and scholarship typically discuss female housemaids in relation to issues of hard working or living conditions, human rights violation, sexual assault, non payment of wages, overwork, or their roles in supporting their family expenses and economies in their country of origin.[3]

Other previous studies and existing literature focusing on Indonesians in Saudi Arabia or the links between Indonesia and Saudi Arabia are concerned about the enormous influences of Mecca-trained Islamic scholars in the past that have contributed to the shape of Islamic teachings, discourses, and Muslim practices in the Malay-Indonesian archipelago. The noted historian of Indonesian Islam Azyumardi Azra (1992, 2004) has examined the transmission of Islamic reformation to Indonesia by examining intellectual networks of the Middle Eastern (particularly Haramain) and the Indonesian Malay ulama in the seventeenth and eighteenth centuries. He argues, among other things, that Mecca-trained Indonesian religious scholars had contributed to the shape of particular Islamic discourses and religious practices in the archipelago. Following Azra's fine study, Basri (1997) investigated Indonesian ulama in the Haramain and the transmission of reformist Islam in Indonesia from 1800 to 1990, while Rachman (1997) examined the contributions of Mecca-trained Indonesian Islamic scholars

(Javanese: *kiais*) for the establishment of Java's oldest and respected Islamic boarding schools (known as "pesantren") during the 1850s–1950s.

Last but not least, the previous studies emphasize the role of Saudi-trained Indonesian Muslim students and scholars in the introduction, spread, and growth of the so-called Salafi *da'wa* movement and some forms of puritanical and reformist Islam in Indonesia. It is obvious that in recent years, particularly after the downfall of dictatorial Indonesian President Suharto in 1998, the country has witnessed the appearance of young men wearing long beards (*lihya*), Arab-style flowing robes (*jalabiyya* or *thawab* in Saudi), turbans (*imama*), and trousers right to their ankles (*isbal*). Not only men, today's Indonesia has witnessed women wearing an *abaya*-type black cloak (a robe-like dress), along with *niqab* (a face veil covering all but the eyes; part of the sartorial hijab).

Identifying themselves as Salafis, these particular Muslim groups are inclined to stand distinctly apart from societies around them. At first, the Salafi movement adopted a stance of apolitical quietism, but in recent years, the Salafis have introduced a new trend in Islamic activism in the country (see, e.g., Hasan 2005: 263–81). Indeed, the growth of Salafism in Indonesia, along with other countries, cannot be separated from the role played by Saudi alumni. However, it should be noted that Indonesian students in Saudi Arabia vary, not only between those of the Islamic sciences and the other secular and social sciences. Even though a student may have studied the Islamic sciences in Saudi Arabia, it does not mean that they automatically follow a strict form of Islam or Salafism.

The bottom line of—and among the reasons behind—this book is to provide a balanced picture and analysis of Indonesian transnational migrants and educational travelers in Saudi Arabia in order to comprehend the variety and density of these groups and their activities, practices, motives, and networks. This book will complement and fill the gap left by previous and existing scholarship on Saudi–Indonesian relations, Indonesians in Saudi Arabia, and the role of Saudi-trained Indonesian Muslims in Indonesia.

Theorizing Muslim travel

There are several types of travel in Islam, namely *hajj* and *umra* (both mean a pilgrimage to Mecca), *hijra* (i.e., migration to other lands for religious, economic, and political reasons), *ziyara* (i.e., visits to shrines and sacred sites), and *rihla* (i.e., travel for learning or educational travel, either religious or secular in nature). As depicted earlier, this book focuses on the study of rihla, namely the links between travel and learning in a Muslim society, particularly Indonesians. Before explaining the notion of rihla and its links to the practices of learning and seeking knowledge among Muslim societies, it is central to describe briefly the ideas of hajj, umra, hijra, and ziyara in Islam as well as some basic theoretical concepts and questions that underline Muslim travel.

Hajj is an annual pilgrimage to Mecca,[4] the most holy city for Muslim's in the world, where Kaaba and Masjid al-Haram, Islam's two most sacred sites, are located. According to Islam, hajj (lit. "to intend a journey") is a mandatory religious obligation for Muslims, which must be carried out at least once in their lifetime by all adult Muslims who are physically and financially capable of undertaking the pilgrimage and can support their family during their absence. Those who are physically and financially limited (e.g., the poor, the elderly, the sick, disable persons) are not required to perform hajj since this pilgrimage needs extra-equipment (e.g., health and wealth). However, in practice, many Muslims across the globe, including those from Indonesia, perform hajj or, at least, umra, although on many occasions they are physically weak and financially restricted (see, for example, Torrance 1930; Tangban 1991; Douwes and Kaptein 1997; DeHanas 2013). Many of them conduct hajj (or umra) after selling their most valuable treasure and property: land, cattle, or even house. They insist on doing so because, for them, hajj is considered the most important worship, ritual practice, and religious journey in Islam that guarantees the believer who performs the hajj entry to paradise in the afterlife.

The hajj is as old as Islam itself. It was instigated by Prophet Muhammad some 1,400 years ago and regularly takes place during the first two weeks of the last month of the Islamic calendar. The hajj itself is a symbol of Muslim solidarity and a mark of submission to God (Allah SWT). Like the hajj, *umra* is also a pilgrimage to Mecca. However, in contrast to the hajj, umra (lit. "a visit to a populated area") is not compulsory, although highly recommended for a Muslim who is capable, physically and financially. As well, unlike hajj, which is performed only once a year in the month Dhulhijjah in the Hijri calendar, umra can be undertaken numerous times and at any time of the year. Sometimes umra is called a "minor pilgrimage" or "lesser pilgrimage," while hajj is the major one. In other words, umra is a "small hajj."

Both hajj and umra connote the outward act of travel and the inward act of intentions at the same time. In the words of Delaney (1990: 513–30), the hajj (and umra alike) is a mixture of sacred and secular practices, meaning that, for Muslims, performing hajj is not simply about "worship to God" but also involves multiple profane activities related to social, economic, and political issues. Whatever its spiritual-religious benefits for the believer (Muslims performing the pilgrimage), foremost the hajj has always been a real journey—tedious, expensive, and often very hot. The nature of pilgrimage is often compared with tourism. Religion motivates people to travel to holy sites that at the same time are tourist attractions (Henderson 2011). While the Eurocentric view of pilgrimage is a serious and meaningful form of travel, tourism carries the connotation of fun, hedonism, and commercialization; thereby, Lucking (2014: 136) uses the term "pilgrimage tourism" to denote the mixture of spiritual and worldly characteristics of this journey. The hajj pilgrimage is also a combination of spiritual fruition, social relevance, economic ability, fun, and refreshment as well as curiosity in other places, which draws people to Mecca. While academic interest in the cultural impacts of today's "pilgrimage tourism" is just emerging in Indonesia, literary travel accounts have a long tradition in the country.

The hajj (or umra) is a risky and hazardous journey. To get to Mecca, pilgrims in the past, including from the Malay-Indonesian archipelago, often had to endure not just heat but far more deadly threats from bad people, rapacious guides, and devastating epidemics (particularly cholera). It is true that in the olden days the hajj was fraught with danger—if they were not robbed or killed by bandits on the way the early pilgrims stood an even greater chance of succumbing to disease and starvation later on. As for hajj groups from the Malay-Indonesian archipelago, or any regions that need a sea voyage to get to Mecca, the journey was even more dangerous in the past (before steamship technology was discovered in the mid-nineteenth century) because hajj pilgrims had to use a small sailing boat and go from place to place to reach Jeddah, which took some six months. There are numerous academic studies from multiple perspectives that underline the complexity of the hajj and the hazards of performing the pilgrimage in the past (see, e.g., Torrance 1930; Chernoff 1984; Delaney 1990; Peters 1994a, 1994b; Douwes and Kaptein 1997).

Hijra is a migration from an unsafe place, arid lands, or dangerous, poor areas to other lands or regions that are safer, securer, and prosperous. In Arabic, hijra literally means "to abandon," "to break ties with someone" (e.g., a bond of kinship or other personal association), or "to migrate" (Watt 1971: 366). This type of journey dates back from the time of Prophet Muhammad, where in 622 CE, he and his companions traveled (hijra) from Mecca to Yathrib (then Medina) in order to avoid attacks and threats from his rivals and foes (i.e., Meccan tribes). Prophet Muhammad, accompanied by his companions, secretly left his home in Mecca to emigrate to Medina after being warned of a plot to assassinate him. Not only to Medina, history also notes that Prophet Muhammad and his companions—male and female—emigrated to Abyssinia (Ethiopia) between 615 and 622 CE to seek shelter. Masud (1990: 30–1) argues that although the hijra to Abyssinia was voluntary and limited in scope, the hijra to Medina was obligatory and involved almost Mecca's entire Muslim community. No Muslim was supposed to stay behind in Mecca. Exemption was allowed only for the weak—women, children, and the sick—and those who could not afford to migrate.[5]

It is tempting to see the fact that the concept and meaning of hijra varies as complex and fluid. Some argue that hijra means the compulsion to migrate from non-Muslim lands (*dar al-kufr*) to Muslim lands (*dar al-Islam*), others define the notion as principally metaphorical, implying only a "spiritual migration." In contemporary Indonesia, especially among pious urban Muslims, hijra means a conversion from non-Muslim to Muslim or a migration from a "less-Islamic Muslim" (e.g., nominal Muslims) to a "more Islamic one" by expressing or implementing what they deem "Islamic symbols and identities" such as wearing the hijab for women and growing a beard and wearing jalabiyya for men. Still, for some Muslims, hijra means the transition from accommodating state authority to resisting it because of a growing realization of its legitimacy. For others, it means the transition from poverty to a better life through affiliation with specific Islamic movements. For some Arabs, hijra means a transition from a nomadic to a settled life. For Muridiya of Senegal, hijra means emigration from a land where Muslims are in a majority but face famine and poverty to prosperous places such as New York City or Paris, where under the direction of their spiritual leaders and largely perhaps for their benefit, they find economic opportunity (see Eickelman and Piscatori 1990: 10–2). In brief, in contemporary era, the uses of the concept of hijra vary, not only in religious-cultural terms but also in political-economic terms. Also, the driving forces for contemporary Muslims to do hijra are not only because of political and security reasons (such as wars, riots, or pogroms) but also due to economic conditions. Many Muslims today migrate to other places to find a better job in a stronger economy with higher wages.

Furthermore, ziyara (etymologically "visit" in Arabic) is a form of pilgrimage to special sites that are considered by some Muslims to be sacred, important, and meaningful.[6] For Muslims, objects or places of ziyara vary, and what is considered to be a sacred site for one Muslim is not always holy for another, except Kaaba for sure. For example, Karbala is widely considered a sacred place for Shiites but not for non-Shiites. Shrines of Muslim saints, most notably Walisongo (the nine saints) in Indonesia, are only deemed holy for (some) Muslims in that specific country. Some Muslims consider tombs of some Islamic clerics sacred, while others do not. Some Muslim groups (e.g., Salafis) do not practice ziyara to a holy shire since they regard it as unlawful (*haram*), sinful, and a form of *shirk* (lit. ascribing or establishing "partners" beside God). This is to say that, for Muslims, the idea of ziyara or visits to holy places is relative, particular, and strongly connected to specific Islamic forms (e.g., Sufism, syncretism, heterodox Islam) and theological schools (Sunni, Shia, etc.) as well as local historical contexts and experiences of Muslim societies.

Moreover, objects of ziyara can be caves, mosques, battlefields, mountains, or graves of particular, special persons (Prophet Muhammad and his companions, Sufis, saints, Islamic scholars or ulama, Muslim leaders, Muslim kings and nobles, warlords, etc.). Ziyara can also refer to a form of supplication made by Shia, in which they send salutations and greetings to Prophet Muhammad and his family. Furthermore, the idea of ziyara is not always linked to a visit to a sacred shrine. In many Muslim societies, visiting graves of family members is also called ziyara. Undertaking a pilgrimage to a potent and special holy site is also popular in Indonesia, including Javanese Muslim society. To quote Catholic scholar Franz Magnis-Suseno: "Faced with important events of life or in need, the Javanese will perform prayers, and possibly undertake a pilgrimage to a magically potent site" (quoted in Van Doorn-Harder and de Jong 2001: 325–26). Moreover, Van Doorn-Harder and de Jong said that, broadly speaking, for Javanese Muslims, ziyara takes place to three types of sites: Javanese-syncretic places; Muslim, Christian, Hindu, or Buddhist locations; and places that are officially considered Muslim but, in reality, are Javanese-syncretic places (326).

Why do Muslims travel?

Why do Muslims travel? What motivates Muslims to travel? What does travel mean to Muslims? What are the effects of Muslim travel? It is undoubtedly difficult to answer such questions. However, it seems obvious that literal readings of hajj, hijra, ziyara, rihla, or any type of contemporary Muslim travel (e.g., labor migration, tourism, scientific expedition, educational/intellectual journey) are inappropriate since travel—any kind of travel—is a complex, plural phenomenon in terms of motivations, rationales, and purposes of journey. A sojourn is not a uniform, monolithic action. For Muslims, and non-Muslims alike, the nature of a journey is not simply about religion. As a human act, its nature can be profane, religious, or a combination of both religion and secular. Some argue that Muslim travel (like all travels) is principally a journey of the mind. Obviously, all sorts of journey in Islam constitute physical movement from one place to another. Although they owe it to the power of the "religious imagination," Muslim travel involves both spiritual, unworldly and temporal, worldly movement at the same time.

Studies on Muslim travel (e.g., Eickelman and Piscatori 1990) also indicate the complexity and plurality of Muslim travel. For example, in his study about the doctrine of hijra in Islamic law, Muhammad Khalid Masud (1990: 29–49) demonstrates that one sense of hijra is movement of the soul from a state of corruption to one of purity. Julia Clancy-Smith (1990: 200–16), in her study on Rahmaniya tariqa (Sufi order) in North Africa, wrote that, for the followers of this Sufi order, ziyara to the shrine of the founder of the Rahmaniya guarantees movement from unhappiness to happiness in this world, and from damnation to salvation in the next world (afterlife). Originally known as Khalwatiya (the Khalwati order or Halveti in Turkey), the Rahmaniya is a Sufi Muslim brotherhood founded by Sidi Muhammad Bou Qobrine in Algeria in 1774. However, this Sufi order only gained popularity (having a strong audience) in the nineteenth century and successfully spread across North African regions and other parts of the world. Today, the Khalwatiya, along with the Naqshabandiya, Qadiriya, and Shadhiliya, constitute the most famous Sufi orders in the Muslim world.

There may also be imagined movement across gender or ethnic lines. As Nancy Tapper (1990: 236–55) has pointed out, for Turkish women, performing hajj or umrah, conducting ziyara (Turkish: ziyaret) to local shrines, and undertaking religious festivals, all become an act of affirmation that before God they are equal to men and that they too can attain salvation. Some Muslims, moreover, may also envision travel across time as a substitute for a physical sojourn. They do not need to voyage across lands and seas to trace their line of intellectual descent (*isnad*) back to eminent Muslims of the early Islamic period. Travel may project Muslims across spiritual space and time, to overcome barriers of gender and politics, and to envisage home. The concept of home does not always refer to the birthplace (or point of origin) of the sojourner but can be a site where the traveler feels tranquil, comfortable, safe, and, above all, at home. Accordingly, for many non-Saudi Muslims in the world, including Indonesians, Mecca is considered to be "the second homeland." This is to say that travel is also a form of an inventive or imaginative journey.

Another important point to highlight here is that travel in Muslim societies (indeed, in all societies) can also be seen as a form of social and political action. These forms of action raise some basic questions for the contemporary social scientific study of Islam. The most basic issue is how to understand such action in various places and times—past and present. Comprehending Muslims's actions, along with the thoughts, notions, and tenets that are presumed to guide them, is certainly a difficult task, in part because a "Muslim world" is not a monolithic world. Muslims—just like Christians, Jews, Buddhists, Hindus, and others—are always plural, not singular, thereby multifaceted in terms of their travel motives, rationales, and purposes. Each Muslim has their own history, experiences, and settings as well as individual and social contexts that in turn could influence and shape their actions.

As Eickelman and Piscatori (1990: 3–25) have aptly noted the problem of understanding Muslim actions is especially acute because it leads to the opaque realm of reasons for actions (e.g., why is it undertaken?) as well as of the meanings that various actors impute to action (e.g., what impact or change is generated by it?). Moreover, Eickelman and Piscatori highlight several reasons why travel can be seen as a specific form of social action within Muslim religious traditions. These reasons are, first, "Islam" itself (like other religions), in which these actions take place, is a "social phenomenon." Although the nature of Islam is for all humanity, this religion was born within a specific social context of Arab societies, especially those of the Arabian Peninsula. Also, although Muslims believe that Islam is a divinely inspired religion, its primary subject is human beings, and its settings and the historical process in which this religion came into being cannot be separated from social issues facing human (Arab) societies.

The second reason is that the specific importance of travel as a process of social action is significant for understanding "Islam" and the ideas of Muslim communities. The third reason is the notion of motives and interests, those culturally and materially informed incentives to travel. It is imperative to notice that Muslim motives and interests vary and, again, can be shaped by multiple factors such as social status, class position, educational background, economic conditions, and the like. Educated and intellectual Muslim elites, for example, might be influenced by doctrinal considerations for their journeys (whether hajj, umra, hijra, ziyara, or rihla), while non-educated Muslims might be shaped by the desire to get God's blessings. The so-called lower class of a given society (defined by ethnicity, schooling, prosperity, authority, caste, etc.) might be motivated primarily by social, political, and economic deprivation for their travels and migrations. Many Indonesian Muslims from middle-class or elite families who perform hajj or umra are motivated by the wish to maintain their prestige and social status in society. It is true that historically and traditionally, the title *haji* (those who have already performed a hajj pilgrimage) is "prestigious" in Indonesian societies, signifying their wealth, status, and religious authority. The rational choices made by Muslim sojourners are also vital for understanding the plurality and intricacy of their motives and interests. Last but not least, the fourth reason is the complementary issue of effects and identities, those specific social and religious meanings created through travel that inspire changes in how Muslims conceive of and experience "Islam" and the community in which they live.

As in other civilizations and traditions, travel is particularly important when considering changes in imagined Muslim communities past and present. Travel creates boundaries and distinctions, even as travelers believe that they are transcending them. In the hope of creating new horizons, travelers set off from home, encounter others, and return with a sharpened awareness of difference and similarity. Moreover, travel of all sorts is significant for Muslim self-expression, and travel is of course informed by the cultural and social contexts in which Muslims are located. This is to say that although Islamic doctrine explicitly enjoins or encourages certain forms of travel—hijra, hajj, umrah, ziyara, rihla, and others—this does not automatically mean that Muslim travel is only inspired by and for the purpose of religion. This is exactly what this book is about. Although the book underscores the vitality of Islamic teachings in influencing travel of some Muslims, this, however, does not mean that all Muslim travels were influenced by religious doctrines, norms, and narratives as well as for the sake of seeking blessings from God. Many Muslims sojourn in this world actually not because of religious command but due to political, security, or economic issues.

As discussed earlier, travel is undoubtedly complex, and this book tries to explain this complexity of Muslim travel. Anthropological studies of travel in Muslim societies such as those of Eickelman and Piscatori (1990) help frame theoretical foundations of this work, especially in dealing with the examination of the nature, plurality, and complexity of Muslim travelers, including those who were and are in search of knowledge and of learning the sciences. This study, furthermore, benefited from Edward Said's (1983) traveling theory, which states that the idea and concept of travel is not only from "person to person, from situation to situation, from one period to another" in a sociohistorical vacuum but is also a response to specific historical and social changes. In this regard, the study not only investigates the role of human agency (i.e., teachers, scholars, students, and alumni) but also the historical dynamics and sociocultural shifts in both Saudi Arabia and Indonesia that might contribute to the changes and developments of Indonesia's Islamic schooling and cultures.

Rihla *and learning tradition in Islam*

The word rihla is rooted from *rahala*, which was originally linked to camel husbandry. In Arabic, *raḥl* is a camel saddle; thereby, there is a phrase *rahala al-baʿīr* (he saddled the camel). The word *riḥla* thus connoted the act of saddling one or more camels and, by extension, a journey. The person endowed with skill in the saddling of a camel, or one who traveled much, was called a *raḥḥāl* (Netton 2016). In the Qur'an and hadith, there is a rich vocabulary of words related in one way or another to travel or rihla. For example, the Qur'an states: "Their [Quraish tribe] accustomed security [in] the caravan of winter and summer" (Sura Quraish 106: 2). This verse refers rihla to the special accomplishments of the Quraish tribe and how much they owe their success to God's providence. Concerning this verse, Gellens made an interesting note as follows: "The Qur'an intends us to understand here that the Quraish above all, with their talents for 'journeys south and north' (presumably meaning to Yemen and Syria), should accept God's commends. Thus, embedded deep in Muslim consciousness is an identification of travel with pious activity, an appreciation that achievement in such endeavour is a sign of divine approval and munificence" (1990: 53).

It is thus obvious that the origin of the word rihla simply means sojourn. This word, originally, had nothing to do with the pursuit of knowledge or a voyage for learning. It was only in later centuries that the word rihla was associated with a specific journey in search of knowledge. Some scholars of Islam (see, e.g., Eickelman and Piscatori 1990) said that it was during the tenth and eleventh centuries that the expressions of rihla (travel) and thalab al-ilm (journey for learning and pursuing knowledge) could almost be used interchangeably. Gellens notes that throughout the Spanish literature on *tabaqat*[7] (in this case, the biographical dictionary of Muslim scholars), the two terms—rihla and thalab al-ilm—are often linked together, and when both are not linked they bear the same general meaning (i.e., travel for seeking religious knowledge) (1990: 53). There are references to the rihla as a hajj (pilgrimage), but it is the former usage that is dominant. It was not until the late twelfth century that the two terms diverge: rihla became identified primarily with the hajj experience, while thalab al-ilm retains its original meaning (i.e., seeking knowledge). This change may reflect the institutionalization of the madrasah system in place of the formerly more individualized, orally oriented relationships that prevailed between students and teachers in early medieval Islamic history (see Gellens 1990: 50–65).

Moreover, it is vital to note that the bulk of the references in the hadith literature are concerned with thalab al-ilm, not rihla. Accordingly, thalab al-ilm, not rihla, is the more precise term and an accurate way to describe a specific aspect of movement and exchange among Muslims. However, the hadith literature also reminds us that the search for knowledge is closely tied to the physical act of travel. It is hence understandable that in the classical Muslim conception, travel was "conceived to be like study and its fruits were considered to be the adornment of the mind and the formation of the traveller" (Fussel 1980: 39).

This is to say that although the terms rihla and thalab al-ilm originally had different meanings, there is an intimate link between travel and learning in Islam, a tradition that has been preserved until the present-day in many religious centers of education in the Muslim world. Accordingly, in this book, I use the term rihla for a particular voyage for learning. Prophet Muhammad himself emphasized the vitality of rihla for the pursuit of knowledge and the sciences. "Seek ʿilm (knowledge, science) even unto to China," "Pursue knowledge from the birth to the death," and "Obtaining knowledge will not be possible with bodily ease" are among the Prophet's famous sayings (hadith) that acknowledge and underscore the significance of travel in search of knowledge or thalab al-ilm (Shalabi 1954: 181; Abaza 1994).

Due to the strong injunction of the significance of thalab al-ilm, endorsed by the Qur'an and hadith, it is, hence, unsurprising if Sunnis, Shiites, Ibadis, Mu'tazilis, and other "Muslim denominations" (followers of other branches of the Islamic school of thought) have maintained a learning tradition from the early periods of Islamic development to the modern era. From the past to the present, the teaching-learning process (*ta'allum*) through both formal and informal schooling has become a Muslim habit and culture. Many Muslims throughout the ages were keen to establish a variety of learning centers and educational institutions as a means of transformation and distribution of knowledge. Moreover, Islam considers rihla and ta'allum not only the pursuit of knowledge and wisdom but also a means of obtaining God's reward (*makafiyat*) of entry to Paradise after their death. Accordingly, the concepts of rihla and ta'allum are linked with the idea of *tabarrukan* or *baraka* (seeking blessings from God) and *ridha* (Allah compliance) (see Wha 1991). This book is part of an endeavor to understand these concepts and their implementation in Muslim societies, especially from the perspective of Indonesian Muslims who have been trained in the Arabian Peninsula.

Scholars disagree on when the rihla tradition as a sojourn for learning began. Ignaz Goldziher, for example, said that it was specialists in hadith (so-called *as'hab al-hadith* or *ahl al-hadith*, "traditionists") who initiated the rihla-voyage in the early eighth century. Goldziher states that the "traditionists" made use of the voyage as a war machine to combat the opposing group of "reasoners" (*as'hab al-ra'y* or *ahl al-ra'y*, "people of reason") in the task of collecting, authenticating, and harmonizing the sayings of Prophet Muhammad (Goldziher 1889–1890: vol. 2, 33–4). Other scholars such as Ziyad M. Mansur (1990) and Ian Richard Netton (1993) argue that the idea of rihla (again, as a journey for the pursuit of knowledge) was inextricably intertwined with the history of Islam from the start. Criticizing Goldziher, Mansur states: "the rihla began in the era of the companions of the prophet. When Prophet Muhammad died and the wars of conquest scattered the troops of the warriors for God among the companions in the newly Islamized regions, the rihla arose" (1990: vol. 1, 102). Netton also observes that the idea of rihla as travel for learning in Islam is as old as the religion itself, as some primary Islamic texts (Al-Qur'an and Hadith) clearly underline the vitality of seeking knowledge (1993: x).

Indeed, some historians (see Abaza 1994) have said that the rihla tradition in Islam dates back to the years after the death of Prophet Muhammad in 632 CE. At the time, when Prophet Muhammad passed away, problems arouse among Muslims, as they struggled to know and understand the prophet's words, counsels, and instructions on Islamic teachings and everyday living in general. Following the prophet's demise, Muslims' interest in searching and learning from his sayings and practices grew rapidly. Early Muslims interested in the prophet's traditions (hadith and sunna) learned from an authentic source such as the prophet's companions and the chain of people who heard them. They usually traveled from region to region to sit personally with transmitters of hadith called *hamala* (carriers of traditions) aiming to check and recheck whether a hadith was valid or not. As noted by Ibn Sa'd, some, if not many, early Muslims even waited for several days until a hadith specialist returned to that city in order to hear and collect the prophet's sayings (Touati 2010: 11–43). Hijaz (Mecca, Medina), Iraq (Basra, Kufa), and Syria (Damascus) had been particularly important places for hadith seekers in the early period of Islam. It is thus clear that the rihla tradition in early Islam was strongly linked to the Muslim desire to hear, search, and comprehend sayings and deeds of the prophet. With the increase of conquered territory and the growing body of problems and questions that needed answers, hadith and sunna became the second authority to be relied upon after the Qur'an.

Besides hearing and gathering hadith, rihla is also linked to the notion of Islamic propagation (*dakwah*). The conquest of new lands encouraged the first generation of Muslims to travel for learning, preaching, and trading in the newly conquered areas. The second generation of Muslim scholars and laypeople expanded this interest and journeyed to even more remote areas in South and Southeast Asia. Later, these scholars and preachers succeeded in Islamizing some local societies of South and Southeast Asia. Some of the scholars and preachers even succeeded in influencing elite members of the societies they visited, including royal families of local palaces, to embrace Islam. The fact that in Aceh on Sumatra Island in today's Indonesia, there were two Islamic Sultanates in the twelfth and thirteenth centuries, namely Perlak (founder: Alauddin Shah) and Samudera Pasai (founder: Merah Silu or Malik al-Salih), prove the interlink between rihla and proselytization. The flow of Muslim scholars and preachers who came to Aceh from the Middle East, particularly from Hijaz, Egypt, Yemen, and Turkey, dates from the eleventh and twelfth centuries, leading to a very enriching intellectual renaissance in the archipelago (see, e.g., Bowen 1991; Azra 1992; Abaza 1994).

An extension of religious-intellectual-trade networks was established during the twelfth to fifteenth centuries through the expansion of Muslim trade routes in the Indian Ocean. Historians note that a pattern of cosmopolitan traveler shaikhs or a community of religious scholars sharing similar cultural traits and knowledge played a crucial role in the spread of Islam in the Malay-Indonesian archipelago, including Java (see, e.g., Ricklefs 1993; Lombard 1994). Today, some Muslims still travel to remote areas across the globe for learning and preaching at the same time. Some of them journey independently and individually, while others voyage as a member of an Islamic group that are devoted to Islamic propagation such as, for example, Tablighi Jamaat (lit. "Society for Spreading Faith"), a transnational non political Sunni Islamic missionary movement. One of the most influential religious movements in twentieth-century Islam, Tablighi Jamaat was founded in 1927 by Muhammad Ilyas al-Kadhlawi in India. An offshoot of the Deobandi movement, Tablighi Jamaat have now spread across the globe, including to Indonesia.

A journey of Indonesian Muslims to Arabia

As stated above, rihla as a journey for learning has a long tradition in Islam. Since the early periods of Islamic formation, Muslims have traveled from place to place to find learned scholars in order to hear the prophet's sayings, understand Qur'anic verses, or study Islamic sciences under their direction. Since Islam greeted the Indonesian archipelago, probably around the twelfth century, some Indonesian Muslims also traveled from region to region within the archipelago to learn Islam from learned Muslims (scholars, teachers, Sufi masters, etc.). This "journey for learning" tradition became common and popular among Indonesian Muslims from the establishment of informal centers for Islamic learning such as *pondok pesantren* or Islamic boarding school (and later madrasah or Islamic school) in Java in the eighteenth and nineteenth centuries.

Not only practicing rihla within the archipelago, Indonesian Muslims have long voyaged to Arabia, especially Hijaz, to purse Islamic knowledge. Historians have also noted that Malay-Indonesians have long established contacts with the Arab world; and Arabs have long traveled to the Malay-Indonesian archipelago for multiple reasons. It is obvious that both regions have established relationships long before European colonials landed in the archipelago in the sixteenth and early seventeenth centuries. The contact and interaction between the two areas continues today, albeit for different factors, rationales, and purposes. Although people from Arabia and Indonesia traveled long before European colonial times, the intensity of their travel to these regions increased after the discovery of steamship technology and the opening of the Suez Canal in 1869, which made it easier for people to travel between the two areas by sea. I explain briefly the history of Saudi Arabian–Indonesian contact in Chapter 1.

Historically, Arabs, particularly Arab-Hadramis in the southern Arabian Peninsula, who traveled to the Malay-Indonesian archipelago, traveled mainly for trade, to settle, or for Islamic propagation (da'wa). Indonesians, by contrast, voyaged to Saudi Arabia, especially Hijaz, due to three main factors: (1) to perform the hajj pilgrimage, (2) to conduct rituals and religious-spiritual activities in the Holy Cities of Mecca and Medina, and (3) to learn Islamic knowledge and sciences in the birthplace of Islam and Prophet Muhammad. At first, Indonesians initially traveled to Mecca mainly for the hajj as one of Islam's main pillars and an important religious compulsion. After performing the hajj, the majority of Indonesians returned to their country. However, a small minority chose to stay in Mecca and Medina to learn and study Islam and at the same time perform religious rituals at Haram Mosque (Mecca) and Nabawi Mosque (Medina), the two most sacred places in Islam. Muslims believed that worshipping and conducting any religious activities in these two areas, unlike in other places, would result in hundreds of thousands of rewards from God that could guarantee worshipers' entry to Paradise after their death.

The desire for both learning Islam and performing rituals drove some Indonesian Muslims to stay longer in the Haramain (Mecca and Medina). While some stayed months or years before returning to their home country, others lived in Mecca until their death. The type of religious and intellectual nature of contact between Indonesia and Saudi Arabia was obvious at least until the Second World War. After the Second World War, however, particularly since the 1980s, the nature of travel and migration of Indonesians to Saudi Arabia began to change, typified by the pursuit of employment following the oil boom. The large number of Malay-Indonesians who had remained in Mecca created small Indonesian enclaves and helped to build a "Kampung Jawa" (lit. "Javanese Village") in the holy city. Located in the district of Shamiah or Shi'ib Ali, the district of Kampung Jawa became one of Islamic training and learning centers, besides a temporary residence for new Indonesians arriving in Mecca. Even today, the Kampung Jawa is an important site for Indonesians, either temporary or semi permanent residents of Saudi Arabia, from various ethnic groups, who either work or study in Mecca.

In the past, while some Indonesians returned home after completing their studies in Mecca, others chose to stay and dedicate their life to teaching there. As a result, there was a great deal of Indonesian Islamic scholars and teachers in Haramain, whose legacy can still be witnessed today. Shaikh Abdallah Abdulrahman al-Moalimi (2000) has documented the respected Islamic teachers and scholars who have taught Islam at Mecca from the past to the present era, and many of whom were Indonesian. Saudi Arabian-trained Indonesian ulama who chose to return to Indonesia also contributed significantly to the development of Islam, Islamic education, and Muslim organizations that played a great role in the history and growth of Indonesian Muslim cultures and civilizations.

It is imperative to note that Indonesians in Mecca in the past not only taught students or wrote scholarly work but also built schools (madrasah) and centers for Islamic learnings, including women's or girls' schools (Madrasah Khuttab al-Banat, established in the early 1940s, is considered to be Saudi Arabia's first female school). Unfortunately, however, the great legacy of Indonesian scholars from the past has been "damaged" by the surge of Indonesian unskilled migrants, such as menial laborers and housemaids, since the late 1970s, who sought unprofessional jobs in the kingdom. Since then the image of Indonesians in Saudi Arabia is no longer one of educational travelers or educated/learned scholars but of uneducated workers.

Contemporary developments, in contrast with the previous era, also indicate the growing influence of Wahhabi-Salafi thoughts and religious practices on Indonesians studying in several Saudi Arabian Islamic universities. As with past generations of Hijaz-trained ulama, the new generation of Saudi Arabian-educated Muslim scholars has also contributed to the development of particular Islamic discourses, teachings, and movements, linked in particular to Wahhabism-Salafism, which have received a mixture of support and opposition from Indonesian society. The label of "Wahhabi" is an exonym generally considered derogatory by those to whom it is applied. I use the term in this book not for pejorative purposes but simply because of the lack of a better alternative and due to the significance of distinguishing the Wahhabi tradition from the broader Salafi tradition (see, e.g., Voll 1975; Delong-Bas 2004; Nafi 2006; Commins 2009; Hegghammer 2010; Farquhar 2015). It is also vital to understand and underline here that not all adherents of Wahhabism are conservative or "radical" as people commonly misunderstand, many of them are moderate, open-minded, modern, and progressive (see, e.g., Raphaeli 2005; Meijer 2010). Further, unlike in previous centuries when all Indonesians learned the Islamic sciences in Mecca or Medina, since the 1990s (especially since the 2000s) some Indonesians began to study the secular sciences (chemistry, physics, engineering, etc.) at universities across the kingdom. Moreover, whereas in the past, Indonesian Islamic scholars at Mecca taught the Islamic sciences, in the contemporary era, a few Indonesian scientists teach secular sciences such as math, chemistry, aerospace, computer science, and so on.

Methods applied in this study

This book is based on, built upon, and developed from my research and fieldwork in both Saudi Arabia and Indonesia during 2014 to 2016. The research combined quantitative and qualitative methodologies and analyses. The quantitative method included administering a questionnaire survey to Indonesian students studying in the kingdom, especially at Umm Al-Qura University (Mecca), Islamic University (Medina), King Fahd University of Petroleum and Minerals (Dhahran), King Saud University (Riyadh), and Imam Muhammad Bin Saud Islamic University (Riyadh). I chose these universities because they represent Indonesian students who learn Islamic studies and non-Islamic studies, namely the sciences and engineering. The survey was an effective technique for data collection to sketch students' basic facts including age, institutional affiliations, courses studied, family background, educational background, and so forth.

The qualitative method, moreover, included conducting in-depth interviews and conversations with multiple actors, especially university students in the kingdom, alumni of Saudi Arabian universities in Indonesia, and scholars or experts of Indonesian or migration studies. The interviews and conversations aimed to gather information regarding the following:

- root causes, motives, and objectives of the Muslim students who studied and are studying in the Saudi Arabia
- socio-biographical sketches of the educational travelers
- social, political, and educational activities of Saudi Arabian-trained Indonesian scholars and alumni
- social networks of those students and graduates
- intellectual dynamics of Indonesia–Saudi relations.

During the research period, I also held focus group discussions (FGDs) and carried out participant observation with Saudi Arabia's Indonesian students (graduates and undergraduates) with the aim of getting opinions or point of views "from within," observing their activities and practices, and chronicling students' sociocultural-intellectual settings and family backgrounds.

The research, furthermore, employed historical, archival, and textual analysis to examine the history, trajectory, and current developments of the educational migrants and intellectual travelers in the kingdom. I also applied a network analysis to assess the institutional, individual, and social networks of graduates and current students in Saudi Arabia. This technique in particular was a useful method for identifying a multiplicity of means, actors, and agencies the students used to facilitate their entry into the kingdom and enrolment in Saudi Arabia's universities and schools. I applied a media analysis—print and online, including social media—to examine the socioreligious impacts of these intellectual migrants and travelers. Finally, I employed a content analysis of the research carried out to examine discourses of research participants and informants.

The research findings demonstrate that Saudi Arabian–Indonesian relations are changing, with the dynamics being marked by peaceful contact and energetic cooperation as well as social tension and conflict. Such a tendency is not a new phenomenon but has occurred in the past. Different perceptions and understandings about Saudi Arabia and Indonesia have driven people of both sides differently in the way they see and respond to each other. While some Indonesians see Saudi Arabia as a fine place to study (especially for Islamic disciplines) and work, others view the kingdom as a home to strict Salafism-Wahhabism that potentially contribute to the tensions and clashes with local society. In the past, for instance, Salafi-influenced Indonesian Muslims (i.e., the Padris) created tensions and violence in West Sumatra in Indonesia, and such conflicts have reemerged in the modern era, particularly since the downfall of President Suharto in 1998. Saudi Arabian societies also vary and tend to shift in response to Indonesians. In the past, Saudi Arabians (especially those who lived in the Hijaz area) saw Indonesians as passionate learners of Islam and learned scholars who contributed to the development of Arabia's Islamic education, knowledge, and discourses, nowadays they tend to see Indonesians as unskilled laborers such as drivers or maids.

Another significant finding of the research is that there are multiple types of intellectual sojourners and educational migrants in Saudi Arabia, not only those who are studying or teaching Islamic studies but also those who are studying or teaching non-Islamic disciplines such as the sciences and engineering. These findings are obviously an important addition to previous studies that merely put an emphasis on Indonesian students of Islamic disciplines. Like Indonesian Islamic scholars in the past in Hijaz, who contributed significantly to Saudi's Islamic schooling, knowledge, and intellectual tradition, contemporary Indonesian scientists, scholars, and specialists of the sciences and engineering also have made positive contributions pertinent to their fields and to Saudi Arabian society.

Moreover, Indonesians who have studied Islam in Saudi Arabia have in turn created diverse networks and multiple groups. In order to understand the plurality and complexity of a web of networks created by Saudi's students and alumni, the book applies theories of social networks (e.g., Boissevain 1978; Christakis and Fowler 2009), which is undeniably useful to explore, comprehend, construct, and reconstruct individual, organizational, and intellectual networks of those students and alumni. Social network theories are also helpful to understand the ways students discover and maintain their networks and friendships, connect and reconnect with contacts as well as to understand the intellectual relationships between the students and their teachers (Saudis and Indonesians alike). Less importantly, the social network literature helps provide an understanding of the nature and "politics" of human beings (students included) in achieving their personal goals by making connections, forming allies, and preserving alliances and friendships. The presence of Indonesian students in Saudi Arabia—in the past and the present—cannot be separated from these networks.

The study found that the Indonesian alumni of Saudi's Islamic studies' programs vary in their perspectives, thoughts, understandings, and practices with regard to

Islamic teachings, religious beliefs, and Muslim cultures. It is imperative to note that, in contrast with public opinions and understandings, not all Saudi alumni are conservative, militant, radical-extremist, and anti-local cultures and customs. Many of them are actually quite open-minded, moderate, tolerant-pluralist, and pro-local traditions and cultures. This book, among other objectives, aims to provide a comprehensive study and analysis of the contributions of Saudi graduates of both Islamic studies and the secular sciences in Indonesia that are widely neglected from the scholarship. This study is grounded within these theoretical frameworks and analyses.

Narrative outline

The book is divided into six chapters as follows:

Chapter 1 traces the historical dynamics and contemporary development of Saudi Arabian–Indonesian relations. The chapter outlines a variety of Indonesian groups—past and present—who voyaged to the Arabian Peninsula, ranging from pilgrims and religious scholars to Islamic teachers, scientists, students, tourists, and workers (both professional employees and menial laborers). It also discusses the rationales that motivated Arabs and Indonesians to travel and migrate. More specifically, the chapter discusses multiple reasons and factors for Indonesians who traveled or migrated to Saudi Arabia, ranging from religion and education to tourism and employment. The chapter not only discusses the history of informal contacts but also of formal ties between Saudi Arabia and Indonesia, and explains the factors that contributed to the building of official relations, particularly concerning cooperation in educational, religious, and cultural issues.

Chapter 2 examines the imprint of Saudi Arabia in contemporary Indonesia and Saudi Arabian influences on Indonesian Muslim society from the past to the present. The Arabian influence on Indonesian society is not only in the spheres of Islamic practices, knowledge, education, and cultures but also in Islamic activism (e.g., the Padri movement, pan-Islamism, and anti-colonialism, among others). Indonesian Muslim students have traveled to the Arabian Peninsula, which is considered by most Indonesian Muslims as a sacred place, since the late sixteenth century to pursue Islamic knowledge, sciences, and wisdom, this means there has been an Arabian influence on Indonesian Islam for centuries. However, particular attention in this chapter is given to the late 1960s onward, when Saudi Arabia began to enter Indonesia through the channel of the DDII. Dewan Dakwah Islamiyah Indonesia is an Islamist organization founded by an exponent of Islamic ideology and a former leader of Masyumi, an Islamist political party (banned in 1960) that supported the establishment of an Islamic state in Indonesia. Since then Saudi influences in the country became stronger, thanks to the oil booms that provided an enormous support for dakwah activity in Indonesia. By the 1980s, Saudi Arabia built a branch of Imam Muhammad bin Saud Islamic University in Jakarta, named LIPIA (Lembaga Ilmu Pengetahuan Islam dan Bahasa Arab). Saudi influences continue today, either through Saudi state or government networks or via individual connections between Indonesians and Saudis. Although DDII still plays a significant role, in recent decades the country has witnessed the rise of multiple organizations that have been the channel for Saudi influences in Indonesia through a variety of activities such as building mosques, madrasah, Islamic centers, and so forth.

As an outcome of the opening of the DDII, since the mid-1980s and especially since the downfall of President Suharto, Indonesia has witnessed a surge in Islamist groups and the Salafi movement in urban areas that promote particular forms of Islam typified by conservatism, puritanism, and "Arabism," which in many ways oppose the general practices of Indonesian local societies and cultures. Although Saudi Arabia is not the only source of Salafism, Islamist ideology, and puritanical practices (other countries include Egypt, Yemen, India, Pakistan, Sudan, or Morocco), Indonesians in general mistakenly see Saudi Arabia as the primary, or even the only, source of Islamist and Salafi movements since the Saudi kingdom and society have obviously contributed to building mosques, madrasah, and Islamic centers or sponsored public events for various Islamist groups. Indonesian responses vary in this regard, some pro others contra, and there have been multiple factors and rationales for societal agreement and disagreement. This chapter explains this phenomenon.

Chapter 3 describes Saudi Arabia as a center for learning and education for Indonesian Muslims. It discusses Saudi Arabia, for Indonesians, as not only a pilgrimage or working place but as an educational site. There are currently thousands of Indonesians studying in the kingdom. At the Islamic University of Medina alone there are more than 800 Indonesian students studying multiple Islamic disciplines (Islamic law, theology, Hadith, da'wa, etc.) from undergraduate to graduate levels. At present, Indonesian students, some of whom pursue non-Islamic sciences (e.g., the hard sciences, engineering, computer science, business, geoscience, and banking, among others), favor the following universities in Saudi Arabia: the Islamic University of Medina, Al Imam Muhammad bin Saud Islamic University, King Saud University, King Fahd University of Petroleum and Minerals, and King Abdullah University of Science and Technology, among others. While in the past Al-Azhar University of Egypt was a favorite destination for Indonesian Muslim students, in recent decades Saudi Arabia has also become a popular site of study, either in the field of Islamic studies or non-Islamic studies. Before Saudi Arabia built its universities, all Indonesians studied Islam at madrasah (such as Madrasah Shaulatiyah and Madrasah Al-Falah, among others) and at informal Islamic learning centers (halaqah, ribat, or ma'had) in Mecca and Medina. This chapter also discusses the history and development of Indonesian schools at Mecca and other cities such as Jeddah and Riyadh. It is imperative to note that in the past century Indonesians established several Islamic schools—both for male and female students—such as Darul Ulum al-Diniyah, Madrasah Indonesia al-Makkiyah, Jam'iyah Khairiyah, Madrasah Ibtidaiyah li al-Banat al-Ahliyah, and most recently Sekolah Indonesia Makah. However, only a few (e.g., Sekolah Indonesia Makah) still exist today, while other schools collapsed or were transferred into the Saudi academic system. This chapter discusses the dynamics and development of Indonesian education in Saudi Arabia.

Chapter 4 discusses Indonesian scholars, teachers, and scientists in Saudi Arabia with particular attention given to those who focus on teaching, writing, and researching subjects related Islamic disciplines and "non-Islamic disciplines" (i.e., the sciences—hard sciences and social sciences—and engineering). In this book, I consider "Saudi Arabia" to include past Hijaz (especially Mecca and Medina) before "Al Saud occupation" of this area in the 1920s. This chapter briefly chronicles respected Indonesian Islamic scholars (ulama) who devoted their life to scholarship in Mecca and Medina, discusses their invaluable contributions to the study of Islam, and highlights the challenges they face with the modern Saudi government. The chapter also briefly depicts biographies and contributions of the more recent Indonesian Islamic scholars, scientists, or non-Islamic studies specialists in Saudi Arabia.

Chapter 5 provides an overview of the history, variety, and complexity of Indonesian Muslim students, a group that have historically and traditionally been major transporters of Islamic thinking and cultural practices from the Middle East, especially from Saudi Arabia but also Yemen, Egypt, and other Middle Eastern countries. It discusses the root causes and a set of cultural patterns, practices, motives, and objectives of those students of both religious and secular sciences. It is vital to acknowledge that Indonesian students in Saudi Arabia not only focus on—or pursue degrees in—Islamic studies but also on the sciences and engineering. King Fahd University of Petroleum and Minerals, King Saud University, King Abdullah University of Science and Technology, and King Abdul Aziz University in particular have been the home for Indonesians studying math, chemistry, physics, computer sciences, and so forth.

It is interesting to find the fact that although they study in the fields of the hard sciences and engineering and other non-Islamic study disciplines and academic programs, some of these non-Islamic studies students have been active in Islamic and Qur'anic study circles, organized by associations of Indonesian Muslim students in the kingdom. I briefly chronicle their "life story" and religious activities during their study in Saudi Arabia, including regular visits to Mecca and Medina to perform ritual practices (e.g., umrah), ziyarah, and religious tourism in Islamic and historical sacred places. In addition, fascinatingly, many Islamic studies students do not absorb Salafi-type conservative and puritanical understandings and interpretations of Islam and Muslim cultures in Saudi Arabia. There are indeed multiple streams of Muslim students majoring in Islamic or non-Islamic studies.

The chapter, furthermore, describes students' activities during their studies and in their networks that provide ways and resources for studying in Saudi Arabia and for maintaining social bonds and individual connections. This chapter not only discusses university students but also non university students, particularly those who learn Islam in informal learning centers such as *ma'had, ribat, halaqah*, or madrasah in Mecca. One of the most famous Islamic boarding schools for Indonesian students up until now in Mecca has been Ma'had Sayyid Muhammad

Alawi. Every year this ma'had recruits students from Indonesian pesantren or Islamic boarding schools (e.g., Pesantren Sarang in Rembang, Central Java) through a personal network and then trains them in the ma'had for several years to study a variety of Islamic disciplines.

There is a tendency to change from past to present concerning ulama that shaped and reshaped thoughts and practices of Indonesian Muslim disciples. In the past, Islamic scholars affiliated to Shafi'i, Hanafi, or Maliki schools of thoughts (mazhab) influenced Indonesian students the most, if not solely. However, in the contemporary era, Hanbali and particularly Wahhabi-Salafi ulama influence the new generation of Indonesian students the most, especially university students of Islamic studies in Saudi Arabia. Different teachers and scholars have definitely brought different understandings, practices, and ways of thinking to students. This chapter is not included to discuss teachers or scholars that have taught—or influenced—Indonesian Muslims, it only highlights briefly several influential ones (both Wahhabi and non-Wahhabi ulama from past to present) such as Shaikh Ibrahim al-Kurani, Shaikh Abu Bakar Syato, Shaikh Zaini Dahlan, Sayyid Muhammad Alwi al-Maliki, Muhammad Nasiruddin al-Albani, Abdul Aziz bin Baz, or Shaikh Abdur Razak bin Abdul Muhsin al-Abbad, among many others.

Chapter 6 outlines Saudi Arabian-trained Indonesian Islamic scholars (ulama) and their contributions to Indonesian society. Whereas some Indonesians remained in Mecca and taught there upon the completion of their learning and study, many returned to their home country to implement what they learned during their studies. Many of these graduates became the backbone of the development of Indonesian Islam. Many of them built Islamic learning institutions (*pesantren* or Islamic boarding schools, madrasah, or even universities), created social organizations and other Islamic institutions, and developed Islamic forums for religious sermons and social gatherings. As for their professions, many of them became preachers, educators, politicians, bureaucrats, religious leaders, and so forth. It is imperative to note that the Indonesian alumni of Saudi Arabian academic institutions vary in the way they perceive, understand, think, and practice Islam. While some tend to be more conservative and intolerant of extremists, others are more open-minded and progressive-liberal in interpreting Islamic texts, understanding local cultures and traditions, and in comprehending Islamic discourses. This chapter discusses why and how Saudi Arabian educational institutions could produce plural and complex Indonesian alumni. Also, the chapter briefly describes the pros and cons of the responses from Indonesian societies toward the role and contributions of Saudi Arabian alumni in the country.

Each chapter closes with a conclusion that summarizes and highlights some significant points and analyses.

Chapter 1

SAUDI ARABIAN-INDONESIAN RELATIONS

This chapter discusses the historical dynamics of the contact between the Indonesian Archipelago and the Arabian Peninsula, with a particular emphasis on the northern part of Arabia—both Hijaz in the past and modern Saudi Arabia. It also sketches the contemporary development of the mutual relationships and cooperation between the Kingdom of Saudi Arabia and the Government of Indonesia which have improved significantly. Moreover, the chapter outlines a variety of Indonesian migrant groups—past and present—who traveled to northern Arabia, including pilgrims, religious scholars, Islamic teachers, scientists, students, and workers (both professional employees and menial laborers), and their various motives and purposes for transnational travel and migration. The primary objective of this chapter is to understand the changing nature of Saudi Arabian-Indonesian relations from past centuries to the present era. This chapter concludes that there were, and are, three primary reasons for Indonesians to travel to Arabia: religion, education, and work. The chapter also underlines multiple—regional, national, or international—factors that have contributed to the shape of the dynamics of Saudi-Indonesian relations, ranging from politics and economy to religion and culture.

The aims of this chapter are, among others, (1) to advance knowledge about national interests as one of the main bases of Saudi-Indonesian relations, (2) to gain insight into the "push-pull factors" that drove Indonesians to travel or migrate to Saudi Arabia, (3) to understand types of Indonesian travelers and migrants in Saudi Arabia, (4) to comprehend the historical dynamics and contemporary developments of bilateral relations (diplomatic and non diplomatic) between the two countries, including their societies, and (5) to identify the changing perceptions of Indonesians in Saudi Arabia as well as of Indonesians toward the Saudi kingdom and society since in recent years, particularly since the visit of King Salman to Indonesia in 2017. Like some other societies in the world, Indonesians generally tend to see Saudi Arabia as a site of a strict form of Islamic Wahhabism (or Salafism), terrorism, intolerance, anti-pluralism, anti-empowerment of women, anti-religious dialogue, and many other stereotypes, which are misleading, overgeneralized, and tend to neglect current positive developments and constructive changes in the Saudi kingdom. The brief visit of King Salman has surprised both "liberals" and "radicals" in the Indonesian Archipelago.[1]

Saudi–Indonesian bilateral ties

In March 2017, the King of Saudi Arabia and the Custodian of the Two Holy Mosques, Salman bin Abdulaziz Al Saud (b.1935–), made a landmark visit to Indonesia, the first by a Saudi monarch since 1970, when King Faisal bin Abdul Aziz Al Saud (1906–1975) visited the archipelago.[2] King Salman's visit to Indonesia was considered by Indonesians as extraordinary since he was accompanied by some 1,500 people, including princes, government ministers, businessmen, and so forth. The Indonesians, from elite members of society to ordinary people, were equally eager to impress. Top government officials and politicians highlighted the visit as extremely extraordinary and historic, while enthusiastic crowds, including tens of thousands of students, lined the route of King Salman's heavily guarded motorcade to the Bogor presidential palace of West Java. The Indonesian government deployed some 10,000 security personnel to protect King Salman and his entourage during their important visit to Jakarta, Bogor, and Bali (Al Qurtuby and Aldamer 2018: 121–12).[3]

There were several main reasons for King Salman's celebrated visit to the world's most populous nation: Indonesia. The first reason was to build diplomatic ties. The visit itself was "reciprocal." Previously, Indonesian President Joko Widodo (known as Jokowi) made an official visit to the kingdom of Saudi Arabia in 2015 during which King Salman presented the Indonesian president with the prestigious King Abdul Aziz Medal. Hence, King Salman's official visit to Indonesia was seen as a "return" of President Jokowi's previous visit. The second reason was to establish economic cooperation. More specifically, the visit was connected to the kingdom's plan of the Initial Public Offering (IPO) of 5 percent of Saudi Aramco, the national giant oil company, which is expected to reach a US$2 trillion value, making it the largest IPO ever.

Coupled to this reason, King Salman's tour to Indonesia and several other Asian countries, including Malaysia, Brunei, China, and Japan, was part of an endeavor to advance Saudi's economic and business interests. Broadly speaking, the visit was, of course, to strengthen bilateral ties and mutual cooperation in various fields, including politics, the economy, and culture. The Indonesian Ambassador to Saudi Arabia Agus Maftuh Abegebriel, in a conversation with me, has noted that a joint declaration, a memoranda of understanding, and an agreements between the two countries have been signed in multiple sectors, including trade, education, health, culture, pilgrimage, tourism, information, science, technology, civil aviation, fisheries, defense, security, and combating transnational crimes, among others.[4]

Although only two Saudi monarchs (King Faisal and King Salman) have visited Indonesia, bilateral relations between the two countries date back to the 1940s. Indonesia–Saudi ties were initiated formally in 1948 with the establishment of the Indonesian Embassy in Jeddah and, two years later, a Saudi representative office in Jakarta that was eventually turned into a formal embassy in 1955. It is important to note the kingdom was among the first countries to recognize Indonesia's independence in 1945. Although the formal relations between the Kingdom of Saudi Arabia and the Government of Indonesia began only in post independence

Indonesia, these two Muslim-majority nations and their people had established contact long before Indonesia gained its independence in 1945 and long before Saudi built a modern kingdom in 1932 that united all regions in the Arabian Peninsula from Ahsa in the east to Hijaz in the west.

Surprisingly, despite the long history of Saudi–Indonesian relations, there is limited writing on the topic. In general, existing studies and literature on the links between Indonesia and Saudi Arabia or Indonesians in Saudi Arabia put emphasis on three sets of issues. The first is the role and contributions of Mecca- and Medina-trained Indonesian Islamic scholars (*ulama*), who shaped the archipelago's Islamic, religious education and Muslim practices and cultures. I briefly highlight some eminent Indonesian ulama and their contributions to Indonesian Islam and society in chapters that follow. The second theme is Saudi Arabia's unskilled Indonesian migrant groups, particularly housemaids, drivers, and laborers. These scholars usually discuss issues such as the treatment of workers, including violations of human rights, abuse of domestic workers, working conditions, and the powerlessness of workers. The third focus is on the role of Saudi Arabia in Indonesia's "Arabized Islam," strict Salafism, and other severe puritanical, reformist forms of Islamic practices, understandings, interpretations, and discourses that in turn create tensions and conflict within Indonesia's diverse Muslim and non-Muslim communities. Writings in this category extend to work on the rise of Islamist extremism, intolerance, fanaticism, bigotry, racism, and terrorism in contemporary Indonesia.

This book, however, tries to take a different approach and perspective by focusing on the bilateral relationship between the two countries as one concerning two pragmatic and rational states. Although I realize that social, cultural, and religious dimensions are certainly important factors shaping the dynamics of Saudi–Indonesian relations, the book sees the two countries' ties as fundamentally consistent with the realist emphasis on state calculations, with each country aiming to maximize its own national interests. Religion and people-to-people ties nonetheless play a key role in the relationship, establishing historical patterns, influencing how the two countries assess each other's impact on their national interests, and shaping how the two countries see each other's governments and societies today (Al Qurtuby and Aldamer 2018: 121–44).

Furthermore, contemporary relations between Saudi Arabia and Indonesia are highly dynamics and unpredictable, marked by a constant ebb and flow. The encounters between these two countries, as reflected in this book, have been marked by tensions and conflict as well as by cooperation and dialogue. Domestic, regional, or international religious, social, cultural, economic, ideological, and political developments have influenced the dynamics of Saudi–Indonesian relations. When Ibn Saud took over Hijaz in the 1920s, Indonesia's Nahdlatul Ulama, the country's largest Muslim social organization, tried to approach him because they feared the new ruler would diminish Islamic historical artifacts and Muslim practices of non-Hanbali schools of Islamic law/legal thought (*madhhab*), thereby potentially creating tensions among Muslims of different madhhab and sects.

Moreover, during the anti-Iranian campaign that started in the early 1980s (in the aftermath of the Imam Khomeini-led 1979 Iranian Islamic Revolution), relations between the two countries intensified, partly because of their mutual interests and objectives to diminish the ideological-political influences of the Iranian Shiites in their respected nations and societies (see Lim 2011; Nawab 2011). Saudi Arabian attempts to forge an alliance with Indonesia actually took place long before the historic Iranian Shia revolution in 1979 that brought Ayatollah Khomeini to power. In the 1950s and 1960s, for instance, Saudi Arabia tried to make a global coalition with Muslim-majority nations, including Indonesia, to counter the effect of the Arab Socialist movement and the Middle East's various brands of radical republicanism that Saudi Arabia saw as a potential threat to their kingdom (Hasan 2005, 2007).

However, Saudi efforts to approach Indonesia at that time only brought minor success, in part because President Sukarno of the Old Order government, an admirer of republicanism and socialism, was unenthusiastic to join the campaign. This situation was undoubtedly different when Indonesia, during the New Order rule, saw post-revolution Iran as a real hazard for President Suharto's reign. President Suharto was afraid that the "virus" of Shia revolutionary ideology would influence Indonesian Muslims and, like in Iran, they could potentially declare a political-religious movement against the existing secular government. Because of these suspicion and fear, Suharto had made every effort to weaken—and eliminate, if possible—Iranian influences in Indonesian society, such as banning books authored by Iranian and Shia scholars and ideologues, and any public event that discussed Iranian or Shia politics.

It is true that in general, the Indonesian government did not see the Saudis as a "green peril" in comparison to the Iranians. The perception that Saudi Arabia was not a political menace for the Indonesian government was one of main keys of "success" to building contact. Coincidentally, like Indonesia, Saudi itself was faced with the challenge of the Khomeini-led Iranian Shia regime; thereby, it began to work closely with various anti-Iran Islamist groups around the globe, from Egypt to Indonesia, providing financial support to the groups' educational institutions and religious activities. Saudi–Indonesian relations became more productive after the 1990s, when Suharto began to change his policies and political orientation. This was marked by close connections being built with "Islamic elements" and urban middle-class Muslim groups (Hefner 2000; Van Bruinesen 2002). In Suharto's New Order Indonesia, relations between the Kingdom of Saudi Arabia and the Republic of Indonesia, as this chapter shows, have been even more fruitful, indicated by mutual productive cooperation in multiple sectors.

This chapter does not only discuss contact between government officials (G-to-G relations) but also between business communities (B-to-B relations) and ordinary people (P-to-P relations) of the two countries, building upon the notions of the Realist School of international relations, especially the assumption of pragmatic rationality, namely the realist emphasis on state pragmatic calculations aimed at maximizing their own national interests (Aldamer 2001: 11).

Although the religious dimension of Saudi foreign policy is not an aim itself, religion does matter and has become a significant factor in Saudi foreign relations (Preuschaft 2016: 16–28), and the same is true for Indonesia. In short, while religion is not the primary driving force behind Saudi–Indonesian foreign relations, Islam is a very important factor, shaping many aspects of the bilateral relationship, including education, trade, employment, business, and pilgrimage (hajj and umra). It has also played an important role in the vicissitudes of Saudi–Indonesian ties. In other words, although religion is not the first and foremost driving force behind Saudi–Indonesian foreign relations, it serves as a means for Saudi–Indonesian foreign relations to further some of their major national interests (Patrick 2016).

As scholars of Indonesian Islam and its history have noted, despite formal diplomatic relations between the Kingdom of Saudi Arabia and the Republic of Indonesia that began in the 1940s, informal contacts between the northern (Hijaz) and southern parts (Yemen) of Arabia and the Malay-Indonesian archipelago are actually ancient, thereby producing a sort of a "creole culture" and civilization of great complexity and internal diversity (see, e.g., Azra 1992, 2004; Freitag and Clarence-Smith 1997; Abaza 2007; Tagliacozzo 2010, 2014). Their contact was mainly through the Indian Ocean, which served as a flat field for travel linking the various component (landed) parts of this maritime arena for a very long time. Both regions had established relations long before European colonials landed in the archipelago, and these continue today, albeit for different reasons, motives, and purposes. Historically, Arabs, particularly Hadramis (from South Yemen in the southern Arabian Peninsula), journeyed to the Malay-Indonesian archipelago mainly for trade, residing, or da'wah (spreading Islam).

Historian Eric Tagliacozzo (2014: 565–66; see also Ho 2006) states that Hadrami wanderers were one of the most vital groups who sailed across the ocean to areas like South Asia and Southeast Asia. Eventually, most Hadramis in fact lived in diaspora away from Yemeni shores, spreading Islam and their own business networks as a corollary of their travel, and the Malay-Indonesian archipelago became an increasingly important destination for this group. It is imperative to note that the Hadrami sojourners, as commonly as other travelers and migrant groups, brought—and introduced to the local communities—their own variants of Islam and Arab culture, both material culture (e.g., ceramics, textiles, gemstones, and most importantly coffee) and immaterial culture (e.g., custom, music, dance).

The two most important exports of the Middle East to Southeast Asian societies were Islam and trade goods. Scholars vary in responding to the links between Islam and merchant goods. Some (e.g., Das Gupta 1979) argue that Islam, as a traveling ideological phenomenon, rode existing systems of exchange and thus circulated to the Southeast Asian societies that would eventually receive Islam as a majority faith. In this view, the relationship between religion (Islam) and trade is one of "symbiotic mutualism" in which each helped the other. In fact, it is common to find that when people travel abroad or go to any foreign areas for commerce or other purposes (e.g., seeking a shelter, leisure, education, among others), they usually share their immaterial cultures, including ideas, thoughts, beliefs, and many others, with new acquaintances they encounter. In this regard, it is possible, for instance, that Arab Muslim traders also shared their Islamic tenets and cultures to societies in Southeast Asia, including Indonesia, during their journey to the archipelago.

Other scholars (e.g., Pearson 1994) have contended that the relationship between Islam and commerce was not intertwined: the two entities traveled separately alongside one another rather than as interlinked phenomena. For this view, instead of trade, it was argued that hajj pilgrimage had been the major channel for the introduction of Islam and the production of Muslim cultures in the Malay-Indonesian archipelago. Some studies on hajj pilgrimage have indeed underlined the contributions of hajj or umrah returnees to the development of Islam in Indonesia and other areas of Southeast Asia (see, e.g., Vredenbregt 1962; Douwes and Kaptein 1997; Van Bruinessen 2015). Given the fact that hajj pilgrims always varied in expressing Islamic thoughts, discourses, notions, and the like, the types of Islam that have developed in Indonesia are also heterogeneous. Various forms of, for example, orthodox and heterodox Islam, cultural and political Islam, mystical and rational Islam, and so on are always present—and contested—in Indonesia; accordingly, from its introduction up until today there has never been a single, homogenous sort of Islam in this archipelago.

It is also imperative to note that, as most, if not all, of the travelers were men, the Arabs, particularly Hadramis, intermarried with local women, creating a new "creole" generation of Indo-Arabs across the Malay-Indonesian archipelago. The group of sadah or ashraf (i.e., descendants of the Prophet Muhammad; sing. "sayyid" and "sharif") of both Hadrami and non-Hadrami Arabs are exceptional in this regard since they have practiced for generations an endogamy marriage, namely marriage practice among sadah/ashraf families. The Hadramis then linked themselves through both religion and commerce to other nodes in the Indian Ocean nexus. The Hadrami diaspora is in fact still living proof of the power and unexpected consequences of some of these connections as they evolved across this huge maritime space over several centuries. This is especially true via economic holdings and also through the intermarriage of Hadramis with indigenes in the Malay-Indonesian archipelago. Whereas Hadramis voyaged to the Malay-Indonesian world for centuries, native Indonesians, by contrast, had never (or rarely) journeyed to Hadramaut in South Yemen but had traveled to Hijaz in northern Arabia instead. Only in recent decades, have Indonesian Muslims, especially students, begun to travel to Hadramaut, especially the Tarim region, to study Islam (see Chapter 5). Although people from Arabia and Indonesia had traveled long before European colonial times, their travel to these regions increased in intensity after the discovery of steamship technology and the opening of the Suez Canal in 1869, with the sea route making it easier to access the two areas.

Moreover, it is imperative to note that contact between Arabia and Indonesia not only occurred through informal ways but also formal or official ones. In the late 1920s, for example, a small group of Islamic scholars (ulama) affiliated to Nahdlatul Ulama (NU), Indonesia's largest Muslim social organization, named

Komite Hijaz (Hijaz Committee), visited Saudi Arabia to meet and give a letter of request from NU to King Abdul Aziz bin Ibn Saud (1875–1953). The Committee was concerned about some issues related to the hajj and other socio religious situations in Mecca and Medina following the shifting political regime in Saudi Arabia. Led by renowned and respected ulama K.H. Abdul Wahab Chasbullah, the Committee requested the following of the King: (1) the implementation of four madhhab (schools of Islamic jurisprudence) within the Sunni tradition, namely Maliki, Shafii, Hanafi, and Hanbali for Muslims in Hijaz; (2) the maintenance of Islamic historical sites; and (3) the announcement to the Muslim world about the cost for a hajj pilgrimage, among others.[5]

Another example of formal contact between Indonesian and Saudi Arabia, moreover, happened in 1967, the Saudi government helped set up and develop the Dewan Dakwah Islamiyah Indonesia (DDII—Indonesian Council for Islamic Propagation), which was initiated by Islamist leading figure Muhammad Natsir (1908–1993) and other former leaders of Masyumi, an Islamist political party banned by President Sukarno in 1960 because of the involvement of some of its political leaders in the separatist movements or rebellions against the central government. Due to Natsir's personal closeness and relationships with Saudi elites, the DDII enjoyed the financial and "cultural" support for the development of Islamic da'wa activities such as the establishment of mosques, the founding of madrasah, the training of preachers, the distribution of free copies of the Qur'an and other Salafi-related Islamic books, and so forth (Hasan 2005: 267–28). All these activities and works in turn helped contribute to the spread of the spirit of Islamic resurgence and the growth of Islamist groupings in Indonesia (see Chapter 2).

Contact in the past: Pilgrimage and learning

There were two main reasons for Indonesians in the past to voyage to Hijaz: (1) to perform a hajj pilgrimage and other religious activities in the Holy Cities of Mecca and Medina (known as Haramain), and (2) to learn Islamic knowledge and sciences in the birthplace of Islam and the Prophet Muhammad. The vast majority of Indonesians who journeyed to Mecca in the past certainly did so for a hajj. Only a small minority, particularly travelers from middle-income religious families such as local Muslim elites, santris (students of pondok pesantren), or the *kaum putihan* (lit. the "white people" referring to a devout Muslim community), was driven by eagerness to learn and advance their knowledge on Arabic and Islamic disciplines in the Haramain. Unlike the majority of Indonesians who returned to their country after completing the hajj rituals, this small group of pilgrims chose to stay in the Haramain. Whereas some stayed on for months or several years to study Islam before returning to their home countries, others continued to reside there until their death. By the early seventeenth to mid-twentieth centuries, some of these initial educational travelers who then resided in the Haramain became respected imams of Haram Mosque (Masjid al-Haram), fine teachers of Islam, and noted Islamic scholars (ulama)[6] (see Chapter 4).

Despite facing many difficulties (e.g., uneasy sea transport, disease, lengthy voyage, limited food), the number of Indonesian hajj pilgrims in the past was significant and tremendous. Between 1850 and 1860, there were about 1,600 hajj pilgrims, about 2,600–4,600 in the 1870s, and in the 1880s, more than 15 percent of all pilgrims to Mecca were from the Indonesian archipelago or the Dutch East Indies. Today, based on the data from the Indonesian Ministry of Religious Affairs, almost every year in the past decade about 250,000 Indonesian Muslims set off on the hajj, the largest number of hajj pilgrims from any region in the world. However, demand is much higher, and as the hajj can only be accomplished once a year, and the number of pilgrims is strictly controlled by the Saudi government, there are long waiting lists. Due to a large number of Indonesian pilgrims, it would be surprising if there were not many Indonesians residing in Mecca. Although accurate figures on Indonesians in Mecca are hard to find, Christian Snouck Hurgronje (1857–1936), a Dutch scholar of Oriental cultures and languages and Advisor on Native Affairs to the colonial government of the Netherlands East Indies, estimated that about 8,000–10,000 Indonesians stayed there in the late nineteenth century.

Snouck Hurgronje stayed in Arabia for a year from 1884 to 1885 and spent six months in Mecca disguised as a Muslim under a pseudonym, Abdul Ghaffar, making his personal life both legendary and controversial. Whether or not Snouck Hurgronje was a true Muslim, there was indeed a controversy about his intellectual honesty. However, reportedly, he behaved as a Muslim and married two Indonesian Muslim women. Some Indonesians remember him under a variety of names and titles such as "Abdogapha," "Si Gam," and "Teungkoe Hadji Belanda." Moreover, many Indonesians, particularly in academic circles, accused Snouck Hurgronje of being a Dutch spy and an Orientalist who had a hidden political agenda, and conducted research, studied, and created policy antagonistic to Muslim societies. Some intellectuals and academics, however, considered him an enlightened and concerned scholar (see, e.g., Abaza 2007: 423–4; cf. Laffan 2011). Jan Just Witkam says, "Snouck Hurgronje's realistic approach of Mecca's history does not need to disturb us as anti-Islamic bias on his part, since Muslim historians themselves are quite open-minded on the subject, in the same way, probably, as Roman Catholics think about the secret history of the Vatican; most holy and most unholy often go hand in hand" (Witkam 2007: xiv).

Whatever Hurgronje's motives and intellectual-spiritual honesty, it was obvious that the Dutch rulers sent him to Arabia, especially Mecca but also Jeddah, to make a report on whether Indonesian hajj pilgrims (haji) constituted a danger for the Dutch East Indies. In other words, the Dutch colonial rulers requested Snouck Hurgronje to study activities of Indonesians in Arabia and to make a report to the government about their activities, especially religiopolitical activities that might jeopardize the existence of the Dutch colonial administration in the East Indies. The Dutch rulers sent Snouck Hurgronje to Arabia in part due to a number of anti-Dutch rebellions in the East Indies, particularly in Java and Sumatra, such as the Java War in Central Java (1825–1830) and the Padri War in Minangkabau of Sumatra (1831–1834), which were led by kiai (religious clerics) and haji (returning pilgrims).[7] These incidents made the Dutch curious as to whether or not there was a link between the uprisings and the idea of "Pan-Islamism" brought by the returned hajjis. The Netherlands had also found itself, particularly from 1873 onward, in a state of war of attrition against the Sultanate of Aceh, an independent state on the northern tip of the island of Sumatra, and it was a war with strong Islamic overtones.

There had been a long tradition of suspicion of Muslim pilgrims among European colonial administrators, such as Sir Thomas Stamford Raffles (1781–1826)—a British statesman, Lieutenant-Governor of British Java, and the author of *The History of Java*—as well as the Netherland East Indies Company (VOC), who considered hajj pilgrimage as a peril for the colonial rule. Both the British and the Dutch officials became increasingly concerned with monitoring international webs of anti-colonial radicalism and rebellion, both real and imagined, being forged among diasporic networks of hajj pilgrims. For the European colonial officials, particularly the British and the Dutch, Arabia was the source of religiopolitical fanaticism among Muslims in their colonial territories (especially India and the East Indies or Indonesia). Mecca, in particular, in the eyes of European colonial powers with Muslim subjects, had become a safe haven for fundamentalist activities of what they called "Muslim fanatics." Mecca, the Holy City for some and the Forbidden City for others, was seen by the Europeans as a site from where pan-Islamic ideas could radiate all over the Muslim world unhindered, a large part of which was by then ruled by European nations, the "abhorrent infidels."

In brief, the European colonial nations saw Arabia as the source of the ideologies of Wahhabism and pan-Islamism that could threaten the existence of colonialism since they, according to the colonizers, became the primary roots for spreading unrest, rebellion, and anti-colonial movements in their colonized societies (see also Low 2008: 269–90). Arabia, particularly Hijaz, was the political territory of the Ottoman Sultanate, which, particularly during Abd al-Hamid II (r.1876–1908), sponsored pan-Islamic ideology to fight against the British and other European colonial powers that threatened its authority. This is why the colonials had long been suspicious toward the hajj returnees. In fact, the colonial rulers introduced tough regulations that restricted hajj pilgrimage and discouraged "Indonesians" to visit Mecca. Besides these political reasons, the European colonizers also identified the hajj as the source of a hazardous disease: cholera. In brief, to borrow William Roff's (1982: 143) phrases, the hajj came to represent a source of "twin infection" of sanitary and security concerns. As an outcome of this "twin infection," the Dutch (and also the British) managed to control the administration of the hajj and limit the number of hajj pilgrims.

However, unlike the colonial rulers, Snouck Hurgronje doubted that the great majority of Indonesian pilgrims would be influenced by ideas and movements of pan-Islamism. For Hurgronje, however, those who needed further scrutiny and could be the source of sociopolitical chaos in the East Indies were not the hajj returnees but the mukims, namely the pilgrims (of Indonesia) who resided in Mecca (some until their death) for long periods (Abaza 2007: 424). Many of the mukims at the time, in fact, were influential Muslim teachers, respected Islamic scholars, and tariqa (Sufi order) leaders that became a *guru* (teacher) to—and a spiritual-intellectual inspiration for—many Indonesian pilgrims (see Chapter 4). Figures such as Abdus Samad Palembang, Abdul Karim Banten, Abdullah Muhaimin Lasem, Ahmad Khatib Minangkabau, Muhammad Muchtar, among many others were the leading scholars in Mecca who were in favor of a jihad against the Dutch. The mukims also established an anti-colonial political group, named Perkumpulan Kemerdekaan Indonesia (Association for the Liberation of Indonesia), which propagated the struggle for liberty and independence among Indonesian pilgrims.

The mukims in turn created small Indonesian enclaves and helped to build a "Kampung Jawah" or "Kampung Jawa" (lit. "Javanese Village") in Mecca. Located in the district of Shamiah or Shi'ib Ali, the Kampung Jawa later became one of the Islamic training or learning centers, besides a temporary residence, for new Malay-Indonesians arriving in Mecca for a hajj or umrah pilgrimage. In the 1880s, Snouck Hurgronje himself had already described the Kampung Jawah and its residents in his classic books published in the 1880s. Long before he landed in Mecca in mid-1880 on a "colonial mission," Hurgronje had already written his doctoral thesis, which he defended on November 24, 1880, in Leiden University, entitled *Het Mekkaansche feest* (The Meccan Festival).[8] The presence of Kampung Jawah in Mecca signifies the long contact between the Malay-Indonesian archipelago and the Arabian Peninsula. It tells us that the voyage of Malay-Indonesian Muslims to Hijaz for either hajj pilgrimage or other purposes (e.g., learning Islamic knowledge and sciences) took place long before the opening of the Suez Canal. This uneasy journey did not always end up with a happy ending. Sometimes the pilgrims died because of food shortage, famine, or disease, or were trapped in slavery.

Hijaz was part of the Ottoman Empire at a time when the practice of enslavement in the private sector was allowed. Even when Hijaz was under the control of the Al Saud family, slavery had been common practice among people of Hijaz at the time. Indonesians came to Arabia as free men, but some eventually became heavily indebted after their arrival. Some of them were robbed on the way or upon their arrival, while others had inadequate funds at the very beginning of their trip that took months on sea and were not be able to pay lodgings, foods, and other necessary things upon their arrival in Jeddah or Mecca after their long voyage. In order to pay back the cost of the hajj journey, some had to work for local shaikhs and merchants, some of them were Indonesians, who took advantage of the unfavorable situation of some of their compatriots. According to reports of the Consulate of the Dutch East Indies in Jeddah, they exploited the pilgrims and forced some of them gradually into servitude. Even many of those slaves who had been freed could not make a living by themselves and eventually ended up in the hands of their former owners again.[9]

With regard to Arabia–Indonesian relations, Diederich (2005: 128–46) divides the contact between Arabia and Indonesia into two main phases. The first phase, which concluded at the end of the Second World War, was typified by the predominance of religious contact, and the second phase (post–Second World War) was marked by the increased migration of menial laborers seeking employment and "unskilled" jobs. The first stage, according to Diederich, is marked by the centrality of the hajj pilgrimage in Islam that brought "Indonesians" (including people of the East Indies) to Arabia to perform this vital religious compulsion. As previously noted, after the hajj, the majority of Indonesians returned to their homeland. However, a small minority stayed behind or continued to travel between Hijaz (Mecca and Medina) and Indonesia.

Diederich argues that the first phase of contact had produced intense transnational connections between Indonesians and Muslim societies in Mecca or Hijaz more broadly. Later on, the Dutch viewed both the hajj pilgrimage and transnational networks as a threat for the security, sociopolitical stability, and continuity of Dutch colonial rule in the East Indies, thereby prompting the Dutch authorities to intervene and control the flow of both people and discourses by implementing several strict rules and policies concerning the hajj and travel to Mecca. The second phase, furthermore, is a "function of both the need for expatriate labor in Saudi Arabia and of Indonesia's uneven economic development, which failed to absorb excess human resources in the country itself" (128). Although there has been significant migration of Indonesian menial workers to Saudi Arabia,[10] this group remains marginal transnational actors, whose weak bargaining position in both Saudi Arabia and Indonesia prevents them from playing a leading role in transnational processes.

Unlike Diederich's observation, however, I notice that the first phase of contact was not only marked by religion but also intellectualism. This is to say that Indonesians who traveled or migrated to Arabia in the first phase did not do so only to perform religious-spiritual activities, such as hajj, but also to learn Islamic knowledge and study Islamic sciences. After completing hajj rituals, learning, and studying multiple Islamic sciences, some students decided to stay in Mecca or Medina (known as *mukimin* or the *mukims*) and became teachers and scholars who ran free *halaqah* (study circles) for pilgrims and built *ribat* (Islamic boarding schools). Second, as for the second phase, Indonesians who traveled or migrated to Saudi in the aftermath of the Second World War were not only there to seek unskilled occupation but also to look for professional, skilled jobs as well as to study various sciences and pursue degrees in multiple disciplines (Islamic and "secular" sciences).

However, it should be noted, during the first phase, most, if not all, students learned and studied Islamic sciences at multiple formal and informal learning institutions (madrasah, halaqah, rubat, and mosques) in Mecca in particular. In the second phase, however, there were three types or groups of Indonesians traveling or migrating to Saudi, not to mention hajj/umrah pilgrims. The first group were Indonesians seeking "unskilled" jobs (i.e., menial workers) as well as skilled occupations (professional expatriates) in the oil industry, construction companies, hotels, or hospitals. The second group were Indonesians studying Islamic sciences in multiple Islamic learning centers: madrasah, mosques, institutes, colleges, and universities. This new trend, for sure, differs from the previous one where Indonesian Muslims learned Islam at informal educational sites, particularly at the holy places of Mecca's Haram Mosque and Medina's Nabawi Mosque, or madrasah (Islamic schools). The third group were Indonesian students studying secular sciences and engineering, mostly at graduate levels (master's and PhD). These types of students mostly studied at King Fahd University of Petroleum and Minerals (Dhahran), King Saud University (Riyadh), and King Abdullah University of Science and Technology (Thuwal).

Since the 1980s and 1990s, Indonesian students, all through scholarship provided by the kingdom, learned Islamic studies at universities and colleges, most notably Umm al-Qura University (Mecca), Islamic University (Medina), and Imam Muhammad bin Saud Islamic University (Riyadh). Of these three universities, Islamic University of Media has been the largest host for Indonesian Muslim students pursuing multiple degrees in Islamic sciences and disciplines such as Islamic Law, Hadith exegesis, and *da'wa* (missiology). At present, there are more than 700 Indonesian students at the Islamic University of Medina. I will discuss the debate on Indonesian students at Saudi's academic institutions further in another chapter.

Indonesian Muslim students have not only studied in Saudi at the Indonesian branches of Saudi universities. In 1980, Saudi Arabia built Jakarta-based Lembaga Ilmu Pengetahuan Islam dan Bahasa Arab (LIPIA—Institute for Islamic and Arabic Studies, formerly Lembaga Pengajaran Bahasa Arab or LPBA—Institute for Arabic Teaching), which offers Bachelor degrees in Islamic Studies and Arabic language. LIPIA is an all-expenses-paid university. The institute, housed in a modern building sheathed in blue reflective glass, has produced thousands of graduates trained in a strict, puritanical Salafi Islam that claims to restore the orthodox practices of the early days of the Muslim religion. The curriculum at LIPIA emphasizes learning the Arabic language (in fact, all classes are taught in Arabic) and the study of Islam, particularly Islamic law, theology (tauhid), and *da'wa* (Islamic propagation).

Like most universities and colleges in Saudi, men and women are also segregated. Moreover, men are encouraged to grow beards following Prophet Muhammad's practice and adopt Salafi dress with ankle-length linen pants and sandals, and women must be completely veiled. Jeans, music, and television are prohibited. This "religious practice" of Islamic Salafism is in stark contrast to the relaxed, tolerant, pluralist local Islam (e.g., Islam Nusantara) practiced by many Indonesian Muslims across the archipelago. This sharply different practice of Islam in many cases has created tensions and conflict between Salafi and non-Salafi groups. For many years, the best alumni of LIPIA have had a chance to continue their study and pursue master's or doctorate degrees at the Imam Muhammad bin Saud Islamic University in Riyadh. The Saudi government intends on expanding the university, from 3,500 graduates to 10,000 graduates a year. It will sponsor a brand-new campus in Jakarta as well as branches in Medan, Surabaya, and Makassar (Scott 2016).

Moreover, some Saudi-trained alumni, particularly those who studied Islamic sciences in the kingdom, also built Islamic centers, madrasah, or pesantren (Islamic boarding school), in some areas of Indonesia such as Pesantren Fitra Al Alam Al

Islamy (FIWA) in Bogor of West Java and Pondok Pesantren Islamic Center Bin Baz in Jogjakarta. According to its official homepage, Pesantren Fitra Al Alam Al Islamy, sometimes known as Fitrah Islamic World Academy, is an "international standard" Islamic boarding school which is built based on the Qur'an, Hadith, and the understandings and practices of early generations of Islam (salaf al-shalih). Headed by Erwandi Tarmidzi and Ali Saman Hasan, it intends to prepare for the creation of the cadres of Islamic scholars (ulama) in the future. The pesantren is also supported by some Saudi Islamic scholars such as Shaikh Abu Abdillah Ahmad Abdulah Al Sudais, Shaikh Abdullah Al Matrudy, Shaikh Mustafa Marzuq, and Shaikh Abdulaziz Al Ahmady, among others.[11]

Moreover, Pondok Pesantren Islamic Center Bin Baz (known as ICBB) has several chapters: Raudlatul Athfal (kindergarten), Salafiyah Uwla (Elementary School), Salafiyyah Wustha (Junior High School), and Madrasah Aliyah (Senior High School). The pesantren also specializes in teaching and memorizing the Qur'an (known as *Tahfidh al-Qur'an*).[12] The name "Bin Baz" is attributed to Abd al-Aziz bin Baz (1910–1999), a former Saudi senior Islamic scholar and a leading proponent of the Salafi form of Islam. Bin Baz was appointed as the Grand Mufti of Saudi Arabia from 1993 until his death in 1999.

Migration, workforce, and employment

The educational travelers and intellectual migrants described earlier are only a small portion of the Indonesians in Saudi Arabia. The largest portion, especially since the 1980s, are labor migrants. Saudi Arabia, along with the Gulf states, is one of the world's largest migrant destinations. As one of the world's favorite migrant destinations, Saudi has become a major source for remittances. The wages that migrant workers send home from Saudi Arabia is second only to the United States as the source of the largest amount of remittance payments in the world[13] (Ratha 2003). Remittances from Saudi Arabia totaled some 285.3 billion riyals—about US$76 billion—in the five-year period between 1995 and 1999 (Kawach 2003).

About 33 percent of the total population in the kingdom, which reach more than 31 million people in 2016, are expatriates.[14] The largest expatriate communities in Saudi Arabia include 1–1.5 million people each from Bangladesh, India, and Pakistan, and another 900,000 each from Egypt, Sudan, and the Philippines (Human Rights Watch [HRW] 2004). A much greater increase in the numbers of foreign workers in the kingdom came with the oil-price boom following the 1973 oil crisis. From 1973 to 1974, Saudi's national income rose dramatically, particularly after the soaring oil prices during the Arab–Israeli war. As an outcome of the oil-price thriving, Saudi, which was formerly known as a dry and barren desert nation, later transformed into a rich region and one of world's prospective international markets. Production and exploration costs were quite low, and it increased profits and income for Arab countries from the oil sector. Extraordinary income from the oil industry also gave birth to newly rich businessmen. The economic changes have indeed increased the range of developments and marvelous economic growth in the kingdom.

Moreover, infrastructure and development plans in Saudi led to an influx of skilled and unskilled laborers from such countries as Egypt, Yemen, India, and Pakistan, leading to a doubling of the Saudi population by 1985. Besides the need for foreign workers to work in oil companies and construction, Saudi also opened up great opportunities for domestic workers and housekeepers. Dr. Ali bin Ibrahim al-Namlah, Saudi Arabia's then long-serving minister of labor and social affairs, said that Saudi Arabia is "a land of opportunity" for qualified low-wage workers (Human Rights Watch [HRW] 2004). Indeed, throughout the GCC (Gulf Cooperation Council) states, jobs created in the private sector other than in the oil industry typically require only low skills and pay low wages. The country's improved economy has created a culture of people who do not want to take care of household affairs and rely on foreign workers. Domestic helpers and drivers, therefore, became one of the much-needed services in Saudi Arabia. As a result, beginning in the early 1980s, Southeast Asian countries, such as the Philippines, Indonesia, and Thailand, increasingly provided "unskilled" migrant workers. Although the oil price declined in the 1980s, leading to a decreased demand for foreign labor and resulting in a substantial drop in migration from Asia, there was a significant increase of female guest workers from South and Southeast Asia who filled roles in the service sector, including "menial" domestic jobs.

As for Indonesian migrants in Saudi, there has been a new wave of workers since the early 1980s, typified by in search for menial employment and "unprofessional" jobs. The early 1980s was the period where Indonesia started to "export" menial workers and housemaids to the kingdom as a result of agreements between the two countries. Retired General Sudomo, the minister of manpower in Suharto's New Order administration, was a key figure and decision maker regarding labor migrants being sent to the Middle East. Indonesia's ambassador to Saudi at the time also expressed enthusiasm for the prospects of labor export, in part because he saw overseas employment meant jobs for unemployed Indonesian nationals as well as crucial foreign exchange in the form of remittances. The involvement of the Ministry of Manpower and the Indonesian Embassy to Saudi means that the Indonesian New Order state bureaucracy has shaped men's and women's immigration to Saudi Arabia. At the time, due to the fall of oil price on an international market, Indonesia had been experiencing rising unemployment and economic upheaval. It was expected, therefore, that by sending more domestic workers to Saudi would generate foreign exchange and diminish joblessness in the country.

In 1983, following the agreement between the Indonesian government and the Kingdom of Saudi Arabia, Indonesia formally released 47,000 fully documented workers to the kingdom, and this number grew rapidly every year thereafter. Since the early 1980s, Indonesian domestic workers have overwhelmed Saudi. Between 1980 and 1984, the Indonesian government recorded 55,976 migrant nationals with work contracts destined for Saudi Arabia. Between 1984 and 1989, the number rose to 223,579 and increased again to 384,822 in the following five-year period. The majority (about 59 percent) of documented overseas workers from Indonesia between 1989 and 1994 migrated to Saudi Arabia, growing more than fourfold from a total of 55,967 between 1979 and 1983 to a total of 223,579 during the subsequent five-year period (Hugo 1995: 280; Silvey 2004b: 145), and over 380,000 per year in 1998 (Hugo 2002). At first, the wave of Indonesian workers was still dominated by men who worked in large construction companies and shopping centers across the kingdom, as Saudi started building a modern and industrial country by initiating huge infrastructure and construction projects resulting from the oil-price boom.

Although the oil price dropped in the mid-1980s, Indonesia continued to send workers to Saudi, and the number of these workers sent by the Indonesian government tended to increase year on year. The data from the Indonesian Ministry of Manpower and Transmigration (Depnakertrans 2004) show that in 2001 alone, 244,000 formally documented migrants were placed in Saudi. The Indonesian government through the Ministry of Manpower and Transmigration even intended to send 2 million workers with fixed-term contracts to Saudi within five years from 1998 to 2003. However, this plan was not realized. The overall number of Indonesian migrants in 2004 was roughly between 250,000 and 500,000, making Indonesia the ninth highest country contributing to the Saudi workforce after India, Pakistan, Egypt, Yemen, Bangladesh, Philippines, Sri Lanka, and Jordan. In 2009, reportedly, the number of documented female domestic workers had reached some 700,000[15] (Machmudi 2011). Data from the Indonesian National Bureau for Placement and Protection of Indonesian Workers (Badan Nasional Penempatan dan Perlindungan Tenaga Kerja Indonesia or BNP2KI) shows that the number of Indonesian workers abroad, including in Saudi, from 2005 to 2010 is still dominated by unskilled workers.[16]

The official government figures from the Ministry of Manpower and Transmigration do not include "undocumented migrants," so the figures might be higher than the official ones, since many people travel from Indonesia to Saudi without completing the documentation required by the government. They usually first traveled to Saudi with an umrah visa, since this is the easiest way to enter Saudi. With the umrah visa, they typically came long before the time of hajj. Many of them try to perform the hajj with insufficient funds and have to get informal jobs to survive. Some stay in the Mosque Haram with a very limited budget. Some become sick and starving because they do not want to leave the mosque for fear of police arrest. Others perform the hajj but do not return home, instead choosing to join other compatriots or their families who have settled there, particularly in the cities of Mecca, Jeddah, and Medina. This phenomenon took place long before the Indonesian government officially sent workers to Saudi in 1983.

The *Tempo* magazine reported that in October 1978,[17] there were two truckloads of Indonesians, who initially came to Saudi for hajj but their visa had expired, stopped in front of the Indonesian Embassy in Riyadh. On average, they did not have return tickets, so the embassy refused their entry. Hundreds of Indonesians were sent to jail in Saudi, since the Indonesian authority in Riyadh was unable to handle them. Some of these Indonesians, mostly uneducated people who came from Indonesia's remote villages and were only motivated by the desire to perform the hajj pilgrimage as one of Islam's main pillars, were actually the victims of travel agent brokers who persuaded and cheated them at home to come to Mecca. Many of them came to Saudi, hoping to perform a hajj, after selling their most precious belonging: land. Unfortunately, however, they did not have an opportunity to perform a hajj because the Saudi government issued a new regulation—known as the 1977 Muharram policy—that ordered the forced repatriation of any foreign nationals without resident permits. Sadly, most of these people did not have return tickets, as these were taken by Indonesian intermediaries once they arrived at the Saudi airports.

Apart from this issue, Saudi, in 1978, had opened up opportunities for foreign workers, including Indonesians, to fill the labor market in the kingdom. In addition to the hajj pilgrimage, another channel for undocumented Indonesian migrants in Saudi were family, neighborhood, and friendship networks. Family invited their family members, friends called their friends, and neighbors asked for their neighbors to come to Saudi to pursue jobs in the informal sectors. Informal economies become the main target especially for undocumented migrants. Some informants said that there was a strong network of Indonesians, particularly those from Madura, Java, Lombok, or Sumatra, in the kingdom, especially in the three main areas: Mecca, Medina, and Jeddah.[18] In recent years, however, the number of illegal migrants has tended to decrease dramatically since the Saudi government implements a firm policy toward undocumented immigrants by catching and deporting them to their home countries.

These undocumented migrants, in particular, are vulnerable to abuse by middlemen and employers. By 1984 onward, reports began to occur in the Indonesian media about the widespread problems faced by migrants in the Gulf, including Saudi Arabia. Despite growing recognition of the problems, however, female domestic migrants to Saudi continued to dominate the documented outflow of overseas migrants until 1995. The economic downturn in Indonesia and the attendant increases in unemployment and inflation intensified the pressure on people to seek work abroad. However, since the economic and financial crises hit Indonesia in the late 1990s, the country's out-migration flows began to shift to other countries in Asia, most notably to neighboring countries such as Malaysia, Singapore, and Brunei, because of the lower cost of travel to these Southeast Asian destinations.

At that time, Saudi became the main destination for Indonesian workers largely because earnings were substantially higher than in other possible destination countries in Asia such as Hong Kong, Malaysia, Brunei Darussalam, and Singapore. Women made up the majority of documented migrants (known as *Tenaga Kerja Wanita* or "female workforce") in Indonesia's rapidly growing overseas labor market. Silvey (2004a, 2004b) also notes that of this large number of migrants, the distinct majority have been women: two-thirds of the migrants between 1984 and 1994 were women; and between 1994 and 1999, more than twelve times as many women are estimated to have formally migrated to Saudi Arabia. More than 80 percent of these migrant women were intended to work as domestic workers, particularly housemaids (Indonesian: *pembantu rumah tangga*, or PRT) (Silvey 2004a: 250).

Indonesian drivers were also hired by Saudis but in smaller numbers than maids. The majority of Indonesian drivers in Saudi work as a "personal driver" (*sopir pribadi*), while the rest work as taxi drivers and bus drivers belonging to SAPTCO, Saudi's largest transportation company.[19] Some SAPTCO Indonesian bus drivers whom I met in Riyadh, Medina, and Mecca said that that the company is like a home for them since many drivers are Indonesians, particularly from West Java. They said that not all Indonesians working in SAPTCO are bus drivers. Some work as SAPTCO cab drivers.[20] In March of 2016, when I visited Medina for additional data collection and "religious tourism," I also used a SAPTCO cab, whose driver was an Indonesian, from the Prince Mohammad bin Abdulaziz International Airport to a hotel near Mosque Nabawi. The driver told me that he had been working for several years in the company as a bus driver and then a cab driver. He said that he got the job via a friendship network.

The flow of the menial workers, documented or undocumented, provides an opportunity for Indonesians to get jobs with higher wages than in Indonesia, on one hand. However, the "surge" of these types of workers also means the appearance of new problems, on the other. It is obvious that Indonesians generally had little bargaining power in the Saudi Arabian labor market in part because many of them had no experience of working overseas, professional employment, or developed skills. As stated earlier, with few notable exceptions, most Indonesians who went to Saudi Arabia to work found employment in private households. Although the oil price went down in the 1980s, Saudi citizens could still afford to hire maids and drivers for their homes with modest wages.

Indonesian maids were considered suitable for work in the private sphere because they were (generally) Muslims, except those from Flores, Nusa Tenggara Timur, and other parts of eastern Indonesia where most migrants were Christians. However, unfortunately, many Indonesian maids encountering problems with their employers feel powerless. Given their lack of language skills and the generally poor predeparture training, Indonesian maids are rarely able to contact the police or the Indonesian Embassy/Consulate when problems arise. Lack of appropriate predeparture training for their jobs abroad has also harmed the "reputation" and image of Indonesia in general. Moreover, Saudis are often unhappy with and complain about Indonesians' lack of language skills (Arabic or English) and their unfamiliarity with modern household equipment. Unskilled female workers commonly come from a poor family background in the countryside or rural areas of Indonesia; thereby, it is understandable if they are unfamiliar with such modern household tools as kitchen utensils, cleaning equipment, toiletries. In brief, Indonesian overseas workers are generally considered inflexible, slow, and poorly educated (Diederich 2005: 133–35). The perception of Indonesians is quite different from that of Filipino migrants who, in general, have a better image and impression, in part because they receive good predeparture training, especially concerning English language skills.[21]

Since Indonesian domestic workers have a lack of predeparture training, Arabic skills, and are unfamiliar with modern household equipment, they occasionally make mistakes which can create problems with their landlords and family members. If the problems are left unresolved, violence can occur. Some domestic workers have been given the death penalty, while others have been sent to jail. Some have been arrested by the Saudi authorities on alleged charges of murder, witchcrafts, and sexual offences. There are plenty of media and research reports about the miserable conditions of Indonesian housekeepers and the ill-treatment practices in Saudi (see, e.g., Hugo 2002; HRW 2004; Silvey 2004a, 2004b; Machmudi 2011). The former Indonesian minister of religious affairs, the late Maftuh Basyuni, also recognized such difficult situations when he was requested by the Indonesian government to come to Saudi to deal with such critical issues facing Indonesian domestic workers in the kingdom.

Furthermore, in response to the mistreatment and the abuse of housemaids by some Saudi landlords, many Indonesians have held mass protests in Jakarta and other cities, and criticized both the Saudi kingdom and the Indonesian government. The Indonesian public has criticized (1) the kingdom for neglecting human rights and human needs of housemaids, and (2) the Indonesian government for failing to negotiate with the Saudi landlords and rulers as well as for not addressing domestic violence and death sentences. Interestingly, whereas the Saudi government immediately stopped receiving domestic household workers from Indonesia after getting harsh criticism from the Indonesian public, the Government of Indonesia was quite slow to respond to this issue. At the time, the Indonesian government was still reluctant to end the export of female workers to Saudi. The government officials even glorified female domestic workers as the "heroines of foreign exchanges" or remittances (known as *pahlawan devisa*) for Indonesia, as they significantly contributed to the national income. Only in 2011, did the Indonesian government stop sending female workers to Saudi (Irianto 2011), and five years later, in 2016, the Saudi kingdom and the Government of Indonesia, reached a new deal on the labor contract concerning Indonesian domestic workers in the kingdom.

Although the ill-treatment of female workers is well known, it is a mistake to generalize about the conditions of domestic female workers and maid–landlord relations in Saudi simply because some Saudi employers maltreated them. Saudi educated and religious employers usually treat their housemaids very well and properly by hiring them in accordance with the government policy on foreign domestic workers, giving them a proper room to live in as well as weekend breaks, taking them to tourist places at home and abroad, and so forth. Some generous Saudi employers also take care of the housemaids' family members in Indonesia, sponsor them for umrah and hajj, and even invite them to work in Saudi to accompany their brothers or sisters. Some Saudis have even married their housemaid and treated them as a wife. Other domestic servants have admitted that their employers have even helped them build their houses in Indonesia. These nice stories have been widely circulated among wives of Indonesian professional expats in Saudi who have informal groupings for social gatherings, Qur'anic recitations, or religious sermons.

Changing mutual images and perceptions between Saudis and Indonesians

There is no doubt that the surge of Indonesian menial and unskilled laborers into the kingdom has indeed shifted the picture, perception, and impression of the Indonesian community in Saudi in general, changing from positive to negative. Although not all Indonesian immigrants in Saudi work in informal economies, the presence of the menial workers since the early 1980s have indeed changed the way contemporary Saudis perceive Indonesia and Indonesians in the kingdom. Sociologically speaking, there has been a shift in the nature of the image and perception of Indonesia and Indonesians in Saudi Arabia as a poor country with low-class, uneducated people due to the influx of Indonesian unskilled laborers and undocumented immigrants in the kingdom since the early 1980s or even before. On November 25, 2011, *Saudi Today* raised the issue of "slavery in the modern age," and identified Indonesia as the largest contributor or exporter to this "modern servitude" or "slave trade"—housemaids.

It is important to note that in addition to the unskilled migrants and domestic servants, there is a sizable number of Indonesian professional expatriates who work as engineers or computer scientists in a number of big companies such as Saudi Aramco (Arabian Oil Company; formerly Arabian-American Oil Company), SABIC (Saudi Arabia Basic Industries Corp), and Schlumberger, among many others. There are also some Indonesians who work as professors, teachers, researchers, and analysts in research institutions and universities in the kingdom such as King Fahd University of Petroleum and Minerals, Imam Muhammad ibn Saud Islamic University, King Saud University, and King Abdulaziz University. I explain and analyze this issue in another chapter of this book. However, their presence and contribution are extremely limited; accordingly, they are unable to change the image and perception of the Indonesian nation and its people in the kingdom.

In short, since the 1980s, when Indonesia began to export unskilled workers to the Middle East, the positive image of Indonesia in Saudi began to change and tended to wane. Due to the influx of this unprofessional migrant group, unskilled female and male laborers have dominated public issues of Indonesian migrants in the kingdom, while Muslim teachers and scholars who historically contributed to Islamic education and civilization in Hijaz have disappeared from the news. Since the 1980s, the term "Jawi ulama" (i.e., Islamic scholars from the Malay-Indonesian archipelago) that gained a high esteem in Hijaz in the past has slowly but steadily changed to become "Indunisi workers," namely menial laborers from Indonesia. In the past, Indonesians in Mecca (known as *mukimin* or settlers) were respected as knowledge seekers, but since the 1980s they have become (inexpert) job seekers who have no or limited knowledge of Islamic and other sciences.

Worse yet, some Indonesian workers, dominated by housekeepers, drivers, and laborers of informal economies, have created problems for the Saudi government and society in general as they have committed crimes or "bothered" Indonesian pilgrims by stealing their money (Machmudi 2011: 235). Some of them reportedly became "informal bodyguards" for Indonesian pilgrims who wanted to touch and kiss Ka'ba and Hajar Aswad (the "Black Stone"). For this service (i.e., guarding and protecting the pilgrims from the crowds in order for them to touch and kiss the Ka'ba and Hajar Aswad), they received money from 100 to 300 Saudi riyals (SR). Indonesian informants told me that some Indonesians were engaged in a revenge-motivated killing and other forms of violence due to their girlfriends or "temporary wives" being involved in love affairs with other Indonesian men.[22]

Furthermore, Indonesian female workers, particularly the undocumented workers or those who have escaped from their landlords due to issues, are often involved in underground prostitution practices in Saudi. Reportedly on average Indonesian prostitutes are paid SR 50 for a date; thereby they are known as *abu khamsin* (i.e., goods for SR 50). Another nickname for Indonesian women is *siti rahmah*. This nickname is not a "praise call" as the original meaning of this word (i.e., women who give love and affection) but rather uttered with negative connotations that indicate sexual desires[23] (see Machmudi 2011: 226). This nickname might be commensurate with—or even lower than—the term "Indon" for Indonesian migrants in Malaysia that signifies the "lower status" of Indonesians working in Malaysia's domestic households and informal sectors. As the Saudi government bans prostitution, which is considered "haram" (unlawful) in accordance with Islamic law, they use apartments to conduct this illegal sexual activity. Male migrants from India, Bangladesh, and Sri Lanka, among others, who work in the informal sectors, usually become the "main customers" of this "clandestine prostitution." Besides "undercover prostitution," some Indonesian women also work in "concealed night clubs" in some major cities, especially Jeddah. Sometimes they tape their activities and post the videos on YouTube.

It is unquestionably miserable to see present-day Indonesian migrants become suspects for issues of immigration violation, crime, and prostitution. But this is part of the contemporary dynamics and changes of Indonesians in the kingdom, which is in sharp contrast with the previous centuries described earlier. It is obvious that there are major changes and differences between nowadays and the past concerning perceptions and impressions of Arabians toward Indonesians. In the past, Arabians, or Hijazis in particular, saw people from the Malay-Indonesian archipelago as learned scholars and fervent learners of Islam. In the modern era, however, they tend to see Indonesians as uneducated people and unskilled workers. In other words, for contemporary Saudis, whom I have talked with on various occasions, Indonesians nowadays are better known as a less-educated working class of informal economies than educated professional workforces. Sadly, Saudi youths do not even know that there are some Indonesian professional expats or skilled workers in Saudi who work in a variety of companies, hospitals, or educational institutions. They are also unfamiliar with the history and contributions of Indonesian Islamic scholars in the past in Hijaz or Haramain.

As for educated Saudi people, particularly those trained in Islamic discipline, social sciences and humanities, they generally admitted the constructive role and positive contributions of the "Jawi ulama" in Islamic schooling and religious discourses in the past.[24] Some contemporary Saudi Islamic scholars have even established a private Islamic learning center in Mecca to train Indonesian Muslim students in Islamic sciences in honor of the "Jawi ulama." Moreover, Saudi middle-class families in general, due to their regular travel to Indonesia, either for business or leisure, recognize Indonesia as a Muslim-majority country filled with abundant green islands and stunning seas and beaches. They also recognize that Indonesians are friendly people. However, they also admit that Indonesia is a poor and underdeveloped country that lacks education, industry, and technology. While acknowledging Indonesia as a gorgeous country with polite people, they tend to overlook the quality of its populace.

Moreover, Saudis who are not familiar with the archipelagic country of Indonesia except for their household servants tend to see Indonesia as a deprived nation, since it sent its citizens abroad to work as housemaids and drivers. Judging on their servants at home, they also thought Indonesians were illiterate or "unschooled" people. Other Saudi citizens, based on their impressions from daily contact with Indonesian migrants, tend to see Indonesians as illegal immigrants, perpetrators of black magic, or disobedient of the Islamic religion, as they committed immoral acts and other legal violations. A teacher at the Riyadh-based Indonesian school, Abdullah Khaidir, expressed his feelings about Saudis as follows:

> In general, Saudis only see positive towards Indonesians in terms of their behaviour or attitudes (friendly and charming). As for other sides, such as science and technology, politics, industry, and security, they tend to disregard us, although not too low. Apparently, the impression of Indonesia in relation to economic development, politics, science, technology and security still tend to be negative. (quoted in Machmudi 2011: 236)

Contemporary developments of Saudi–Indonesian cooperation

Apart from the slightly negative image and impression of Indonesia and Indonesians, there is a strong tendency to improve formal bilateral relationships between the Kingdom of Saudi Arabia and the Government of Indonesia. The two Muslim-majority countries have seemingly strengthened their diplomatic and non diplomatic relations on various matters: politics, economy, businesses, defenses, education, among others. "At present, our relationship with Indonesia is in excellent shape," said Saudi Ambassador to Indonesia, Abdulrahman Mohammed Amen Al Khayyat. The ambassador furthermore said that Saudi would like to further strengthen the decades-old relationship with Indonesia.[25]

Taking the same line, the Indonesian Ambassador to the Kingdom of Saudi Arabia and Organizations of Islamic Cooperation (OIC) Agus Maftuh Abegebriel also initiated a long-term diplomatic program called SAUNESA (Saudi Arabia–Indonesia) to boost close relationships between the two nations.[26] The ambassador also brought Saudi philanthropist and businessman Prince Alwaleed bin Talal, chairman of Kingdom Holding Company (KHC), to Indonesia to meet President Joko Widodo and discuss a number of local and regional issues, the global economic climate, investment as well as humanitarian and social issues related to their respective countries. Prince Alwaleed has long-standing business connections with Indonesia, since he has invested in numerous business sectors in the country. Through Alwaleed Philanthropies, the prince also has donated millions of US dollars to charities, humanitarian agencies, and to help with social issues in Indonesia.[27]

As stated earlier, the formal ties between the two countries began in 1948, although informal relations had taken place long before. The long historic and well-nurtured bilateral relationship between Indonesia and Saudi Arabia was evidently preserved with the visit of President Joko Widodo in September 2015 to the Kingdom of Saudi Arabia. The president, along with his accompanying delegation, was warmly welcomed by Custodian of the Two Holy Mosques King Salman bin Abdulaziz Al Saud. King Salman, moreover, decorated President Widodo with the prestigious King Abdulaziz Medal at Al-Salam Palace in Jeddah. This medal is the highest honorary medal granted to foreign heads of state, symbolizing an appreciation of the strong friendship, relationship, and cooperation between the two nations. The two leaders, moreover, held talks on a number of international and regional issues of mutual concern and interest. They also discussed the state of bilateral relations and explored ways of enhancing them.[28]

To follow up this historic meeting, the following month King Salman sent Minister for Foreign Affairs Adel al-Jubeir to meet President Widodo in Indonesia. During the meeting with President Widodo that took place in the Presidential Office in Jakarta, Minister al-Jubeir, reportedly the second person not belonging to the House of Saud to hold the office after Ibrahim bin Abullah Al Suwaiyel, conveyed the greetings of King Salman, the government, and people of Saudi Arabia to Indonesia's president. In turn, the president sent his appreciation to King Salman, expressing his wish to see the relations between the two countries pushed to higher horizons. Former Saudi Ambassador to the United States, Al-Jubeir discussed with the president ways of enhancing cooperation between the two countries in the fields of political consultation and coordination, military, security, economic, investment, cultural, oil and petrochemical industries, among others. The aim of this cooperation is to create a qualitative leap in relations between the two countries in the services of mutual concern as well as the service of the Islamic nation.

Moreover, Minister al-Jubeir held talks with Indonesian Minister of Foreign Affairs Retno Marsudi during which he discussed a wide range of issues relating to bilateral relations and regional and international issues of mutual concern. In a joint press conference following the talks, Minister Retno Marsudi lauded the depth of relations between the two countries, noting that her meeting with al-Jubeir focused on ways of enhancing cooperation between the two countries in the fields of energy, commerce and investments, among others. Al-Jubeir too praised the bilateral relations between the two countries which are based on a number of common factors and recalled that the kingdom was among the first countries to have recognized Indonesia's independence in 1945, confirming the kingdom's hope to see more development and enhancement of the strong relations between the two sisterly countries.

The two nations have reached an agreement to build relations on numerous issues and fields, including security or defense, agriculture, trade and economy, oil and petroleum, culture and education, and so on. On the security issue, for instance, Indonesia and Saudi Arabia had signed the Defense Cooperation Agreement (DCA), which is the first agreement of its sort between Indonesia and Saudi Arabia or any other Middle Eastern country.[29] The DCA covers training, education, counterterrorism, and defense industry cooperation (Panda 2014). Saudi Arabia and Indonesia are among the Muslim-majority countries in the world that suffered from—and was damaged by—Islamist terrorism. Multiple terrorist attacks by radical Islamist groups took place in both countries targeting various sites and properties belonging to the government, the private sector, or particular religious groups. Accordingly, it is understandable if the two countries joined forces to fight against terrorism that has damaged not only the reputation of the nations but also the Islamic religion and the Muslim community as a whole. Another reason for signing the agreement is that both countries have special counterterrorism units. Saudi Arabia, under the chairmanship of Minister of Interior Prince Muhammad bin Nayef, has succeeded in battling against terrorism with a variety of counterterrorism programs. Indonesia, via the special security unit Densus 88, has also gained a reputation for successfully fighting against domestic terrorism since the Bali Blast in 2002. In fact, both Saudi Arabia and Indonesia, in agreeing to cooperate on counterterrorism, noted that terrorism should not be linked to any ideology or religion, in particular Islam. Indonesia's interlocutor adds that "No religion in the world teaches violence."[30] For Saudi Arabia, in particular, the DCA with Indonesia comes on the heels of a similar deal with Pakistan, with both deals highlighting the kingdom's interest in expanding relations with Islamic nations outside its immediate Middle Eastern neighborhood.

In addition to the field of defense, Saudi Arabia and Indonesia have also built strong economic and trade relations, and these ties will expand in the years to come. Naturally, bilateral trade has reflected the predominance of energy in trade between the two countries. However, in recent years, Indonesia and Saudi Arabia has agreed to double their bilateral trade value by 2020, as the two countries believe they have a lot of potential for expansion. The total trade between Indonesia and Saudi Arabia amounted to US$8.6 billion in 2015, with the Saudi investment value in Indonesia reaching US$29.3 million in the first half of 2015. Indonesian exports to Saudi Arabia amounted to US$3.35 billion in 2015, while imports were worth US$5.14 billion.[31] The figures are yet to reflect the potential of both countries, as Saudi Arabia is one of the biggest potential markets for Indonesia in the Middle East.[32]

During his business visit to Indonesia in May 2016, Maher Jamal, head of the Chamber of Commerce and Industry, said that Saudi Arabia has expressed an interest in cooperating with various business players in both countries including those running professional nursing care and producing pharmaceutical products, cosmetics and medical equipment. During his business trip, Jamal was accompanied by some thirty-four Saudi business representatives. The businessmen were later participating in the latest buying mission attended by around 100

Indonesian companies. Both countries reportedly have committed to increasing their trade value by at least 15 percent annually. To reach this goal, Saudi Arabia will participate in exhibitions staged by Indonesia, while Indonesia will also be invited to participate in exhibitions held in Saudi Arabia. In addition, to bolster its commitment, the Makkah Chamber of Commerce is planning to cooperate with the Indonesian government to create an Arabic language website and take other steps to make it easier for Saudi businesspeople to understand details of products being offered by their Indonesian counterparts.[33]

Religious, cultural, and educational issues have been another main concern and interest between the two countries. Beyond the economic/trade ties and defense/security cooperation depicted above, Saudi Arabia and Indonesia also maintain considerably strong religious and cultural links with each other. As discussed previously, Saudi has invested in education. In 1980, Saudi Arabia had already established the LIPIA in Jakarta aimed at teaching Islam studies and the Arabic language. This college has close affiliations to Riyadh-based Al Imam Muhammad bin Saud Islamic University. Over the past few years, the kingdom has sent a number of Arabic teachers to Indonesia and has granted scholarships for Indonesian students to study in a number of universities in Saudi Arabia, including King Fahd University of Petroleum and Minerals (Dhahran), King Saud University (Riyadh), King Abdullah University of Science and Technology (Thuwal), Islamic University (Medina), King Abdulaziz University (Jeddah), Umm Al-Qura University (Mecca), Taiba University (Medina), among others. The Saudi Embassy, particularly through its religious attaché office (opened in 2008) also carries out a number of social and religious programs in Indonesia. These include cooperating with the Indonesian Ministry of Religious Affairs to dispatch Imams during Ramadan to more isolated provinces, printing considerable amounts of religious literature in Indonesian languages, and distributing aid for the needy.

Another significant issue that marks the better relationships between Saudi Arabia and Indonesia is the implementation of a newly signed agreement between the two nations on Indonesian domestic workers in the kingdom. In May 2016, after a five-year period of the Indonesian government not sending female workers to Saudi, the Saudi Ministry of Labor and Social Development and its Indonesian counterpart had reached a new agreement for the recruitment of domestic laborers.[34] The deal stipulated that the Indonesian government should send the workers within a month of the approval of their visas. According to the pact, the ministry will safeguard workers' interest and needs such as keeping their identity cards and travel documents with them as well as freedom to call their families, all of which were absent before. Prior to reaching this new agreement, all travel documents and identity cards belonging to the Indonesian housemaids were kept by their landlords. Accordingly, they were unable to travel outside their masters' houses. If they did so, and were caught by the police, they would be sent to prison because they could not provide legal documents. This new agreement, therefore, is an excellent breakthrough, as it gives more freedom and rights to the workers.

Moreover, the new deal that was signed by both the Saudi and Indonesian governments provided several other helpful provisions to ensure a smooth policy, facilitating better arrangements for Indonesian domestic help in the country. The treaty includes the establishment of a mechanism to employ and a guarantee of the rights and duties of the workers and the employers, as per international norms. Furthermore, the agreement ensured that working contracts are made in accordance with the applicable laws and regulations in the two countries in terms of the time and place of work, the duties and responsibilities of the worker and the employer, the weekly day off, vacations, and the expiry date of the contract. Also, the employer will open a bank account in the name of his worker for the purpose of depositing his/her salary, as stipulated in the working contract. This is to ensure the financial rights of the employees.

Another piece of good news is that the Saudi authorities will facilitate the offering of consular assistance by the diplomatic missions to Indonesian citizens in the event of their arrest or detainment. In this case, the consulate will facilitate the return of Indonesian workers to their home country once their work contracts expire, or in emergency situations, including the issuance of exit visas. Under Article 4 of the agreement, the Indonesian candidate for employment should be within the age group of twenty-one to fifty-five years and must have no prior criminal record. Additionally, they must be trained on the specified skills required in the work contract and must familiarize themselves with the culture, customs, and social norms in Saudi Arabia. Finally, Indonesian domestic workers must also meet the health conditions set by Saudi Arabia. Among other provisions, it stipulates the working contract only comes into effect when the language and wording of the document is understood by all and has been formally agreed by both parties. Any disputes, the agreement says, between the parties should be amicably solved through the use of a joint conflict resolution committee and the engagement of all necessary regulatory channels. The new agreement in 2016 no doubt provided new hope for both Indonesia and Saudi to ensure a mutual relationship between the two countries.

Conclusion

The description and analysis sketched above suggest a few things as follows. The Indonesian immigrants who came to Saudi Arabia in the past and contemporary eras are mainly distinguished by their motives, purposes, social backgrounds, and sponsorships. In this regard, education, religion, and employment have been the major factors for Indonesian migration to Saudi Arabia.

In the past, roughly from the eighteenth to the mid-twentieth century, migrants were primarily driven by the desires to learn Islamic sciences and seek religious knowledge, hoping that, after completing their study in the Haramain, they could preach and spread Islam in the Indonesian archipelago. For devout Muslims, learning Islam in the birth place of Islam and Prophet Muhammad could bring both prestige and blessing (*berkah*) on the part of the learners and therefore they wanted to do so. Other major motives included conducting religious rituals (*ibadah*) in the Holy Lands of Mecca and Medina as well as performing a hajj pilgrimage.

As for social backgrounds, they mostly came from "religious families" who had a strong interest in understanding and comprehending Islamic knowledge, or from elite members of societies who wished to maintain or elevate their positions and status in the given society in part because the title of hajj was considered to be highly prestigious in the Indonesian past. The hajj pilgrimage, hence, was not only about religious obligation but also "social status."

In the contemporary era, however, particularly since the early 1980s, most Indonesian migrants in the kingdom were motivated by seeking jobs (mostly in informal sectors), earning wages, and other economic reasons. These immigrants generally came from rural, poor areas of Indonesia and from non religious, uneducated families. In general, this sort of migrant was not interested in learning Islam or pursuing Islamic knowledge or performing hajj pilgrimage. The deprived condition of the family, with the added dream of improving their life, drove them to work in informal economies in Saudi.

There were also groups of migrants who were initially purely motivated by the desire to conduct a hajj pilgrimage but ended up in illegal working activities, as they needed jobs to survive while at the same time they had limited funds and expired visas. These undocumented migrants and female household workers had occasionally "created" some problems in Saudi that, in turn, created tensions and "unhappy relations" between Saudi Arabia and Indonesia. However, in recent years, there has been the big hope of restoring and improving the relationship, as both Saudi and Indonesia are eager to work together and collaborate in a variety of issues and fields—politics, economy, security, education, and so forth.

Another type of contemporary Indonesians in Saudi are intellectual or educational migrants, either students, professional workers, or scientists and teachers. Unlike Indonesian students in the past who funded themselves for their studies, most contemporary students who study in the kingdom are mostly funded through scholarships provided by the Saudi kingdom. As well, unlike Indonesian students in the past who all studied or learned Islamic sciences in informal Islamic learning institutions and madrasah in the Haramain, contemporary students study either Islamic disciplines or hard and social sciences and engineering in universities across the kingdom, not only in Mecca and Medina but also in Dhahran, Riyadh, and Jeddah, among others.

There are also professional expatriates who work as scientists or engineers in some major firms as well as professors and researchers who work in some major universities and colleges in the kingdom. This is to say that historically and sociologically, there were, and are, multiple Indonesian migrants and travelers in Saudi ranging from menial, unskilled workers and professional, skilled expats to religious persons and knowledge seekers (both scholars and students). I will discuss and analyze further the Indonesian intellectual and educational migrants in other chapters.

In the context of Saudi–Indonesian relations, furthermore, religion (in this case Islam) becomes one of the key factors and means to achieve or capitalize on these national interests of the two countries. Issues discussed in this chapter, such as education, trade, employment, business, and pilgrimage (hajj and umra) as well as those related to politics, security, and the defense sector, most if not all of which utilize religion (Islam) as a channel for building connections and cooperation, cannot be avoided from the perspective of national political-economic interests.

Chapter 2

SAUDI INFLUENCES ON INDONESIAN ISLAM AND SOCIETY

This chapter is devoted to the study of "Saudi influences" on Indonesian Islam and society, from past centuries to the present-day era. Before describing "Saudi influences," let me briefly clarify what I mean by the word "Saudi" in this chapter. First, the term does not only refer to the contemporary Kingdom of Saudi Arabia but also the past Hijaz (especially Haramain, i.e., Mecca and Medina), which was previously an independent region before King Abdul Aziz ibn Abdul Rahman Al Saud (known as Ibn Saud, 1875–1953), the founder of the modern Saudi kingdom, united Hijaz and three other areas (i.e., Najd, Ahsa, and Asir) into a single state (kingdom) in 1932. I have already explained that Muslims from the Malay-Indonesian archipelago traveled to Hijaz, especially to Mecca and Medina, long before 1932; intellectual and religio-cultural interactions between Muslims of the region that today is Indonesia and Islamic scholars residing in Hijaz, especially of Arab origins but also other nationalities (Indian or Kurdish), have taken place for centuries, a vibrant tradition which continues today. Because of this long period of contact it is unsurprising to discover that Islamic intellectual life in Indonesian societies has a lengthy history (see, e.g., Azra 1992, 2004; Riddell 2001; Feener 2011; Laffan 2011).

Second, the term "Saudi influence" can refer to the influence of Saudi government and society; Saudi clerics and Islamic scholars; or Saudi education, tradition, culture, and politic. This is vital to underline in part because Hijaz in the past was a "global metropolitan area" where many people across the globe resided in order to make a living, complete a pilgrimage, worship, or study. Moreover, the status of Mecca as the destination for the hajj ensured that educational settings in the region attracted religious migrants from across the Islamic world. Accordingly, it is unsurprising that Mecca (and also Medina) was, and is, home to Islamic scholars, religious teachers, and Sufi masters from multiple ethnic backgrounds. Many arrived there following long journeys, including some well-known scholars or Sufi gurus such as Ibrahim bin Hasan al-Kurani and his son Abu Tahir Muhammad al-Kurani (Iraq), Muhammad Hayya al-Sindi (Pakistan), Ahmad bin Idris (Morocco), and Nawawi al-Bantani (Indonesia).

According to Dutch Orientalist and scholar Christian Snouck Hurgronje (1857–1936), who arrived in Hijaz toward the end of the nineteenth century, those teaching in Mecca included ulama who had either been born in or traced their family histories back to Egypt, Central Arabia, Hadramaut (Yemen), the Caucasus, India, Central and Southeast Asia, and no doubt many other locations besides (Hurgronje 1970: 197–202). For that reason, like other students, Indonesian Muslim students in the past who studied in Hijaz did not only learn Islam from Saudi teachers but also from other nationalities and ethnicities such as Yemeni, Egyptian, Syrian, Indian, Turkish, Kurdish, and many others. Also, academic institutions (Islamic schools/madrasah) in Hijaz were not only established by Saudi Islamic scholars but also by non-Saudi Islamic scholars and philanthropists, including Indians and Malay-Indonesians (see Chapter 3).

In this chapter, I will briefly outline the historical dynamics and contemporary development of Saudi influences in Indonesia, particularly in terms of intellectual tradition, cultural practices, and religiosity. The chapter aims to provide perspectives on the intellectual trajectory and genealogy of Indonesia's Islamic scholarship and a variety of Islamic traditions that have been initiated, spread, and advanced by the Saudi government, Saudi societies, Saudi's ulama, sheikhs, and institutions as well as Saudi-influenced Indonesian scholars, academics, preachers, clerics, and activists, in the archipelago. More specifically, the chapter places an emphasis on the intellectual, cultural, political, and religious influences of the societies in the Arabian Peninsula toward those of the Indonesian archipelago. The Saudi influence on Indonesian Islam and society, it should be noted, does not only take place in the fields of Islamic scholarship, education (schooling), cultural practices, and social foundations but also in Islamic activism with the rise of neo-Salafi groupings.

Earliest influences: Haramain-trained Indonesian Islamic scholars and Sufi gurus

As discussed earlier, in the past, upon completing their studies and learning in Arabia, particularly in Haramain (Mecca and Medina), Indonesian Muslims brought some Islamic knowledge, religious understandings, and cultural practices they observed and obtained back to Indonesian societies. What they introduced and brought to Indonesia depended on what they learned during their studies, with whom they learned Islam, what type of Islam they received from their Islamic teachers and scholars in Haramain, and so forth. Muslim pupils who studied under reformist Islamic scholars tended to introduce Islamic reformism, whereas those who learned Islam under the guidance of a Sufi master or a *tarekat* guru would most likely develop Islamic Sufism and join a Sufi order.

The growth of some renowned Sufi orders such as Shatariyyah, Naqshabandiyyah, Qadiriyyah, Qadiriyyah-Naqshabandiyyah, among others, in the Malay-Indonesian archipelago cannot be separated out from the role of Haramain-educated Indonesian Sufis. Moreover, Muslim students who learned Islam under the Shafii jurist scholars in Haramain also tended to present and grow the Shafii school of thought in Islamic jurisprudence (Islamic law). In recent years, as many Indonesian Islamic studies students have learned Islam with

Hanbali scholars, the Hanbali school, which is the official madhab of the Saudi kingdom, has also been introduced and developed in Indonesian societies. Some Saudi alumni have even established Islamic centers and learning institutions in the country (e.g., madrasah, ma'had, or colleges) that are in accordance with—and dedicated to—the Hanbali madhab.

The prolonged intellectual, cultural, and religious influence of Arabia toward Indonesian societies can be seen, for instance, in the role and contributions of the Haramain-trained Indonesian Islamic scholars, clerics, teachers, and Sufis, who have been present at least since the seventeenth century. Some of these noted figures were foreign (Arab/Hadhrami or Gujarati) but they lived in—and dedicated their lives to—Indonesian societies. These well-known ulama, Sufi masters, and prolific scholars in the sixteenth and seventeenth centuries included such famous names as Hamzah al-Fansuri (d. *c*. 1607), Shams al-Din al-Sumatrani (d.1630), Nur al-Din al-Raniri (d.1658), Abd al-Ra'uf al-Sinkili (d.1693), and Muhammad Yusuf al-Makassari (d.1699), among others.

Noted historian of Indonesian Islam Azyumardi Azra said that these great ulama were part of intellectual Muslim networks in Mecca and Medina, who later went back to Indonesia and played a very important role in transforming Islamic knowledge by becoming channels for the two distant and different worlds (the Malay-Indonesian archipelago and the Arabian Peninsula) and also by offering new and fresh understanding of Islam to their people and societies (Azra 1992, 2004). One of the earliest agents of Malay-Indonesian archipelago's Islamization were Sufis (many of whom received their mystical training in Arabia), in addition to Arab-Malay Muslim traders. Johns (1961: 10–23) said that Sufism was the most visible picture in the Islamic world of the Malay-Indonesian archipelago from the thirteenth century onward, and this was also applicable in the thirteenth century of Sumatra and Java, the two main islands that transmitted Islam in the archipelago. Islam would have never been "the religion of Java" (also, "the religion of Sumatra") unless Sufism that tolerated Javanese (and Sumatran) tradition and modified it under the banner of Islam had been embraced by Javanese (Sumatran) nobles and many people on the coastal areas of Java and Sumatra.

One of earliest Southeast Asian Muslims who conducted the hajj (Heidhues 2000: 81), Hamzah al-Fansuri, was a Sumatran Sufi (and one of the first Sufi thinkers of the Malay world) who introduced mystical panentheistic ideas, derived from the writings of medieval Islamic scholars and Sufis, into Indonesian/Malay Muslim societies which later was continued by his disciple Shams al-Din al-Sumatrani. These two great mystics had a strong intellectual orientation to philosophical Sufism, mainly Ibn al-Arabi's doctrines of *wahdat al-wujud* (unity of being) (see, e.g., al-Attas 1970; Braginsky 1999: 135–75). Nur al-Din al-Raniri, born into a Gujarati Muslim family of Hadhrami lineage, was another great ulama of Indonesian Islam in the seventeenth century, whose legacy can still be witnessed today. Like Hamzah al-Fansuri and Shams al-Din al-Sumatrani, Nur al-Din al-Raniri was also an Islamic mystic and scholar. However, unlike al-Fansuri and al-Sumatrani who followed philosophical Sufism (*tasawuf falsafi*), al-Raniri was bitterly against this type of Islamic mysticism. Accordingly, al-Raniri, who enjoyed the patronage of Sultan Iskandar Thani of Kesultanan (Sultanate) Aceh, attacked their predecessors (al-Fansuri and al-Sumatrani) and denounced them as heretics for their violation of Islamic beliefs and Islam's theological foundation. Moreover, al-Raniri ordered their books to be burned and replaced them with his many orthodox religious standard books such as, most notably, *Bustan al-Salatin* (The Garden of Kings), a seven-volume encyclopedic work, covering the history of the world from the creation through to the period of the prophets of Islam and the Muslim kings of the Middle East and the Malay area, and *al-Sirat al-Mustaqim*, which is arguably the first text on *fiqh ibadah*[1] (i.e., Islamic jurisprudence of Muslim religious rituals or "fiqh of worship") in Malay (Riddle 2001).

Abd al-Ra'uf al-Sinkili, who was born in Aceh, was another noted ulama in the seventeenth century who tried to reconcile and mediate the two opposing and competing tendencies: heterodox Islam (of al-Fansuri and al-Sumatrani) and orthodox Islam (represented by al-Raniri). Besides many treatises on Sufism, al-Sinkili also produced his two most significant works: *Tarjuman al-Mustafid*, the first complete *tafsir* (Qur'anic exegesis), and *Mir'at al-Tullab*, the first work on *fiqh mu'amalah* (i.e., Islamic jurisprudence related to worldly matters or dealings such as commercial and civil acts). It is true that from the sixteenth century onward there had been hostile conflicts and tensions between supporters of heterodox Islam and orthodox Islam as well as between Sufis and *fiqh*-oriented Muslims, some, if not many, of which had been shaped and influenced by Arabia through the intellectual networks of Haramain Islamic scholars and Sufi gurus and Indonesian pupils who learned Islamic sciences and Sufism in the peninsula. The tensions particularly took place in the islands of Sumatra and Java, the two most important areas of early Islamization in the Indonesian archipelago.

Interestingly, this period of heated controversy had also been noted by Haramain-based ulama Shaikh Ibrahim al-Kurani (d.1689), an eminent *khalifa* of Shaikh Ahmad Qushshashi (d.1661). Shaikh Ibrahim was an important figure for the Malay-Indonesian ulama because he was one of the leading Islamic scholars who taught many Muslim disciples from the archipelago in the Haramain, including Abd al-Ra'uf al-Sinkili and Muhammad Yusuf al-Makassari. A guru of the Shattariya Sufi order (*tarekat*), a Hadith expert, and a specialist of the Shafii school of thought, Shaikh Ibrahim al-Kurani engaged in fierce polemics in defense of Ibn al-Arabi's doctrines (especially *wahdat al-wujud*) against the followers and pupils of the Indian Ahmad Sirhindi (d.1624), the great shaikh of the Naqsabandiyyah Sufi order and the defender of the doctrine *wahdat al-shuhud* ("unity of witness") (Hanif 2000; Azra 2003; Gibson 2010; Van Bruinessen 2015). The position of Shaikh Ibrahim al-Kurani resembles Shaikh Zaini Dahlan (d.1887), a renowned mufti of Mecca in the nineteenth century, as they both played a vital role in educating, transferring, and transforming Islamic knowledge to Indonesian Muslim students.

In the seventeenth and eighteenth centuries, Indonesia also produced a number of Haramain-trained eminent Islamic scholars including, most notably, Muhammad Yusuf al-Makassari (alias Abadin Tadia Tjoessoep, known as Shaikh Yusuf, d.1699), Muhammad Nafis al-Banjari (d.1735), Abd al-Samad al-Palimbani (d. *c.* 1789), and Muhammad Arshad al-Banjari (d.1812). Shaikh Yusuf was a contemporary of al-Sinkili and an influential Islamic scholar and mystic whose work (especially *Zubdat al-Asrar* or "The Essence of Secrets") and anti-Dutch colonial activism have been praised by many Indonesian Muslims today. Reportedly Shaikh Yusuf learned Islam and studied Islamic mysticism in Medina, mainly under the mentorship of Shaikh Ibrahim al-Kurani, for nine years (Gibson 2010: 70–1). Abd al-Samad al-Palimbani, furthermore, was renowned for being the most prolific interpreter of al-Ghazali's Sufism, Muhammad Arshad al-Banjari was author of the famous *Sabil al-Muhtadin* (a work on *fiqh ibadah*), and Muhammad Nafis al-Banjari was the author of the well-known treatise on Sufism entitled *Tuhfat al-Nafis* (Azra 1992, 2004; Gibson 2010).

The period spanning from the seventeenth to the eighteenth century, attested to by the introduction of the original (or, at least, the vernacular) works both in Arabic and especially in Malay marked the earliest heyday of Islamic scholarship in the archipelago, which later contributed significantly to the reform and renewal of Islamic life in the area. The peak in the production of Islamic scholarship in this region was between the nineteenth century and the early decades of the twentieth century. This period generated a great deal of notable Islamic scholars who produced excellent Islamic research on multiple subjects and created Islamic discourses, thanks to European colonialism, on jihadism against colonial rule. This period, as noted by Azra (2001: 103–04), was also marked by the emergence of Islamic modernism, which constituted a response to the need for religious reforms among Muslims and to the intellectual challenges prompted by European concepts such as nationalism, the nation-state, and democracy.

As explained in the previous chapters, the rise of Islamic scholarship in the Malay-Indonesian world had much to do with intense and continued links between the archipelago and Arabia. At the time, Mecca was not only a home to those in search of Islamic knowledge and a place to perform religious ritual practices but also a meeting place for Indonesian nationalists who wanted to liberate the archipelago from colonial power. The tradition of searching for Islamic knowledge (*rihla 'ilmiyyah*), which had begun in earnest in the sixteenth century, created a community of Malay-Indonesian students (*ashab al-Jawiyyin*) in the Haramain, who learned Islam with a great number of prominent Islamic scholars (of Arab or non-Arab origins, including Malay-Indonesians) and, therefore, were involved in the cosmopolitan networks of ulama. When these Jawi students returned to the Malay-Indonesian archipelago, they became the most important channels for transmission of Islamic knowledge and tradition. Later on, particularly since the late nineteenth century, Cairo became a major source of Islamic knowledge for the Malay-Indonesian world (Roff 1970; Abaza 1990; Laffan 2011). Later developments, after Indonesia gained its independence, produced a multifaceted Islamic intellectual life, and the channels for transmission as well as responses are also increasingly complex. In the post-New Order era (since the 2000s), Islamic intellectual life is more complex than ever since sources of Islamic knowledge are more diverse, not only from Arabia or the Middle East but also other parts of Asia and the West. However, one thing is clear: the indigenization of Islamic scholarship in Indonesia is continually gaining momentum.

It is worth noting here that although the Haramain-trained Islamic scholars played an enormous role in the growth of Islam in the region, this does not mean that all Indonesian Islamic teachers, fiqh scholars, or Sufi masters in the past were educated in the Haramain. In fact, many of them received Islamic training in their homeland from their local gurus, without traveling to Islamic learning centers in the Middle Eastern world. In recent years, as many Indonesian students learn Islam outside Saudi Arabia, sources of Islamic knowledge, traditions, and cultures in the country have been deeper, more plural, and more complex than previous ones.

The Wahhabi-influenced Padri movement in Minangkabau, West Sumatra?

Besides influencing the growth of Islamic scholarship, mysticism, education, and cultures in general through the hands of the Haramain-educated talented Islamic scholars, teachers, and mystics, Arabia, in the past, also contributed to the rise of Islamic activism in Indonesia. One of the earliest evident examples of Islamic activism is the occurrence of the Islamic revivalist movement (known later as the Padri movement) in the early nineteenth century in Minangkabau,[2] West Sumatra. Some scholars (see, e.g., Azra 2005; A'la 2008; Indra 2017) identify the Padri movement as a Saudi Wahhabi-influenced religiopolitical activist movement. The Sumatran hajj returnees that later led the Padri movement, according to every written history, had been influenced by the teachings and practices of the Wahhabis who conquered Mecca in the early nineteenth century.

However, it is still unclear and disputed among scholars and historians of Sumatran Islam, whether or not the Padri movement was influenced or shaped by Wahhabism. Some argue that the Padri's ideology is Wahhabi, while others contend that the movement is purely a harsh critical response toward local religious developments and social phenomena, triggered by a local economic transformation in Minangkabau or West Sumatra in general (Dobbin 1977: 1–38). Nonetheless, apart from this disagreement, there are indeed some similarities and differences between the Padri and Wahhabi movements, for instance, both are concerned with purification of Islamic doctrine of *tauhid*. Below I will explain the pros and cons concerning the Padri movement provided by scholars, along with their arguments. Viewed from another standpoint, the rise of the Padri signifies the upsurge of Minangkabau's Islamic revivalism and "renewalism," albeit, it has been hard to supply any accurate dates for the birth of these movement.

The term Padri is synonymous with three famous hajis (i.e., Haji Miskin of Luhak Agam, Haji Abdur Rahman of Piobang, and Haji Muhammad Arief of Sumanik) who arrived in Minangkabau from Mecca in 1804, which would have enabled them to witness the capture of the holy city of Mecca by the Wahhabis. Scholars vary concerning the origins of the term Padri. Some argue that the term originated from the name of a site in Aceh: Pedir, from which Islam spread to Minangkabau (Van Ronkel, cited in Zakaria and Salleh 2011: 200–01). Known as "Serambi Mekah" (the Verandah of Mecca), Aceh is renowned as the oldest

Islamized area in the Indonesian archipelago, from which Islam was introduced and developed to other regions not only Sumatra but also other islands in Java, Kalimantan, and the Moluccas. Muslims from different parts of the archipelago flocked to study Islam in Pedir under the mentorship of local ulama whom they called "Padris" (Steenbrink 1993). Others argue that the word Padri is derived from "Pidari," referring to hajj pilgrims who had returned from Mecca by way of Aceh (Dobbin 1972). Still other scholars contend that the term "Padri" was a modification of the Portuguese word "Padre," priestly zealots of all faiths as well as a term used by Westerners for a religious scholar (Hadler 2008: 272). It has been argued that the Minangkabau people and those of other areas in Sumatra also used the word since the Islamic/Arabic term of religious scholars at the time was not yet familiar in the society. Historian of Southeast Asia Anthony Reid, for instance, said that the term "Padri" originated from European usage, "presumably because they first heard the Islamic party described by analogy with the priests" (Reid 1967: 272). Interestingly, local sources such as *Surat Keterangan Jalaluddin* did not use the term Padri but *kaum putih* (white people) and *kaum hitam* (black people) instead. Whatever the origins of the term Padri, it is obvious that the Padris were a puritanical, reformist, and revivalist Muslim group in Sumatra Island.

They later called themselves *orang/kaum putih* (white people) and their opponents *orang/kaum hitam* (black people), terms which appear to have had a moral connotation for them in which "white" represents piety, goodness, morality, or religiousness whereas "black" denotes the opposite: impiety, badness, immorality, or lack of religiousness. For the European colonials at the time, *putih* (white) referred to the white robes of the Padris and *hitam* (black) referred to the dark colors traditionally worn by the penghulus, signifying conflict and tensions between shariah-oriented groups and *adat*-driven societies (Dobbin 1974: 330–31). Similar terms, more or less, appeared in Java, especially from the eighteenth century onwards, referring to "pious, good people" for white (*kaum putihan*—the white group or *wong santri*—the santri people, or simply *wong kaum*) and "impious, bad people" for red (*kaum abangan*—the red group or red people) (see, e.g., Geertz 1976; Hefner 1989; Ricklefs 2007). Although the connotations of the terms have slightly shifted from the past, some contemporary Indonesian Muslims still use color as a metaphor to signify a particular socio religious group.

The Mecca sojourn of the three well-known hajis depicted above that later led the puritanical reformist movement in the early nineteenth century in Minangkabau raises the problem of whether, and to what extent, the Padri movement was influenced by foreign Wahhabi ideology, teaching, practice, and example. Should, after all, the Padris be considered as the "agent" or "channel" of Wahhabism in Sumatra Island, particularly Minangkabau? The Dutch intellectual P. J. Veth (1814–1895) was arguably the first scholar who argued that the Padris were primarily influenced by Arabia's Wahhabi devotees and ideology. Veth based his argument on the similarities between Padris and Wahhabis practices, such as their ban on tobacco and wearing ornaments and silk. More specifically, this alleged Wahhabi "infiltration" in Minangkabau is based on the oft-cited incident when the three hajj pilgrims who returned from Mecca in 1804 started to pledge a radical and occasionally violent movement of religious and social reforms in the region (Zakariya and Salleh 2011: 201).

It is true that, coincidentally, in early 1803, the Wahhabis took Mecca, and it is not to be supposed that, as Dobbin (1972: 332–31) has argued, the Sumatran hajis did not observe their reforms relating to dress, prayers, and tobacco-smoking, and, indeed, pilgrims in the holy city of Mecca at the time were obliged to comply with the Wahhabi precepts. Since the Padri movement took place after the arrival of these three hajj pilgrims, Dutch observers (such as P. J. Veth) soon assumed that the hajis (pilgrims) had been influenced by Wahhabism during the Najdi occupation of Hijaz in 1803, and this postulation has been adopted by most scholars and authors (home and foreign) of Minangkabau's social and Islamic history (see, e.g., A'la 2008: 267–99). The late Harry J. Benda, a renowned Indonesianist, coined the term "Pax Wahhabica" to explain the historical link between the Saudi Wahhabi and the Padri movements as well as the influence of the former on the latter. Benda, moreover, argued that this "Arabian dogma" (i.e., Wahhabism) was also able to transcend the doctrinal differences existing among the Indonesian adherents and united them in the pursuit of their ideological cause (Benda 1958: 73).

The prominent Indonesian scholar and historian of Islam Azyumardi Azra also sees the resemblances between the Padri movement and the Wahhabi movement in Arabia. He stated:

> One should not be misled, however, with these current developments; in fact, radicalism among Indonesian Muslims in particular is not new. Even though Southeast Asian Islam in general has been viewed as moderate and peaceful Islam, but the history of Islam in the region shows that radicalism among Muslims, as will be discussed shortly, has existed for at least two centuries, when the Wahabi-like Padri movement, in West Sumatra in late eighteenth and early nineteenth [centuries] held sway to force other Muslims in the area to subscribe to their literal understanding of Islam. The violent movement aimed at spreading the pure and pristine Islam as practiced by the Prophet Muhammad and his companions (the salaf). The Padri, however, failed to gain support from majority of Muslims; and, as a result, the Padri movement was the only precedent of Muslim radicalism throughout Southeast Asia. (Azra 2005)

Other scholars disagree with the Wahhabi influence on—or Wahhabi-like reformist Islamic movement of—the Padri. One of the noted scholars of Indonesian Islam Martin van Bruinessen, for instance, said that the evidence that supports arguments on the Wahhabi influence of the Padris is weak and unconvincing. It is true, Van Bruinessen said, that "the large Indonesian community resident in Mecca was a medium through which knowledge about Wahhabism reached Indonesia, but the community itself appears to have remained virtually immune to Wahhabi influences" (Van Bruinessen 2002: 1).[3] Likewise, in a brief comment on Wahhabi influence in Indonesia, Van Bruinessen wrote:

Wahhabism became a hotly debated issue after the second Wahhabi conquest of Mecca in 1924. Indirectly it gave rise to the major traditionalist organization, Nahdlatul Ulama [NU], that had as its chief objective the defense of beliefs and practices that were attacked by the Wahhabis: *wasila, ziyara, tariqa, taqlid, fiqh*. The middle part of the 20th century was characterized by often fierce debates over traditional practices, in which their opponents were invariably dubbed Wahhabis by the traditionalists. In reality there was little direct influence of [the Saudi version of] Wahhabism on Indonesian reformist thought until the 1970s. There was, however a certain convergence: the puritan Persatuan Islam [lit. "the Union of Islam"] movement appears to have developed its strict Salafi ideas almost in isolation from the contemporary Middle East, but evolved towards positions that were almost indistinguishable from those that were internationally sponsored by the Saudis. The *fatwa* rubric of Persatuan Islam journal *Al Muslimun* is indicative of the strict Salafi approach adopted by this organization. (Van Bruinessen 2002)

B. J. O. Schrieke (d.1945) was another scholar who argued that the Padri was not a Wahhabi-influenced puritanical movement. Schrieke, who was a Dutch professor of ethnology and history of the Dutch East Indies (formerly Indonesia) in Batavia (now Jakarta), argued that the evidence P. J. Veth used to support his argument on the Wahhabi influence on the Padri movement (i.e., the similar practices and behaviors between the Wahhabis and the Padris, namely the ban on tobacco and wearing ornaments and silk) is thin since these practices and behaviors were not exclusively linked merely to Wahhabi; hence they cannot be considered as definitive evidence of the influence of Wahhabism to the Padris. Schrieke, furthermore, clarified different religious practices between the Padris and Wahhabis that signify the distinction between the two such as the veneration of saints, which Padris do not prohibit whereas Wahhabis ardently oppose the practice. Similarly, according to Schrieke, the Padris, unlike Wahhabis, did not ban the celebration of Prophet Muhammad's birth (called *maulid*).

Another important marker, for Schrieke, is that the origins of the rise of the Padri, in contrast with the Wahhabi movement, were more than a religious puritanical reform since it entailed a conflict and tension between the religious clerics (represented by the Padris) who favored reform-minded ideas and puritanical Islamic practices and the *adat* leaders who backed the Minangkabau's social institutions and traditional cultural practices. In brief, as for Wahhabis, it was the emergence of Sufis or mystics that mostly provides a basis for the theological reform movement. The Padris, however, emerged mostly as a critical reaction against the adat defenders. The traditional leaders of adat (customary law), dominated by local aristocrats, had long been the dominant group that shaped and influenced the region's social system and societal practices, while the religious clerics and scholars (i.e., the Padris) had been marginalized. In this regard, the Padri movement, Schrieke affirmed, can be seen as the uprising of the religious clerics against the adat guardians (Schrieke 1973).

The late Jeffrey Hadler also refuted the argument that Wahhabism influenced the three hajj returnees stating that the "coincidence [of the three hajj pilgrims being in Mecca at the same time with the Wahhabi presence] is not proof, however, and in no Padri-war era Minangkabau text do we find mention of Wahhabism" (Hadler 2008: 979). In the case of Tuanku Imam Bondjol[4] (d.1854), one of the most prominent leaders of the Padri movement, Hadler stated that the Tuanku Imam was a "putative Wahhabi, and a leader of the Padri War, which is often described as the first Muslim-against-Muslim jihad in Southeast Asia" (972). However, Hadler said that there are indications of his "apparent renunciation of this Wahhabism" (979). Scholars of Indonesian Islam have usually traced the genealogy of Indonesia's Islamist extremism back to the Padri War and to the Tuanku Imam Bondjol, albeit a religious-driven violence took place before the war and the Tuanku Imam. The word "Bondjol" (or Bonjol for the new spelling) refers to the name of the town where the Tuanku Imam Bondjol led the fight against the Dutch colonials, backed by local *adat*-oriented Muslim leaders, which annexed the highlands of Minangkabau from 1833 to 1837. While most contemporary Western and Indonesian sources on the Padris clearly claim that these religious clerics were strongly influenced by Wahhabi doctrines and practices, Hadler argues that such claims are based on poor evidence. He wrote: "it is impossible to know with any certainty whether the three [Minangkabau] hajji were directly influenced by Wahhabism while in Mecca ... What is clear is that for these returning hajji, traditional Minangkabau culture was unacceptable; matrilineal and matrilocal longhouses could not be reconciled with the essential teachings of Islam" (980).

Generally speaking, in brief, the "Wahhabi-centered thesis" on the Padri movement relies on two main arguments, namely (1) the role of the three famous hajis who returned from Mecca in pioneering the socioreligious movement in Minangkabau, and (2) some similarities in socioreligious practices between the Wahhabis and the Padris (e.g., the two groups prohibited tobacco as well as wearing ornaments and silk, as Veth pointed out). Moreover, those who are against this "Wahhabi-centered theory" have based their arguments primarily on the uncertainty of the Wahhabi influences on the Padris (especially the three hajj returnees). In other words, there is no obvious indication or mark to prove the influence of the former on the latter. They have also claimed that there is not a single word of "Wahhabi" or "Wahhabism" in the nineteenth-century local texts of Minangkabau, signifying that there is not a direct link between Wahhabism and the Padri movement. Moreover, they have argued that the reformist movement in Minangkabau actually long predated the advent of the Padri movement in 1803/04.

It is true that, as stated earlier, the puritanical socioreligious movement and the occurrence of reformist Muslims had apparently existed in Minangkabau long before the nineteenth century when the Padris began to take a radical reform in the society (see Abdullah 1966; Reid 1967; Hamka 1981). It began with a clash between followers of the Naqsabandi Sufi order and those of Shattariya, a well-established dominant Sufi order in the region. Here is the story. Islam has a long history in Minangkabau. It greeted the region before the European colonials landed in the Malay-Indonesian archipelago and long before the Dutch arrived in the Minangkabau area. Historian Merle Ricklefs predicted that Islam arrived and then flourished in Minangkabau around the sixteenth century (2007: 304–05). By that time the king of Minangkabau and hundreds of his relatives and partisans had already embraced Islam, and since the characteristics of society in the past in Indonesia was "raja-centric," it meant that whatever religion was adopted by the raja (king), the masses would soon follow.

Since its formation, Minangkabau's Islam was identical to its Sufistic or mystical form.[5] The predominant school of Sufism in Minangkabau was Shattariya, a Sufi order known for its ability to absorb local cultures and customs. This Sufi order was first introduced by Burhan al-Din from Aceh, a brilliant student (*murid*) of the famous Shaikh Abd al-Ra'uf al-Sinkili (d.1693), who studied Islam and mysticism for many years in the Haramain with prominent Islamic scholars, most notably Shaikh Ibrahim al-Kurani. Later on, Burhan al-Din's main disciples and successors (*khalifahs*) developed and spread Shattariya to neighboring areas and by the second half of the eighteenth century the order had become the sole religious power in Minangkabau (Fathurrahman 2003). For many years, the Shattariya had played a key role in the peaceful reform and reconciliation of Islamic values with local cultures and traditions; thereby it has left a marked imprint on the local Muslim society and guided them to a form of tolerant Islam that respects local society's traditional and cultural practices that existed (and was practiced by society) for centuries before the advent of Islam in the region.

However, by the end of the eighteenth century, Islam was no longer what it was. By this period, the face of Islam was about to shift to another type of Islam that neglected or undermined the centrality of local cultures and traditions, *adat* guardians, the *tuanku shaikh* (guru) of the Shattariyya, and centers of traditional Islamic learning (i.e., *surau*). The main agent of this dramatic change was the Naqshabandiyya Sufi order, a sort of sharia-based Islamic mysticism. When the adherents of the Naqshabandiyya initiated and introduced this Sufi order to the local society of Minangkabau, it soon shocked the people and generated early tensions and conflict with local Muslims, most notably followers of the Shattariyya. The campaign of the "return to the sharia" became the norm among local Muslims and widespread toward the end of the eighteenth century that in turn challenged the religious authority of the Shattariyya. This marked the beginning of the Muslim–Muslim clash in the region. The conflict and violence were mainly due to two things: (1) the failure of the Naqshabandiyya followers to respect different religious views, understandings, and practices; and (2) the political struggle for domination over social, political, economic, and religious scarce resources.

When the Padris came in as the patrons of the Naqshabandiyya, the situation became even worse. Violence in the name of religion prevailed and intimidation became the rule of the day (A'la 2008: 267–96). Noted historian Azyumardi Azra said that the peaceful reforms initiated by the surau-based Sufi *tuanku shaikhs* (Sufi gurus) underwent a process of radicalization after the return of the three renowned hajis from Mecca in 1803, resulting in the break of the long Padri wars in the first decades of the nineteenth century, the first ever major blow on the *suraus* and its Sufi *tarekats*. Of the three hajis, Haji Miskin was the first Padri who initiated radical reform. Soon after coming back from Mecca, Haji Miskin embarked on a reform mission in his homeland, believing that the Minangkabau society's structure was not at all in line with the teachings of the Qur'an and the Sunna and therefore must be reformed. He sought to replicate the Arabian style of reform where the old structure of society is totally replaced by a new one, regardless of the different nature of the existing social structure (Dobbin 1977: 30). This idea of total reform was welcomed by a great deal of local reformist clerics, most notably Haji Abdur Rahman and Haji Muhammad Arief. Together these three hajis reached the conclusion that a common platform must be formulated and a "holy" mission should be commenced, and soon, with that the seeds of the Padri movement were sewn and intellectual agendas to launch what subsequently appeared to be a furious onslaught on the foes were tabled.

Like the Wahhabis in Arabia, Azra said, the Padris condemned the *suraus* as the centers of unorthodox beliefs, ungodly practices, and un-Islamic rituals. Not only condemning the suraus and tarekats, the Padris also burned many suraus to the ground and murdered many *tuanku shaikhs*, surau teachers, and Muslim clerics whom they dubbed "deviant" due to their views, notions, understandings, and practices that, according to the Padris, contradicted the Islamic sharia and theology (Azra 2006: 68–9). The Padris' efforts to undertake a radical reform met strong opposition from local Muslims, particularly the adherents of the Shattariyya Sufi order. One of the Padris' opponents, Tuanku Nan Tuo (a religious leader and a former business partner of Haji Miskin) denounced Haji Miskin and rejected entirely his puritanical reform ideas. At first, the Padri movement was sporadic and unsystematic, but later (from the 1810s onward) it became more organized and systematic, following the support of several local strong leaders known as *Harimau Nan Salapan* (the "Eight Lions").

Against this backdrop, it can be said that the appearance of the three celebrated hajis only radicalized the lengthy Islamic reform process that had already taken place in the region. In the words of historian Anthony Reid (1967: 272): "It was only galvanized into aggressive action with the return in 1803 of three hajis." Although the overstatement of the Wahhabi effect on the Padris might be misleading, I contend that, neglecting their influence completely is also unfair. It is a fact that the three hajis who radically led the reform in Minangkabau had just returned from a hajj pilgrimage in Mecca, where they witnessed and experienced the Wahhabi-directed puritanical Islamic reform in the holy city. This is not just simply a coincidence. The three hajis may have gained radical ideas, understandings, strategies, or tactics of conducting puritanical Islamic reform (and then applied them in the Minangkabau society) after they saw the Wahhabi movement in Mecca. The fact that there is no single word of "Wahhabi" or "Wahhabism" in nineteenth-century local texts in Minangkabau cannot be used as a basis or argument to cast-off the "Wahhabi thesis" on the Padri movement, in part because the words "Wahhabi" or "Wahhabism" are new terms created recently (in the twentieth century) by Western academia, not by adherents of Shaikh Muhammad ibn Abdul Wahab, the founder of the movement (see DeLong-Bas 2004; Commins 2016). The local Muslim people of Minangkabau in the nineteenth century were certainly not familiar with these words.

In brief, the Padri movement was not merely a local phenomenon in Minangkabau without any relationship with the regional or global world. It was also not simply a purely religious reform movement. Furthermore, the violence that the Padri movement committed throughout the reform period was neither simply ideological nor theological in nature. The Padri was a mixture of local, regional, and global socioreligious reformers whose main objectives were, among others, (1) to purify Islamic ritual practices and theology with the aim of preventing them from being corrupted by un-Islamic local customs and beliefs, and to conform with the sharia, (2) to diminish the influences of heterodox Sufism and its mystical orders, and (3) to establish a religious authority centered primarily around the figure of a reformist ulama (Padris), who would be the main socioreligious leader, and not Sufi masters, aristocrats, or adat guardians. The "drama" of the Padri movement, hence, can be seen as a socioreligious contest between the orthodox, reformist, puritanical religious clerics vis-à-vis heterodox Sufi mystics and adat leaders. A'la (2008: 269) stated: "Although the Padri movement might have developed its own normative values, agendas, and obsessions, an ideological and perhaps pedagogical relationship [between the Padris and the Wahhabis] remains possible."

Java's pesantren tradition and the Sunni-Shafi'ite madhhab

Other Arabian influences on the Malay-Indonesian archipelago are the "pesantren tradition" and the practice of Sunni-Shafi'ite schools (madhhabs in Islamic theology and jurisprudence) among Muslim societies, especially in Java but also in outer Java. A traditional educational institution, pesantren or pondok pesantren[6] (sometimes just called "pondok" or "surau" in West Sumatra), is Java's oldest Islamic boarding school and a center of Islamic learning that has existed in the archipelago for centuries. (Male) students who learn Islam in the pesantren are called *santri*[7] (or *santriwati* for female pupils), thereby pesantren is a site where santri (or *santriwati*) reside for learning and seeking wisdom. The words "santri" and "pesantren," hence, are interlinked. Throughout the centuries, pesantren tradition has displayed its dynamism and flexibility by absorbing local and foreign elements whilst remaining uniquely based on Islamic principles, tenets, and values. Since its inception, pesantren has played a great role not only in the field of religious education but also in politics, the economy, literature, and cultures in general. It also contributed significantly to the ideologies of pan-Islamism, nationalism, and anti-colonialism (against both Dutch and Japanese rulers of the East Indies) (see, e.g., Dhofier 1982; Rahardjo 1985; Nilan 2009; Wahid 2014; Van Bruinessen 2015). What I meant by "pesantren" here is a "traditional pesantren" linked mostly to Nahdlatul Ulama, Indonesia's largest Muslim social organization.

Reports vary regarding when the first pesantren was established. Historian Michael Laffan (2003a) has pointed out that small *pesantren* had existed in Java since the sixteenth century, especially in the northern coastal regions which were the first to convert to Islam, and by the late eighteenth and early nineteenth centuries the pesantren had spread into the interior of Java (*Jawa pedalaman*), as a fast-growing community of returning pilgrims (*hajis*) and students trained in Mecca and Medina took advantage of the colonial peace to establish schools in territories which prior to this time had been only nominally Muslim (Hefner and Zaman 2007: 172-98). However, it seems that pesantren were first initiated around the seventeenth century. Sultan Agung Hanyokrokusumo of "Islamic Mataram" (or Sultan Agung for short, 1593-1645) played a vital role in the development of pesantren. During his reign, Sultan Agung offered *tanah perdikan*[8] to the santri community so that they could develop as many as three hundred pesantrens, which were divided into several categories: a large and master pesantren, *takhassus* pesantren with specialization in specific Islamic knowledge, and a *tariqa* pesantren (Darban 1988: 32-8). At present, Indonesia has more than 47,000 pesantren and madrasah (Hefner and Zaman 2007: 191).

Due to the dynamic process of Muslim education together with the major increase of the pesantren in Java before the nineteenth century, it is not an exaggeration to consider the Islamic Mataram period, chiefly during the reign of Sultan Agung, "the golden age" of the Islamic educational system. Before the seventeenth century, Muslims probably studied Islam and the Qur'an with local Qur'anic teachers, Islamic clerics, or mystical masters at *langgar* (a small mosque) or a house of local *kiai* (Islamic scholar). It is unclear which pesantren is the oldest in Java. However, reportedly, the oldest pesantren in Central Java (or perhaps Java in general) is Pesantren Dondong, located in the village of Wonosari, a subdistrict of Ngaliyan in the western part of Semarang (now renamed Yayasan Luhur). Local sources have noted that the pesantren was established between 1609 and 1612 by Kiai Syafii Pijoro Negoro bin Kiai Guru Muhammad Sulaiman Singonegoro. At present, this pesantren is directed by Tobagus Mansyur (Gus Toba), the seventh generation of Kiai Syafii Pijoro Negoro.[9]

Although the institution of pesantren might have existed in the archipelago since the seventeenth century, it was not until the nineteenth century that its existence and contribution became more visible and widespread in the Muslim communities of Java and Madura. It was also after the nineteenth century when the pesantren began to be the backbone of traditional and orthodox Islam associated with the Sunni-Shafi'i schools. Those who contributed significantly to initiate, develop, and design the intellectual tradition of pesantren were mostly, if not all, alumni of Arabian (Hijaz/Haramain) academic centers of Islamic learning. In 1997, Abd. Rachman wrote a doctoral thesis at the University of California, Los Angeles, entitled "The Pesantren Architects and Their Socio-Religious Teachings (1850-1950)." This dissertation discusses the roots of Islamic teaching, the santri Muslims of Indonesia (together with the intellectual masters of the pesantren tradition), and the pesantren strategists during the nineteenth and the first half of the twentieth centuries. It also elaborates on the intellectual biographies, including the historical background, socioreligious roles in society, and the religious principles, of these pesantren architects, namely the ulama (or "kiai" in Java), who contributed to the proliferation of the pesantren tradition as a primary institution of Islamic learning in Java (and Madura), respectively.

Rachman, in particular, emphasizes the role of five influential Islamic scholars whom he calls "the pesantren architects," two of whom were classified as "intellectual masters" (of the pesantren) and the rest as the "pesantren strategists." For Rachman, the intellectual masters of the pesantren were Kiai Nawawi Banten (d.1897) and Kiai Mahfudz Termas (d.1919), while the pesantren strategists were Kiai Khalil Bangkalan (d.1924), Kiai Hasyim Asy'ari Jombang (d.1947), and Kiai Asnawi Kudus (d.1959). The classification of "pesantren intellectual masters" and "pesantren strategists" was based on the fact that, according to Rachman (1997: 4), even though their pesantren socioreligious background and environment were typical, their contribution to the pesantren was different. The "pesantren intellectual masters" (i.e., Kiai Nawawi Banten of West Java and Kiai Mahfudz Termas of East Java) were identified with their prolific scholarly works and their honored status as the "*Imam al-Haramain*" during their stay in Hijaz. Their writings and academic works have been widely used by pupils of pesantren in Java, Madura, and other parts of the Muslim world (see Chapter 3).

Moreover, their significant heritage to the pesantren tradition rested on their devotion to transfer their knowledge (and wisdom) and to educate many renowned pesantren founders (including Kiai Khalil Bangkalan, Kiai Hasyim Asy'ari Jombang, and Kiai Asnawi Kudus themselves) in the Haramain (Mecca and Medina). It is true that even though the two great scholars spent most of their lives dedicated to the transmission of knowledge in the remote area of Arabia in the nineteenth and early twentieth centuries (and in fact, both ulama died and were buried in Mecca), "their position of the intellectual masters of the pesantren tradition was undoubted since they persistently remained the inspirers and real *qibla* ['center'] of the pesantren founders" (Rachman 1997: 4–5). Furthermore, the second group of ulama (i.e., the "pesantren strategists") apparently founded their own pesantrens in Java (East and Central Java) and Madura after they finished their Islamic studies in Hijaz. Their actual involvement in the pesantren community made them very respected and important models for other pesantren's leaders. Additionally, they masterminded the institutionalized an organized pesantren community on the national level by establishing the Nahdlatul Ulama (the Revival of Religious Scholars) in 1926.

In brief, those five Islamic scholars were central to inspiring and designing the pesantren tradition. As Rachman has argued, the authority of these five ulama is "demonstrated by the fact that their students became the leaders of the pesantren community all over Java [and Madura islands], and that the latter not only glorified them as actual masters and leaders but used the works of these ulama as well until now" (xi–xii). Interestingly, the "ulama of pesantren" (i.e., ulama who inspired, designed, and ran the traditional pesantren affiliated to Nahdlatul Ulama) are mostly adherents of Sufism and Sufi orders (tarekat), Sunniism (especially Ash'ari) in theology, and Shafi'i in Islamic jurisprudence. Accordingly, the discussion of pesantren tradition cannot be separated from that of Islamic mysticism, Sunniism-Ash'arism, and the Shafi'i school of thought, since they are all interconnected, and all of these dynamics were strongly linked to the intellectual tradition of Hijaz in the past where these "designers and developers of pesantren" pursued Islamic knowledge with many Arab and non-Arab Islamic scholars, *fuqaha* (Islamic jurists), and Sufi masters.

Although in his study, Rachman emphasized the vital role of the five ulama in initiating and designing pesantren in accordance with Mecca's Islamic schooling system in the nineteenth and early twentieth centuries, this does not mean that they were the only Arabian-educated Islamic scholars who contributed to the establishment and development of the pesantren tradition in Java. There were other Hijaz-trained great Javanese ulama of the nineteenth and early twentieth centuries who contributed significantly to the founding and growth of the pesantren tradition and Sunni-Shafii schools. These ulama included, among others, Kiai Saleh Darat Semarang (d.1903), Kiai Ma'sum Lasem (d.1972), Kiai Bisri Shansuri Denanyar (d.1980), Kiai Munawwir Krapyak (d.1942), Kiai Wahab Chasbullah Tambakberas (d.1971), Kiai Bisri Mustafa Rembang (d.1977), Kiai As'ad Syamsul Arifin Situbondo (d.1990), Kiai Zubair Sarang, Kiai Abdullah Abbas Cirebon, Kiai Muslih Mranggen, Kiai Abul Fadhol Senori Tuban, Kiai Abdullah Termas, Kiai Ihsan Muhammad Dahlan Kediri, Kiai Muhammad Siddiq Jember, Kiai Manaf Abd al-Karim Lirboyo, and Kiai Abdullah Mubarak Suralaya, among many others.

Kiai Saleh (or Salih) Darat Semarang (Muhammad Salih bin Umar al-Samarani), for instance, had been instrumental in the pesantren tradition. Kia Saleh Darat was contemporaneous with Kiai Nawawi Banten, and they shared several teachers. However, unlike Kiai Nawawi who settled in Mecca and wrote books in Arabic, Kiai Saleh Darat returned to Java, settled in Semarang, and wrote books all in the Javanese language with Arabic script (known as "Arab Pegon"). Kiai Saleh Darat is known for his printed Islamic texts in Arab Pegon. Kiai Saleh Darat was one of few local ulama in Java who consistently produced Islamic texts in Arab Pegon. Other Javanese ulama who wrote Islamic scholarly works in Arab Pegon included Kiai Ahmad Rifai Kalisak (d.1875), a prolific Islamic scholar and anti-colonial activist, and Kiai Bisri Mustafa Rembang (b.1915), author of the Qur'anic exegesis, entitled *Tafsir Al-Ibriz*. Kiai Saleh Darat was deeply concerned with educating people so that they could acquire sufficient knowledge of Islam to perform their religious observances properly. For that objective, Kiai Saleh Darat utilized all his potential, from teaching both students (santri) in his pesantren (Pesantren Darat, Semarang of Central Java; founded around 1870) and ordinary people in religious circles (halaqa) in mosques and prayer houses to composing Arab Pegon Islamic texts. During his life, Kiai Saleh Darat wrote at least twelve printed works, ranging from prayer manuals, theology (tauhid), Islamic jurisprudence (*fiqh*), Qur'anic exegesis (tafsir), to a hagiography of Prophet Muhammad (see Umam 2013: 243–74).

All of these noted ulama learned Islam with Malay-Indonesian Islamic scholars as well as Arab ulama in both Java and Hijaz. Some famed ulama where these "pesantren architects" studied Islam of the Sunni-Shafi'ite schools included Shaikh Ahmad Khatib Sambas, Sayyid Ahmad Dimyati, Shaikh Ahmad Bafaqih Ba'lawi, Shaikh Abd al-Ghani Bima, Shaikh Ahmad Zaini Dahlan, Shaikh Ahmad bin Sayyid Abd al-Rahman al-Nahrawi, Sayyid Abu Bakr bin Sayyid Muhammad Shata, Shaikh Muhammad Sa'id al-Hadrami, Muhammad Shalih al-Zawawi, Sayyid Alawi bin Abbas al-Maliki, Shaikh Yusuf Sunbulawi, Shaikh

Umar al-Syami, Kiai Abdullah Termas, and Shaikh Abd al-Karim Banten, among many others. It is also imperative to note that these "pesantren architects" were not only students but also teachers at the same time. Kiai Saleh Darat Semarang, Kiai Nawawi Banten, Kiai Mahfudz Termas, and Kiai Khalil Bangkalan, for instance, became teachers of many Indonesian ulama and founders of pesantren. Suffice it to say that nineteenth-century Java was typified by a more intense quest for learning in Arabia. Their status in Mecca and Medina as teachers after they succeeded in mastering the core Islamic knowledge undoubtedly contributed to the creation of an extremely favorable atmosphere of Javanese intellectualization among the future Javanese, Sundanese, and Madurese kiais with their educational institutions: the pesantren.

The ideology of pan-Islamism and anti-colonialism

As discussed in the previous chapters, ties between Indonesian Muslims and Muslims from the Middle East have existed for hundreds of years, dating back to the Islamization of the Malay-Indonesian archipelago, which started around the thirteenth century. The Arab Middle Eastern Muslim traders, Sufis, and scholars (in addition to Kurdish, Persian, Indian, and Chinese Muslims) played a central role in the Islamization process. By the mid-eighteenth century onward, Arabs (particularly the *sadah* group) assumed the position of *qadis* (religious judges) and *sultans* and acted as royal envoys and advisors in the islands of Borneo (Kalimantan), Sumatra, and Java (Al Qurtuby 2003, 2017). This earlier contact was an important precursor to subsequent connections between the Malay-Indonesia archipelago and the Middle East that started to escalate its intensity in the eighteenth century, and particularly in the nineteenth century after the discovery of steamship technology and the opening of the Suez Canal in 1869.

Two important places in the Middle East that have long attracted many Muslims from the Malay-Indonesia archipelago are Hijaz and Egypt. Indonesian Muslims voyaged to these sites for various reasons ranging from pursuing Islamic knowledge and performing a hajj pilgrimage to seeking title, religious legitimacy, or "divine supernatural power" (*kesaktian*). Toward the mid-seventeenth century, the rulers of Banten (west Java), Mataram (central Java), and Makassar (south Sulawesi or Celebes), for instance, sent envoys to Mecca to request recognition of their kingdoms from the "caliph-sharif" and to be given the Muslim title of sultan. Apparently, the rulers—and, in fact, most Indonesian Muslims at the time—were confused and unable to distinguish between the titles of "Caliph" (the Ottoman) and Grand Sharif (the de facto ruler of Mecca). The Grand Sharif of Mecca did not further enlighten them but gave them the requested titles and new, royal Muslim names (Djajadiningrat 1983; Van Bruinessen 1995: 115).

For Indonesian Muslims, furthermore, Hijaz or Arabia not only brought religious knowledge and sciences but also ideologies of pan-Islamism and anti-colonialism. Historians and scholars of Indonesian society (Benda 1958; Van Niel 1960; Reid 1967; Ricklefs 1993) have already pointed out that, for many

Indonesian Muslims, in the past, especially since the Dutch colonial era until the Japanese occupation, the hajj pilgrimage was not simply about performing Islamic rituals, fulfilling the fifth *arkan al-Islam* (the Islamic precept or foundation), or seeking Islamic knowledge in the holy city of Mecca, but also a medium of gathering and consolidating to fight against colonial powers. At the time, many Indonesian Muslims in Hijaz, some influenced by the Middle Eastern reformist Islam and pan-Islamic ideas of such figures as Jamal al-Din al-Afghani (1838–1897) or Muhammad Abduh (1849–1905), held strong nationalist beliefs that the Indonesian world and society should be freed from colonial rule. Coincidentally, the trend for greater intensification in transforming Islamic learning in Southeast Asia came at a time when Britain and the Netherlands were shaping their colonial entities and being forced to come to terms with Islam as a cultural force.

It is common to acknowledge that many native "Indies leaders" and founding fathers of the Republic of Indonesia, hosted by Indonesian ulama who resided in Mecca, had made the holy city of Mecca (and also Medina) a safe place to strengthen bonds of nationality and to discuss and consolidate for the struggle against the colonial authorities (Dutch and Japanese). Indeed, some "Muslim unrests" (e.g., the Banten Revolt of 1888) against the Dutch had been controlled by Indonesian Sufi gurus and Islamic scholars in the Haramain that utilized their *tariqa* and Islamic student networks to fight against the colonial rulers. The eagerness to be free from the colonial powers had been the norm among Indonesian Muslims in previous centuries, and the hajj pilgrimage, in this regard, was a vital source of inspiration for the emergence of "pan-Islamism" and the spirits of nationalism. However, it should be noted, for Indonesian Muslims, the pan-Islamist movement in the past had nothing to do with the desire of founding an Islamic state but instead was closely linked to the spirit of nationalism and anti-colonialism.

Although Mecca had long inspired Indonesian pilgrims to fight against the Dutch (see the case of Shaikh Yusuf al-Makassari), it was not until the nineteenth and early twentieth centuries that the hajj gained a significant momentum, in part because throughout this period many protests and rebellions against the Dutch were widespread across the archipelago (take, e.g., the Banten Revolt, the Java War, the Padri War, the Aceh War), many of which, especially in Java and Sumatra, were led by hajj returnees, in addition to local ulama and clerics (see, e.g., Kartodirdjo 1966, 1979). It is true that *haji* (hajj pilgrims), along with ulama, were the first to arouse distrust whenever anti-European movements started, and hajj returnees were indeed indiscriminately regarded by the Dutch rulers as potential subversives. Dutch Indies officials were highly suspicious of the hajis since they dubbed them as anti-government agitators that could provoke local masses and Muslim societies to wage jihad against the Dutch.

It is worth noting that by the end of the nineteenth century there was a sizable community of resident Malay-Indonesians in Mecca (collectively known as the "Jawah" or "the Jawi"). Occasionally there were reports of a returning pilgrim bringing an Ottoman flag with him and proclaiming nominal allegiance to the "sultan-caliph." Although Hurgronje, in 1885, suggested to the Dutch East Indies government that Hijaz or Mecca was not the hotbed of anti-colonial conspiracies for which some Dutch administrators took it, he, nonetheless, made a remark that the Meccans, local and foreign residents alike, including Southeast Asians, were acutely aware of the advance of European imperialism and its growing domination of the Muslim world as well as of the resistance movements it engendered (Van Bruinessen 1995: 156–57). Unlike the Dutch rulers, Hurgronje championed a more intelligent approach at the end of the nineteenth and the start of the twentieth centuries.[10] The Dutch oracle on Islam, Hurgronje said that it was not the hajj returnees but the caliphate (the Ottoman) and the *mukimin* (Meccan residents of Malay-Indonesian origins) that constituted the real political threat to Dutch rule.

Against this backdrop, accordingly, the closer nineteenth- and early twentieth-century connection between Southeast Asia and Arabia deserves and merits special attention. Some scholars (e.g., Benda 1958; Van Niel 1960) have examined the complex and intimate relationship between Islam and nationalism, and indeed the nineteenth century became a starting point to analyze the link between Islam, anti-colonialism, and a sort of nationalist movement. The nineteenth century also marked the beginning of anxiety on the part of the European colonial rulers toward Mecca. Historian Michael Laffan (2003b: 402) also notes that some Dutch (and British) officials were worried about the role of Mecca in the 1870s and pointed out that their subjects would be exposed to an unhealthy mix of ideas in that holy city. Their worries were not only about the hajj pilgrimage but also Mecca's Saulatiyya Madrasah, where many Southeast Asian Muslims, including those from Indonesia, enrolled. Founded by an exile from the Indian Mutiny and a propagandist for the Ottoman Caliphate, Rahmat Allah Kairawi (1818–1890), the Saulatiyya Madrasah was seen by the European colonials as a perilous site that could potentially influence its students to form pan-Islamism and to wage jihad against the colonial authorities. It was true that in the early 1880s, for example, the Dutch and British consuls in Jeddah were convinced of an impending plot hatched in Mecca and Istanbul to activate the mystical orders and to declare global jihad (Laffan 2003b). For obvious reasons, then, the later Dutch government sent Hurgronje to oversee and monitor the activities of Jawi residents in Arabia.

Although the Dutch authorities imposed restrictions through regulations on the hajj pilgrimage and limited the number of hajj pilgrims, there was a remarkable number of Indonesian Muslims who made the pilgrimage to Mecca.[11] It was reported that, in the last three decades of the nineteenth century, there were 4,000–8,000 Indonesian pilgrims each year, forming on average of about 15 percent of the total overseas arrivals in Hijaz. Indeed, for centuries, the holy city of Mecca has been a very popular destination for Indonesian Muslims. Many Indonesian Muslims considered Mecca their "second homeland" and many of them wanted to die and be buried there, since they believed it was a way to enter paradise. Hurgronje, who visited Mecca in 1885, made a remark that the Jawis could be distinguished by their scorn for their own half-pagan country and their naïve respect for the idealized land where all institutions were presumed to be in accordance with the law of the Prophet.

For nineteenth-century Indonesian Muslims, the hajj was the principal source of foreign ideas, including those of pan-Islam and anti-colonialism. Coincidentally, many Muslim-majority areas in the nineteenth- and early twentieth-century world from Africa and the Middle East to South and Southeast Asia had faced the same problem: foreign (mostly European) colonialism and imperialism. Thus it is understandable that the Mecca and hajj pilgrimage became a vital niche and a central instrument of sharing—and spreading—the notions and spirits of nationalism, anti-colonialism, and contra-imperialism. Reid (1967: 269) has noted that even though the majority of the Jawis only spent a few weeks in Hijaz (a small minority chose to stay longer in Mecca, either to seek Islamic knowledge, to live, or to work to pay debts or for the money to return home), they made contact there with a remarkably large number of their countrymen and foreign people residing semi permanently in Mecca, who had come to share the international and distinctly anti-colonial outlook of the holy city. This connection should only throw into sharper light the scandal of infidel rule over a Muslim people. In a time where communal gatherings and discussions in Indonesia had been outlawed—or at least restricted—by the Dutch authorities, Mecca became an alternative place and a secure haven for Indonesian pilgrims to hold meetings with their compatriots and discuss ideas of how to free their homeland from the colonial power.

This caused a vicious cycle of tension and conflict between the Dutch rulers and the religious leaders, particularly the hajis and ulama; the Dutch, in turn, actively favored the secular, non religious leaders of the *adat* (customary law) (e.g., the Minangkabau case previously depicted) over the Muslim leadership whenever there was a chance to exploit the split. It was common for Indonesian pilgrims to have conversations and compare notes in Mecca on discrimination, injustice, immorality, or evilness practiced by the Dutch rulers upon Muslim society. The multiple immoral, severe, and unjust practices of the Dutch toward the Muslims, added to their support of the *adat* and secular leaders, resulted in their bad standing in the Middle East, namely as a fervent adversary of Islam and an ardent foe of Muslim society. The Dutch adviser Hurgronje was alarmed that "in the Muslim daily press our government is frequently derided as the enemy of Muslims, while in geographical textbooks used in Turkish and Arab schools the Netherlands is tersely indicated as a Power unfamiliar with the principles of tolerance, under whose yoke millions of Muslims suffer" (quoted in Reid 1967: 270).

It should be noted, however, that although foreign ideas and movements of pan-Islamism might have been a vital addition to the anti-Dutch movements, the biggest factor that contributed to the anti-colonial protests and upheaval, however, was still local socio economic-religious situations and political dynamics in the Malay-Indonesian archipelago, all of which were connected to the Dutch policy and authorities. In other words, the rise of pan-Islam among Indonesian Muslims linked to the anti-Dutch sentiment would not have emerged on the political stage in the East Indies if there had been no feelings of humiliation and subjugation on the part of Muslims and the Dutch had not made trouble with, and problems for, local Muslim societies by implementing unfair policies, making alliances with other social groupings that divided local communities, and generating rules that disadvantaged Indonesian Muslims in the archipelago.

Most, if not all, anti-colonial movements waged by Muslims from Banten and Central Java to West Sumatra and Aceh in the nineteenth and early twentieth centuries were successfully cracked down on by the Dutch rulers who joined forces with the local authorities. In Java, for instance, the alliance between the VOC (the Dutch East Indies Company) and the aristocracy of "Islamic Mataram" succeeded in impeding the growth of a middle-class Muslim leadership which elsewhere provided the source and inspiration for the ideology of pan-Islamism. In Minangkabau on Sumatra Island, after a long period of conflict and skirmish, the coalition of the Dutch and the adat chiefs finally succeeded in defeating the Padris in 1837 (see Dobbin 1974; Hadler 2008). Since the 1820s, Dutch military intervention on the side of the adat leaders had gradually transformed the Padri cause into a patriotic one, representing broader interests than the militant puritanism with which it had begun. Although the alliance of Dutch and adat chiefs crushed the Padris, their legacy was undoubtedly important in bringing Indonesian Islam closer to that of western Asia (the Middle East).

The occurrence of the spirit of pan-Islamism in the nineteenth century can be seen as a form of pre-nationalism that grew significantly from the early twentieth century with the emergence of several Islamic organizations, political parties, ethno-linguistic groups, and civil society associations: Sarekat Dagang Islam, Sarekat Islam, Muhammadiyah, al-Irshad, Persatuan Islam, Nahdlatul Ulama, Partai Nasionalis Indonesia, and Partai Komunis Indonesia, among others. A considerable number of these organizations, which espoused an Islamist political ideology, were formed by energetic "*Kaum Muda*" (lit. young people) nationalists, both from the reformist and traditionalist camps. However, it is imperative to note that unlike the current Islamist groupings that seek to build an Islamic state or Islamic government, or to implement Islamic laws in every realm of life, the Islamist ideology they absorbed was simply a channel to fight against colonialism and colonial power. This sort of Islamism also tended to be less concerned with the application of Islamic law (see Nawab 2011: 42–3). However, this phenomenon changed, especially from the 1930s onward, when some Islamist leaders (e.g., the cofounder of Persatuan Islam [the Islamic Union] Ahmad Hasan, 1887–1958, and the cofounder of Masjumi [the Indonesian Muslim Advisory Council] Muhammad Natsir, 1908–1992), influenced by the Egyptian Ikhwanul Muslimin (Muslim Brotherhood), used Islamism to transform Indonesia into an Islamic state.

Unfortunately, "pan-Islamism" did not have a happy ending, since leaders of local Muslim organizations in the archipelago (founded by both native and Arab Muslims), which were initially established from the 1900s onward to challenge the Dutch, were involved in tensions and conflicts with one another. Conflicts between leaders of Sarekat Islam and of Muhammadiyah, for example, became more frequent, and by the end of the 1920s, the All Islam Congress, a series of meetings previously attended by representatives of multiple Muslim organizations and backgrounds, was exclusively a Sarekat Islam affair. In 1929, Sarekat Islam gave up its pan-Islamism in favor of Indonesian nationalism. Other Muslim organizations (Nahdlatul Ulama, al-Irshad, and Persatuan Islam, among others) turned their attention to more strictly religious, educational, and social concerns. As a result, the pan-Islamic ideals no longer received much attention in the Dutch East Indies, and the first brief chapter of Islamic internationalism was closed. However, one thing that is clear is that, although pan-Islamism failed to unite the archipelago's Muslim societies, Mecca had still been a vital niche for Indonesian Muslims that contributed to the emergence of the spirit of nationalism and the anti-colonial movement.

The Saudi imprint in contemporary Indonesia: The rise of modern neo-Salafism

Beginning in the 1980s, Indonesia witnessed a new religious movement in its social and religious history: Salafi da'wa (Islamic propagation). The emergence of the Salafi da'wa movement can be seen, first and foremost, in the way young Muslim men and women (Muslimah) wore their clothes (and other attributes) that emulated Arab Salafis. As for the young men, they wore long, flowing robes (*jalabiyya*), turbans (*imamah*), trousers right to their ankles (*isbal*) as well as growing long beards (*lihya*), while the women wore a black veil covering their faces (*niqab*). These young men and women called themselves "Salafi." At first these Salafis (or perhaps "neo-Salafis"), who were attired in Arab-style dress, appeared in the areas around university campuses, where they formed an exclusivist current of Islamic activism, before they spread into the wider community.

For this particular group, a commitment to wear jalabiyya (or grow *lihya*) for men and niqab for women is much more important than taking part in political activities partly because they are considered to be an integral part of Islamic doctrine and a Qur'anic injunction, and a way to follow the practices of Prophet Muhammad and the early generations of Islam. For this group, wearing jalabiyya and niqab is not a cultural practice of Arab Muslims but a religious or doctrinal one (i.e., Islamic doctrine and teaching). To strengthen their understanding of Islam and to reinforce their group solidarity, they openly organized a series of meetings called *halqa* (study circle, namely a form of study in which participants sit around the teacher to hear and scrutinize the lessons) and *daura* (a type of workshop held for a certain length of time) in mosques located on the outskirts of cities and in rural villages. As a result, enclaves of members sprang up, followed by the construction of mosques and Islamic schools under the banner of the Salafi da'wa movement.

Furthermore, unlike any reformist, modernist Muslim organizations, either in Indonesia or abroad, the Salafi da'wa movement was squarely within the puritanical classic Salafi-Wahhabi tradition, typified by its concern with matters of creed and morality such as strict monotheism, anti-Sufism, anti-*ziyara* (shrine visits), divine attributes, purifying Islam from accretions, and developing the moral integrity of the individual (see Wahib 2006; Hasan 2007, 2010a, 2010b; Chaplin 2014: 217–36).

In other words, the group's primary concerns were (1) the purity of the concept of the oneness of God (*tauhid*), (2) the call for a return to strict religious practices, and (3) the subsequent moral integrity of individuals. Noorhaidi Hasan (2007: 84–5), a specialist of Indonesian Salafism study, calls this movement a form of "reconstituted Wahhabism."

The indication that this group is a sort of "reconstituted Wahhabism," Hasan has argued, can be viewed from the determination of its proponents to codify and follow more systematically the thoughts and ideas formulated by (1) the three main classic Salafi-Wahhabi inspirators, namely Ahmad ibn Hanbal (780–855), Ahmad ibn Taimiyya (1263–1328), and Muhammad ibn Qayyim al-Jawziyya (1292–1350), (2) the founder of the then "Wahhabism" (i.e., Shaikh Muhammad ibn Abd al-Wahhab [1703–1792]), and (3) the contemporary Wahhabi authorities such as, among others, Shaikh Abdul Aziz bin Baz (1912–1999) and Shaikh Muhammad Nasir al-Din al-Albani (1914–1999). The two latter Wahhabi scholars were famous for their campaign for the revival of the Sunna (Prophetic traditions) and for their notions that political activism (*hizbiyya*) is a form of *bid'a* (heretical religious innovation) and hence anathema to Islam (Hasan 2005, 2007, 2010a, 2010b). Derived mainly from thoughts of these two leading Islamic scholars, the Salafi da'wa movement adopted an apolitical quietism in its doctrine. The salafi has been used as the banner of this movement partly because of the pejorative connotation of the term "Wahhabi" among many Muslims in the world. In other words, although their dress is Salafi, its content is Wahhabi.

To make it clearer, at this point, it is necessary to situate Wahhabism in relation to Salafism, and, more broadly, Islamic belief and praxis. If Islam is understood as a discursive tradition, then Salafism amounts to a subcultural "tradition within a tradition," marked out by a distinctive set of principles and points of reference. Whereas the label of Salafism is contested among scholars and, in reality, often vaguely applied, Michael Farquhar (quoting Bernard Haykel) has defined contemporary Salafism as typified by several interconnected features: (1) a focus on the purity of the beliefs and praxis of the *salaf al-salih* (pious ancestors); (2) a distinctive understanding of *tauhid* (the oneness of God), which in turn tends to give rise to the view that many traditional Islamic practices constitute *shirk* (polytheism); (3) a stress on combating perceived unbelief, particularly *shirk*; (4) an insistence that the Qur'an, the Sunna, and "the consensus of the Prophet's companions" are the only legitimate bases of religious authority; (5) an emphasis on purging illegitimate religious innovations (sing. *bid'a* or pl. *bida'*) understood to have corrupted Islamic belief and praxis; and (6) a conviction that the Qur'an and the Sunna are clear in meaning and offer sufficient counsel in all circumstances (Farquhar 2015: 704–05).

In this regard, Wahhabism displays all of these features and those who are labeled Wahhabis would typically prefer to think of themselves simply as Salafis (see, e.g., Voll 1975; Cook 1992; Nafi 2006; Ochsenwald 2007). In fact, many contemporary adherents of Wahhabism prefer to be called "Salafis" or "Hanbalites." Wahhabism, nevertheless, has certain additional characteristics that justify treating it as a distinguishable subcultural tradition within the broader

Salafi fold. One of these characteristics is the central place given within it to works authored by the eighteenth-century Najdi reformer Muhammad ibn Abd al-Wahhab and certain of his descendants. Another feature of the Wahhabi tradition is a distinctive approach to Islamic jurisprudence. In principle, Wahhabism shares with many other modes of Salafism a commitment to rejecting blind emulation (*taql'id*) of the rulings of the mainstream Sunni schools of law, in favor of verifying legal rulings by independent reasoning (*ijtihad*) with direct reference to the Qur'an and the Sunna. However, in practice the Wahhabi tradition has historically been very closely associated with Hanbali jurisprudence and Ibn Taimiyya's religious notions.

While wearing *jalabiyya* and *imamah* or growing long beards are not new phenomenon for Indonesian Muslims since some Muslim groups in the past (see, e.g., the Padris of West Sumatra or Java's traditionalist ulama) did perform all of these practice, their main concerns with the strict "pristine *tauhid*" and the "puritanical creed" typical of the Middle Eastern (chiefly Saudi) Salafi-Wahhabis are somewhat new phenomena in the history of Indonesian Islam. The efflorescence of the Salafi da'wa movement has indeed marked a new trend in Indonesia's Islamic activism. The prototype of the Salafi movement to a large extant resembles what Oliver Roy (1996: 25) refers to as neo-fundamentalism, which he defines as a nonrevolutionary Islamic movement attempting to re-Islamize society at the grassroots level without being formed within an Islamic state. The rise of transnational Salafism might be due to the failure of Islamism, a modern political Islamic movement that claims to recreate a true Muslim society by establishing a new Islamic order through revolutionary and militant political actions.

The questions remain: Where did this Salafi da'wa movement come from? Why and how did this movement emerge on the stage of Indonesian Islam?

Let me explain briefly the origins of the Salafi da'wa movement. Although Saudi was one of the earliest countries in the world that recognized the independence of the Republic of Indonesia in 1945, and one of the initial nations that opened its embassy in Jakarta (in 1947), it was not until the late 1960s that the Saudi kingdom began to contribute to the development of Indonesian Islam and Muslim cultures that later helped to create the appearance of Salafism (or "neo-Salafism"), the Salafi da'wa movement, and a particular form of Islam typified by an exclusivist tendency and rigid ritual practices as well as avoidance of any local practices that were viewed as aberrant from foundational Islamic doctrines and theology (*aqidah* or *tauhid*). Seen from the Indonesian perspective, it was local political dynamics and developments following the late reign of Sukarno that pushed a segment of the country's Islamists and reformist Muslims, most of them linked to the banned Masjumi Islamist political party, toward closer cooperation with the Saudi government. At the same time, Saudi Arabia itself, especially from the 1950s onward, made attempts to look for international partnerships with Islamic groupings that could cooperate with the kingdom and help fight against the influence of (1) Egyptian Nasserism (pan-Arab Socialist-Nationalist movement, initiated by the then president of Egypt Gamal Abdel Nasser, 1918–1970), and, since the late 1970s, (2) "Iranian Shiism" (especially the revolutionary ideology of

Shiites and Ayatollah Imam Khomeini, 1902–1989), both of which were viewed as a menace for the Saudi central government.

Ever since King Abdul Aziz Al Saud (known as Ibn Saud, 1875–1953) took over Mecca in the 1920s, he had played an enormously important role in initiating endeavors to make Saudi become the center of the Muslim world and the leader of Muslim societies across the globe, and in preparing the ground for the sustainability of this position. Various efforts had been made by Ibn Saud and his successors (King Saud, King Faisal, and others) to create a global coalition with international Muslim communities with Saudis as their leaders. Already in 1926, for instance, Ibn Saud organized the World Muslim Congress, with the aim to forge solidarity between Muslim-majority nations and to place Saudi as an epicenter of pan-Islamism out of the hands of the Ottoman Empire. After the Second World War, and particularly since the 1950s, Saudi Arabia adopted the strategy of spreading Wahhabism as a major part of its foreign policy primarily to counter the effect of Arab Socialist Nationalism launched by Gamal Abdel Nasser, which Saudi saw as a potential threat to the existence of its kingdom (Hegghammer 2010). The 1950s is a moment in history when Saudi rule faced serious challenges from the Middle East's political dynamics and developments. In Egypt and elsewhere in the Middle East, the 1950s witnessed the rise of various brands of radical republicanism that decried the hereditary privileges of monarchy and whose opponents (especially Gamal Abdel Nasser) were actively engaged in efforts to destabilize Riyadh.

It is within this context that Saudi sponsored the founding of several Islamic organizations and universities aimed at spreading Salafism-Wahhabism across the Muslim world and protecting the Saudi kingdom and society from the political movement of leftist republicanism. In 1957, Saudi sponsored the founding of the Organization of Islamic Conference (later the Organization of Islamic Cooperation), whose objective was to organize the foreign politics of the Muslim world in accordance with Saudi's political interests. In the early 1960s, the Saudi kingdom founded the Islamic University of Medina (IUM), whose main objective was to counter the transnational extension of leftist republican projects by advancing a competing program grounded in claims to historical and religious authenticity. Since opening its doors in 1961, the IUM has been a central pillar of efforts by Saudi actors to promote the global proliferation of Salafi understandings of Islam, broadly aligned in core matters of creed and praxis with Wahhabism. The IUM from the start was committed to recruiting over 80 percent of its all-male student body from outside Saudi Arabia, with a comprehensive state-funded scholarship program covering their travel, living costs, tuition, and other expenses. The hope was that after several years of religious studies, they would return to their home communities or settle elsewhere to promote the particular conception of orthodoxy they had learned in Medina. By around 2001, tens of thousands of non-Saudis had been offered scholarships to study at the IUM and nearly 11,600 had secured undergraduate qualifications from its constituent colleges (Farquhar 2015: 701–21).

Around the same period, in the early 1960s, furthermore, Saudi also set up the Rabitat al-'Alam al-Islami (hereafter the Rabita-Muslim World League), which was responsible for the institutionalization of its influence in cultural and religious activities across the Muslim world. The rise of the Rabita has contributed a great deal to the further spread of Saudi influence in the Muslim world, which has steadily gained momentum since the beginning of the 1970s, thanks in particular to the skyrocketing of the world oil prices and the defeat of Muslim countries in the Arab–Israeli War that elevated the Saudi role in the Muslim world to replace the "failed Egypt." To accentuate the spread of its influence, Saudi urged the Rabita to take part as its philanthropic agent in the liberal distribution of money to Islamic organizations and Muslim institutions, particularly those having, more or less, similar concerns, principles, and objectives with Saudis and Wahhabis, all over the world (Hasan 2007, 2010a, 2010b). Saudi attempts and roles in forging a global alliance with the Muslim world and in spreading Wahhabism became more active and enthusiastic after the 1979 Shia Iranian Revolution. It is within this context that Saudi built connections with factions of Indonesian Islamist and Muslim reformist groups.

In short, the Saudi imprint and the emergence and development of Salafism-Wahhabism in contemporary Indonesia since the 1970s and 1980s was mainly due to the local political dynamics and global changes within Indonesia, Saudi, and the Middle Eastern world, especially Egypt and Iran. In the context of Indonesia, more specifically, the rise of Salafism-Wahhabism, particularly among youths, university students, and urban Muslims, which initially adopted a stance of apolitical quietism primarily because of governmental policies of—and local political conditions during—the Old Order and the New Order regimes that disadvantaged the Islamist-reformist group. As historians have noted, because some top leaders of the Masjumi Islamist political party were involved in the political rebellions against the Indonesian central government (e.g., the case of PRRI, Pemerintahan Revolusioner Republik Indonesia—the Revolutionary Government of Republic of Indonesia), Sukarno caught and jailed some elite members of the Masjumi and shut down the political party in early 1960s.

When Suharto took over the government through a series of brutal anti-communist campaigns and the bloody revolutions of 1965–1966 that marked the founding of the New Order regime, the fate of the Indonesian Islamists was even worse than under the Old Order rule since Suharto did not give them a chance to be actively involved in the political domain, albeit at first he utilized the Islamist group and a variety of Islamic groups as "foot soldiers" to fight against the Indonesian Communist Party's members, activists, and fans (Hefner 2000). President Suharto also caught and jailed Islamist leaders and activists who tried to challenge his political authority. Suharto's rejection of the "political Islam" espoused by Islamist groups, mainly ex-Masjumi, marked the beginning of an era of marginalization of Muslim politics, reinforcing the policies of the preceding Sukarno regime.

Because of the hostile situation and unpleasant political developments for the reformist-Islamist factions, leaders, activists, and sympathizers of these groups, especially those connected to the banned Masjumi, found alternative ways to be active and exist on the Indonesian cultural stage. Some of them, especially the famed and influential Muhammad Natsir (1908–1993), founded the Dewan Dakwah Islamiyah Indonesia (DDII, the Indonesian Council for Islamic Propagation) in 1967. The decision to establish the DDII was a strategic choice to disentangle themselves from the political standoff and, at the same time, to avoid Suharto's pressures on the Islamist and Muslim political groups. To circumvent Suharto's ill treatment toward the Islamist political faction, the DDII embraced multiple strategies and tactics, including mobilizing religious preachers (*dai, muballigh,* and *khatib*) across the Indonesian archipelago to hear briefings by government officials about Suharto's and the New Order's policies. More importantly, the DDII soon associated itself with Saudi Arabia and, in fact, this organization became the primary Indonesian representative of the Saudi-sponsored Muslim World League (the Rabita). This connection reinforced the very existence of the DDII in Suharto's eyes. Suharto's steadfast determination to marginalize Muslim politics and wipe out its radical expressions encouraged the DDII to reaffirm its position as an exclusively da'wa movement (Hefner 2000; Hasan 2007).

Although ideologically, at first, its leaders and activists remained closer to the Muslim Brotherhood of Egypt (Ikhwanul Muslimin, founded by Hassan al-Banna, 1906–1949, in the late 1920s as a response to the Ottoman Empire's collapse and the establishment of the secular Republic of Turkey by Mustafa Kemal Ataturk, 1881–1938) due to their long admiration of this Egyptian Islamist group rather than to Wahhabism of Saudi Arabia, the DDII later became one of the primary conduits for introducing and spreading Salafi and Wahhabi ideas in Indonesia, especially since the 1970s. It is the DDII that initially played a major role in bringing the Saudi kingdom, along with its Salafism-Wahhabism, into contemporary Indonesian Muslim society. Moreover, through the DDII activists and other Islamist channels, the Saudi kingdom began to formally finance some Muslim organizations and to sponsor educational, cultural, and religious programs that later helped to shape and influence some Indonesian Muslim individuals and groups.

Indeed, in Indonesia, Saudi funding has had a more wide-ranging impact. Some scholars have identified numerous Islamic organizations that have benefited from Saudi funding, most, if not all, of which have adopted a form of reformist puritanical Islam, including the DDII, Persatuan Islam (Islamic Union), and al-Irshad, an Arab-sponsored educational institution (Fealy and Bubalo 2005). Of these organizations, the DDII was the most "politically" active ("clandestinely"), while others were more concerned with the cultural, educational, religious, and da'wa movements and were less active in the political arena. As stated earlier, the DDII's chairman, Muhammad Natsir, who was widely respected in Middle East Wahhabi and Salafi circles, became the most important channel for Saudi funds flowing into Indonesia during the 1970s and 1980s. Of all the early generation of Islamist leaders (especially during the Old Order and the New Order) Muhammad Natsir was exceptional in part because he had direct links with leaders of multiple worldwide Islamist groups ranging from Egypt's Ikhwanul Muslimin to Pakistan's Jama'at-i-Islami. Natsir's close relations with these international Islamist leaders and players was partly because of his active involvement and leadership in the world's various Islamic organizations such as the Organization of Islamic

Cooperation and the Muslim World League. Natsir also sat on the international advisory board of the Islamic University of Medina, along with several prominent Salafi and Islamist thinkers from Saudi, Egypt, Syria, India, Pakistan, and other nationalities.

Beyond this direct funding, the Saudi government also provided financial support, mostly through the DDII, to madrasah (Islamic schools), *ma'had* (Islamic learning centers), modern Salafi pesantren, and higher institutions of Islamic learning (e.g., LIPIA, the Institute for the Study of Islam and Arabic, based in Jakarta) in order to introduce, teach, and indoctrinate students with Salafism-Wahhabism. The Saudis, moreover, (financially) sponsored a range of educational activities, even among moderate traditionalists, with the effect that Hanbalite or Hanbali *fiqh* (i.e., Islamic jurisprudence following the madhab of Ahmad bin Hanbal, 780–855) conquered a place beside, or even instead of, Shafiite or Shafi`i *fiqh* (i.e., Islamic jurisprudence following the madhab of Muhammad bin Idris al-Shafii, 767–820), which has been dominant in traditional pondok pesantren linked to Nahdlatul Ulama since the last century, in several traditional pesantren and madrasah (Wahid 2014). Financial provision was also given to individual students in the form of bursaries and scholarships to universities in Saudi Arabia and elsewhere in the Middle East (Von der Mehden 1993). In fact, the DDII actively recruited talented students to study Islamic subjects in Saudi universities, particularly the Islamic University of Medina, Al Imam Muhammad bin Saud Islamic University, and Umm al-Qura University.

The "success" of the Saudi project to popularize its Hanbalite and Wahhabi doctrines in Indonesia (and elsewhere in Southeast Asia, see Nawab 2011: 42–9) was largely due to the fact that the Indonesian rule (and the governments of Southeast Asian countries in general) did not see the Saudis as a "green peril" for its political authorities in comparison to the Iranians. It is true that, for the New Order regime, after the 1979 revolution that brought Ayatollah Khomeini to power, the Islamic Republic of Iran was viewed as a real hazard for Suharto's reign. He was afraid that "the virus of Shia revolutionary ideology" would influence Indonesian Muslims and, like in Iran, they could potentially declare a political-religious movement against the existing secular government. Because of this suspicion and fear, Suharto made every effort to diminish (and eliminate, if possible) Iranian influences in Indonesian society by, for instance, banning books authored by Iranian and Shia scholars and ideologues (e.g., Ali Shariati or Imam Khomeini) which once gained popularity among young Muslim activists and university students.

This situation for sure differs from Saudi Arabia in which the New Order generally did not view it as a political threat to the Indonesian administration and society. In fact, in the aftermath of the Iranian revolution, the Saudi kingdom, like the Indonesian government, was faced with the challenge of this Shia regime; thereby, it began to work closely with various anti-Iran Islamist groups around the globe from Egypt and Pakistan to Malaysia and Indonesia by providing financial support to the groups' educational institutions and religious activities. At the time, Saudi Arabia was haunted by the possibility that a similar revolution to that in Iran could wipe out its own kingdom. This worry was indeed justified by a series of anti-Saudi government protests orchestrated by pro-Khomeini Shiites of Saudi Arabia as well as by the rise of a revolutionary Islamic group within the kingdom that in 1979, under the leadership of Juhayman al-Utaybi, seized the Grand Mosque of Mecca (see Hegghammer 2010; Matthiesen 2014).

Here we can see that the New Order's Indonesia and the Kingdom of Saudi Arabia shared a similar concern: how to rub out the influence of—and to protect society from—the Shia Iran. In this case, the DDII benefited from the success of the Imam Khomeini-led Iranian Islamic Revolution in toppling Shah Muhammad Reza Pahlavi (1919–1980) from his throne. As the primary agent of the campaign against Shiites in Indonesia, the DDII received more generous influxes of money from Saudi Arabia than before, through such channels as the International Islamic Relief Organization, the World Council of Mosques, the Committee of Islamic Charity, and the World Assembly of Muslim Youth, among others. The DDII then used the large financial support given by Saudis to fund projects in the da'wa activities and social fields, such as building mosques, orphanages, hospitals, and Islamic schools (madrasah). The funds were also used to produce free copies of the Qur'an and Salafi books as well as to train preachers who later were sent to remote transmigration areas in the archipelago. Moreover, beginning in the 1980s and 1990s, as noted by Martin van Bruinessen (2002: 1), "an unending stream of anti-Zionist, anti-Semitic, anti-Christian, anti-Shi`a, anti-Ahmadi and anti-liberal tracts, many of them of Saudi or Kuwaiti provenance, flooded the cheap book market in Indonesia." Indonesian graduates of Saudi institutes of learning also had an increasing impact on public debate on religious issues. The impact of the intensification of Islamic revitalization launched by the DDII was felt most significantly on university campuses (especially non-Islamic, secular universities) that witnessed the rapid expansion of Islamic activism and Salafi groups.

The Saudi imprint in contemporary Indonesia: Education, publication, and foundation

In addition to supporting programs and activities of the DDII and other Indonesian Islamist-reformist Muslim institutions, the Kingdom of Saudi Arabia, in 1980, also set up the Lembaga Pengetahuan Islam dan Bahasa Arab (LIPIA, the Institute for the Study of Islam and Arabic), again through Muhammad Natsir, who mediated between the Saudi kingdom and the Indonesian government. Based in Jakarta, the LIPIA, initially established as the Lembaga Pengajaran Bahasa Arab (LPBA, the Institute for Arabic Teaching), is a branch of Riyadh-based Al Imam Muhammad bin Saud Islamic University. The LIPIA emerged as the first foreign institution to open formal educational activities in Indonesia. To lead this institution, the university appoints a Saudi director whose responsibilities include directing administrative and academic affairs under the direct supervision of the Saudi embassy in Jakarta. The university also selects and recruits lecturers (on a contract basis) from multiple countries including Saudi Arabia, Egypt, Sudan, Jordan,

Somalia, and Indonesia. The LIPIA, furthermore, printed many Islamic books (particularly those linked to Salafism-Wahhabism) and distributed them (free of charge) to many Islamic educational institutions and religious organizations across the archipelago. Also, the LIPIA sponsors translations of these Islamic books, which are written in Arabic, into Bahasa Indonesia. The Islamic books translated and printed include those authored by leading authorities of Salafism-Wahhabism such as Ibn Taimiyya, Ibn al-Qayyim al-Jauziyya, Muhammad ibn Abd al-Wahhab, Abd al-Aziz ibn Baz, Muhammad bin Salih al-Uthaymin, Muhammad Nasir al-Din al-Albani, Abd Allah ibn Jibrin, and Muhib al-Din al-Khatib, among many others. Initially, these translations were circulated by the LIPIA. However, it has now spread to an insurmountable number of publishers scattered across the archipelago such as At-Turots (Yayasan Majelis al-Turots al-Islami), YPIA (Yayasan Pendidikan Islam al-Atsari), and Wahdah Islamiyah, among others. The International Crisis Group (ICG 2005) has listed twenty-four prominent publishers that publish Salafi-Wahhabi research (past and present) written by, mostly, Saudi Islamic scholars.

As a Saudi-sponsored higher Islamic learning institution, the LIPIA certainly introduces Wahhabite doctrines to its students who mostly come from modernist-reformist backgrounds (DDII, Persis, al-Irshad, or Muhammadiyah). Although the exact extent of their influence cannot be assessed, many aspects of the Wahhabite doctrines have been espoused by the students, around 25 percent of whom are female (Jahroni 2013). Since its inception, the LIPIA has produced thousands of graduates, more than thirty of whom (the best ones) received a full scholarship to continue their Islamic studies at Al Imam Muhammad bin Saud Islamic University in Riyadh. The return of LIPIA graduates who had completed their studies in Saudi Arabia and undergone a combat experience in the battlefield of Afghanistan during the Soviet–Afghan War marked the birth of a new generation of "reformist Muslims" in present-day Indonesia that explicitly identified themselves as "Salafis." It is true that many contemporary Salafi leaders, some of whom later became radical Islamists and jihadists, were trained in the LIPIA. This new generation of Salafi-Wahhabis clearly differs (in thoughts, understanding, strategies, and practices) from that of the Islamist-reformist groups of the previous centuries described earlier.

Although the LIPIA has been central as the "producer" of Indonesian Salafi-Wahhabis, it is not the only academic institution and channel that contributes to the spread of Salafism-Wahhabism in the country. The Islamic University of Medina (IUM), Saudi's first Islamic university, is another higher institution of Islamic learning that has greatly contributed to the production and expansion of Salafi-Wahhabi ideas in Indonesia through the role of its extensive number of graduates (see Chapter 5). As depicted earlier, since its inception in the early 1960s, the IUM has been committed to recruiting Muslim students from Muslim-majority countries, including Indonesia, and has provided them with full scholarships to study Islam (in accordance with Hanbalite madhhab and Wahhabite doctrines). Furthermore, the role of Al Imam Muhammad bin Saud Islamic University cannot be underestimate. There is no doubt that the alumni of these three Islamic institutions (i.e., the LIPIA, the IUM, and Al Imam Muhammad bin Saud Islamic University), many of whom became leaders and activists of multiple Islamist organizations (e.g., the Islamic Defenders Front, the ex-Laskar Jihad or Jihad Forces, and the Islamic Umma Union, among others) or members of the Indonesian Council of Ulama (at the central, provincial, or district levels), have played a major role in producing and developing Salafism-Wahhabism in the country.

Indeed, there are Islamic study graduates of other Saudi universities (e.g., King Saud University) but their role in the introduction and development of Indonesia's Salafism-Wahhabism is peripheral. Also, there are non-Islamic studies (i.e., technical and engineering) alumni from Saudi universities (e.g., King Fahd University of Petroleum and Minerals; and King Abdullah Science and Technology) but their roles, contributions, and influences in the country are peripheral since these non-Islamic study programs have been offered (or opened) only recently for Indonesian students, and Indonesian graduates of these programs are very limited. It is also significant to note that, as I described in the previous chapters, Saudi Islamic universities and learning centers not only produce conservative, hardline Salafis but also generate moderate Muslim groups.

From the 1980s onward, graduates of Islamic study programs from some Saudi Islamic universities (especially the LIPIA, the IUM, and Al Imam Muhammad bin Saud Islamic University) have organized religious activities that in turn have helped create a sense of group solidarity and identity that has fostered a growing network. The publication of pamphlets, bulletins, journals, and books that are distributed through (and displayed in) mosques, madrasahs, offices, and other places provided communication channels through which Salafi-Wahhabi messages were disseminated to a broader audience not only limited to youths and university students but also the urban middle class, townspeople, and villagers. The multiplication of Salafi activism and various religious activities have led seamlessly to the birth of Islamic foundations with names such as al-Sunna, Ihya al-Sunna, al-Turath al-Islami, al-Sofwa, Lajnah al-Khairiyya, and Wahda Islamiyya, among many others; Islamic schools (e.g., Pondok Pesantren Islamic Center Bin Baz), Islamic centers (such as those of Khalid Basalamah), higher learning institutions (e.g., Sekolah Tinggi Dirasat Islamiyah Imam Syafii, Jember and Sekolah Tinggi Agama Islam Ali bin Abi Thalib, Surabaya), television channels (e.g., Mufid TV, Rodja TV), radio stations (e.g., Rodja), and many others.

The fruits of Suharto's fall for neo-Salafis

It seems that the fall of Suharto's authoritarian government in May 1998, which marked the "new-born" democracy in Indonesia was a "blessing in disguise" for the Salafi-Wahhabi group (known in Indonesia for its nickname "Sawah"). The long-ruling Suharto (1967–1998) was toppled by an alliance of secular Muslims and non-Muslims, middle-class societies, democracy activists, students, and some political elites, following the economic crises that hit the archipelago and other Southeast Asian countries beginning in late 1997. The emerging Muslim democrats and a new class of intellectual Muslims played a key role in the political reformation intent on providing solid Islamic bases for democracy, pluralism, egalitarianism, liberalism, and civil society (Hefner 2000; Mujani 2003). This new class of Muslim intellectuals, scholars, and activists, in particular, had emerged since the early 1990s when Suharto energized them by establishing the state-sponsored Association of Indonesian Muslim Intellectuals (Ikatan Cendekiawan Muslim Indonesia, or ICMI). Since that time, Indonesia has had a wealth of activists and intellectuals involved in religious discourses aimed at a foundational reorientation of Muslim politics (Abdillah 1997; Hefner 2000).

However, it should be noted, Suharto's collapse not only brought the space for democracy but also for the proliferation of anti-democracy movements. Moreover, despite some notable social, political, and economic growth, post-Suharto Indonesia has also been marked by the influx of transnational Islamist groups from multiple foreign countries (e.g., India, Pakistan, Egypt, Yemen, Saudi) as well as international and local Salafis (or neo-Salafis) and other conservative Muslim groups. Unfortunately, many Islamists and some Salafi-Wahhabi groups that formerly adopted apolitical quietism, in the post-Suharto era, turned out to be a group of "political activism" that were actively involved in the campaign (at the central, regional, and local levels) to transform the country into an Islamic government (or governance) that would espouse sharia and replace "secular law," or even an Islamic state that would substitute the principal philosophical, ideological, and constitutional foundations of the Republic of Indonesia (including *Pancasila* [Indonesian state ideology] and Undang-Undang Dasar [UUD] 1945).

While some Salafi-Wahhabi groups promote nonviolent ways for their Islamic da'wa activities by emphasizing on *amr m'ruf* (commanding right), other Islamist groups have supported and committed acts of intolerance, anti-pluralism, and radicalism across the country. Examples of the latter type of group include the ex-Laskar Jihad (Jihad Forces), the Islamic Defenders Front, the Islamic Umma Union, and the National Coalition of Anti-Shia Movement, among many others, which have been notorious for their intolerant, radical, and violent actions against minority groups, local sects, and even Muslim groups deemed "deviant." The Islamist groups that formerly conducted religious activities clandestinely, in the post-Suharto period, now do all activities publicly. As a result, the rise of the Islamist groups has provoked tensions, conflict, and collective violence in some regions of the archipelago.

The increase of multiple Islamist and Salafi groups (Saudi or non-Saudi influenced) was the product, directly or indirectly, of the political reformation and democracy following the downfall of Suharto. As stated before, during the early years of the New Order, following Suharto's 1965 coup and persecution and mass murder in the name of anti-communism, his regime was ruthless in severely controlling both Muslim reformist groups and supporters of Islamism. Suharto's collapse was thus seen as giving momentum for Islamist, extremist, and conservative groups to express their political and religious interests (Van Bruinessen 2002). Indeed, democracy and its guarantees of civil liberty ironically provides room for Islamist groups and Muslim hardliners to flourish. In the name of democracy and civil liberty, conservative Muslim groups have established Islamic centers, organizations, schools, and even political parties. They freely produce Islamic books and distribute them to society. However, paradoxically, although these groups enjoy living in a democratic system, they use these Islamic institutions to disseminate antidemocratic ideas, religious hatred and intolerance and to oppose democracy, which they saw as a Western secular product.

Although political efforts to replace the country's secular-pluralist constitution (UUD 1945) and Pancasila with a national Islamic ideology and constitution failed to receive majority support from political elites and high-ranking bureaucrats in the national parliament and central government, the conservative Muslims' agenda, however, has gained some support from a number of local governments, at both provincial and district levels, for inserting elements of, or even applying the whole of, sharia (Islamic Law) into their regional laws, resulting in what is known as *Perda Syariat* (see, e.g., Hefner 2011).

The growth of Islamist, radical, and conservative Muslims has indeed raised worries among religious minorities and moderate Muslims because they could challenge Indonesia's nascent democracy and fragile pluralism as well as the image of Indonesian Muslims as tolerant and moderate when compared to their coreligionists in central Asia, the Indian subcontinent, or the Middle East. The threat presented by religious violence and Islamic militancy to Indonesia's plurality and civility needs to be taken into consideration by those concerned about the future of democracy, tolerance, and peace in this archipelagic nation. The Indonesian case has also shown that there are many factors and obstacles, including those coming from the state as well as non-state anti-democracy actors and Islamist paramilitary groups that have contributed to the development of ethnoreligious violence, anti-pluralist movements, and steps backward in the democratic political transition from authoritarian rule.

Conclusion

A few conclusions can be drawn as follows. The linkages between Saudi Arabian religious institutions (and actors) and Indonesian religious institutions (and actors), maintained through personal, professional, and even virtual ties, are central in boosting the significance of the Arabian Peninsula among Indonesian Muslims interested in this movement. In recent years, more specifically, as noted by Chaplin (2014: 226), "not only do they increase the resonance of Salafi claims to represent an Islam in line with the practices of Islam's most holy places but also, logistically, they increase access to funding and private donations from abroad. Yet, such connections are reified through the dissemination of Salafi-Wahhabi scholastic works," published by Saudi/Wahhabi-influenced Indonesian publishing houses and distributed through a network of Salafi-affiliated religious bookstores, schools, mosques, and organizations. The distribution of the works of Arabian-based ulama also provides insight into the modes through which Salafi Islamic authority is constructed in Indonesia.

The depiction sketched above also suggests that the past Hijaz and contemporary Saudi Arabia have produced multiple variants of Islam and religious activism in the Indonesian archipelago: Sufism, Sunnism, Shafiites, reformist Islam, traditionalist Islam, Hanbalites, Salafism, Wahhabism, and moderate Islam, among others. The Arabian Peninsula also contributed to the emergence of various types of Islamic education (e.g., pesantren, ma'had, madrasah) along with their educational systems and teaching-learning methods, pan-Islamism, anti-colonial movements, and the spirit of nationalism in the past. Furthermore, equally important, Saudi learning institutions not only brought Islam to Indonesia but also generated non-Islamic study fields by producing alumni of (secular) science and engineering, albeit their roles and contributions are not observable yet due to their limited number in comparison with Islamic study graduates.

This fact suggests that Arabia, compared to other foreign Muslim-majority regions, has played an enormous role in designing the face of Indonesian Islam and society in the past, present, and perhaps in the future.

Chapter 3

SAUDI ARABIA AS A CENTER OF LEARNING AND EDUCATION FOR INDONESIANS

Hijaz in the western Arabian Peninsula, where Mecca is located, has been a center of learning and education for Muslims worldwide for centuries. Long before the advent of the Kingdom of Saudi Arabia in the twentieth century, Hijaz was well established as a terminus for pilgrim scholars and students from across the Muslim world. For centuries, as Farquhar (2017: 23) has rightly noted, "the mosques, madrasas, Sufi lodges that hosted these migrant seekers of knowledge served as nodes in a cosmopolitan religious economy, encompassing circulations of knowledge, qualifications, funds, and pedagogical techniques from as far afield as West Africa and Southeast Asia." Since the region transformed into part of the Kingdom of Saudi Arabia, it has still been a vital niche for studying and learning Islam for Muslims across the globe.

This chapter outlines the history and recent development of educational institutions or learning centers in the Arabian Peninsula (Hijaz in the past and the Kingdom of Saudi Arabia in the modern era), which has been a vital site for learning and education for Muslims worldwide, including Malay-Indonesians. This chapter, more specifically, describes and identifies institutions of learning and schooling—both formal and informal, public and private, universities/colleges or non universities/colleges—for Indonesians, both in the preceding centuries and the contemporary era. Informal and private educational institutions such as madaris, mosques, Sufi lodges, and *ribat* or *ma'had* were significant places of learning for Indonesian Muslim students in the past. In the modern era, however, although some Indonesians continue to learn Islamic sciences in such informal Islamic learning centers, particularly in Mecca (but also in Medina, particularly in Nabawi Mosque), many have began to study in universities and colleges across Saudi Arabia.

Still, while in the past most, if not all, Indonesians studied the Islamic sciences, there has been a significant number of Indonesian students since the late 1990s who have studied the secular sciences—hard sciences, engineering, computer sciences, social sciences, among others. This is to say that there is a significant change and development regarding students' orientation and their focus of study from the past to the present. This new development is part of Saudi's change in educational policies, especially those of higher education, that emphasize not only Islamic studies but also the secular sciences. Finally, yet importantly, this chapter sketches Indonesian schools in Mecca and other areas in the kingdom, highlighting factors that have contributed to their emergence, decline, and/or survival.

Learning institutions in the Islamic past of Arabia

Unlike Egypt, Morocco, and Iraq where universities had already existed since the Middle Ages, there was no single formal university in the Arabian peninsula until 1957, when the Saudi government built King Saud University in Riyadh, which is now the largest university in the kingdom and offers a wide range of courses in the sciences, humanities, and professional studies. Previous to this, the College of Sharia in Mecca had been built by the Saudi kingdom in 1947, which was later (in 1981) transformed into a university (i.e., Umm al-Qura University). This, however, does not mean that there were no institutions of education and learning centers in Arabia, especially Hijaz. Like the other main cities of Islamic and Muslim civilizations in the Middle East such as Damascus, Baghdad, Cairo, or Fez, Mecca and Medina in Hijaz have long been the sites of Islamic learning and religious education. Traditionally and historically, there were several important centers for Islamic learning in Hijaz and other "civilizational regions" of the Islamic Middle East, particularly during the medieval period, including mosques, houses, ma'had, Sufi lodges, and most notably madaris.[1] Other important centers for study and discussion in the past were Dar al-'Ilm, Dar al-Kutub, and Majelis al-Nadar or Majlis al-'Ilm.

Mosques, indeed, were not religious schools or madaris in the full sense because their key function was to conduct prayers, recite Qur'anic verses, practice devotions, or perform ritual activities. The chief function of a mosque was as a place of worship, where daily canonical prayers were performed. The primary purpose of madaris, by contrast, was the teaching of Islamic law (*fiqh*) within the Sunni school of thought. Also, unlike madaris, mosques lacked the necessary accommodation and certain other aspects of colleges. However, although the main function of a mosque is for performing worship or conducting religious sermons, there were many mosques in the early and medieval period of Islam (in fact, until today) that functioned as a site for the teaching-learning process, or "mosque-college," in addition to other activities such as meeting, socializing, devotional gatherings, discussions, and daily conversations.

Moreover, prior to the introduction of the madrasah institution in the eleventh century, mosques had played a central role for the distribution and transformation of Islamic knowledge and sciences. Indeed, mosques far preceded madaris; therefore it is plausible that Muslims in the past relied on this institution for Islamic education and other religious-secular activities. Even after the creation of madaris, many mosques (which far outnumbered madaris) were still used for teaching Islamic law, the Qur'an, or Arabic, and sometimes even by an endowed teacher with stipends for the students. However, not all mosques have been centers of schooling or, more particularly, of teaching Islamic law. One particular exception in this case was the role of cathedral mosques (*masjid jami'*) that retain their significance in the field of education.

Makdisi (1961: 4–6) said that before and after the eleventh century, when madaris were first introduced to the Arab world, Islamic scholars and teachers continued to teach in mosques such as, most notably, Masjid Jami' al-Mansur, Masjid Jami' al-Mahdi, and Masjid Jami' al-Qasr in Iraq, and Masjid Haram and Masjid Nabawi in Arabia. Masjid Haram (Haram Mosque or the Grand Mosque) in Mecca, for instance, served as the most prestigious setting for instruction in the area. In this mosque, many Islamic scholars disbursed knowledge and qualifications in study circles (*halaqat*). Masjid Nabawi (Nabawi Mosque) in Medina had also long been a vital place of religious education, albeit the scale of teaching in this mosque appears to have been significantly more limited than in the Haram Mosque.[2]

Sufi lodges or *zawaya* (sing. *zawiya*) had also been an important place of religious education in the past in Hijaz before the Saudi kingdom banned them, albeit not all *zawaya* were used as teaching-learning places. In the history of Islam, Sufis had for centuries been both numerous and influential in the Hijaz, playing a vital role in the spread of mysticism or Sufism (*tasawuf*), the creation of Sufi orders (*tariqat*), and the distribution of Islamic knowledge. Their zawiya had been used as learning centers for centuries, as many Sufi masters or gurus were also Islamic scholars. Many Indonesian Islamic scholars in Hijaz had also been the Sufi gurus or masters or devout followers of particular Sufi orders (see Chapter 4). Reportedly, there were forty different Sufi orders in seventeenth-century Mecca and Medina (these included the major Sufi orders such as Sanusiyya, Naqshabandiyya, Qadiriyya, and Shadhiliyya), maintaining a total of fifty-three lodges.

Of all these Islamic learning and discussion institutions in the historical Muslim world, madaris were the most famous and important as training centers of Islamic law in the Sunni tradition. Houses of shaikh, ulama, or rich merchants sometimes were used to run an Islamic school. But their role is restricted and marginal. The Ma'had or ribat (a sort of informal Islamic boarding school) was no doubt a vital institution for Islamic schooling. In fact, the ma'had or ribat still exists in the contemporary Arab world and the Middle East. However, in the context of the Arab world and the Middle East, its contribution was, and is, limited. Its role and impact is also minor. This fact is in sharp contrast to the role and contribution of the pesantren (Java-type Islamic boarding school) in Indonesia that has played a great role in the shaping of Islamic cultures, knowledge, discourses, and traditions in the archipelago (see, e.g., Dhofier 1982; Rachman 1997).

The role of the madrasah, with few notable exceptions, in the distribution, formation, and transformation of Islamic discourses and civilization in Indonesia is peripheral and limited. This is because Indonesia's madaris, unlike pesantren, have never been a solemn and profound training center of the Islamic sciences and classical religious texts. The pesantren has a long-standing reputation for being a somber center of Islamic studies and of the study of Islamic scriptures. Also, the madrasah, in contrast with the pesantren, has never become a center or a network of the spread of Sufism and tariqa (Sufi order) which is an integral part of Indonesian Islam. Still, while the madrasah is isolated from society, the pesantren has played an active role in the process of changes in society, neighborhoods, and local communities. Students of pesantren are often involved in—and work together with—society to help overcome their social problems.

No doubt the madrasah was the chief vehicle for training in Sunni's Islamic law. In the modern era, the role of the madrasah is still important, particularly for elementary education. Gary Leiser (1986: 16) notes that the madrasah's "religious, educational, political, and social significance far overshadowed that of other Muslim institutions such as *bayt al-hikma* or *dar a-'ilm* (libraries), *dar al-hadith* (school for teaching hadith), *dar al-qira'ah* (school for teaching the Qur'an), *khanqah* (Sufi convent), and *ribat* (fortified Sufi retreat)." In the past in Islam, the madrasah had an endowment providing for a single chair for a single teacher of Islamic law (*mudarris*), an income for other faculty or staff, scholarships for students, and funds for the maintenance of the building. Although usually translated as "college," the madrasah was much different from modern colleges and universities. The word madrasah itself was derived from the Arabic root *darrasa* or *tadris* meaning to teach or teaching *fiqh* (Islamic law). The mudarris was the one who taught fiqh and the madrasah was the site where fiqh was taught. Today the word has lost its original technical meaning, and the Arabic word madrasah in the contemporary era simply means school.

The general use of the term "madrasah" began in the late Middle Ages. An example is the famous Dar al-Hadith, built by the Ayyubid Sultan al-Malik al-Kamil in Cairo in 1225, which was sometimes referred to as a madrasah (Leiser 1986: 16–23). The Seljuq Dynasty, an Ogush Turk Sunni Muslim kingdom whose territory stretched from Central Asia to Byzantium, was perhaps the first Muslim empire that contributed to the introduction and development of the madrasah as a center of Islamic learning. Abu Ali Hasan ibn Ali Tusi (1018–1092), better known by his honorific title of Nizam al-Mulk, the grand vizier during the two Seljuq rulers, Alp Arslan and Malik Shah, was the man behind the founding of the madrasah. Under the auspices of the Seljuq Empire, Nizam al-Mulk did much to encourage the formation and spread of madrasah in most of Seljuq's major cities. He also founded one of his own in Baghdad in 1065 by the name of Nizamiyya of Baghdad that later became famous. All of the madaris he built were called Nizamiyya. The name of Nizam al-Mulk was actually linked to this extensive network of learning institutions (i.e., Madrasah Nizamiyya) throughout the lands of the Seljuq Empire (see, e.g., Makdisi 1961: 1–2).

Richard Mortel (1997: 236–37) argues that the madrasah as an educational institution was initially dedicated to the teaching of one or more of the four schools of thoughts (sing. madhhab, pl. madhahib) of Sunni Islamic jurisprudence, namely Maliki, Hanafi, Shafii, and Hanbali. The teaching was often in conjunction with the ancillary Islamic sciences, including Arabic grammar, the study of Qur'anic exegesis (tafsir) and Hadith. Occasionally, secular disciplines such as history, literature, rhetoric, mathematics, and astronomy were also taught in the madrasah. Even though its origins are traceable as far back as the early tenth century in eastern Iran, the madrasah began to proliferate in the eastern Islamic lands from the eleventh century. As the religion of Islam and its accompanying civilization spread into new territories in sub-Saharan Africa, Anatolia, and the Indian subcontinent, the madrasah not only accompanied this diffusion but also lent it active support.

After the collapse of the Shi'i Fatimid Dynasty (Daulah Fatimiyya) in Egypt in 1171, the madrasah made their debut not only in Egypt (the first madrasah in Egypt was formed in 1100) but also in North Africa, Spain, Iraq, and neighboring lands such as Syria and the Hijaz, which had hitherto been under the suzerainty of the Fatimid. Between 969 and 1171, the Fatimid Empire ruled Egypt and dominated other regions such as North Africa, Syria, Yemen, and even Sicily. However, Shia Muslims naturally and historically had no Sunni institution like the madrasah. From the late twelfth century, individual rulers and representatives of the wealthy elites began to endow the madrasah in the major cities of the Islamic world, including Mecca and Medina. As a result, between the eleventh and fourteenth centuries, the madrasah had spread from the east to the west of the Muslim world. This book does not focus on the origin and history of the madrasah; therefore I will not explain this institution in detail. However, it is enough to state that the madrasah played an enormous role in the transmission of Islamic knowledge and discourse.

There were several main reasons for the creation of madaris in the past. The first and foremost reason was to fortify Sunni Islam against the tenth-century challenge of Shiism. Two Shi'i Empires that occupied the Middle Eastern lands that made Sunnis worry at the time were the Fatimids (centered in Egypt) and the Buyids (based in Iraq). Shi'i propagandists were also active throughout the Islamic domain. They also had many academic institutions for intellectual training and education such as the famous Al-Azhar of Cairo and numerous institutes, Dar al-'Ilm or Bait al-Hikmah. After the Sunni Seljuqs succeeded in driving out both the Fatimids and the Buyids, the madrasah became the primary ideological tool for rooting out Shiism. Mahmud Ghazni (d.1030) of the Ghaznavid Empire and Nizam al-Mulk (d.1092) of the Seljuq Dynasty were perhaps the main advocates of Sunnism at that time who saw the institution of the madrasah as a strategic and effective vehicle of thwarting the Shi'i threat, on one hand, and as means to revive, strengthen, and promote Sunni Islamic jurisprudence, on the other.

As mentioned before, Nizam al-Mulk built a number of madaris (all under the name of Madrasah Nizamiyya) in Iraq, particularly in Nisabur and Baghdad, as a buttress of Sunni Islam. The eminent orientalist Ignaz Goldziher said that the Nizamiyya, with its Shafi'ite teachers, represented the success of the resurgence of the dogmatic theological movement, namely "Ash'arism, which linked to the Shafi'ite school of Islamic law. Interestingly, for Goldziher, the establishment of the Nizamiyya marked the victory of the Ash'arite school (i.e. Sunni) over Mu'tazilism (a rational faction of Islamic schools of thought) as well as Shiism and its radical aberration: Batinism" (cited in Makdisi 1961: 2–3).[3] This is to say that the history of the madrasah is the history of both education and dogmatic theology (within the Sunni tradition).

The second reason for establishing madaris was to create a loyal cadre for the new government. It is imperative to note that madaris, particularly those built by the government, not only trained students to become religious functionaries such as muftis or imams but also judges, ministers, administrators, and bureaucrats of all kinds. In other words, the madrasah was set up as a site to educate students hoping that in the future, upon finishing their studies, they could govern, influence, and contribute to the "state" (kingdom) and society. This is to say that the madrasah would guarantee its alumni loyalty and devotion to Sunnism as well as their practical expertise to work in the government and other state institutions.

Lastly, the founding of the madaris was driven by the desire of the ruling authorities to dominate the religious elites so that they could be used (or abused) to provide the "religious stamp" for the stability of the government and its subject. However, it should be noted, not all madaris were founded by the ruler and designed to create government workers or "loyalists" of an Islamic dynasty. Many madaris were built by wealthy merchants or Islamic scholars as a mainstay of Islamic education or *thalab al-ilm* (seeking knowledge and science) and of teaching and preserving Sunni schools and traditions that have nothing to do with political issues or governmental matters. Moreover, the madrasah was not the only vehicle for the distribution of knowledge and transformation of Sunni teachings, traditions, and discourses in the Islamic world. Besides those three primary functions mentioned above, madaris also performed other functions, for instance, as a hostel for travelers (see Leiser 1986: 18-9). Furthermore, some wealthy people or bureaucrats founded madaris in order to burnish their reputation in front of publics and/or rulers such as in the case of Zainuddin Abdul Basith ibn Khalil, a Mamluk Dynasty bureaucrat in the fifteenth century, who built five madaris (all named Madrasah Basitiyah) in Cairo, Jerusalem, Damascus, Mecca, and Medina (see Igarashi 2013: 79-93).

In the context of Hijaz, in particular, the great mosques of Mecca (Masjid al-Haram) and of Medina (Masjid Nabawi) have long fulfilled the function of a sort of madrasah (i.e., as a center of learning or schooling of Islamic law) from the earliest times, long before the founding of the "real" madrasah in the tenth or eleventh century. Even after the establishment of the madaris, these two holy mosques have continued to function as an Islamic learning site, in addition to being a place of worship and religious sermons. From generation to generation, scholars of Islamic law and the allied Islamic sciences, including those from the Malay-Indonesian archipelago, expounded their curricula in the arcades of the Mosque Haram and Mosque Nabawi. Muslims in general see learning Islam in these two mosques as exceptional and it acquires special merit since they consider both the most sacred spots on earth.

Although madaris already existed in Mecca from the twelfth century, many Muslims persisted to learn the Islamic sciences in Masjid al-Haram and Masjid Nabawi in part because they believed that studying Islam in these two holy mosques was distinctive and blessed with abundant rewards from God. Christian Snouck Hurgronje, who visited Mecca in the nineteenth century and had conversations with many Muslims there, also made this point (Hurgronje 1970: 172). It is thus not surprising, as depicted later, if Indonesian Muslim pupils in the past learned

Islamic disciplines and pursued Islamic knowledge in these two mosques, besides madaris and other places, for sure. In other words, the founding of madaris in Hijaz could not replace the role and function of Mosque Haram and Mosque Nabawi as the center of Islamic learning and education.

Institutions of learning and education for Indonesian students

Before the founding of Madrasah Shaulatiyah in 1874, it was unclear what formal learning institutions were available for Indonesian Muslims who studied in Hijaz. Indonesian Islamic scholars (ulama) who studied in Hijaz in the past did not reveal the types or models of schools for their studies, either in formal (e.g., madaris) or informal (e.g., mosques, houses, etc.) educational institutions. Biographies of Indonesia's great ulama who learned Islam in Mecca between the seventeenth and nineteenth centuries such as Yusuf al-Makassari, Muhammad Arsyad al-Banjari, and Abdus Shamad al-Falimbani only mention book titles they used to study as well as some of their teachers such as Muhammad bin Abdul Karim al-Salman (a Sufi master), Muhammad bin Sulaiman al-Kurdi (a mufti of Medina), and later Shaikh Ahmad Zaini Dahlan (a respected scholar in Mecca).

Although these Indonesian ulama did not mention in what sort of school they studied, it is almost certain that, as described earlier, in the past, they mostly learned the Islamic sciences in informal settings (usually by using the *halaqa*, or study circle, system), particularly at the two great mosques in Mecca and Medina (i.e., Masjid al-Haram and Masjid Nabawi), ribat, or perhaps houses of their teachers. After the building of formal Islamic schools (madaris) such as Madrasah al-Falah and Madrasah Shaulatiyah (both founded by Indian Muslims), many Indonesian Muslim students learned Islam in madaris, albeit the learning tradition continued in informal settings. After some Indonesians established their own schools such as Madrasah Darul Ulum (built in 1934), many Indonesian students studied at these institutions while at the same time continuing their tradition of study in Masjid al-Haram.

Dutch Orientalist Christian Snouck Hurgronje (1970), who stayed in Mecca in 1885, reported that by the end of nineteenth century, education in Hijaz was centered in Masjid al-Haram of Mecca, which at the time had become a sort of "university." The rector of this "university" was called Shaikh al-Ulama, who was appointed by the Ottoman Empire (through the Grand Sharif of Mecca), and only noted Islamic scholars could teach at this institution. Less-notable scholars taught at other learning centers in both Mecca and Medina. The educational system used in the "University" of Masjid al-Haram differed from that of the madaris, for instance, there were no fixed curricula in Masjid al-Haram. Books studied and read during the learning process mostly depended on the decision of the teachers and their pupils. In the past, Indonesian students mostly stayed in the "Kampung Jawah" and came to the holy mosque of Masjid al-Haram for prayers, learning, or social gatherings.

Generally speaking, most Indonesian students of the Islamic sciences in Hijaz studied at informal centers of learning (e.g., mosques, houses, ma'had) not in the Ottoman-type madaris, until the establishment of Madrasah Shaulatiyah in 1874. An Indian-type reformist Islamic school, Madrasah Shaulatiyah later became popular among Indonesians, before the founding of Madrasah Darul Ulum in 1934 by a group of Indonesian teachers and students. Van Bruinessen (2015: 103–04) argued that Madrasah Shaulatiyah, in addition to Al-Azhar University of Cairo, became a model for some of Indonesia's reformist madaris and traditional pesantrens (Islamic boarding schools) in terms of class, curricula, or dormitory (*riwaq*) systems (see also Steenbrink 1974; Yunus 1979). In brief, Indonesian students in Hijaz learned Islam in both Indonesian schools and non-Indonesian educational institutions. While some Indonesians studied Islam in Masjid Nabawi in Medina, most of them studied Islamic sciences in Mecca, which is considered by some Indonesian Muslims as their "second homeland."[4]

Indeed, Mecca's Masjid al-Haram, especially Ma'had al-Haram and Halaqa Masjid Haram, had been famous for Indonesians. In the past, each main gate of Masjid al-Haram (i.e., Abdul Aziz, Malik Fahad, Bab al-Salam, Bab al-Fattah, and Bab al-Umrah) and the mosque's yards (i.e., Hijir Isma'il and Rukun Yamani) historically and traditionally became a place for halaqa (a study circle) after Maghrib and Subuh prayers. There were multiple methods or ways of schooling and knowledge transmission in the history of Islam, some of which through formal madrasah, informal *halaqa, khuttab* (lecture), *zawiyah* (pesantren-type education), and *niqash* (discussion), among others. Indonesians, along with others in Hijaz, also learned Islam through these multiple formal and informal learning centers and teaching methods.

As previously depicted, Mecca has long had a reputation as a center for religious learning and education for Muslim societies across the world. Prophet Muhammad put a high value on seeking knowledge and studying the sciences (*thalab al-'ilm*) as one of Islam's main tenets, some of Mecca's rich inhabitants historically and traditionally endowed their houses for learning activities. Al-Fasi (1985) noted that in fifteenth-century Mecca, there were some eleven endowed schools (madrasah waqf), fifty-two endowed ribat, and tens of halaqah (informal gatherings for learning and studying Islam). One of these ribats, named Ribat Hashim al-Rusaifah, where some Indonesian students learned, still exists today.

As for madaris in Mecca, the earliest madrasah (i.e., Madrasah al-Arsufi) was founded in 1175–1176, by Afif Abdullah bin Muhammad al-Arsufi, a wealthy Syrian merchant who settled in Egypt. The fifteenth-century historians of Mecca, Taqiyuddin Muhammad bin Ahmad al-Fasi and Najmuddin Umar bin Fahd, dubbed the twin pillars of medieval Meccan historiography, documented several madaris in the medieval Islam of Hijaz prior to the Ottoman occupation in 1571. Both historians (cited in Mortel 1997: 237–39) documented some twenty-three madaris in Mecca in the medieval period including Madrasah of Amir al-Zanjili, Madrasah Tab al-Zaman al-Habashiyya, Madrasah of Muzaffar al-Din, Madrasah of al-Nihawandi, Madrasah of Abu Ali Abi Zakariyya, Madrasah of Ibn al-Haddad al-Mahdawi, Madrasah of Amir Fakhruddin al-Shalah, and Madrasah of al-Malik al-Mansur, among others.

It is interesting to note that the founders of these madaris were not only political rulers or bureaucrats but also generous merchants, ulama, shaikhs, and even freed slaves. Madrasah Tab al-Zaman al-Habashiyya, for instance, was founded by an Abyssinian slave woman who had been manumitted by the Abbasid Caliph al-Muhtadi. All of the madaris mentioned here were dedicated to teaching Islamic law of the Sunni school. Unfortunately, however, most, if not all, of these madaris disappeared during the Saudi-led ambitious expansion projects undertaken in the Meccan Haram beginning in the 1950s.[5] Actually, already in the eighteenth and nineteenth centuries, where Mecca was under the control of the Ottoman Empire, which followed the Hanafi school, the role of formal madaris as a focal institution of learning tended to be waning (see Van Bruinessen 2015: 103).

Although the role of madaris tended to decrease in the nineteenth century, this, however, does not mean that madaris had completely disappeared in Mecca. A number of popular schools and learning institutions in Mecca remained, including madaris, where many Malay-Indonesians learned. These included Madrasah Shaulatiyah, Madrasah Al-Falah, Madrasah al-Usrufiyah, Madrasah al-Bashithiyah, Madrasah al-Sanjariyah, and Madrasah al-Sulaimaniyah, among others. Of all these formal schools, Madrasah Shaulatiyah had been the most favorite place of Islamic learning for Malay-Indonesians before the founding of Mecca's Indonesian schools, notably Madrasah Darul Ulum. Another popular school for Malay-Indonesian students was Madrasah al-Falah, founded by an Indian, albeit it was not as famous as Madrasah Shaulatiyah. Many Sunni teachers of Masjid al-Haram were also teachers of Madrasah al-Falah, such as Sayyid Alawi al-Maliki, Sayyid Amin Kutbi, and Shaikh Hasan Al Masyyath, among others. Sayyid Muhammad bin Alawi al-Maliki said that the Madrasah al-Falah prioritized not only teaching Islamic knowledge but also morality (*ahlaq al-karimah*) to its students and teachers (Al Jufri 2017: 56–7).

Madrasah Shaulatiyah, moreover, was founded in 1874 by Begum[6] Shaulah al-Nisa (a female merchant and philanthropist) and Abdul Khaliq al-Banggali (a founder of Madrasah Dar al-Faizin), both of whom were from India. In particular, it was through generosity of Shaulah al-Nisa, who donated a considerable amount of money to set up the school that made the building plan of Madrasah Shaulatiyah became a reality. Furthermore, Madrasah Shaulatiyah was led by Rahmatullah bin Khalil al-Utsmani al-Hindi or Maulana Rahmatullah Kairanavi (1818–1891), an Indian reformist scholar, an Al-Azhar University graduate, and a teacher at Masjid al-Haram.

Prior to coming to Hijaz, Rahmatullah, reportedly a descendent of the third Caliph Usman bin Affan, was a noted Muslim scholar and anti-colonial activist in India. He was famous in particular for being successful in defeating a German missionary, Pfander, in a religious debate and in struggling against the British colonial government in 1857. After his anti-colonial political movement was crushed by the British, Rahmatullah fled to Mecca via Mocha, Yemen, where he became a celebrated Islamic scholar and a strong adversary of colonialism and Westernization (see Van Bruinessen 2015: 103–06).

After having migrated to Mecca, Rahmatullah intended to set up an Islamic school but scarcity of financial resources proved to be a real hurdle. It was during this hard time that Shaulah al-Nisa finally helped Rahmatullah to actualize his dream, establishing an Islamic school (i.e., Madrasah Shaulatiyah). Prior to building the madrasah, Rahmatullah was a teacher at Masjid al-Haram (appointed by leading scholar of Shafii school Shaikh Ahmad Zaini Dahlan), where he taught the Islamic sciences. However, he was unhappy with the teaching methods used in the mosque, which were more like sermons than planned academic lectures. Rahmatullah wanted to have an Islamic school where he could teach lessons based on a sound curriculum.

Under the leadership of Rahmatullah, Madrasah Shaulatiyah transformed itself into one of Mecca's most renowned foreign Islamic learning centers, where many non-Arab students studied. It is important to note that Madrasah Shaulatiyah was a part of India's Islamic educational reform that had succeeded in establishing Madrasah Darul Ulum in Deoband (founded in 1867, about ten years before the establishment of Madrasah Shaulatiyah). Like Darul Ulum of Deoband, the curricula developed at Madrasah Shaulatiyah was still traditional with an emphasis on the study of hadith. It was a "modern" institution because it applied a class structure, fixed courses, and exams.

Some respected teachers and well-known ulama at Masjid al-Haram, both Arab and non-Arab, have taught at Madrasah Shaulatiyah including, among others, Hasan bin Muhammad al-Mashshath, Shaikh Daud Dihan, Habibullah bin Maya'aba al-Shinqithi, Mukhtar bin Utsman Makhdum, Abdullah bin Al Hasan al-Kuhaji, and Mahmud bin Abdulrahman Zuhdi. Madrasah Shaulatiyah's popularity, quality, and esteem had attracted Malay-Indonesian pilgrims, many of whom chose to stay at Mecca after the *hajj* to learn Islam in this school. Among notable Malay-Indonesian students who studied at this school are the cofounders of Madrasah Darul Ulum, Mecca's first Indonesian school, including Muhsin bin Ali al-Musawa (from Palembang, Sumatra), Zubair bin Ahmad (from Pinang, Malaysia), Abdullah Muhaimin (from Lasem, Central Java), and Yasin bin Isa (from Padang, Sumatra).

Saudi's Indonesian schools

Besides Meccan schools and learning centers, Malay-Indonesians also learned and studied Islam at their own schools. The oldest Indonesian school in Mecca was Darul Ulum, a name that reminded me of two renowned reformist madaris from the nineteenth century, one was in Deoband (built in 1867) and the other was in Cairo (founded in 1872). In 1934, initiated by Sayyid Muhsin bin Ali bin Abdurrahman al-Musawa (1905–1936) and Muhammad Yasin bin Muhammad Isa al-Fadani (1915–1990), a group of Indonesian scholars, teachers, and students opened an Islamic school (located in the district of Shieb Amir) by the name of Darul Ulum al-Diniyyah al-Jawwiyah (or Darul Ulum for short; lit. "House of Sciences"). Abdul Manan reportedly was a coordinator who organized fundraising among Indonesian pilgrims in Mecca to support the founding of the madrasah whose building was provided by Shaikh Yakub Perak (Aboebakar 1957: 100–01).

Madrasah Darul Ulum was built after Indonesian students of the Madrasah Shaulatiyah, which had until then been one of the most favored Islamic schools for Indonesians in Mecca, were involved in a dispute with the madrasah's non-Indonesian teachers. The dispute was driven by an incident between Shaulatiyah teachers and Indonesian students over the use of the Malay language (i.e., Bahasa Melayu). Madrasah Shaulatiyah's non-Indonesian teachers said that Malay language was not a religious language; therefore it could not be used in the discussion, conversation, writing, or teaching of Islam. The madrasah was said to have strict rules including banning students from reading books, journals, articles, and other readings irrelevant to the courses.

There were several stories about the root causes or the origins of the dispute. Some said that the conflict was driven by a teacher of Madrasah Shaulatiyah who tore a Malay/Indonesian language newspaper being read by Indonesian disciples in the madrasah. Shaikh Muhammad Yasin al-Fadani, who was a student at the madrasah who later became a principal of Darul Ulum, added that the teacher mocked nationalist aspirations of Indonesian students, saying that a "stupid nation" like Indonesia will never gain independence. Another account said that Indonesian students would like to talk in the Malay/Indonesian language to their teachers but that it was forbidden since Arabic was the only language used in the madrasah for both teaching and everyday conversation (see Aboebakar 1957: 88–90). Still, another source said that the dispute was triggered by the madrasah's teacher who tore and threw the *Berita Nahdlatul Ulama* magazine being read by Indonesian students in the classroom. Not only tearing up and throwing the magazine, the teacher also looked down at the students saying that "The Jawi [Malay-Indonesian] people are people who have bad and low manners" (Aboebakar 1957: 100–01).

Whatever the nature and root causes of the dispute and conflict, it was obvious that Indonesian students were angry due to their language and sense of nationality being offended. The incident disappointed Indonesians from different ethnicities and regions, and they decided to split from Madrasah Shaulatiyah and to establish their own school that used the Malay language or Bahasa Indonesia as a language of teaching instruction. It was reported that following the incident, the Indonesians organized fundraising to build their own madrasah and, at the time, hundreds of Indonesians formerly studying at Madrasah Shaulatiyah moved to the new Madrasah Darul Ulum, which later became Mecca's most notable Indonesian Islamic school, which trained many students and scholars, both Indonesian and others, before its collapse in the late 1980s.

Nationalist movements and ideas were strong at the time, and the Malay language had been a lingua franca of the Malay-Indonesian archipelago as well as a "nationalist language" for Indonesians who struggled against the Dutch and pursued an independent nation-state. The Malay language also became a sort of "national identity" for Indonesians, so disparaging this language is equal to looking down at their "Indonesian identity." Within this political-cultural context, it is understandable why Indonesians in Mecca became reactive, mad, and sensitive where the Shaulatiyah teachers underestimated and insulted the Malay language. Mecca, particularly since the early twentieth century, had been one of the centers of the nationalist movement. It is imperative to note that before Indonesia gained its independence in 1945, Indonesian ulama, activists, and intellectuals in Mecca also formed the Perkumpulan Kemerdekaan Indonesia (Association for Indonesian Independence) as a medium to discuss anything related to the nation's ideas of freedom, sovereignty, and autonomy.

Mecca became a strategic meeting point for Indonesian nationalists to discuss and organize nationalist movements against the Dutch and Japanese, in part because the region, unlike in East Indies at that time, was a secure place. In addition, many Indonesians visited Mecca for the hajj pilgrimage every year, and many religious elite members of Indonesian society lived in the holy city. Mecca, furthermore, is a transnational city in which people from different parts of the world come and stay; accordingly, transmissions and flows of anti-colonial thoughts, ideas, and movements from countries experiencing colonialism could not be avoided. All of these factors helped to create and strengthen nationalist notions and movements for Indonesians in Mecca. Apart from the tensions and conflict, however, both Madrasah Shaulatiyah and Madrasah Darul Ulum have strongly shaped a culture of traditional religious learning and an educational system in Indonesia.

After the founding of this madrasah, Mecca's Indonesians held a meeting to choose a chairman and board members of the Darul Ulum Foundation. Founders and elite members of Darul Ulum included Tengku Mukhtar (the foundation's chairman), Sayyid Muhsin bin Ali al-Musawa, Muhammad Yasin al-Fadani, Zubair Ahmad al-Mandili, Raden Atmojo, Abdul Majid, M. Abdullah Muhaimin, Dahlan Hasan al-Kadiri, and Ahmad Mansuri. The board chose Sayyid Muhsin al-Musawa as its first principal (*mudir*). Under the short leadership of Sayyid Muhsin al-Musawa, Darul Ulum was transformed into a prestigious teaching and research center. Sayyid Muhsin also built a vast library in the madrasah that housed many books, including rare books and unpublished manuscripts authored by both Malay-Indonesian ulama and others. Shaikh Mahmud Said Mamduh, a noted Egyptian ulama and a graduate of the Darul Ulum, said that the library became Mecca's largest library that collected books and manuscripts in the Shafiite School.

At first, Darul Ulum had four school/learning divisions: *al-tahdiriyah* (preparatory school), *ibtidaiyah* (elementary), *tsanawiyah* (junior high school), and *aliyyah* (senior high school). Following the Saudi government educational policy, the elementary school's length of study increased from four to six years. In 1964, the name of tsanawiyah was replaced by mutawasithah and aliyah became tsanawiyah. Although founded by Indonesians, school certificates from Darul Ulum were recognized by the University of Al-Azhar (Egypt) and the Islamic University (Medina).

The founding of Darul Ulum had attracted hajj/*umroh* pilgrims of Indonesian, and even Southeast Asian, origins. Many of them spent time—months or years—learning a variety of Islamic sciences (Islamic jurisprudence, Islamic legal theory and legal maxims, Qur'anic exegesis, hadith, Islamic theology, and many others) at the school. For a long time, Darul Ulum succeeded in producing many great teachers, scholars, and thinkers, including Abdul Qadir al-Mandili and Abdul Karim al-Banjari. A graduate of Umm al-Qura, Mecca, Abdul Adzim Irsad (2015), noted that the Islamic knowledge and intellectual quality of Darul Ulum's alumni had been recognized by many academic institutions in Saudi Arabia and Egypt. The alumni also played a vital role in spreading Islam and developing Islamic education in Indonesia and beyond. At first, the financial support for running Darul Ulum mainly came from Indonesian pilgrims' endowments (hibah), whilst funds for purchasing foods and to pay other expenses came from teachers and students occasionally working as pilgrim guides (hajj and umroh).

Unfortunately, however, in the 1980s the financial support and endowments from the pilgrims decreased dramatically. Due to this financial crisis, Darul Ulum finally accepted funds from the Saudi government with a special note that all the school programs, curricula, and teaching-learning processes should be based on the kingdom's educational policy and system. However, since Indonesians were no longer interested in supporting and developing the school, added to the lack of respected and influential Indonesian Muslim ulama in Mecca, the historic Darul Ulum finally collapsed in the late 1980s, and in 1990 Shaikh Muhammad Yasin bin Isa passed away, the last bastion of Darul Ulum and arguably the last influential Indonesian Islamic scholar in Mecca.

Besides Darul Ulum, there was another Indonesian school in Mecca, named Madrasah Indonesia al-Makkiyah (MIM). Founded in 1947 by Janan Muhamamd Tayyip (a graduate of Al-Azhar University, Egypt) and Muhammad Nur Salim al-Khalidi, this private school (*al-madrasah al-ahliyah*) was run in Bahasa Indonesia (Malay: Bahasa Melayu). Built in the district of Gararah near Haram Mosque just two years after Indonesia gained independence, the school became an "Indonesian identity" and was a symbol of the country's political autonomy and sovereignty from the colonial power. This school also became a marker of the birth of the Indonesian nation-state; therefore many Indonesian pilgrims felt proud of this school and spent time studying there. MIM's students were not only from Indonesia but also from today's Malaysia. Interestingly, the school not only offered courses in the Islamic sciences but also those related to cultures (*tsaqafah*). However, unfortunately, like Darul Ulum, MIM was ill-fated. The school "died" with its founders. The school existed for forty years and served as an Islamic learning center for Indonesians and Malaysians before it closed.

Other centers of learning for Indonesians were Ma'had al-Muallimat al-Ahliyah, a non-formal Islamic boarding school, and Madrasah Ibtidaiyah li al-Banat al-Ahliyah, a special school for female students (both located at Shami'ah, Mecca). The founder of the two educational institutions was Yasin bin Isa al-Fadani (known as Shaikh Yasin, 1915–1990), a renowned Indonesian Islamic scholar in Mecca from Padang, Sumatra (see Chapter 4). It is interesting to see a rationale behind the founding of the Madrasah Ibtidaiyah li al-Banat al-Ahliyah (built in 1957). Shaikh Yasin said that mothers in general have more opportunity than fathers to engage with their children. Mothers also have more responsibility (than fathers) to teach and educate their children. Accordingly, it is understakable if mothers (women) need to be educated and schooled first before teaching and educating their offspring.

It is true that in a patriarchal kinship system and culture, where women mostly are responsible for "domestic matters," women (mothers) have more opportunities and time to be involved with and to oversee their children; accordingly, their role is vital in the upbringing of their progenies. Islam is clearly influenced by a patriarchal Arab culture; thereby it is understandable if this religion puts an emphasis on the "domestic role" (instead of the "public role") of women. Derived from some Islamic texts, teachings, and discourses that are "unfavorable" about women and without examining and analyzing within the socio historical and politico-cultural context of Arabia, some ulama prevent and discourage women from pursuing education. Unlike this type of ulama, however, Shaikh Yasin affirmed that education for women is a compulsion in Islam. The founding of the female school Madrasah Ibtidaiyah li al-Banat al-Ahliyyah was driven by multiple factors including the enthusiasm of the girls and women who informally learned Islam with Shaikh Yasin in his house in Mecca.

Jam'iyyah Khairiyah was another learning institution for Indonesians in the past. Like Madrasah Ibtidaiyah li al-Banat al-Ahliyyah, Jam'iyyah Khairiyyah is also a female school or a learning center for women. Founded by Siti Aminah, the wife of Shaikh Yasin bin Isa al-Fadani, the creation of Jam'iyyah Khairiyah was in honor of—or dedicated to—Khairiyah, the wife of Mecca-based ulama from Lasem of Central Java Kiai Abdullah Muhaimin Lasem (b.1890) and the daughter of Kiai Hasyim Asy'ari (1875–1947) (fahmialinh 2016), the founder of Indonesia's Nahdlatul Ulama. In 1942, Khairiyah initiated and established a female school named Madrasah Khuttab al-Banat, which may have been the first female school in Arabia (Ulum 2015: 182–87). In 1955, the Kingdom of Saudi Arabia transformed the Jam'iyyah Khairiyah school into a government school.

The collapse of Darul Ulum and MIM did not make Indonesians in Mecca or the Hijaz in general give up on building their own schools. Endorsed by Muhammad Ilyas, the Indonesian Ambassador to Saudi Arabia, some members of Saudi's Indonesian Consulate in Jeddah (i.e., Lillahi Grahana Sidharta, Zainal Arifin al-Abbasyi, and Emzita) built a school in 1963 that later became Sekolah Indonesia Jeddah (SIJ, Indonesian School of Jeddah, formerly Sekolah Indonesia Pancasila). At first, the school, located in the region of Bagdadiyyah al-Sharqiyyah, was for elementary schooling but later it was transformed into a secondary school that opened junior and senior high schools.[7] The establishment of this school initially was aimed at providing educational training for Indonesian parents' children in Jeddah. Unlike Madrasah Darul Ulum and MIM, Sekolah Indonesia Jeddah was not purely designed for teaching Islamic studies but rather a sort of combination between Islamic and secular disciplines. Further, this school is sort of a foreign branch of an Indonesian school; hence, it adopts the Indonesian school curricula. However, the school also accommodates the Saudi educational curriculum system.

A similar school to SIJ was built in 1985 in Riyadh, named Sekolah Indonesia Riyadh (Indonesian School of Riyadh), providing for the need of education for Indonesians residing in Riyadh. Historically, this school to some extent was a continuation of SIJ. Jeddah was the capital of the Kingdom of Saudi Arabia before it was moved to Riyadh. Once the capital had moved there was a need for the children of the Indonesian Embassy's staff to continue their education there; thereby they established Sekolah Indonesia Riyadh. However, the school was not only for the staff's children but for those of Indonesians in Riyadh in general. The Saudi government through its Directorate General of International School recognized, or legalized, the existence of Sekolah Indonesia Riyadh under the name of the International Indonesian School.[8]

Furthermore, in the late 1990s, in Mecca, a group of Indonesians built a school, named Sekolah Indonesia Makkah (SIM, officially founded in 2000), which has a division or a chapter from elementary to senior high school. There were a number of Indonesian figures who contributed to the founding of this school, including the late Baharuddin Lopa (a former Indonesian ambassador for Saudi Arabia) and, most notably, Fuad Abdul Wahhab (Kiai Fuad), a respected Indonesian ulama in Jeddah, who had been living for many years in the kingdom. For Indonesians in the Hijaz, Kiai Fuad is called "the father of Jeddah" due to his long presence in the region and his vital role in organizing—and building ties with—the Indonesian community in the Hijaz area. An activist of several Islamic organizations, including NU (Nahdlatul Ulama), ICMI (Association of Indonesian Muslim Intellectuals), and FORMIDA (a Forum for Indonesian community in Jeddah), Kiai Fuad is not only a cleric but also a businessperson who runs a shipping company named Amer Cargo.

As chairman (Ketua Tanfidziyah) of the Saudi Arabian branch of Nahdlatul Ulama, Kiai Fuad supported the founding of SIM not only morally and intellectually but also financially. Kiai Fuad not only endorsed Sekolah Indonesia Makkah (SIM) but also Taman Pendidikan Al-Quran (TPQ—a school for learning Al-Qur'an), Al-Nasiriyah, and Sekolah Indonesia Jeddah (Jeddah Indonesian School). The Indonesian community in the Hijaz area (Mecca, Medina, and Jeddah) whom I met and interviewed also noted the vital role of Kiai Fuad, stating that he is a *ruh* (spirit or soul) who has devoted his life for the development of Indonesian education in Saudi Arabia.[9] According to the principal of Sekolah Indonesia Makkah, Sinsin Rasyidin, the school currently has 447 students and 26 teachers.[10] However, unlike in the past, students at SIM are children and teenagers, since the founding of the school aimed at providing "elementary education" for children of Indonesian parents residing at Mecca.

Non-Indonesian educational institutions for Indonesian students

Besides Saudi's Indonesian schools, Indonesian students also study Islamic and non-Islamic sciences at Saudi academic institutions or Saudi Arabia's non-Indonesian learning centers (e.g., madrasahs, ribats, and universities) such as, most notably, Madrasah Shaulatiyah, Madrasah al-Falah, Ma'had/Halaqah al-Haram (at Masjid Haram), Ma'had Sayyid Muhammad Alawi, and Ma'had Shaikh Ismail (all in Mecca), among others.

In Medina, besides the Islamic University of Medina, which I will explain in the next few paragraphs, Indonesians learned Islam at Masjid Nabawi and Ribat Abdurrahman bin Hasan al-Jufri (known as Ribat al-Jufri). This ribat was founded by Habib Zain bin Abdurrahman bin Zain bin Smith Ba'alwi (known as Habib Zain bin Smith, b.1936). Born in Jakarta, Habib Zain bin Smith is a renowned Islamic scholar on Arabic grammar and Islamic law. Zain's father was an imam at Masjid Abdullah bin Muhsin al-Attas in Bogor, West Java. After learning the Islamic sciences, Arabic, and classical Islamic texts in Java, Indonesia, and Hadramaut, Yemen, Habib Zain settled in Medina to build and teach Islam at the Ribat al-Jufri. Habib Zain's students were not only from Indonesia but also from other parts of the world. However, sadly, the Saudi government shut down the ribat after twelve years of operation partly because it taught materials that opposed Saudi Salafis' religious beliefs, teachings, tenets and understandings.[11]

While Madrasah Syaulatiyah was one of the famous religious learning sites for Indonesians in the past (in addition to Masjid al-Haram and Masjid Nabawi, for sure), since the 1970s, Ma'had Sayyid Muhammad Alawi al-Maliki has been the most popular. Located in the district of al-Rusaifah, Mecca, the Ma'had was founded by the late Sayyid Muhammad bin Alawi bin Abbas ibn Abdul Aziz al-Maliki (known as Sayyid Muhammad Alawi, 1947–2004), a descendent of Prophet Muhammad through Imam Hasan ibn Ali. A graduate of Al-Azhar University of Egypt, Sayyid Muhammad Alawi was the most highly acclaimed and respected scholar in Mecca. A former professor of Islamic studies at Mecca-based Umm al-Qura University, Sayyid Muhammad Alawi was a contemporary Meccan scholar of tafsir (Qur'anic exegesis), hadith (Prophet Muhammad's sayings), fiqh (Islamic law), aqidah (religious beliefs), and *sirah* (Prophet Muhammad's biography). Sayyid Muhammad Alawi's family were traditional Maliki scholars with an ancestral residence in the holy City of Mecca. His grandfather was a qadi (judge) of Mecca and an Imam of the Mosque Haram, and his father was a well-known Maliki ulama and a teacher in the precincts of Mosque Haram for nearly thirty years until he passed away in 1971.[12]

As stated before, Ma'had Sayyid Muhammad Alawi has been Saudi Arabia's most popular non-university Islamic learning center for Indonesian Muslim disciples. Although religious sermons and public lectures conducted in the Ma'had were open to a general audience, the Ma'had itself was solely designed for—or dedicated to—Indonesian students. Prior to becoming an organized ma'had for Indonesian disciples, this place was at first (during the time of Sayyid Abbas and then his son, Sayyid Alawi) a *majelis al-ilm* (an informal place for teaching and preaching Islam) for all Muslims from any country. It was Sayyid Muhammad bin Alawi, who transformed an informal majelis al-ilm into a sort of formal organized ma'had exclusively dedicated to Indonesian students. The reason for providing the Ma'had for Indonesian students was to "pay an intellectual debt" because Sayyid Muhammad, his father (Sayyid Alawi), and grandfather (Sayyid Abbas) had studied under the mentorship of Indonesian Islamic scholars in Mecca such as Imam Nawawi Banten, Shaikh Mahfud Termas, Shaikh Zubair Sarang, and Shaikh Yasin bin Isa Padang, among others (see Chapter 4).

Sayyid Muhammad Alawi himself had occasionally visited Indonesia to meet his teachers, friends, and Ma'had alumni, from which Saudi–Indonesian intellectual networks were established. It is imperative to note that all Indonesian students who study in the Ma'had do not pay a tuition fee. The students even receive a modest monthly stipend from the Ma'had for food and other expenses during their studies in Mecca. All students also live in the dormitory of the Ma'had free of charge. Due to limited spaces, the Ma'had only accepts around forty Indonesian students during each period of study. The Ma'had will not accept new students unless there are spaces (due to students leaving or graduating).[13] The selection criteria are based on an individual relation between Sayyid Muhammad Alawi and his Indonesian teachers, friends, and Ma'had alumni. Pesantren Sarang of Lasem, Central Java, led by Kiai Maimun Zubair, has been one of the primary channels of the Ma'had. Students are not allowed to return home to Indonesia until they complete the materials/courses taught in the Ma'had. Students usually need ten years to finish their studies in the Ma'had. Alumni of the Ma'had, many of whom have established a pesantren or Islamic boarding school in Indonesia, are scattered across the Indonesian archipelago creating a web of Mecca-trained intellectuals or Islamic scholars in the country. Alumni of the Ma'had, some of whom became prominent advocates of anti-Shia campaigns, also shaped an association to channel and preserve Saudi–Indonesian contact. Since the death of Sayyid Muhammad Alawi in 2004, the Ma'had has been run by his son Sayyid Ahmad bin Muhammad bin Alawi al-Maliki.

In recent decades, particularly since the 1980s and the 1990s, there has been a new trend for Indonesians to study in Saudi Arabia. While some continued to learn Islamic disciplines and Arabic grammar at madrasah, ma'had, or ribat and Mosque Haram, many began to shift their studies to university- or college-based learning institutions. There are at least three universities in the Kingdom of Saudi Arabia, where most Indonesians learn the Islamic sciences, namely the Islamic University (Medina), Umm al-Qura (Mecca), and Imam Muhammad bin Saud Islamic University (Riyadh). Of these three universities, the Islamic University of Medina (al-Jami'ah al-Islamiyyah bi al-Madinah al-Munawarah) has had the largest body of Indonesian students of Islamic studies.

Founded in 1961 by a group of Salafi and Wahhabi scholars from Saudi, Egypt, Syria, and Indo-Pakistan (among others), the Islamic University of Medina follows the strict Salafi/Wahhabi ideology; thereby many of its alumni have been the main supporters of the spread of Salafism-Wahhabism in Indonesia. I will discuss this issue in a later chapter. Like Ma'had Sayyid Muhammad Alawi of Mecca that maintains intellectual networks with some Indonesian Islamic boarding schools, the university also builds close relationships with some Indonesian Islamic learning centers such as Pesantren Gontor (Ponorogo of East Java) and Pesantren Darun Najah (Jakarta). Many alumni of these two large pesantrens have continued their studies at the Islamic University of Medina, mostly at the undergraduate level but some at the postgraduate level.

Another fascinating phenomenon is that many Indonesians, particularly since the 1990s and the 2000s, have studied and pursued degrees in "secular sciences" such as the hard sciences (physics, chemistry, math, etc.), engineering, computer sciences as well as in social sciences, especially sociology. Three universities have been the famous destination for Indonesian students in these fields, namely King Saud University (Riyadh), King Fahd University of Petroleum and Minerals (Dhahran), and most recently King Abdullah University of Sciences and Technology (Thuwal).

These three universities are famed in the kingdom for being an educational center for secular "hard sciences" and engineering that have vitally helped contribute to the transformation of Saudi Arabia from a desert kingdom to a modern technology-based society. The universities offer scholarships for international students, including those from Indonesia, to pursue master's and doctorate degrees in these particular fields. At present, hundreds of Indonesian students pursue postgraduate studies in the hard sciences and engineering in these three universities (for more details, see Chapter 5).

Factors contributing to the decline of Indonesian schools

There are multiple factors that contributed to the collapse of the past Indonesian Islamic schools and learning centers in Mecca and Medina, more specifically. One of the important aspects that contributed to the waning of Indonesian schools in Hijaz was the lack of financial support from Indonesian pilgrims. In the past, many Indonesian pilgrims supported Mecca's Indonesian madrasahs, especially Madrasah Darul Ulum and MIM, by giving an endowment (*waqf*) and charitable funds to the schools. The funds were used to finance the madrasah's teaching-learning and daily administrative expenses. Teachers and students alike could also survive in Mecca by working as an umrah/hajj guide for the pilgrims, a shopkeeper, or a small business owner. Unfortunately, since the 1970s and 1980s onward, the tradition or practice of giving donations to the madrasah discontinued. Contemporary Indonesian pilgrims also no longer utilize Indonesians residing in Mecca as guides but rather a travel guide provided by their travel agents or the Indonesian government (i.e., the Ministry of Religious Affairs) instead. As a result, the madrasahs suffered financially and were unable to run the schools and continue their educational programs.

Another factor is the shortage of influential prominent Indonesian Islamic scholars (ulama) in contemporary Hijaz. Again, in the past, there were plenty of esteemed Indonesian Islamic scholars in the holy cities of Mecca and Medina (see Chapter 4) who functioned as an engine or "prime mover" of the madrasahs and other Indonesian-linked Islamic learning sites. Their voices and power were able to influence Indonesian pilgrims to give financial and moral support to the madrasahs, majelis al-ilm, and other institutions of learning for Indonesians. Unfortunately, however, since the mid-twentieth century or so, Mecca was no longer a home to Indonesian eminent Islamic scholars who could utilize their leverages and charisma to influence Indonesian pilgrims. Following the death of Shaikh Yasin bin Isa al-Fadani, arguably the most influential and respected Indonesian ulama in Mecca in the twentieth century, Saudi Arabia has been almost entirely absent of eminent Indonesian Islamic scholars.

The shrinking interest to study the Islamic disciplines on the part of Indonesians also has contributed to the decay of Hijaz's Indonesian Islamic learning centers. In the past, many Indonesians who visited Mecca were not only driven by the desire to perform the hajj but also to learn the Islamic sciences. However, in recent decades, Indonesians coming to Saudi Arabia were mainly seeking jobs, performing hajj or umrah, conducting rituals at Mosque Haram and Mosque Nabawi, or doing "religious tourism" by visiting a variety of historic Islamic sites. The rise of pilgrimage and the religious tourist industry following the growth of the country's economy and middle-class families has indeed contributed to the increased interest from Indonesians to perform the hajj and, notably, umrah. However, this increased interest in the hajj/umrah is not followed by the desire for pursuing Islamic knowledge and learning. Indonesian hajj/*umrah* pilgrims nowadays are not interested in the study of Islam or pursuing knowledge but "gathering *pahala* (reward)" by performing ritual practices or making as many payers as possible, instead. This is to say that, unlike the hajj pilgrims in the past, in the contemporary era, there is a tendency for "religious conservatism" to grow but "intellectual tradition" to shrink.

Of all these factors, the sociopolitical change in the Arabian Peninsula is the most important root cause of the collapse of the Indonesian schools and the decrease of Indonesian ulama in Mecca. Since Al Saud family occupied Hijaz in the 1920s, especially since the founding of the modern Saudi kingdom in 1932, the nature of the religious milieu, education, and Islamic learning slowly began to change. In the past, before and during the Ottoman era, Hijaz was an arena of religious contestation of multiple Islamic schools of thought (i.e., Hanafi, Maliki, Shafi'i, and Hanbali), sects (mainly Sunni and Shia or Mu'tazilah), streams (Sufism, reformism, traditionalism, among others), and practices (e.g., heterodox and orthodox Islam). This religious/Islamic plurality is no longer the case since Hijaz has been under the control of Saudi rule. Since then the government has imposed strict interpretations of Islam in accordance with Salafi/Wahhabi teachings and understandings, and Hanbali madhhab.

The introduction of national curricula into the Saudi academic system is another reason for the waning of the Indonesian schools. In order to survive, foreign schools have to follow the rules set up by the kingdom concerning materials or courses taught in the schools, school management, educational curricula, and so forth. Saudi Arabia's education has four defining characteristics: a focus on the teaching of Islam, a centralized system of control and educational support, state or government funding, and a general policy of gender segregation. Agencies that have responsibility for the implementation of education policy include the following: the Ministry of Education (responsible for elementary schools, years 1–6, intermediate schools, years 7–9, and male secondary schools, years 10–12), the Ministry of Higher Education (responsible for universities, now merged with the Ministry of Education), the General Organization for Technical Education and Vocational Training (responsible for technical colleges and training), and the General Presidency of Girls' Education (responsible for the segregated education of girls and women) (Smith and Abouammoh 2013: 1–3).

It is imperative to point out that even though the Al Saud family took control of Hijaz from the 1920s and the modern Kingdom of Saudi Arabia was built in 1932 marking the unity of the Arabian Peninsula, it was not until the 1960s that the kingdom began to realize the importance of religious educational institutions as a vanguard of Salafism and Wahhabism. More specifically, the shift in education policy related to Islamic matters started taking place in the 1960s when the Saudi government founded the Islamic University of Medina (al-Jami'ah al-Islamiyah bi al-Madinah al-Munawarah) in 1961. However, serious attempts in reformulating the national educational system took place in the 1970s following the oil boom and in the 1980s following the Iranian/Islamic Revolution and the Mecca uprising in 1979. In these periods of political sensitivity, the ulama were able to strengthen their influence on the kingdom's policies including those related to education.

In the context of Saudi Arabia, as noted by Michaela Prokop (2003: 77–8), the evolution of education, the structure of educational apparatus, and the content of teachings in schools (home and abroad) and in textbooks have been circumscribed by the concern to preserve the religious foundations of the regime (i.e., Wahhabism-Salafism). Unlike in other countries in the Gulf, the ulama (i.e., Muslim scholars with authority to pronounce on religious questions) or the religious authority has a vital role in Saudi Arabia. The Grand Mufti, whose office was created in 1953 by the founder of modern Saudi Arabia, King Abdul-Aziz Al Saud (1875–1953), is Saudi's most senior and most influential Muslim religious and legal authority. Like Iran, the religious establishment in Saudi Arabia has also had a bargaining position with the political authorities. In order to get the approval and the acquiescence of the ulama, for instance, the government has made concessions to the religious authority in the fields of culture, curriculum development, and control over the educational apparatus (Prokop 2003: 77–89). In brief, religious and political authorities have worked hand in hand to design a national curriculum that is strong with religious content.

The story of political–religious collaboration in education as well as the production of "Saudization" of religious schooling within the framework of Salafism-Wahhabism began in the late 1950s when Saudi rule faced serious challenges on multiple fronts. Outside the kingdom, at the time, there was a strong movement of radical republicanism in Egypt, and the Middle East in general, that decried the hereditary privileges of monarchical governmental system. As a state that follows a monarchical political system, Saudi Arabia had been a routine target of criticism from advocates of pan-Arabism and Republicanism. The proponents of this movement, especially Gamal Abdel Nasser (1918–1970), were actively engaged in attempts at destabilizing the Saudi rule that made the kingdom feel threatened. Inside the kingdom, moreover, the ruling family was fractured by the competing claims of King Sa'ud (a successor of King Abdul-Aziz), his brother Faisal, and a faction of more junior princes.

All of these political dynamics and changes within and outside the kingdom provided the impetus behind the founding of the Islamic University of Medina (IUM) in 1961, Saudi's first religious university and an influential Wahhabi missionary project with global ambitions that has functioned as a beacon of ultraconservative religious practices and understandings. The objectives of the founding of IUM were (1) to buffer the kingdom from "outside influences" (particularly the political movements of Egyptian-type Republicanism and Middle Eastern pan-Arabism) and (2) to bolster and promote Salafism and Wahhabism at home and abroad. As Farquhar (2015: 703) has rightly pointed out, the founding of IUM mainly aimed "to counter the transnational extension of leftist republican projects by advancing a competing program grounded in claims to historical and religious authenticity." Insofar as IUM represented an award to the Wahhabi religious establishment, it also stood to bolster patronage relations between dynastic actors and this key constituency.

At first, IUM was pioneered by a group of Salafi scholars—Saudi and non-Saudi alike—including Abu A'la Maududi of the Jama'ati Islam (South Asian Islamist movement), Abu al-Hasan Ali Nadwi of India's Nadwat al-Ulama, and some leading figures of Ikhwanul Muslimin (Muslim Brotherhood). Saudi-Wahhabi scholars involved in the initiation and establishment of IUM were the first Grand Mufti Muhammad bin Ibrahim Al al-Shaikh and Abdul Latif bin Ibrahim Al al-Shaikh, who was charged with overseeing a system of religious colleges in the kingdom. In fact, from the founding of IUM to the 1990s, foreign Salafi teachers and scholars from, notably, Egypt, Syria, Iraq, India, and Pakistan were dominant at the university. However, by the early 1990s the practice of co-opting foreigners to work at IUM was coming to an end, and toward the end of that decade, there were no more than a handful of non-Saudi staff left on campus (see Farquhar 2017).

The process of "Saudization" and "Wahhabization" of religious education became much stronger than before following the Iranian/Islamic Revolution and the upraising in Mecca (both in 1979). The two religiopolitical events have marked another new stage of the development of Wahhabism in the kingdom. Moreover, after these religiopolitical events, the Islamic content of the school curriculum was reinforced. The kingdom also allocated huge sums of money to build mosques, Islamic institutions, and missionary centers that promoted Islam in accordance with Salafi-Wahhabi beliefs, practices, and understandings. Since that period, the percentage of religious television and radio programs rose significantly, schools promoting summer programs to further the Islamic education of students grew, and funding for religious colleges and universities was increased. To complement the Medina-based IUM mission and to strengthen the promotion of Wahhabism and Salafism, King Fahd opened the Mecca-based Islamic University of Umm al-Qura (previously the College of Sharia) in 1981. Such policies continued even during the mid-1980s, when oil revenues fell dramatically. By 1986 more than 16,000 of the kingdom's 100,000 students were enrolled in Islamic studies, and by the early 1990s, one-quarter of all university students were studying in religious institutions (see, e.g., Abouhaseira 1998; Okruhlik 2002; Prokop 2003: 77–89).

The influence of ulama in the educational and social domain is felt particularly strongly in respect of women's education and the role of women in public life (from a few years ago, however, this feature has been dramatically changed since the kingdom has adopted a new policy on women's emancipation in education and the public sphere). This sociopolitical-religious background provides a clue that Saudi Arabian religious education is emphasized at all levels of education. According to the Saudi Ministry of Education on "Educational Policy," the kingdom's educational objectives underscore the significance of creating a sense of loyalty and obedience, and the duty of spreading the message and defending it against the "enemies." Education, furthermore, should promote a spirit of loyalty to Islamic law by denouncing any system or theory that conflicts with it and by behaving with honesty and in conformity with Islamic tenets. It also should "awaken the spirit of Islamic struggle, fight our enemies, restore our rights, resume our glory and fulfil the mission of Islam" and "project the unity of the Muslim nation" (Saudi Ministry of Education 1978: 5–9). The main religious subjects taught in Saudi schools are the Qur'an, tawhid (declaration of the oneness of God), tajwid (a science of Qur'anic reading and recitation), tafsir (the Qur'anic exegesis and commentary), hadith (Prophet Muhammad's sayings), and fiqh (Islamic Jurisprudence).

The politicoreligious movements in the forms of Saudization of national education and Wahhabization of religious education at all levels of schooling provided a historical setting and rationale for the deterioration of the Indonesian schools and Islamic scholars in the kingdom. The shortage is understandable in part because most, if not all, of the Indonesian ulama and schools in the kingdom followed non-Wahhabi Islamic interpretations and practices. Furthermore, many of them had been the devout followers of Sufism and tariqa (Sufi order) which were outlawed by the Wahhabi religious establishment. The closure of Rubath al-Jufri (built by the Indonesian ulama Habib Zain bin Smith) in Medina and, more importantly, of madrasahs founded by Shaikh Yasin bin Isa Padang, is a strong indication of Wahhabi-imposed religious teachings and national curricula on foreign religious educational institutions.

The terrorist tragedy of September 11, 2011, has marked another change in Saudi's educational system which differed substantially with the previous one in terms of school curricula and other educational policies. In the aftermath of 9/11, the relationship between Washington, DC, and Riyadh has been fraught with tensions, and transnational pressure has been put on the Saudi government to reform education in the kingdom. Thus, the educational change and reform in the kingdom was due to widespread international criticism against the Saudi religious education system which had been viewed or dubbed as partly responsible for producing Islamist extremism and terrorism. Notwithstanding the international pressures brought about by 9/11, as in the earlier stages of Saudi educational reform, the foreign factors are not the only ones that have contributed to the change and reform in education. Domestic factors, such as the economy, have also been one of the primary pushes toward curriculum changes and neoliberal reform in higher education.

There are a number of indicators of the changes and neoliberal reforms to the higher education system, for instance, the founding of King Abdullah University of Science and Technology, which is the first co-educational university in the kingdom; changes to university curricula to include more globally recognized subjects;

and an increased push to educate Saudi nationals abroad. The most significant exemplar is the "Tatweer Project" for the development of general education in Saudi Arabia. Tatweer is an Arabic expression for the "development of oneself." Beginning in 2007, this ambitious project was allocated US$293 million. The project has four stated purposes: enhancing teachers' skills, improving curricula, developing school activities, and improving school facilities and infrastructure. On its official website, it states that the primary objective of this program will be "to focus on the quality of education to ensure that students of public education in the Saudi Kingdom are equipped with the necessary skills to participate in an increasingly globalized society and engage with the complex and myriad problems that globalization brings" (Elyas and Pichard 2013: 31–41).

Despites the shrinking of the Indonesian schools and Islamic scholars depicted earlier, the founding of Salafi-based Islamic universities such as IUM (1961), Imam Muhammad bin Saud Islamic University (1974), and Umm al-Qura (1981) have attracted a new generation of Indonesian Muslim students pursuing degrees in Islamic studies. Many alumni of this new wave of Islamic studies have become the guardians and promoters of Wahhabism and Salafism in contemporary Indonesia. This phenomenon is the subject of analysis in Chapters 4 and 5.

Conclusion

The description and analyses sketched above suggest the following. First, the Arabian Peninsula—past and present—has long been a center for Islamic education for Indonesians and others. As Arabia is the birthplace of Islam and Prophet Muhammad, it is plausible that this is the reason it has become a focal point for Islamic learning for Muslims. Since learning in Islam is not simply about an "intellectual tour" to pursue knowledge and sciences but also a "spiritual excursion" (i.e., learning is a worship), Arabia—as the home of numerous sacred sites and Islamic historical places—has long attracted Muslims from all over the world who visited Arabia, not only for performing hajj and other religious rites but also for learning Arabic or studying Islam. Even though less intensive than in the past, this intellectual–spiritual tradition has continued to the present day.

Second, in the past, Indonesians studied Islamic sciences at Hijaz-based non university Islamic learning centers—formal and informal alike—such as madrasahs, mosques, ma'hads/ribaths, and houses, among others. In contemporary Saudi, however, Indonesian disciples, with a few notable exceptions (e.g., Muslim students at Ma'had Sayyid Muhammad Alawi in Mecca), mostly learn Islamic disciplines at universities and colleges not only in Hijaz (Mecca and Medina) but also in other areas (e.g., Riyadh, Dhahran, and Thuwal) within the kingdom. This is to say that, to some extent, modern-type educational institutions (i.e., universities or colleges) have replaced traditional learning centers (e.g., madrasahs, ma'hads, mosques). However, this does not mean that the traditional institutions of learning and education have completely disappeared from the land of Arabia since some of them (e.g., Ma'had Muhammad Alawi in Mecca) still exist today. Moreover, Saudi

Arabia has not only attracted Indonesian "Islamic studies" students but also those, particularly postgraduate ones, of the hard sciences as well.

Third, the fate of Indonesian schools in Arabia varies: some completely declined (e.g., Madrasah Indonesia al-Makkiyah and Ribat al-Jufri in Medina), others survived (e.g., Sekolah Indonesia Jeddah and Sekolah Indonesia Makkah), and the rest have been transformed into part of the Saudi educational system (e.g., Madrasah Darul Ulum and Madrasah Ibtidaiyah li al-Banat al-Ahliyat). With few notable exceptions, there are indeed multiple factors that contributed to the decline of madrasahs and other learning and educational centers established by Indonesian scholars and teachers in both Mecca and Medina such as the sociopolitical shifts taking place in Saudi Arabia, the kingdom's educational policies, state-controlled education, the religious policies implemented by the government, the lack of funds and support from Indonesian pilgrims and residents in Hijaz, and the lack of influential Indonesian scholars in Hijaz, among others. Despite the dearth of the schools, Indonesian students continue to learn in non-Indonesian learning institutions and Saudi universities and colleges (see Chapter 5).

Chapter 4

INDONESIAN ISLAMIC SCHOLARS, TEACHERS, AND SCIENTISTS IN SAUDI ARABIA

Who lives sees, but who travels sees more.

Ibn Battuta

In the past, as I have noted earlier, Indonesian Muslims who traveled to the Arabian Peninsula were initially driven by the desire to perform the hajj as one of Islam's main pillars and an important religious compulsion as well as to visit Mecca as Islam's most sacred site. After performing the hajj, the majority of Indonesians returned to their home country. However, a small minority chose to stay in Mecca and Medina for various reasons: studying Islam, deepening Islamic knowledge, and at the same time performing religious rituals at Masjid al-Haram (Haram Mosque at Mecca) and Masjid al-Nabawi (Mosque Nabawi at Medina).[1] Muslims believed that by performing worship, prayers, devotions, and any religious activities in these two holy mosques, unlike in other mosques, they would be granted hundreds of thousands of rewards by God and that could guarantee them entry to Paradise after their death.

The desire for learning Islamic sciences, hunting religious knowledge, and performing ritual practices drove some Indonesian Muslims to stay longer in the Haramain. Other reasons for staying longer in Hijaz (in Mecca and Jeddah in particular) included pilgrims losing their travel equipment (goods and money), so they needed to work there for a while to pay for food and their return travel to the Malay-Indonesian archipelago. While some stayed months or years before returning to what is now Indonesia, others lived in Mecca until their death. The type of religious and intellectual nature of contact between Indonesia and Arabia was obvious at least until the Second World War.

There were a great deal of Indonesian Islamic scholars and teachers in the past in Hijaz, whose legacy can still be witnessed today. As for Indonesian Islamic teachers and scholars in Saudi Arabia, there is a big difference between the past and the present. While in the past there were plenty of Indonesian Muslim teachers and Islamic scholars who taught in Mecca (and Medina as well) and wrote numerous books (in Arabic or Malay) on Islamic knowledge and sciences, at present it is almost impossible to find such Islamic teachers and scholars in the kingdom. There are only a few Indonesian Islamic scholars and teachers in Mecca and Medina.

Why is it hard to find Indonesian Islamic scholars in contemporary Saudi Arabia? What factors contributed to this reduction? This chapter will try to explain this shifting phenomenon. Furthermore, whereas in the past, most, if not all, Indonesian teachers and scholars in Arabia focused on Islamic studies, nowadays there are a few Indonesian teachers and scholars who teach and write about secular sciences such as math, chemistry, physics, engineering, computer science, aerospace, and the social sciences, among others. In the past, Indonesian Muslim teachers and scholars taught at non university formal educational institutions (e.g., *madrasah*) and informal centers for Islamic learning (e.g., *halaqah* and *rubat*), in the modern era, they teach at colleges and universities across the kingdom.

More specifically, this chapter sketches a short biography of these scholars who were dedicated to teaching and working in Mecca in the past, in addition to contemporary Indonesian teachers, scientists, and scholars who teach at universities across the kingdom. In brief, this chapter outlines Indonesian Muslim educational sojourners or intellectual travelers in Saudi Arabia from the past to the contemporary era, with particular attention to the discussion of the role and contributions of Indonesian scholars, teachers, and scientists—both religious and secular sciences scientists from the past to the present—in the kingdom. This chapter also examines the root causes and various motives of this group for seeking sciences (religious and secular) and for pursuing knowledge in the kingdom—and then teaching there—and investigates whether or not Islamic doctrines have contributed and motivated them. It, moreover, discusses whether or not their intellectual journey was motivated by social, economic, and political reasons, holy, religious/Islamic concerns (e.g., the idea of Arabia as a "sacred geography"), or inevitably a mixture—a combination of profane and sacred rationales. It also scrutinizes the transnational and local significance of *rihla* and explores how this particular journey has heightened a universal sense of "being Muslim" while also inspiring the redefinition of the frontiers of sect, language, territory, and nation.

Indonesian scholars and teachers in Mecca in the past

As noted by some studies (e.g., Azra 1992; Basri 1997; Rachman 1997), in the past (from the seventeenth to the early twentieth century) there were a great number of Indonesians who studied and pursued Islamic knowledge in Mecca, in addition to Cairo, Egypt. Mecca and Cairo have long been sources of Islamic knowledge and civilization for Indonesian Islam and Muslims. From these two cities, multiple types of Islam—Salafism, reformism, traditionalism, Sufism, modernism, among others—have spread to the Indonesian archipelago, brought back by the country's alumni who studied at Mecca and Cairo.

Although many of these educational travelers returned to their home country upon completing their studies, some of them taught, lived, and died in Mecca. So far no data has been found of whether or not there were Indonesian scholars who dedicated their lives until their death in Cairo. However, history has noticed that there was a significant number of Indonesian Islamic scholars in the past who played an enormous role as both teachers and scholars and who greatly contributed to the growth of Islamic education and discourses in Arabia and beyond. Their profound legacies and heritage in teaching students, advancing Islamic educational institutions, and producing religious scholarly works (mostly in Arabic, some in Malay) can still be witnessed in the modern Indonesian archipelago and Arabian Peninsula. This is among many reasons why during the nineteenth and early twentieth centuries, Indonesian teachers and scholars received great esteem from Arabs and other ethnicities in Hijaz.

Not only those who taught and worked in Mecca but also Indonesian Islamic teachers and scholars (ulama) who chose to return to their home country also played a vast role in the process of Islamization as well as in the creation and development of Islamic education, social organization, and Muslim civilization in the country. Many of these ulama occupied high positions in local palaces (e.g., as a judge or an adviser to a king or sultan) and enjoyed prestige among local societies due to their knowledge and status as a *wong alim* (a learned person). These ulama had also contributed to the shape of *pesantren* (Islamic boarding schools), Indonesia's oldest Islamic learning institution, which have played a gigantic role in the transformation of Islamic knowledge and the spread of Islamic culture. Renowned Arabia-trained Indonesian ulama include Kiai Saleh Darat Semarang, Kiai Kholil Bangkalan, Kiai Ahmad Rifai Kalisalak, Kiai Muhammad Hasyim Asy'ari, Kiai Ahmad Dahlan, Kiai Faqih Maskumambang, Kiai Baidhawi bin Abdul Aziz, Kiai Wahab Chasbullah, Kiai Ridwan Mujahid, and Kiai Ma'shum bin Ahmad. Many of these eminent ulama were involved in the founding of Nahdlatul Ulama, Indonesia's largest Muslim social organization, on January 31, 1926. Others (e.g., Kiai Ahmad Dahlan) founded reformist-modernist Islamic organizations such as Muhammadiyah in the early twentieth century.

As for Indonesian notable Islamic scholars who studied (and those who also taught and worked) in the Haramain and later became part of intellectual networks in Arabia–Indonesia and transmitters of Islamic knowledge, cultures, traditions, and discourses can be divided into two waves. The first wave was between the seventeenth and eighteenth centuries. The respected and influential scholars from these centuries included Nuruddin al-Raniri, Abdurrouf al-Sinkili, Yusuf al-Makassari, Shamsuddin al-Sumatrani, Hamzah al-Fansuri, Muhammad Arshad al-Banjari, Abdusamad al-Palimbani, Muhammad Nafis al-Banjari, Shihabuddin bin Abdullah Muhammad, Kemas Fakhruddin, Kemas Muhammad bin Ahmad, Abdul Wahhab al-Bugisi, Abdurrahman al-Batawi, Abdul Muhyi Waliyullah Pamijahan, and Kiai Ahmad Mutamakkin. An eminent Indonesian historian of Islam Azyumardi Azra in his numerous studies (e.g., 1992, 2004) have discussed the noticeable roles and contributions of what he called reformist ulama in the transmission and spread of Islamic reformism and renewal from the Middle East to the Indonesian archipelago. In his studies, Azra mainly pays attention to the roles played by renowned reformist or renewalist Islamic scholars in the seventeenth and eighteenth centuries such as Nuruddin al-Raniri (d.1658), Abdurrouf al-Sinkili (d.1693), and Yusuf al-Makassari (d.1699), as well as Abdus Samad al-Palembani (and other ulama from Palembang, South Sumatra),

Muhammad Arshad al-Banjari, and Daud al-Fattani (from South Thailand). Azra (1992, 2004) argues that through the lens of the intellectual career and teachings of these scholars, it becomes obvious that Islamic developments in the archipelago were to an extent influenced by those in the Middle East, particularly Arabia and Egypt. It should be noted, however, that although Middle Eastern influences on Indonesia's Islamic reformism began to take place in the seventeenth century, Arabs had reached the archipelago long before then. Moreover, Arabs were not the only agents to spread Islam in Indonesia, other ethnic groups that played a vital role in the process of Islamization in the Malay-Indonesian archipelago included the Chinese, Persiand, Gujarati, and Bangla (e.g., Al Qurtuby 2003).

Along with other prominent Indonesian ulama in the seventeenth and eighteenth centuries, the ulama mentioned above provided a vital link with a number of important scholars in the centers of networks in the Hijaz (as well as Cairo). Azra (2004: 127), moreover, said that these Islamic scholars served as a connection for later Indonesian scholars and students, who came in ever-increasing numbers to the Haramain. Their links with Jawi (Indonesian) students in the nineteenth and twentieth centuries, which involved a number of leading scholars in Mecca and Medina, created similarly complex webs of scholarly networks. I will return to the discussion of their contributions to the creation of some forms of Indonesian Islam—reformism or traditionalism—in the chapters that follow. For the moment, it is imperative to point out that some notable ulama (e.g., al-Raniri and al-Sinkili) contributed to the transmission and diffusion of ideas of Islamic reformism that places an emphasis on the practices of shari'at and orthodox forms of Islam while demonizing *tasawuf* (mysticism) and local religious practices. Others (e.g., Hamzah Fansuri, Shamsuddin al-Sumatrani, and Kiai Ahmad Mutamakkin) had introduced and contributed to the transmission and development of some forms of heterodox Islam that embrace Sufism and local customs and traditions.

While al-Raniri, al-Sinkili, and al-Makassari have attracted scholars, Indonesian ulama who lived between the eighteenth and early twentieth centuries, unfortunately, have been less researched and studied. Only a few scholars are interested in the research of these remarkable ulama. Although few resources are available, mainly in the Malay and Indonesian languages, they simply narrate biographical aspects of these Islamic scholars without critical examination of their socioreligious-intellectual roles in the society, their positions versus Islamic development in the Malay-Indonesian world, or their links to the teachings introduced by their predecessors (i.e., al-Raniri, al-Sinkili, and al-Makassari). Furthermore, with a few notable exceptions (see, e.g., Azra 1992, 2004), no effort has been made so far to trace their connections with the scholarly networks of the larger Muslim world that could provide a better picture of the continuing religious and intellectual relations between Indonesia and Arabia/the Middle East.

Although Indonesian scholars were present in Haramain from the seventeenth century, they only began to teach (and write scholarly works) there in the nineteenth century. As described below, some scholars continued to teach Islamic disciplines in Haramain until the middle—or the second half of—the twentieth century. Since the 1960s, particularly following the 1970s oil boom, the Saudi government started to implement a new teaching and religious policy that limited non-Wahhabi/Salafi scholars to teach Islamic sciences at Haram Mosque, Nabawi Mosque, madrasahs, and universities in the kingdom. Even though Indonesian Islamic scholars had been in Haramain since the seventeenth century, their contributions to Islamic discourses and scholarship were not visible to the public until the late nineteenth and early twentieth centuries. These two centuries were the second wave that marks the "golden age" of Indonesian Islamic scholars and teachers in the holy cities of Mecca and Medina.

During their academic careers at the Haramain, students who learned and studied Islam with these notable ulama were not only from the Malay-Indonesian archipelago but also from the Middle East, Africa, and South Asia. Their constructive role and contributions in teaching Islamic knowledge and sciences as well as in writing academic works on Islam that have been used in academic circles across the Arab regions, and South and Southeast Asia, had helped to create a positive image about the Malay-Indonesian archipelago in Arabia in the past. This constructive picture contrasts with the contemporary era in which Indonesians in general in Saudi Arabia are portrayed as "coolie class" or "unskilled laborers."

Distinguished Indonesian Islamic scholars in Haramain during this period included the following (among many others):

- Muhammad Nawawi bin Umar al-Bantani
- Akhmad Khatib al-Minangkabawi
- Kiai Mahfudz al-Turmusi
- Kiai Abdul Hamid bin Muhammad Ali al-Qudsi
- Muhammad Yasin bin Isa al-Fadani
- Muhammad Uhid bin Idris al-Bughuri
- Abdullah Dardum al-Fadani
- Abdul Ghani al-Bimawi
- Usman bin Shihabuddin Pontianak
- Asy'ari bin Abdurrahman al-Baweani
- Ahmad Nakhrawi al-Banyumasi
- Muhammad Zainuddin al-Baweani
- Ahmad Khatib Sambas
- Ismail al-Khalidiyah al-Minangkabawi
- Muhammad bin Umar al-Sumbawi
- Sayyid Muhsin bin Ali al-Hasani al-Palimbani
- Abdul Fattah Rowah
- Abdul Qodir bin Abdul Muttolib al-Mandili
- Baqir bin Muhammad Nur al-Jukjawi
- Abdullah Muhaimin bin Abdul Aziz al-Lasemi
- Junaid al-Batawi
- Muhammad Mukhtar bin 'Atharid al-Bughuri
- Abdul Karim al-Bantani
- Ali bin Abdullah al-Banjari

- Jinan Muhammad Thayyib al-Sariaki
- Abu Bakar bin Syihabuddin al-Tambusi
- Abdul Qadir al-Mandili
- Abdullah bin Hasan al-Jawi
- Muhammad bin Muhammad al-Jawi
- Marzuki al-Jawi
- Muhamamd Abdul Malik
- Muhammad Ilyas Sukaraja
- Abdul Qadir Banten
- Muhammad Thalhah Cirebon

This chapter will certainly not describe the roles and contributions of all of these noted Indonesian Islamic scholars in Mecca from the past, particularly from the nineteenth to early or mid-twentieth century. This chapter, moreover, only sketches biographies and contributions of the most renowned and influential figures of these ulama who played a vital role in inspiring other Islamic scholars and who became the primary intellectual networks of Arabia–Indonesia. Without nullifying the roles and contributions of other Indonesian Islamic teachers and scholars in the past in Mecca or Medina, this chapter will mainly focus on the analyses of four leading esteemed ulama, creative thinkers, and prolific authors, whose teachings, thoughts, and writings have influenced many Indonesian ulama, kiais, Islamic scholars, and religious leaders. They were Imam Nawawi Banten, Shaikh Ahmad Khatib Minangkabau, Kiai Mahfud Termas, and Shaikh Yasin bin Isa Padang, all of these productive ulama lived in the nineteenth and twentieth centuries. Imam Nawawi Banten was an immense scholar of Islamic law, Kiai Mahfud Termas was a brilliant Hadith scholar, Ahmad Khatib Minangkabau was an icon of reformist Islam, and Shaikh Yasin Padang was a multitalented ulama: activist, educator, writer.

Prior to describing contributions of these four leading distinguished scholars, it is useful to highlight briefly some other past notable Indonesian scholars in Mecca. One of them was Abdus Samad al-Palembani[2] (b.1704?), one of the most eminent Indonesian Islamic scholars in the eighteenth-century intellectual networks. A noted Indonesian historian Azyumardi Azra (2004: 112–17) said that Abdus Samad almost entirely established his career for teaching and writing in the Haramain and never returned to his home island of Sumatra. Even though Abdus Samad never returned to the Indonesian archipelago, he nonetheless kept a deep concern for the development of Islam and Muslim societies in the Malay-Indonesian world. To maintain his knowledge, understanding, and religiopolitical development in the archipelago, Abdus Samad was involved in the Jawi community in the Haramain. Abdus Samad was a fellow student of Muhammad Arshad al-Banjari (Kalimantan), Abdul Wahhab Bugis (Sulawesi), Abdur Rahman al-Batawi (today's Jakarta), and Dawud al-Fatani (Thailand), all of whom were prominent ulama in their time. Reportedly, Abdus Samad and his cohorts had the same teachers, most notably Muhammad bin Abdul Karim al-Sammani, Muhammad bin Sulaiman al-Kurdi, Abdul Mun'im al-Damanhuri, and Siddiq bin Umar Khan, the Sufi from whom Abdus Samad obtained his first initiation into the tariqa Sammaniyya. Abdus Samad's writings were widely read in the Malay-Indonesian world, especially in the ulama circles, pondok, surau, pesantren, and other Islamic educational institutions. Azra (2004: 117) notes that the scholarly works of Abdus Samad contains teachings of neo-sufis as well as of jihad against the European/Dutch colonizers who had intensified their efforts to subdue Muslim political entities in the East Indies (Indonesia).

While Abdus Samad played a vital role in the eighteenth-century intellectual network, Ahmad bin Abdul Ghaffar bin Abdullah al-Sambasi (popularly known as Shaikh Ahmad Khatib Sambas, 1802–1872?) was one of key intellectual figures in the nineteenth-century network. Ahmad Khatib was renowned as a founder and *mursyid* (a *tariqa* master or guru) of the Qadiriyya wa Naqsabandiyya Sufi order (tariqa), which has attracted many Indonesian Muslims, particularly on the island of Java, since its inception up until today. Although this tariqa won the hearts of Muslims in Java, it is, however, not well developed in areas outside of Java because of the lack of pesantren institutions there as the "guardians" of Sufi orders (Van Bruinessen 2015). Ahmad Khatib was born in the Sultanate of Sambas in West Borneo (Kalimantan) and died in Mecca. He claimed that both Qadiriyya and Naqsabandiyya were an evolution from the Sammaniyya Sufi order. Dubbed as the "first Indonesian sheikh" in Haramain, Ahmad Khatib, who left for Mecca at the age of nineteen, soon became extremely influential throughout Indonesia primarily due to his roles as a *tasawuf* (mysticism) teacher or a Sufi master.

Martin van Bruinessen (1998: 16; cf. Laffan 2011: 61) said that Ahmad Khatib did not write any religious treatises himself. Succinct summaries of the tariqa Qadiriyya wa Naqsabandiyya teachings can be found in two modest treatises that were written by his disciples. These are (1) *Fath al-'Arifin* (The Victory of the Gnostics) by a Balinese Muslim scholar Muhammad Ismail bin Abdul Rahim, which was translated into English by Shellabear (1933), and (2) *Futuh al-'Arifin* (The Victories of the Gnostics) by Muhammad Ma'ruf bin Abdullah Khatib from Palembang in Sumatra. Due to the lack of publications, his influence in Nusantara (Indonesia) was mostly through the network of his students (or *murid* in tariqa). Through his disciples, the tariqa Qadiriyya wa Naqsabandiyya has spread in some major areas of the Malay-Indonesian archipelago. Some important students of Ahmad Khatib who later became "transmitters" of Qadiriyya wa Naqsabandiyya and introduced this Sufi order to Malay-Indonesia included Kiai Abdul Karim (Banten), Kiai Kholil Bangkalan (Madura), Kiai Ahmad Thalhah (Cirebon), Kiai Ahmad Hasbullah (Madura), Muhammad Isma'il bin Abdul Rahim (Bali), Shaikh Yasin (Kedah, Malaysia), Haji Ahmad (Lampung), and Muhammad Ma'ruf bin Abdullah al-Khatib (Palembang). All of these ulama helped develop the tariqa Qadiriyya wa Naqsabandiyya in their regions. As for Sambas in West Borneo, the birthplace of Ahmad Khatib, his other disciples, such as Muhammad Sa'ad and Shaikh Nuruddin, helped to set up and spread this tariqa there.

The historian of Indonesian Islam Michael Laffan said that after the death of Ahmad Khatib,[3] the mantle of Qadiriyya wa Naqsabandiyya was passed to his talented disciple from Banten, Kiai Abdul Karim, who went on to win many more adherents of this tariqa from West Java to Madura (Laffan 2011: 54; see also Van Bruinessen 2015). Born in Tanara, Serang of Banten, in 1830, Kiai Abdul Karim was an influential religious leader and Sufi master who also taught in the Haramain. Kiai Abdul Karim was not only a well-known Sufi master of Qadiriyya wa Naqsabandiyya but also a nationalist ulama and a heroic spiritual leader against the Dutch during the Banten Revolt of 1888. Along with Imam Nawawi al-Bantani (described later), Kiai Abdul Karim became a key figure and an "architect" that inspired his students and followers of Qadiriyya wa Naqsabandiyya to take a lead in the religiopolitical revolt. Kiai Abdul Karim's disciples, who later became the "field commanders" and "foot soldiers" of this civil unrest, included Kiai Wasith, Kiai Tubagus Ismail, Kiai Abdurrahman, Kiai Arshad Thawil, Kiai Harris, Kiai Aqib, Kiai Arshad Qashir, among others. They all mobilized local people (notably peasants) and santris (students of pesantren) in order to fight against the European colonials (Kartodirdjo 1966; Ulum 2015: 232–41). Kiai Abdul Karim's teachings and writings on the compulsion of jihad against the colonial oppressors were able to influence his students and networks and awake a "spirit of struggle" among them to fight against the Dutch.

A descendent of a celebrated legend Sultan Maulana Hasanuddin, the founder of Banten Sultanate (Ambary and Dumarcay 1990), Kiai Abdul Karim was a respected religious figure not only by his students and kiais (ulama) but also local political leaders and bureaucrats. Following his teacher Ahmad Khatib Sambas's example, Kiai Abdul Karim also trained many students that later became leading figures in their regions. Some noted students of Kiai Abdul Karim include Kiai Asnawi Caringin-Banten, Kiai Thalhah Cirebon, Kiai Kholil Bangkalan-Madura, Kiai Marzuki Tanara-Serang, Kiai Sadzili Kaloran-Serang, Tubagus Falak Pandegelang, Shaikh Abu Bakar Pontang, Tubagus Ismail Gulacir, Ajengan Abdullah Mubarak Suryalaya, Muhammad Amin Lombok, Muhammad Siddik Mataram, among many others.[4]

Interestingly, however, in the document that contains the *silsilah* (chain) of tariqa Qadiriyya and Naqsabandiyya in Pesantren Suryalaya in West Java, one of the strongest mainstay of this tariqa, Kiai Abdul Karim was not mentioned as the successor of Ahmad Khatib Sambas. Instead, it mentions Kiai Thalhah bin Talabuddin of Cirebon as the master of this tariqa. From Kiai Thalhah, the spiritual leadership cloak of this tariqa was passed to his favorite student Ajengan Abdullah Mubarak bin Nur Muhammad (known as Abah Sepuh), who was the founder of Pesantren Suryalaya. After the death of Abah Sepuh at the age of 120, the tariqa's headship went to his student and son: Ajengan Ahmad Shahibul Wafa Tajul Arifin (known as Abah Anom, 1915–2011).[5]

From Sumatra (Abdus Samad Palembang), Kalimantan (Akhmad Khatib Sambas), and Banten (Kiai Abdul Karim), now we move to Sumbawa in eastern Indonesia. From this island, there emerged prominent scholars in the Haramain, namely Shaikh Umar al-Sumbawi and his son Muhammad bin Umar al-Sumbawi. Shaikh Umar was a teacher of Shaikh Ahmad bin Yusuf al-Qisti, one of notable Meccan ulama who taught at the Madrasah Darul Ulum. Besides learning Islam with his father, Muhammad bin Umar studied Islam with other scholars in

Haramain including Shaikh Saleh Bafadhal, Shaikh Umar Bajunaid, and Shaikh Muhammad Ali. Muhammad Umar reportedly not only taught at the Haram Mosque but also in his house in Mecca's Qishashiyya (see Ulum 2015: 313–14). Muhammad Zainuddin al-Sumbawi was another Indonesian scholar in Hijaz from Sumbawa in the late nineteenth century. The same as other Indonesian ulama in the Haramain at the time, Muhammad Zainuddin taught at the Haram Mosque. Muhammad Zainuddin's teachers included Shaikh Abdul Hamid al-Shirwani al-Daghistani, Shaikh Ahmad Zaini Dahlan, and a Pattani scholar: Dawud bin Abdullah, who initiated him into the tariqa Shattariyya. During his academic career in the Haramain, Muhammad Zainuddin taught simpler courses in *fiqh* (Islamic law) and tasawuf (mysticism). He wrote at least two books including *Siraj al-Huda* and *Minhaj al-Salam*, which are still used in the Malay-speaking regions.

Usman bin Shihabuddin al-Funtiyani al-Sarawaki (known as Usman Pontianak) was another Indonesian scholar of Borneo origins teaching in Mecca in the late nineteenth and early twentieth centuries. Little is known of his life, Usman Pontianak, as he mentions in his work *Taj al-Arus*, apparently learned Islam under the guidance of Abdul Qadir bin Abdurrahman al-Fatani. However, informants in West Borneo said that Usman Pontianak was a disciple of Muhammad Salih al-Zawawi, whom initiated him into the tariqa Naqsabandiyya. During his academic career in the Haramain, Usman Pontianak had primarily taught fiqh and Arabic grammar to many Malay students including those from West Borneo. According to Martin van Bruinessen (1998: 8), Usman Pontianak wrote several scholarly works, all of which are Malay translations of Arabic originals, such as *Taj al-Arus* (a translation of Ibn 'Ata'illah's *Al-Hikam*) and *Tanwir al-Qulub* (a translation of Ibn 'Ata'illah's *al-Tanwir bi Isbat al-Tadbir*), both are on Sufism. Usman Pontianak also translated the works of Mecca's renowned Shafii scholar Ahmad Zaini Dahlan (i.e., *Fath al-Mutafakkirin*) and of Ja'far al-Barzanji's well-known *Maulid*.

Another of Mecca's Indonesian Islamic scholars who deserves to be highlighted for his constructive role is Sayyid Muhsin bin Ali al-Musawa. Born in Palembang, Sumatra Island, he was cofounder and the first rector of Madrasah Darul Ulum al-Diniyah (established in 1934), Mecca's first Indonesian Islamic school, whose students were not only from today's Indonesia or Southeast Asia but also from other parts of the world, including Africa and the Arab region. Darul Ulum's teachers were not only from the Malay-Indonesian archipelago but also from Haramain and other regions. Two notable non-Jawi ulama who taught at Darul Ulum are Shaikh Muhammad Ali bin Hussein al-Makki, who visited Sumatra in 1924, and Shaikh Ahmad bin Yusuf al-Qisti, who was the former student of Indonesian scholar Shaikh Umar Sumbawa. Sayyid Muhsin bin Ali was thirty years old when a group of Jawi ulama selected him to be the principal of Darul Ulum. The appointment was a sign of his deep knowledge of Islam. Prior to directing and teaching at the Darul Ulum, he was a teacher at the Madrasah Shaulatiyya, one of the favored Islamic learning centers for "Jawi students" before the founding of Darul Ulum. Once Darul Ulum was founded most Jawi students moved there to study (for more on Darul Ulum, see Chapter 2). Darul Ulum was successful at training many students who later became noted Islamic (Indonesian or non-Indonesian) scholars including Sayyid Alawi bin Abbas al-Maliki, who later became part of one of the main intellectual networks for Indonesians in Haramain. Sayyid Awalwi's house at Mecca has been used for generations to train Indonesian students in Islam. Sayyid Muhsin al-Musawa wrote several important works including *al-Rihlah al-'Aliyyah ila Diyar al-Hadramiyya, al-Nafhatu al-Tsaniyah Syarh Tuhfatu al-Tsaniyah,* and *Wa Madkhalu al-Wushul ila 'Ilm al-Ushul,* among others.

The role of Kiai Abdullah Muhaimin bin Abdul Aziz bin Baidlowi al-Lasemi in the Haramain also deserves a special mention here. Born in 1890 in the district of Lasem on the north coast of today's Central Java province, Kiai Abdullah Muhaimin played a vital role during his residency in Mecca. Known as a "Little Chinese Town," Lasem has also had a long reputation of being a "santri area," mainly because this small town has produced so many eminent ulama who later helped to establish centers for Islamic learning such as pesantren, surau, madrasahs, or mosques in the area.[6] This region was also home to one of nine legendary Muslim saints (*Walisongo*), namely Sunan Bonang, who played a large role in the introduction—and the process—of Islamization in Java from the fourteenth to the sixteenth century (Al Qurtuby 2003; Sunyoto 2015). Another legendary Islamic figure in Lasem was Sayyid Abdurrahman (popularly known as Mbah Shambu), who was the grandson of a well-known Pajang Sultanate ruler, Joko Tingkir or Sultan Hadiwijaya. Kiai Abdullah Muhaimin was the offspring of Mbah Shumbu and Joko Tingkir.

Before traveling to Mecca, Kiai Abdullah Muhaimin studied under the direction of multiple distinguished "Jawi ulama" such as Kiai Umar bin Harun of Pesantren Sarang (Rembang, Central Java), who was the student of Mecca's Imam Nawawi Banten and Shaikh Abu Shatta, and Kiai Hasbullah of Pesantren Tambak Beras (Jombang, East Java), the father of Kiai Abdul Wahhab Chasbullah (1888–1971), one of the founding fathers of the Republic of Indonesia. Later, Kiai Hasbullah requested that Kiai Abdullah Muhaimin teach at Pesantren Tambak Beras and marry his daughter. After the death of his wife, Kiai Abdullah Muhaimin remarried the daughter of Shaikh Hashim Asy'ari (1875–1947), the founder of Nahdlatul Ulama. After years of study in multiple pesantren in Java (i.e., Lasem, Sarang, and Tambak Beras), Kiai Abdullah Muhaimin departed to Mecca and arrived there in 1924.

It is unclear with whom Kiai Abdullah Muhaimin studied during his stay at Mecca. However, some sources say that he learned Islam under the guidance of notable Indonesian ulama in Haramain at the time such as Sayyid Muhsin bin Ali al-Musawa, Shaikh Baqir al-Jukjawi, and Shaikh Muhammad Mukhtar bin 'Atharid al-Bughuri (Ulum 2015: 156–57). Due to his deep knowledge of Islam, Kiai Abdullah Muhaimin was requested by a group of Meccan ulama to teach Islam at the Haram Mosque. Not only teaching at the Haram Mosque, Kiai Abdullah Muhaimin was also appointed to be Rector of Madrasah Darul Ulum al-Diniyah to replace Shaikh Zubair bin Ahmad al-Filfulani. Under his leadership, Madrasah Darul Ulum (established in 1934) grew significantly. Besides directing Madrasah Darul Ulum, Kiai Abdullah Muhaimin also built a discussion forum, named Raudlatul Munadzirin, which became an academic meeting site for Indonesian students and scholars at Mecca and Medina to discuss any issues related to Islam and social phenomena. Kiai Abdullah Muhaimin analyzed, summarized, and gathered the discussions' outcomes for further reference in Islamic law. Another contribution of Kiai Abdullah Muhaimin is that he saved many classical Islamic books of the Sunni school from the hands of the newly Saudi-Wahhabi rule that banned non-Salafi books for use in teaching Islam in the kingdom (Ulum 2015: 143–65).

A less well-known scholar but who nonetheless contributed to teaching in Mecca was Shaikh Junaid al-Batawi. It is unclear when he was born, but Christian Snouck Hurgronje said that in 1834 Shaikh Junaid was already an imam of the Haram Mosque. Born in the district of Pekojan, in today's Jakarta, Shaikh Junaid was married to an Egyptian woman. After learning some basic Islamic teachings in his home village, Shaikh Junaid journeyed to Mecca for the hajj pilgrimage and to pursue knowledge of Islam, the Qur'an, Hadith, and the like. Reportedly, he was the student of the well-known Syafi'i scholar Shaikh Zaini Dahlan and Sayyid Abdus Samad Palembang. In Mecca, he lived in the Kampung Jawi, as most Indonesians did at the time, along with other notable people such as Shaikh Arshad bin Abdus Samad Banjar and Shaikh Mahmud bin Kinnan Palembang. Together they were the teachers of Mecca's foremost Indonesian Islamic scholar: Imam Nawawi Banten, who I am going to explain in the following paragraphs.

Four leading Indonesian Islamic scholars from the past

As mentioned earlier, besides the scholars discussed above, there were at least four leading Indonesian ulama at Haramain, who played an enormous role in the development of Islam. They were Nawawi Banten, Muhammad Mahfud Termas, Ahmad Khatib Minangkabau, and Muhammad Yasin Padang. What made these four scholars distinctive and different from other Indonesian scholars in Haramain in the past was their scholarly productivity, intellectual charisma, religious-academic influences, and social networks.

Nawawi Banten (1813–1897)

Let me start with a depiction of Imam Nawawi bin Umar al-Bantani or Imam Nawawi Banten (1813–1897), who was perhaps the most famous and influential Indonesian ulama and the most admired Indonesian scholar, who had achieved the highest clerical career in the holy cities of Mecca and Medina. The name "Nawawi" refers to the great ulama in medieval Islam, Abu Zakaria Muhyiddin Yahya ibn Sharaf al-Nawawi (known as Imam Nawawi, d.1277) from Nawa, Syria, an influential Shafi'i jurist and *hadith* scholar. His father, Kiai Umar Banten, gave him the name "Nawawi" because he admired this ulama hoping that in the future his son would be like him, a wish or a dream that later became a reality. Although there were many Indonesian ulama in Mecca who played a vital role in creating a web of intellectual networks between Mecca (Arabia) and Indonesia, Imam Nawawi might be considered the most prominent one and the primary "intellectual axis" of these networks.

Born in the village of Tanara in Serang, Banten of West Java, the young Nawawi, before departing to Mecca, received Qur'anic and Islamic trainings from a number of respected ulama in his region, including Kiai Sahal Banten and Kiai Yusuf Purwakarta, in addition to his father. Accompanied by his brothers, Imam Nawawi voyaged to Mecca and arrived there in 1828. Upon arrival, he soon stayed at Kampung Jawah, a popular district for Malay-Indonesian pilgrims and students. At Mecca, Imam Nawawi studied Islam with both Arab and Indonesian ulama. Among Nawawi's Indonesian Islamic teachers were Shaikh Ahmad Khatib Sambas, Abdul Gani Bima, Junaid al-Batawi, Mahmud bin Kanaan al-Palembani, Abdush Shamad bin Abdulrahman, and Yusuf bin Arshad al-Banjari. As for non-Indonesian teachers who taught Imam Nawawi at Haram Mosque, they included Shaikh Ahmad al-Nakhrawi al-Makki, Shaikh Ahmad al-Dimyathi, Shaikh Hasbullah, Shaikh Zaini Dahlan, Shaikh Abdul Hamid Daghastani, and Shaikh Muhammad Khatib Hanbali, among others.

After years of studying various Islamic disciplines and subjects under the guidance and mentorship of both respected Arab and Indonesian ulama in Mecca, Imam Nawawi then taught Islam first at the Kampung Jawa and later at the Haram Mosque upon the agreement of a group of ulama and teachers in Mecca. Imam Nawawi's students, it should be noted, were not only from the Malay-Indonesian archipelago but also from other parts of the world, many of whom became great scholars, teachers, or preachers. His notable Indonesian students include Mas Abdurrahman, Zainuddin bin Badawi, Abdul Ghani bin Shubuh, Mahfudz al-Turmusi, Asy'ari al-Baweani, Abdul Karim al-Bantani, Jum'an bin Ma'mun al-Tangerangi, Abdul Hamid al-Qudsi, Hasyim Asy'ari, Arsyad Thawil al-Bantani, Khalil Bangkalan, and Umar bin Harun Rembang, among many others. Furthermore, Imam Nawawi's Arab students who later taught at the Haram Mosque include Sayyid Ali bin Ali al-Habsyi, Shaikh Abdul Satar al-Dahlawi, and Shaikh Abdus Satar bin Abdul Wahhab al-Shadiqi al-Makki.

At the time, his students called Imam Nawawi "Imam al-Manthuq wa al-Mafhum," namely an imam or a teacher who comprehends Islamic knowledge and understands ways of teaching the knowledge. Due to his expertise and masterpiece, Imam Nawawi was granted multiple religious titles by Arab ulama such as "Sayyid al-Ulama al-Hijaz" (the lord of Hijaz ulama), "Alim al-Hijaz" (the scholar of Hijaz), "Imam Ulama al-Haramain" (the leader of ulama of Haramain), "Hukama al-Mutaakhirin" (the Last Jurist or Judge), or Shaikh al-Hijaz (the "prince of scholars" in Hijaz). Moreover, Imam Nawawi was appointed as a mufti of the Grand Mosque of al-Haram and earned the highest religious authority in Mecca (Machmudi 2011: 229–30; Ulum 2015: 51). Not only a teacher at the Haram Mosque, Imam Nawawi was also invited by Shaikh Ibrahim al-Baijuri, the grand mufti of Egypt, to give a religious lecture at the mosque of Al-Azhar. Due to Imam Nawawi's great contributions in teaching Islamic knowledge the Haram Mosque,

Shaikh Abdallah Abdulrahman al-Moalimi (2000) included him as one of the most distinguished teachers and scholars in Mecca's history.

Imam Nawawi was not only a great teacher but also a truly productive scholar and a prolific writer who, according to Egyptian Islamic scholar Shaikh Umar Abd al-Jabbar, wrote more than 100 books and publications in Arabic on various subjects (hadith, *tafsir* or Qur'anic Exegesis, Islamic law, theology, Islamic history, Arabic grammar, literature, etc.). Many of his works have been widely used in traditional Islamic boarding schools (pesantren) across Indonesia and beyond, in addition to Mecca, where he ran a *halaqah* (a circle for learning and studying Islam). When I was in pesantren in Pekalongan and Semarang (both in Central Java, in the early 1990s), I also studied Imam Nawawi's books.

Imam Nawawi's monumental work on Qur'anic exegesis *Tafsir al-Munir* (two volumes, written in 1866) was examined—and then recognized—by a group of ulama in Egypt and Mecca. Imam Nawawi wrote several books on Islamic law (fiqh), including *Fath al-Qarib, Kasyifat al-Saja, Nihayat al-Zain, Sullam al-Munajat*, and *Uqud al-Lujain, al-Aqdu al-Samin, Mirqath al-Shu'ud al-Tashdiq*, among others. His books on theology (*aqidah*) and morality (*akhlaq*) include *Bahjat al-Wasa'il, Fath al-Majid, Tijan al-Durari, al-Najah al-Jadidah, Salalim al-Fudhala*, and *Nashaih al-Ibad*. On history, Imam Nawawi wrote *Targhib al-Mustaqim, al-Ibriz al-Dani, Madarij al-Shu'ud*, and *Fath al-Shamad*.

In brief, Imam Nawawi was the legend whose teachings, knowledge, and charisma have inspired many Indonesian Muslims. After years of teaching, lecturing, and acting in the service of developing Islam, Imam Nawawi died in 1879 and was buried at Ma'la, Mecca, close to the graveyards of Ibn Hajar al-Asqalani (a medieval Shafi'ite Sunni scholar of Islam and a Hadith expert, d.1449) and Asma' bint Abu Bakar (d.692), one of the companions of Prophet Muhammad peace be upon him.

Ahmad Khatib Minangkabau (1860–1916)

Another outstanding Indonesian ulama who deserves to be mentioned is Ahmad Khatib bin Abdul Latif al-Minangkabawi (known as Shaikh Khatib Minangkabau, 1860–1916). Ahmad Khatib was born in Kota Gadang, Minangkabau, West Sumatra, and died in Ma'la, Mecca. Like Imam Nawawi Banten and Shaikh Mahfud Termas he was a celebrated teacher and a prolific author. Reputed to have been a "troublemaker" in his childhood and youth, Ahmad Khatib was actually a gifted and ambitious person who later sojourned to Mecca in 1881 to perform the hajj and learn Islam, accompanied by his younger cousin Muhammad Tahir Jalaluddin (1869–1956). A historian from Jeddah, Abd al-Jabbar, said that Ahmad Khatib's grandfather, who was later appointed as a preacher in Kota Gadang, Minangkabau, had been a Salafi sojourner from the Hijaz during the first Wahhabi occupation (Laffan 2011). Ahmad Khatib's father (named Abdul Latif Khatib Nagari) was the brother of Datuk Rangkayo Mangkuto, a Nagari (village) chief and part of the local elite in Kota Gadang.[7]

For many years, after studying at Mecca under the mentorship of Indonesian and Arab ulama (such as Imam Nawawi Banten, Shaikh Abu Bakar Syatha, Shaikh Usman Syatha, Shaikh Ahmad Zaini Dahlan, and Shaikh Muhammad bin Sulaiman Hasbullah al-Makki), Ahmad Khatib later taught and became a prayer imam and a khatib (preacher) of the Friday prayer at the Haram Mosque. The positions of teacher, imam, and khatib at the Haram Mosque are very esteemed and prestigious since they need approval from a group of respected ulama and local political leaders in Mecca. Some scholars have said that Ahmad Khatib's rise to prominence as a scholar and a teacher dates to the 1880s and was due to an "advantageous marriage" to the daughter of Shaikh Saleh al-Kurdi (named Khadijah), one of Ahmad Khatib's teachers, a respected ulama, and a rich merchant that owned a large book store in Mecca. It was Shaikh Saleh who requested Ahmad Khatib marry his daughter (Ulum 2015: 65–7). Shaikh Saleh was an ulama of the Shafi'i school who had a close relationship with the rulers (Sharif) of Mecca[8] such as Sharif 'Awn al-Rafiq Pasha (r.1882–1905), Sharif Ali Abdullah Pasha (r.1905–1908), and Sharif Husein bin Ali Pasha (r.1908–1916), who later claimed to be the King of Hijaz before being defeated by the Al Saud family in 1924.[9] Even though this marriage might have provided additional leverage for him to be an eminent scholar, Ahmad Khatib's talent, ingenuity, and knowledge should be taken into consideration as the major factor for his fame at the time. Ahmad Khatib's children were also quite successful but in business and political careers. His eldest son, Abdul Karim owned a bookstore in Mecca, while some of his other sons served as ambassadors, such as Abdulmalik Alkhatib, ambassador of the Ashraf to Egypt, and Shaikh Abdulhameed Alkhateeb, the first Saudi ambassador to the Islamic Republic of Pakistan. Ahmad Khatib's grandson Fouad Abdulhameed bin Ahmad Alkhateeb was an author, businessman, banker, humanitarian activist, and Saudi ambassador to Bangladesh and Malaysia.

Whilst Ahmad Khatib was head of the Shafii school of law, his students came from different parts of the world, including Indonesia. His Indonesian students, upon completing their studies, played a huge role in transforming Islamic knowledge into Indonesian settings and in developing Muslim education and organization in the archipelago. Some of Ahmad Khatib's notable students include Abdul Karim Amrullah or Haji Rasul (the father of the well-known Haji Abdul Malik Karim Amrullah, or HAMKA), Muhammad Jamil Jambek, Sulaiman al-Rasuli, Muhammad Jamil Jaho, Abdullah Ahmad, Abbas Abdullah, Khatib Ali, Hasan Maksum, Muhammad Saleh, Muhammad Zain, Muhammad Nur Ismail, Muhammad Thaib Umar, Agus Salim, Kiai Mas Mansur, among others. Many of Ahmad Khatib's students became mufti, judges, reformers, educators, political leaders, religious leaders, and so on. The founder of Nahdlatul Ulama (KH Hasyim Asy'ari, 1875–1947) and the founders of Muhammadiyah (KH Ahmad Dahlan and KH Muhammad Darwis, 1868–1923), Indonesia's first and second largest Muslim social organization, respectively, were also the students of Ahmad Khatib.

Not only that, Ahmad Khatib's students also became strong supporters of anti-colonialism against the Dutch upon their return to Indonesia. Ahmad Khatib, like other Indonesian ulama in Mecca at the time, was renowned for his ideas about the anti-colonial movement and the unity of Islam. His anti-colonial notions are unsurprising, in part because he himself was said to be the descendent of a judge of the Padri movement, a movement initiated and led by Padris (ulama) of Minangkabau to erect Islamic sharia and reformist Islam in the area. This movement later turned into the Perang Padri (Padri War) from 1803 to 1837 between the Padris (Salafi or reformist Muslim clerics, led by Tuanku Imam Bonjol) and the adat (customary law) supporters comprising Minangkabau nobility and traditional chiefs. The war was driven by the Padris' want, and acts, to impose a strict form of Islam based on sharia that opposed adat-based local practices, cultures, and traditions. The adat group later requested the help of the Dutch, who intervened from 1821 onward and helped the nobility and traditional leaders defeat the Padri faction (see, e.g., Dobbin 1983; Ricklefs 1993; Graves 2009). Although the war was painful for many people, it had a "blessing in disguise," namely, in the aftermath of the war the two factions (sharia and adat groups or religious and traditional leaders) increasingly met to resolve their contrasting visions and ideas. This led to the creation of a new "reconciled religious formula" that met the needs of the two conflicting parties, namely *adat basandi syara', syara' basandi Kitabullah* (customs or traditions should be built based upon sharia and sharia should be built based upon customs or traditions).

As with his ancestors, Ahmad Khatib was a strong voice of reformist Islam or Islamic reformism, whose intellectual foundations were built based on an austere form and strict understandings of sharia, anti-Sufism, and tariqa, and intolerance with local traditions and customs that contrast with the general principles of Islamic law and the Islamic belief system (aqidah). A sharia-minded scholar and a firm believer of Islam, Ahmad Khatib, for instance, disagreed with and opposed the practice of adat-based inheritance (waris) in Minangkabau, which is based on a matrilineal system, namely wealth (particularly lands and others) is passed on to nieces from the mother line, while nephews were charged to help them and oversee and protect their wealth. Ahmad Khatib argued that this practice contrasts with the Islamic law of inheritance in which the wealth should be given priority to children of the deceased where sons receive more wealth than daughters, since the former has more responsibility than the latter. Ahmad Khatib wrote a special book (known *Manhaj al-Mayru'*) to address this issue.

Moreover, Ahmad Khatib also opposed Sufism (mysticism) and was involved in an open conflict with a local Sufi order, Thariqat Naqsabandiyah al-Khalidiyah, which he accused of practicing heretical innovations. To defend his notions of anti-Sufism, Ahmad Khatib wrote a book (published in 1906 and printed in Padang, Sumatra) titled *Izhar Zaghl al-Kadhibin* (Explanation of the Contamination of the Liars), drawing on canonical collections of Prophetic tradition and Qur'anic exegesis, including that of Shihabuddin Mahmud al-Alusi. Accompanied by a *fatwa* (non-binding Islamic legal opinion) issued by Meccan muftis, such as Ba Busail, Abdulkarim Daghistani, and Shuaib bin Abdulkarim al-Maghribi, the book caused a storm among the local Khalidis (Laffan 2011: 179–80). As a result, followers of the Khalidiyah and other Sufi groups were angry with Ahmad Khatib. In response to his writing, Shaikh Muhammad Sa'ad Mungka, who was a spiritual leader of the Naqsabandiyah Sufi order and Ahmad Khatib's friend, wrote a book, titled *Irghamu Unufi Muta'annitin fi Inkarihim Rabitat al-Washilin* (1907).

Unlike Imam Nawawi Banten, mentioned earlier, Ahmad Khatib Minangkabau was an expert in multiple subjects and disciplines including astronomy, inheritance, math, geometry, and history, besides Islamic jurisprudence (fiqh), Islamic legal theory (usul al-fiqh), and theology. A truly prolific scholar, Ahmad Khatib wrote at least forty-nine books (in Arabic and Malay) on these subjects, some of which have been taught and studied at traditional Islamic boarding schools (pesantren) across Indonesia. Ahmad Khatib's scholarly publications include *Raudat al-Hussab fi A'mal Ilm al-Hissab, al-Jawahir al-Naqiyah fi al-A'mali al-Jaibiyah, Hasyiyat Nafahat ala Syarh al-Waraqatuhar, al-Riyadhu al-Waradiyyah fi Fiqh al-Syafi'iyyah, al-Natijah al-Mardhiyah, al-Durratu al-Bahiyyatu fi Kaifiyati Zakati al-Durrati al-Habasiyyati*, and *Fath al-Mubin Liman Salaka Thariqa al-washilin*, among many others.

Muhammad Mahfud Termas (1868–1920)

Another noted Indonesian scholar and a respected teacher in Mecca was Muhammad Mahfud bin Abdullah al-Turmusi (known as Shaikh or Kiai Mahfud Termas, 1868–1920). Born in Termas in the regency of Pacitan, East Java, Kiai Mahfud was another leading scholar who, like Imam Nawawi Banten and Shaikh Ahmad Khatib Minangkabau, became a primary source of the intellectual network of Arabia–Indonesia. Most influential Javanese traditional ulama (kiai) of the early twentieth century became Kiai Mahfud's students. A brilliant hadith scholar, Kiai Mahfud was credited for his endeavors in widening the range of works studied in the Javanese pesantren (Islamic boarding school) to include hadith collections and usul al-fiqh (Islamic legal theory), themes that were not previously studied in this traditional educational institution. Kiai Mahfud's paternal grandfather, namely Kiai Abdul Manan Dipomenggolo, was the founder of Pesantren Tremas in 1830, which is one of the oldest traditional Islamic boarding schools in the archipelago. After the death of Kiai Abdul Manan Dipomenggolo, who also learned Islam in Mecca, Kiai Mahfud's father Kiai Abdullah took the lead of Pesantren Tremas.

Before traveling to Mecca, Kiai Mahfud learned Islam in the famous Pesantren Tegalsari under the guidance of Kiai Kasan Besari (Hasan Basri), who was also the teacher of the famous Surakarta court poet-philosopher Raden Ronggowarsito. When Kiai Mahfud was six years old his father Kiai Abdullah took him to Mecca for the hajj and introduced him to respected Indonesian ulama residing in the Kampung Jawa such as Imam Nawawi Banten and Ahmad Nahrawi Banyumas, both of whom were Kiai Abdullah's teachers. After completing the hajj, Kiai Abdullah and Shaikh Mahfud went home. But later, when he was thirty years old, in 1897, Shaikh Mahfud, accompanied by his younger brother, Kiai Dimyathi, returned to Mecca to continue learning Islam with several notable scholars at the Haram Mosque including Shaikh Abu Bakar bin Muhammad al-Shatha, an eminent Shafi'i scholar, originating from Egypt. Kiai Mahfud's other teachers were Muhammad

Sa'id Ba-Basil (a successor of Shaikh Ahmad Zaini Dahlan as Mecca's Shafi'i mufti), Sayyid Hussein bin Muhammad bin Hussein al-Habshi, Shaikh Muhammad al-Sarbini, and Sayyid Muhammad Amin bin Ahmad Ridwan al-Madani. Kiai Mahfud also studied Islam with some Indonesian ulama in Mecca such as Imam Nawawi Banten, Abdul Ghani al-Bimawi, and Muhammad Zainuddin al-Sumbawi, all of whom taught at Haram Mosque (Van Bruinessen 1998: 3–4).

Although Shaikh Mahfud learned and studied various subjects of the Islamic sciences he was most renowned for his expertise in the hadith and Islamic law. After years of studying Kiai Mahfud taught at the Haram Mosque, whose students were not only from the Malay-Indonesian archipelago but also from other regions. Some of his notable non-Indonesian students included Shaikh Habibullah al-Shinqithi, Shaikh Umar Hamdan al-Mahrusi, Shaikh Ahmad Abdullah al-Shami, Qadhi Yahya Aman al-Makki, Shaikh Abdullah Hamid al-Makki, and Shaikh Sa'dullah al-Maimani (a mufti of Bombay). Kiai Mahfud also educated numerous Indonesian students who later became eminent Muslim figures in their areas. They included Ali al-Banjari, Muhammad Baqir al-Jugjawi, Muhammad Maksum Lasem, Abdul Muhit Panji Sidarjo, and the "trio" of prominent figures of the Nahdlatul Ulama, Indonesia's major traditionalist Muslim organization, namely Kiai Hasyim Ash'ari, Kiai Abdul Wahhab Chasbullah, and Kiai Bisri Syansuri.

Many of Kiai Mahfud's Indonesian students established pesantren upon their return to Indonesia that later contributed significantly to the shape and growth of Islamic education and knowledge. Moreover, through his students, Kiai Mahfud also made a significant contribution to the development of the pesantren curriculum such as the introduction of hadith and usul al-fiqh (Islamic legal theory) works, previously never taught in this traditional Islamic learning institution. Under Kiai Mahfud's influence, Kiai Hasyim Asy'ari, who was one of Kiai Mahfud's favorite disciples, built Pesantren Tebuireng in Jombang, East Java, and introduced the works of Imam Bukhari, namely *Sahih Bukhari*, a canonical hadith collection and the most authoritative hadith collection in the Sunni tradition. Kiai Hasyim Asy'ari, the father of the first Indonesian Minister of Religious Affairs (KH A. Wahid Hasyim) and the grandfather of the late President of Indonesia (KH Abdurrahman Wahid), was the first kiai in Java who taught hadith in a pesantren, which later influenced other kiais in the archipelago. Besides hadith, Kiai Mahfud also influenced his disciples in the field of usul al-fiqh; thereby the works of, for instance, Imam Subki (*Jam' al-Jawami'*) and of Ibn Hajar (*Sharh Mukhtasar*), unlike before, were familiar in the pesantren.

Kiai Mahfud wrote several books including commentaries of some works on Shafii jurisprudence such as *al-Minhaj, Fath al-Wahhab,* and *al-Iqna*. Some of his commentary works were later known as *Hashiyat al-Turmusi* and written in several volumes. His other publications include *al-Fawa'id al-Turmusiyah fi Asma al-Qira'ah al-'Asriyah* (Qur'anic Reading Skills), *Manhaj al-Nazhar fi al-Manzumat Ahl al-Athar* (Methodology of Hadith), and *al-Siqayah al-Mardiyah fi Asma fi al-Kutub al-Fiqhiyah Ashab li al-Shafi'iyah* (The Encyclopaedia of Shafii Jurisprudence School). In making a comment about the legacy of Kiai Mahfud, KH Maimun Zubair (b.1928–), one of Indonesia's most respected Islamic clerics today, said that he was "Shaikh al-mashayikh al-alam wa qudwah al-anam min al-ulama al-barizin fi al-qorni al-rabi 'ashar'" (the professor of professors and a role model for people in the fourteenth century of Hijri) (Ulum 2015: 85–6). KH Maimun Zubair is one of key leading religious figures who has been a main channel for Indonesian students to study at Mecca's Islamic learning centers, especially at the Ma'had Sayyid Muhammad Alawi al-Maliki al-Makki.

Muhammad Yasin Padang (1916–1990)

Shaikh Muhammad Yasin bin Isa al-Fadani (born and died in Mecca, 1916–1990; hereafter Shaikh Yasin) was another one of Mecca's eminent teachers and Islamic scholars of Indonesian origins, whom anthropologist Martin van Bruinessen (2015) called "Begawan [Maestro] Sumatra," referring to the ancestral root of Shaikh Yasin, namely Padang of Sumatra Island. Like other Indonesian ulama at Mecca at the time, Shaikh Yasin also learned under the guidance of Arab and non-Arab ulama, including Indonesians such as Shaikh Mahfud Termas (East Java), Shaikh Abdullah Uhid Bogor (West Java), Shaikh Mahmud bin Uqid Padang (Sumatra), and Sayyid Muhsin al-Musawa (Sumatra), among others. Some sources said that Shaikh Yasin studied Islam at Mecca with hundreds of Muslim scholars (*ulama* and *fuqaha*) from many regions: Hijaz, Yaman, Egypt, India, Syria, and Thailand (Pattani), among many others; hence, it is unsurprising that later he became a noted scholar of Islam whose intellectual works are able to shine many students from different parts of the world.

Shaikh Yasin wrote ninety-seven books (some have said 100), all of which used an excellent, systematic classical Arabic (*fushah*), on multiple disciplines and themes, particularly hadith, Arabic grammar/linguistic, Islamic jurisprudence (*fiqh*), Islamic legal theory (*usul al-fiqh*), and astronomy (*falak*). Many of Shaikh Yasin's works have been widely used as references in many Indonesian pesantren (Islamic boarding schools), Islamic schools, and universities, including Al-Azhar University (Egypt) and Umm al-Qura (Mecca). Due to Shaikh Yasin's exhaustive knowledge and masterpiece on hadith, many Islamic scholars granted him a prestigious respected title "Al-Musnid al-Dunnya," namely the expert or scholar of sanad—the chain of narration of hadith—in the world. A well-known hadith scholar Sayyid Abdul Aziz Al-Ghumari also said that Shaikh Yasin was the "pride of Haramain ulama." Some important academic works of Shaikh Yasin include *al-Dar al-Mandlud Syarah Sunan Abu Dawud* (twenty volumes, on Hadith), *Fath al-A'llam Syarah Bulugh al-Maram* (four volumes, on Hadith), *Bughyah al-Musytaq Syarah Luma' Ab al-Ishaq* (two volumes, on fiqh and usul al-fiqh), and *Hasyiyah ala Asybah wa al-Naza'ir fi al-Furu' al-Fiqhiyyah li al-Suyuthi* (on fiqh and usul al-fiqh), among others. Although a Shafi'ite scholar, Shaikh Yasin, it should be noted, was also acknowledged as an expert on non-Shafi'i schools of thought (*mazahib*) such as Hanafi, Maliki, and Hanbali.

As a teacher, Shaikh Yasin taught at the Haram Mosque (particularly at the Bab [Gate] Ibrahim and Bab al-Shafa), Madrasah Dar al-Ulum, and his residences at

Misfalah and Utaibiyah. Since he specialized mostly in hadith, Shaikh Yasin taught many hadith books within the Sunni tradition including *Shahih Bukhari, Shahih Muslim, Sunan Abi Dawud, Sunan Al-Tirmidzi, Sunan Ibn Majjah,* and *Musnad Ahmad ibn Hanbal,* among others. Shaikh Yasin's students were not only from the Malay-Indonesian archipelago but also from other areas of the "Muslim world," many of whom became respected ulama in their countries, and functioned as an "intellectual channel" between their home countries and Hijaz/Arabia.[10]

It is imperative to note that Shaikh Yasin not only taught students and wrote scholarly works but also pioneered the founding of Mecca's Indonesian schools and women's education. As depicted earlier in this chapter, Shaikh Yasin was among the founders of Madrasah Dar al-Ulum in 1934, the first Indonesian school at Mecca, which became an educational base for Malay-Indonesian students in the Hijaz. Shaikh Yasin not only participated in the building of the school but also was actively involved in fundraising and teaching, and later served as principal. Shaikh Yasin, moreover, also founded Ma'had al-Muallimat al-Ahliyat, a non-formal Islamic boarding school, and Madrasah Ibtidaiyah li al-Banat al-Ahliyah, a special school for female students located at Shami'ah, Mecca. Shaikh Yasin affirmed that schooling for women is an obligation in Islam arguing that since a woman has the responsibility to teach her children she therefore needs an education. The primary question behind Shaikh Yasin's support for a female schooling was: How can a woman educate her children if she never receives an education? The founding of this female school in 1957 was driven by the enthusiasm of girls and women who informally learned Islam with Shaikh Yasin in his house. Interestingly, Shaikh Yasin's wife Nyai Aminah, also established a learning center for women, named Jam'iyyah Khairiyah. This name was dedicated or attributed to the wife of Kiai Abdullah Muhaimin Lasem (b.1890), namely Khairiyah Hasyim, the daughter of KH Hasyim Asy'ari (1875–1947) (fahmialinh 2016). In 1942, Khairiyah Hasyim initiated and established a female school, named Madrasah Khuttab al-Banat, which may have been the first female school in Arabia (Ulum 2015: 182–87). In 1955, the Kingdom of Saudi Arabia transformed this school into a government school.

Contemporary Indonesian Islamic teachers and scientists in Saudi Arabia

The death of Shaikh Yasin in 1990 brought deep sorrow for Indonesians and non-Indonesians alike, not only those who lived in Saudi Arabia but also those across the world. Many Muslims mourned and felt the loss of a respected teacher and a prolific author whose life was dedicated to teaching Islam. Since then there has been almost no eminent Indonesian Islamic scholar teaching Islam in Mecca, Medina, or other areas of Saudi Arabia. It does not mean, however, that there have been no Indonesian Islamic teachers and scholars in the Haramain in the aftermath of Shaikh Yasin. The newest generations of post-Shaikh Yasin Indonesian ulama at Mecca have included Sayyid Hamid bin Alawi al-Kaff Banjarmasin (d.2015), Shaikh Muhammad Husni Tamrin Banjar (d.2014), Kiai Ahmad Damanhuri

Arman Banten (d.2007), Kiai Husein Palembang, Kiai Yasin Barhamin, and Kiai Mukhtar Palembang, among others, all of whom were the disciples of the late Shaikh Yasin. Even though they made a vital contribution to the teachings of Islamic sciences, their roles, influences, and productivity cannot be compared with those of Shaikh Yasin.

As did Shaikh Yasin, these ulama also comprehended various Islamic disciplines. However, they were mostly renowned as hadith scholars. When he was alive, Shaikh Yasin used his house as a place (*majelis al-ilm*) to learn and recite hadith. After he passed away, these ulama continued the hadith learning tradition in the Shaikh's house. Abdul Jalil, who was a disciple of students of Shaikh Yasin, said that students learned hadith under the mentorship of these Indonesian ulama who were not only from Indonesia but also from Malaysia, Thailand, Syria, Yemen, and India. Jalil (2016) notes that various types of hadith were studied with these Indonesian scholars ranging from small collections of hadith (e.g., *al-Adab al-Mufrad* or *Musnad* of Imam Shafii) to large ones such as *Shahih Bukhari*, and *Sunan Abi Daud, Sunan Tirmidi*, among others.

Some informants[11] also said that there are two Indonesians who currently teach Islam in Mecca and Medina, namely Ustadah Soraya, who teaches at Taibah University (Medina), and Dr. Ahmad Fahmi, who teaches at Madrasah Shaulatiyah (Mecca). Founded in 2003 with some 7,000 students enrolled, Taibah University now has more than 60,000 students (both male and female). The university has some twenty-two colleges focusing not only on Islamic studies but also the sciences, engineering, medicine, the arts, and the social sciences. Madrasah Shaulatiyah, as described earlier, founded in the nineteenth century, put emphasis on Islamic studies. Some informants said that Ustadah Soraya, a female teacher from Sumatra, is a strict follower of Salafism who practices a puritanical form of Islam and rejects any religious innovation (*bid'ah*) and local traditions and cultures for the pristine and pureness of Islamic belief and teachings. In addition to teaching at the Taibah University, Ustadah Soraya also preaches at the Nabawi Mosque of Medina for Indonesian hajj/umrah pilgrims.

Besides the Haram Mosque in Mecca, the Nabawi Mosque in Medina is also considered to be a special place for Muslims, dubbed the second holiest site in Islam. In this Nabawi Mosque area, Prophet Muhammad and some of his close companions were buried; accordingly, it is unsurprising that many Indonesian pilgrims traditionally visited Medina after or before the hajj and umrah in Mecca. In each sermon, Ustadah Soraya always requests Indonesian pilgrims not to pray and recite any religious prayers and recitations at the Prophet Muhammad graveyard since it considers it to be *haram* (unlawful) and *shirk*[12] in Islam and could "contaminate" Islamic doctrines.[13]

Unlike Ustadah Soraya, Dr. Ahmad Fahmi, a native of Lombok in Nusa Tenggara Barat, is quite moderate and flexible in understanding, implementing, preaching, and teaching Islam for Muslim communities. A follower of the Shafi'i school, Dr. Fahmi is also a chairman of the Mecca branch of the Indonesian Association of Muslim Intellectuals (ICMI) and the supreme leader (Ra'is Shuriyah) of the Saudi branch of Nahdlatul Ulama, Indonesia's largest Muslim organization. Having been trained in Saudi Arabia, Sudan, and England, Dr. Fahmi specializes in the study of Islamic philosophy.

Another teacher—or a preacher more precisely—at the Nabawi Mosque is Firanda Andirja (known as Ustad Firanda), who earned a doctorate degree in theology (aqidah) from the Islamic University of Medina.[14] Like Ustadah Soraya, Firanda is also an austere follower of Wahhabism-Salafism who teaches (or preaches) at the Nabawi Mosque for Indonesian hajj/umrah pilgrims. An active resource for Rodja Radio, a Salafi radio channel in Bogor, West Java, Firanda is able to give sermons at the Nabawi Mosque due to his teacher at the Islamic University of Medina, namely Shaikh Abdur Razak bin Abdul Muhsin al-Abbad, being a Saudi senior ulama and a permanent teacher at the Nabawi Mosque. It is worth mentioning that Shaikh Abdur Razak's father Shaikh Abdul Muhsin al-Abbad was a member of the first Advisory Council of the Islamic University of Medina and taught at the university when it first opened and later took charge of the university for a period following the departure of Shaikh Abdulaziz bin Baz (Farquhar 2015: 707–08). Ustad Firanda also invited Shaikh Abdur Razak to visit Indonesia and give lectures and sermons at several locales including in the Istiqlal Grand Mosque in Jakarta.

Still, some Indonesians only teach at the Indonesian schools in Mecca (Sekolah Indonesia Makkah), Jeddah (Sekolah Indonesian Jeddah), or Riyadh (Sekolah Indonesia Riyadh). These schools run from elementary to junior and senior high schools, designed particularly for children of Saudi Arabia's Indonesian expatriates. These schools, unlike Mecca's past Indonesian schools described earlier, follow Indonesian state schools' curricula, not specifying the study of Islamic knowledge and sciences, albeit there are some local (Saudi) components in the curriculum. Although at first the schools were initiated and founded by Indonesian individuals residing in Saudi Arabia, later the schools were transformed and administered under the Indonesian Embassy in the kingdom (see Chapter 3).

Apart from the lack of Islamic studies teacher, there are several Indonesian scientists, Muslim and non-Muslim alike, specializing in the hard sciences, engineering, computer sciences, information technology, management, or the social sciences, among others, who teach at several Saudi universities. They are, among others, Bambang Trigunarsyah, Oki Muraza, Prasetyo Edi, Khairul Saleh, Yose Kadrin, Sumanto Al Qurtuby, I Putu Danu Raharja, Anton Satria Prabuwono, Setiyadi Umar, Ali Rinaldi, and Farid Fadlilah. Of all the Saudi universities, KFUPM (King Fahd University of Petroleum and Minerals) seems to be the largest university in the kingdom that hosts Indonesian scholars and teachers.

I will briefly highlight some of them. Bambang Trigunarsyah, a faculty member in the Department of Construction Engineering and Management at KFUPM and a former professor at Queensland University of Technology, Australia, specializes in construction management and economic, constructability and operability of infrastructure projects, knowledge management in project-based organization, post-disaster reconstruction project management, project and program governance, infrastructure project delivery, and infrastructure asset management. Bambang said that his move to Saudi Arabia was due to a number of reasons, including the eagerness to expand his geographic areas of research related to the kingdom's oil and non-oil industries and the opportunity to visit Mecca and Medina on a regular basis as the holy cities of Islam.[15]

Moreover, Anton Satria Prabuwono, who teaches at King Abdulaziz University, specializes in the studies of multimedia technologies, web systems and technologies, computer architecture, machine vision, intelligent robotics, and autonomous systems, among others. While Khairul Saleh is a mathematician and expert in statistics, Oki Muraza is a chemist specializing in structured catalysts and structured reactors. Both scientists teach at KFUPM. Speaking on the reasons for pursuing an academic career in Saudi Arabia, both Khairul and Oki said that Saudi is a good place to raise his children as well as a fine site to conduct more research since the university has a lower teaching load. Both agreed that Saudi is a comfortable, safe, and secure place for both living and work.

Another scientist is Prasetyo Edi, a faculty member in the Department of Aerospace Engineering at KFUPM and a specialist in the studies of aircraft design, aerodynamics, and helicopters. A firm believer of Islam, Prasetyo is not only an aerospace engineer but also a devout Muslim who practices fundamental Islamic teachings and actively attends religious sermons and gatherings. A regular visitor of the holy cities of Mecca and Medina, Prasetyo, in several conversations with me,[16] expressed his pride and happiness in Saudi. For Prasetyo, there are several reasons for his pleasure of living in Saudi. First, in the kingdom, unlike in the West or Indonesia, his country of origin, there is no sites for *maksiyat*, namely religiously sanctioned wrongdoing or unlawful activities such as night clubs, brothels, gambling centers, alcohol selling shops, among many others. Second, Saudi is a home to halal foods; accordingly, he is not afraid of, say, mistakenly eating Islam-banned foods or meats such as pork or any meats whose slaughtering process and technique are not in accordance with Islamic law. The third factor is a religious tourism, which is to say that, by living in Saudi, a Muslim can easily visit Haram Mosque, Nabawi Mosque, and many historic Islamic sacred sites. He believes that worship and prayers conducted in the two holy mosques result in thousands of *pahala* (rewards from God) that guarantee the worshipers entry into paradise after their death. Another factor for choosing Saudi as a place for pursuing an academic career is about the safety and security of him and his family.

The same reason was given by Yose Kadrin, a faculty member in the Department of City and Regional Planning at KFUPM. A native of Padang, West Sumatra, Yose told me that he dreamt for a long time, particularly when he was in Switzerland (both for studying and working), of how to find the best way to enter and live in Saudi Arabia. Finally, he found working at a Saudi university would be the best channel for entrance to the kingdom. Fortunately, KFUPM opened a position in the Department of City and Regional Planning that Yose thought fitted his qualifications, expertise, and specialty. He then applied, and when he finally got an offer for the position, he was very excited and thankful to God for listening to his prayers and wishes. There was a strong reason for his excitement. Saudi, for Yose, is not only as an Islamic country per se but also a "sacred geography," in part because Mecca and Medina are located in the modern Saudi territory.

Yose argued that Saudi is the world's most Islamic Muslim-majority country where the government's rules and policies as well as societal behaviors and attitudes follow Islamic rules, doctrines, and teachings exactly.[17] Although Egypt, Qatar, Oman, Kuwait, United Arab Emirates, and many Arab countries have shared Arab cultures, traditions, and identities, the Kingdom of Saudi Arabia, according to Yose, is distinctive and exceptional. Compared to other Arab countries or Muslim-majority nations, he explained, Saudi is the most religious and faithful. "Look at Bahrain, Saudi's neighbours. Bahrain completely differs from Saudi in ways of appreciating and implementing Islamic norms and teachings," Yose affirmed. Unlike other Muslim majority countries, much less Western societies, he said, there are no places in Saudi that offer or sell Islam-sanctioned unlawful stuffs such as alcohol, drugs, pork and other haram meats. Yose is very happy since there are no such places in Saudi.

Furthermore, Yose, who wears *jalabiyya* (Arab-style flowing robes) in everyday life, is not afraid of eating any meats in Saudi since the slaughtering process of animals are in-line with Islamic law. Another indicator of "Islamic Saudi," for him, is a gender segregation. Schools and universities in Saudi are gender based. Most Saudi universities have a separate female and male college. While KFUPM is the only all-male university, Princess Nora University in Riyadh is the only female university in the kingdom.

> When I was in Swiss, Yose told me, non-Muslims were very friendly. Even though they knew I am a Muslim, they respected my faith and me. This is why they understood when I left office during certain times for praying or when I was fasting in Ramadan. However, I felt my inner heart was in conflict or tensions living in a country where Islam has not become the norm in the society.[18]

A faithful Muslim and an active member of religious sermons and gatherings, Yose is typical of a contemporary Salafi, who strictly embraces Islamic norms and teachings and follows paths or traditions of the pious ancestors or early generations of Islam (*salaf al-salih*).

Social changes and the shifting nature of intellectual travel

Based on the description and analyses sketched above it is obvious that there was a vast decline of Indonesian scholars who taught the Islamic sciences in Mecca's (and Medina's) Islamic learning centers (madrasahs, Masjid al-Haram, Masjid Nabawi, ribats, etc.). There were many reasons and factors that contributed to this reduction, some of which I have explained in Chapter 3. However, one of the major aspects of its deterioration was Saudi sociopolitical changes and government educational policies that limited non-Wahhabi/Salafi scholars of Hanbali madhhab (pl. *madhahib*; Islamic schools of thought) teaching Islam and Islamic jurisprudence. In the past, Hijaz was occupied by the Sharifate of the Ottoman Sultanate, which first took control of the area in 1517 under Sultan Selim I, which gave more freedom and flexibility in the study of Islam that allowed teachers and scholars from multiple madhahib, particularly in Islamic jurisprudences (fiqh) but also in Sufism. The Sharifate permitted Islamic teachers and scholars from the Sunni's four main madhahib (Maliki, Hanafi, Shafii, and Hanbali) to teach at the Haram Mosque, Nabawi Mosque, madrasahs, and other Islamic learning institutions. Also, the Sharifate allowed Sufi masters from multiple Sufi orders to teach (and practice) Sufism in Sufi lodges and other places.

Because of the vibrant intellectual environment, many types of Islam— reformist, traditionalist, or rationalist Islam, among many others—had grown significantly in the Haramain (Hijaz). Although learning Islam with Shafii scholars had been dominant for Indonesian students in the past, they also studied the Islamic sciences with scholars from non-Shafii Sunni ulama. Moreover, Sufism and various Sufi orders or tariqa (such as Qadiriya, Naqsabandiyya, Qadiriyya wa Naqsabandiyya, Shadhiliyya, and Shamaniyya, among many others) were also well developed in the past in Hijaz. It is hence not surprising to find the fact that, in the past, many Indonesian students not only learned Arabic and the Islamic sciences but also followed Sufi tariqa. In fact, many Indonesian Islamic scholars in the past, as described earlier, became devout followers and even the leaders or masters of particular Sufi orders such as Ahmad Khatib Sambas and Kiai Abdul Karim Banten. Other Indonesians, particularly the reformist-minded students and scholars (e.g., Ahmad Khatib Minangkabau), rejected Sufism and tariqa, arguing that both are an aberration of Islamic doctrines. Both supporters and opponents of Sufism and tariqa were clearly present in Hijaz. While some Indonesian Islamic scholars were fervent adherents of—and strong advocates against—Sufism and tariqa, others (such as Imam Nawawi Banten) took a middle ground, allowing Sufism and practicing tariqa as long as the two were in line with Islamic law.

When King Abdulaziz (Ibn Saud) took over Hijaz in the 1920s, intellectual, educational, and religious conditions in the region slowly began to change since the new rule disheartened the growth of non-Salafi/reformist forms of Islam, including Sufism, tariqa, and non-Hanbali schools of thoughts. The Saudi government also controlled Islamic education and learning in Haram Mosque and Nabawi Mosque, allowing only those that are in line with the Saudi madhhab. This change, however, did not take place over night. It occurred gradually. In the early years of the Saudi government, they still allowed scholars from some Sunni madhahib of non-Hanbali Islamic jurisprudence to teach in some madrasahs and learning centers. The government started systematically implementing Salafi-affiliated educational systems and curricula following the founding of the Islamic University of Medina (IUM) in the early 1960s and reached its peak in the aftermath of the Iranian/Islamic Revolution in 1979 (see Chapter 3). IUM was created as a means to counter the radical Republicanism movement in Arab countries and the Middle East that endangered social stability and the political existence of the Saudi government (Farquhar 2015).

However, this does not mean that the new Saudi government was completely intolerant and did not allow all non-Hanbali scholars or Sufi masters to teach and practice their madhhab and Sufism in the kingdom. In some cases, the government still gave them an opportunity to teach and practice in the kingdom. In fact, some non-Hanbali Indonesian Islamic scholars still taught in the kingdom such as Shaikh Muhammad Yasin (1916–1990), who taught in his madrasah Darul Ulum or in his house up until his death. Also, the noted Maliki scholar and follower of the Shadhili Sufi order Sayyid Muhammad Alawi al-Maliki (1944–2004), with whom many Indonesians studied (see Chapter 3), also taught the Islamic sciences in Masjid al-Haram (and occasionally in Masjid Nabawi) and Umm al-Qura University as well as in his home, ribats, and mosques in the Rusaifah district of Mecca until his death, albeit he was previously engaged in tensions and conflict with Wahhabi scholars, including Shaikh Bin Baz (Abd al-Aziz ibn Abdullah ibn Baz, 1910–1999).[19]

In the early 1980s, the Council of the Senior Scholars of Saudi Arabia, chaired by Shaikh Bin Baz, issued a fatwa denouncing Sayyid Muhammad's religious beliefs, including his Sufi practices, as deviant and misguided and in violation of the purity of Islam's monotheistic principle (*tauhid*). Due to this fatwa, Sayyid Muhammad relinquished his teaching position at Umm al-Qura University, where he started teaching in 1970 after his graduation from Al-Azhar University of Egypt, as well as his ancestral chair of teaching in Masjid al-Haram, a position he had held since 1971 following the death of his father (Sayyid Alawi). The Maliki family, to which Sayyid Muhammad belonged, had been teaching in this Grand Mosque for more than a century. Many Indonesians studied (and continue to study today) with Islamic scholars of the Maliki family and vice versa: some Islamic scholars from this family, including Sayyid Muhammad, along with his father and grandfather (Sayyid Alawi and Sayyid Abbas), learned Islam with noted Indonesian Islamic scholars (e.g., Kiai Mahfud Termas, Imam Nawawi Banten, Kiai Zubair Sarang, and Shaikh Muhammad Yasin, among others).

Regardless of criticisms against Sayyid Muhamamd Alawi, the Maliki family retained their prominence. Sayyid Muhammad's regular religious sermons and lectures in his mosque and house were attended by hundreds of Muslims and his devout followers. Notwithstanding the fatwa that disparaged his religious understandings and practices, the kingdom began to support Sayyid Muhammad, along with practitioners and followers of Sufism in Hijaz, in an attempt to counter the radical Islamist revival that undermined Saudi authority from the early 1990s, as a way to bolster religious support of the state. Since then, Sayyid Muhammad became the self-imposed leader of Hijazi Sufism under state sponsorship, with several thousand supporters. Following the death of Sayyid Muhammad in 2004, the Maliki family is now headed by his son: Sayyid Ahmad. Currently there are about forty Indonesian students studying Islam under his mentorship in Mecca, excluding irregular Indonesian visitors (i.e., umrah pilgrims or students of Saudi universities).

Another major factor in the decline of Indonesian scholars in Hijaz was the lack of financial support to sustain them living in Mecca. Equally important, the decrease of intellectual eagerness and religious motivations for (free) teaching (without salary) the Islamic sciences in the Haramain. In the past, Indonesian scholars and teachers who dedicated their life and academic careers to Hijaz were primarily driven by religious motives, namely the Muslim obligation to learn (Islamic) knowledge and then teach or share it with other people. Since they saw the teaching-learning process and the search of knowledge (*thalab al-ilm*) as "God's mandate" in Islam, they did it with *ikhlas* (lit. "purity," "sincerity," or "refinement") and without getting any payment or salary from students or other people.

To fulfill their living expenses, they mostly brought supplies (money and provisions) from their home country, Indonesia, entrusted it to someone to bring it to them during the hajj sessions, worked as a hajj guide, or worked other jobs (e.g., as a shopkeeper) in informal economies. It is imperative to note that most Indonesian teachers and scholars in the past were mostly from a middle-class background and a religious family. Since traveling to Saudi at the time was hard, dangerous, and costly, it was almost impossible for "ordinary people" and "nominal Muslims" to voyage to Arabia. They believed that God would "pay" them and reciprocate their sacrifice in teaching-learning activities. What they expected was a "ridha Allah." However, due to the long journey, many of them ran out of supplies; therefore they needed to work to support themselves.

In contrast with the past ulama, Saudi's contemporary Indonesian scholars are motivated by a combination of religious–spiritual–emotional motives (e.g., easy access to Mecca and Medina, the chance to visit many sacred historic Islamic sites, no "haram" places and foods) and secular–rational–intellectual reasons such as good salaries and benefits, no income taxes, a low teaching load, more funds for research, a secure place to live, and family comfort, among others. This is to say that religious, economic, and intellectual motives have been common for contemporary Indonesian scholars and scientists in Saudi Arabia. The combination of religious–secular factors are clearly expressed by modern Indonesian scholars, teachers, researchers, and scientists, whom I met and talked with, as well as professional expatriates who work in various companies or industries across the kingdom. In the past, there were certainly no Indonesian scholars who taught in the Hijaz for money, well-being, their children's education, research, family comfort, and the like.

It is true that Saudi is the best place for devout Muslims since it is in this kingdom where the Haramain is located, but this does not mean that religion and spirituality are the only reasons for driving contemporary Indonesian academics and professional expats to the kingdom. Some scholars and anthropologists (see, for instance, Eickelman and Piscatori 1990) have examined the plurality and complexity of motives and objectives of human travel. In this regard, Indonesian intellectual and educational travelers in Saudi Arabia are not exclusive or unique.

In brief, there was a change in the nature of Indonesian intellectual/educational sojourners in Saudi Arabia from the past to the present. Apart from the shift and differences, however, it is central to acknowledge that both past and present scholars have shared the same view, namely they consider Saudi Arabia as a source of learning, knowledge, spirituality, and religious wisdom.

Chapter 5

INDONESIAN STUDENTS IN CONTEMPORARY SAUDI ARABIA

One of the central focuses of this study is to underline the centrality of Saudi Arabia as a major source of learning, schooling, and knowledge that in turn help understand rationales of why so many Muslims from around the world, including Indonesians, are attracted to travel, emigrate, and study in the kingdom. Saudi Arabia for many Indonesians—from the past to the present era—is a vital niche not only for pursuing Islamic education or performing religious ritual practices but also for tourism and making a living. Moreover, for contemporary Indonesian Muslims, Saudi Arabia is not only seen as an ideal place for learning Islamic studies but also for non-Islamic studies such as the hard sciences and engineering. For Indonesian Salafis,[1] including Salafi students, in particular, Saudi Arabia has been viewed as a source of educational and financial sponsorship as well as a site of religious authority and ideals.[2] The image of Saudi, furthermore, is used by contemporary Salafis in Indonesia to construct an imaginary ideal through which social and religious issues are reflected. Any religious decision, for these groups, must find its legitimacy in Saudi sources. Not only that, Saudi society itself is utilized as a model of piety that adherents should strive toward (Chaplin 2014: 217–36).

This chapter, in particular, focuses on Indonesian students, a group that has historically and traditionally been one of the most important conduits for Islamic thinking and practices from the Middle East. It is these students (or former students) who have played an enormous role in introducing and transforming knowledge, ideas, and practices in the society. In the context of Indonesia, their role and contribution to the shape and enrichment of Indonesian cultures are also critical. Focusing on students provides an insight into the impact of Middle Eastern notions, concepts, thoughts, practices, and influences on the broader Muslim community in Indonesia. For centuries, as discussed earlier, a small but substantial amount of the Indonesian Muslim community traveled to the Arab Middle East to study at a variety of Islamic institutions, from leading centers of Islamic learning such as al-Azhar University of Egypt to informal madrasahs or mosque-based schools. Indonesian students studying in the Middle East do not only represent Indonesia's mainstream Muslim groups affiliated to Muhammadiyah and Nahdlatul Ulama (NU) but also other smaller Muslim organizations and social groups such as Al-Irshad, Persatuan Tarbiyah Islamiyah (Perti), Persatuan Islam, and Washliyah.

This chapter outlines the history and diversity of Indonesian students from past Hijaz to the modern Saudi kingdom as well as describes their motives and purposes of study. It also briefly sketches the students' activities during their studies and the networks that provide ways and resources for studying in Saudi Arabia, and for maintaining social bonds and individual connections. Further, this chapter not only outlines students who learned (or are learning) at formal educational institutions (madrasahs in the past or universities in the present) but also at informal centers of learning and education (e.g., *ma'hads, ribats*, or mosques), particularly in Mecca and Medina.

It is central to note that Indonesian Muslims who studied (or are studying) in the kingdom varied in terms of the subjects or courses they learned, the social backgrounds of their family, the economic conditions, and so forth. As for subject of study, many of them (both past and present) learned the Islamic sciences, while others studied the hard sciences and engineering. In the past, most, if not all, Indonesian Muslims learned the Islamic sciences (e.g., Islamic law, Islamic legal theory, Qur'anic exegesis, *hadith* science, theology, and Sufism or Islamic mysticism, among many others), a tradition that continued up until the past two decades or so, when a great deal of Indonesian disciples studied non-Islamic "secular" sciences (e.g., math, physics, chemistry, engineering, or computer science) in multiple universities across the kingdom.

The Middle East: Educational institutions for Indonesian students

The Middle East, both in the past and the present, has always played a vital role in shaping Islamic thought, practice, and activism in Indonesia (Fealy and Bubalo 2005). Whereas Islam in the Indonesian archipelago has largely evolved in line with local cultural and social outlooks (Woodward 1989, 2010; Hefner 1989), Indonesian Muslims, as discussed in the previous chapters, have long journeyed to the Middle East to learn Islam and deepen their knowledge of their faith. Not only studying Islamic sciences in the Middle Eastern centers of Islamic learning, Indonesians have also invited and welcomed Islamic preachers, scholars, and activists from the Arab Middle East to Indonesia, either through direct contacts or via the translations of their scholarly work. Until now, some Islamic groupings in the country have often organized public events to welcome Arab Muslim preachers and Islamic scholars. Some Salafi groups have even had special radio and television programs to broadcast Islamic preaching from Arab regions or online interviews/open-answer questions with Arab Muslim scholars and preachers.

Even though in the past there were some competing countries as the destination of Islamic learning (e.g., Malaysia or even countries in the West such as Australia, the United States, and some western European states), the Middle East is still seen by some Muslim groups, particularly students with Salafi or Islamic traditionalist backgrounds, as the most prestigious site to study Islam. Although there are some new nonreligious developments concerning the Middle East's influence in Indonesia (e.g., business, economy, or politics), the greatest impact has been in the area of religious education and Islamic practice. Some Indonesian Muslims have even adapted their religious practices and everyday life to accord more closely with what are seen as more authentic Islamic practices in the Arab Middle East. Most Indonesian Muslims in general cannot distinguish between Islamic/Muslim practices and Arab customs and traditions. Accordingly, they think and consider what they view in everyday practices of the Arabs in the Middle East from dresses to greetings as Islamic/Muslim cultures, values, and norms.

In the past, Egypt in North Africa and Hijaz (now part of Saudi) in the Arabian Peninsula were the most common and popular learning sites for Indonesian Muslim students. Cairo, Egypt, and Mecca, Hijaz, had long been the homes to learn Islam for many Muslim students from the Malay-Indonesian archipelago. The two cities, thanks to the fame of Mecca's Masjid al-Haram and Cairo's al-Azhar University (but also Madrasah Dar al-Ulum, now part of Cairo University, known as the Faculty of Dar al-Ulum), have long enjoyed prestige among Indonesian Muslim students. Alumni of Mecca and Cairo have also played a major role in the creation, spread, and development of Islamic education, social organizations, religious movements, and other sectors related to Muslim politics and cultures of Indonesian society.

In the past, while Cairo was linked to Muhammadiyah (founded in 1912) as a symbol of modernist Islamic movement, Mecca represented a traditionalist one with Nahdlatul Ulama (founded in 1926) as its primary emblem.[3] At present, characterizations of Muhammadiyah as a modernist and Nahdlatul Ulama as a traditionalist Muslim social organization are no longer accurate since there are traditionalist elements within Muhammadiyah and there are modernist components within Nahdlatul Ulama. Apart from this classification, it is valid to state that Cairene and Meccan communities (i.e., Indonesian students and graduates of Cairo and Mecca in the past) have historically played a great role in the shape of Indonesia's Islamic education, economy, discourses, practices, cultures, and politics, and Muslim civilization more broadly. Whereas Mecca has been the site of learning for Muslims from the Malay-Indonesian archipelago since the seventeenth century (or even before that period), Cairo was not visible as a home of Islamic learning for Indonesian students until the mid-nineteenth century. Historian Michael Laffan (2004: 2–3) has noticed that despite the long-standing renown of Cairo's al-Azhar mosque (and university), there is "little hard evidence of a Southeast Asian student in Egypt before the 1860s."

In the contemporary era, however, a great deal of Indonesian students not only study in Egypt and Saudi Arabia but also in Yemen, Sudan, Morocco, Syria, Turkey, Jordan, Libya, Tunisia, Iraq, Algeria, Iran, and the United Arab Emirates. In addition to the Middle Eastern region, a tiny group of Indonesian Muslim students also study the Islamic sciences in multiple universities and madrasahs in Pakistan[4] and other countries such as Malaysia, Brunei Darussalam, and Western countries. As for the Middle East, recent data indicates that the largest population of Indonesian students in the area are in Egypt, Saudi Arabia, and Yemen (see Bubalo, Jones, and Nuraniyah 2016). Egypt, a country linking northeast Africa to the Middle East, has the single largest concentration of Indonesian students (approximately 4,500),[5] followed by Saudi (over 2,000 students), and then Yemen (reportedly about 2,000 students before evacuations in 2015, but this decreased dramatically due to violent conflicts in northern Yemen).

In Egypt, most Indonesian students are in the Egyptian capital Cairo, while others can be found in smaller cities such as Tanta, Mansoura, and Samanoud. The latter two areas have a concentration of students with Salafi backgrounds. Most Indonesian students in Egypt study at al-Azhar University, followed by Cairo University (the country's premier public university, located in Giza), and then some small universities such as the American Open University (al-Jamiah al-Amrikiyyah al-Maftuhah). Associated with al-Azhar Mosque in the era of Islamic Cairo, al-Azhar University, initially founded as a mosque and madrasah in 975, is Egypt's oldest degree-granting higher learning institution and is renowned as the most prestigious Sunni Islam university in the world. Besides higher education, al-Azhar oversees a national network of schools with approximately two million students. As of 1996, over 4,000 teaching institutions in Egypt were affiliated with the university (Roy 2004: 92–3).

At first, before transforming into a Sunni educational institution, Al-Azhar (Jamiah al-Azhar) was founded in 970/972 by the Fatimid Dynasty, particularly the commander Jauhar (al-Gawhar) on the orders of the Caliph and Ismaili Shia Imam Abu Tamim Maad al-Muizz li Dinillah (932–975) as a center of Islamic learning and the study of Arabic literature, where its students could study the Qur'an, Islamic law, and other sciences. Arguably, Al-Azhar, whose mission is to propagate Islam and Islamic culture, was one of the first universities in the world and the only one in the Arabic world to survive as a modern university. Beginning in 1961, additional non religious subjects were added to its curriculum.

In the past, Indonesian students could go directly to al-Azhar without undergoing any selection process at home. Since 2010, however, all Indonesian disciples who want to study at al-Azhar must pass a written exam administered by the Indonesian Ministry of Religious Affairs and an interview with a panel of al-Azhar professors. Because many Indonesian students in the past did not have sufficient Arabic proficiency to understand the lectures, the new regulation was initiated to ensure more qualified applicants. As a result, only a few applicants are able to pass the test and interview, and receive a scholarship to study at al-Azhar. Indonesians in Egypt are called Masisir (Masyarakat Indonesia di Mesir). Egypt's Indonesian High School and University Students Association (Persatuan Pelajar dan Mahasiswa Indonesia, or PPMI) was established in 1927, while an association of Pelajar Islam Indonesia (Indonesian Muslim Students, or PPI) was founded in 1947. Most Indonesian students in Egypt, from the past to the present, study Islamic sciences such as Islamic law and jurisprudence, Islamic philosophy, hadith science, Qur'anic exegesis, and Islamic legal theory, among others.

Yemen is another destination for Indonesian Muslim students in the modern era. Since the last decade, the Indonesian student population in Yemen has grown from 200–300 students before 2000, with the majority going to madrasahs rather than universities, to some 1,500–2,200 students. According to the PPI, there were some 1,500 students who were formally registered as members of their association, with around 700 students who were reportedly not registered. As contact between Yemeni and Indonesian ulama and teaching institutions have developed, visas have become easier to obtain and scholarships offered, the numbers have grown rapidly. Indeed, a number of Yemeni universities now have branches in Indonesia that help facilitate student travel to Yemen. They include al-Ahgaf University, Rub al-Tarim, and Dar al-Mustafa, all of which are in Tarim in the governorate of the Hadramaut.

In fact, the largest concentration of Indonesian students in contemporary Yemen is in Hadramaut, particularly in the city of Tarim. Historically, Tarim is indeed an important site for Yemeni–Indonesian connections since most Hadramis who journeyed (or lived) in the Malay-Indonesian archipelago came from Tarim (Ho 2006). Indonesian students in Tarim, moreover, are spread between four large institutions: Dar al-Mustafa and its sister institute for women, Dar al-Zahra; al-Ahgaf University; and Rubat Tarim (Bubalo, Phillips, and Yasmeen 2011: 33). These educational institutions follow the Shafi'i school of Islamic jurisprudence, which is the school of thought (*madhhab*) of most Indonesian Muslims, and Sufi Islam practices. Yemen's other Islamic learning institutions where some Indonesian students study Islamic sciences include Jamiat al-'Uloom al-Shari'a (in Hodeidah), Rubat al-Batah, Rubat al-Idreesy, and Rubat Yahia (located in Zabeed), Rubat al-Aidrous (in Eden), and Yamenia University (in Sana'a), a private university run by the Yemeni branch of the Egyptian Muslim Brotherhood.

A small number of Indonesian students, particularly those having strict Salafi backgrounds, study at Salafi educational institutions such as al-Iman University (Sana'a) and the Dar al-Hadith (in Dammaj, al-Fiyoush, al-Shihr, Marib, and Ma'bar). More specifically, al-Iman University, founded by Abd al-Majid al-Zindani, who was a confidant of Osama bin Laden in the 1980s and is listed by the United States as a "specially designated global terrorist," has long been a key destination for Indonesian "Yemeni-Salafis," particularly tiny radical Salafi groups. Having been accused of having connections to some international terrorist groups, the university is very sensitive on the topic of foreign students and instructs students not to speak with outsiders on issues relating to the way the university is run. This is a reflection of the university's notoriety, particularly since the terrorist attacks in the United States in 2001, where the university was dubbed as a home for a number of high-profile terrorists and terrorist suspects, perhaps most famously the American extremist John Walker Lindh. The university was closed down temporarily after 9/11 and a large number of foreign students and former students received terrorism-related charges.[6]

It is worth mentioning that Indonesia has a small "Yemeni-Salafi" circle that traditionally sends students to a variety of Salafi institutions in Yemen in the south of the Arabian Peninsula. The term "Yemeni-Salafi" here does not necessarily mean a Salafi group of Yemeni descent, albeit many are, but refers to those that follow the religious teachings of well-known Salafi scholars of Yemeni nationality such as the late Shaikh Mukbil bin Hadi al-Wad'i, Shaikh Yahya al-Hajuri, and Shaikh Abdulrahman al-Adeni as well as Saudi ulama who have close relations with Yemeni Salafi scholars and shaikhs, most notably Shaikh Rabi al-Madkhali (Bubalo, Phillips, and Yasmeen 2011: 37). However, it is central to understand that

Indonesian Salafi groups are not monolithic having similar concerns, networks, and objectives. They are divided, and the division reflects (but also interacts with) a conflict within Yemen's Salafi community (e.g., a conflict between Shaikh Yahya al-Hajuri and Abdul-Rahman al-Adeni) (40–2). This conflict in turn influences Indonesian Salafi groups in the decision of selecting Yemeni Salafi learning centers.

There are various reasons why Indonesian students study Islam in Yemen. The first reason is that Yemen is a country with low living expenses, which suits students with a modest budget. Second, tuition fees are very low. Third, a number of academic institutions in Yemen provide modest scholarships in which room and board (not airfares) are provided for students. Some universities and madrasahs also provide full scholarships, including a monthly stipend. Fourth, the standard and quality of Islamic education, especially in al-Ahgaf University, is highly regarded by Indonesian students. Fifth, Yemen has many things in common with Indonesia regarding their Islamic school of thought (both countries follow Sunni-Shafi'i) and Sufi Islam practices (Sufism is very strong in both countries). Sixth, there are ancestral connections between Yemen and Indonesia, including the existence of a small but important Indonesian Yemeni community in various parts of Indonesia. As discussed in the previous chapters, the Hadramis of southern Yemen had voyaged to the Indonesian archipelago long before European colonialism, many of whom chose to stay there while others went back to their place of origin. However, their intensity of travel has increased since the discovery of steamship technology and the opening of the Suez Canal in the mid-nineteenth century. Accordingly, it is understandable if Indonesians are familiar with Yemen (especially Hadramaut) and, in fact, if they have shared traditions, cultures, customs, or even religious practices. In brief, rationales of why Yemen has found favor with Indonesian students include "its low cost, its exoticism, but also familiarity in an Islamic cultural sense, as well as the Yemeni heritage that many Indonesian have" (Bubalo, Phillips, and Yasmeen 2011: 31–2).

The new favorite destination for Indonesian students is Turkey. In Turkey, the number of Indonesian students is estimated at 728, most of them from Aceh on the northwest tip of Sumatra Island. Acehnese students have been the majority due to the scholarships provided by Turkish non governmental institutions for Acehnese as part of several recovery programs following the tsunami in 2004. Unlike in the Arab Middle East, where Indonesians have studied for many centuries, Indonesian students in Turkey are a relatively new phenomenon. Despite the fact that Turkey has a great deal of highly regarded universities, there were only a few Indonesian Muslims who were attracted to study at Turkish universities. According to the PPI homepage,[7] there were only a few dozen Indonesian students in Turkey before 2005. After the December 2004 tsunami in Aceh, more Indonesian students went to Turkey, thanks to the scholarships provided by various Turkish private organizations. Furthermore, whereas Indonesian students in the Arab Middle East are at both university and non university educational institutions (e.g., madrasahs or informal schools like *rubat*), Indonesian students in Turkey are mostly university students from undergraduate to masters and doctoral students, and most likely with scholarships.

As for scholarship, there are at least three agencies that provide fellowship to Indonesian students: the Turkish government, the Indonesian government, and Turkish private institutions. In 2008, the Turkish government introduced a scholarship program for Indonesians to study in Turkey's senior high schools. In 2012, the Turkish government launched a new international scholarship program for university students (Duncan 2014). The Indonesian government, in 2014, through the Ministry of Religious Affairs, also launched a scholarship for the country's university lecturers, mainly those who teach in Islamic universities, to pursue a PhD in home and foreign countries. Since then, there have been more Indonesian students studying at various Turkish universities.

As of October 2014, four hundred Indonesians were in Turkey as part of that program. Reportedly, Indonesian students are spread across fifteen regions in Turkey with the largest populations found in Ankara, Istanbul, Bursa, Sakarya, Izmir, Kayseri, Konya, Samsun, Trabzon, and Gaziantep. The Turkish non-government institutions that sponsor Indonesians to study in Turkey include the Pacific Countries Social and Economic Solidarity Association (PASIAD—in its Turkish acronym), the United Islamic Cultural Center of Indonesia (UICCI), and Nurcu (Jamaat al-Nur). PASIAD is a nonprofit organization affiliated with the Gulen movement, a transnational religious, social, and political initiative of Turkish Islamic scholar Fethullah Gulen. Gulen has operated in Indonesia since 1995 and provides scholarships for students to study in Turkey and Indonesia.

The rest of the Middle Eastern countries, such as Sudan, Morocco, Libya, Qatar, United Arab Emirate, Bahrain, have a small populace of Indonesian students, from tens to hundreds of Indonesian disciples. Of all these countries, the largest concentration of Indonesian students is in Sudan and Morocco. Others are below 100. In Sudan, as at 2011, there were 315 Indonesian students, most of them study at the University of Khartoum, Sudan's largest and oldest university, and the International University of Africa (in Khartoum),[8] all with scholarships provided by the Indonesian and Sudanese governments. Morocco, a North African country bordering the Atlantic Ocean and the Mediterranean Sea, is also home to some 200 students (in 2014), a big jump from just ten people in 1995 (*The Jakarta Post* 2014), most of whom study at the Mohammed V University in Rabat and other smaller universities such as the University of Sidi Mohammed Ben Abdellah in Fez (Rakhmat 2016). In addition to scholarships provided by both Moroccan and Indonesian governments, the Agence Marocaine de Cooperation Internationale also allocates funding for some fifteen students from Indonesia every year to receive scholarships to study in Morocco.

Indonesian students in Saudi Arabia: Past and present

Of all Middle Eastern countries, Saudi Arabia is distinctive and exceptional for students from Indonesia due to a number of fundamental reasons. First, Saudi Arabia (both Hijaz in the past and the modern Saudi kingdom) is the only country where lots of students from the Malay-Indonesian archipelago have sought Islamic knowledge and sciences for centuries; accordingly, Saudi has been the oldest and longest country in which Indonesian students pursue Islamic knowledge and learn the Islamic sciences, thanks in particular to the two holy cities of Mecca and Medina (the Haramain), which many Muslims in the world desire to visit. Long before the nineteenth century, Indonesian Muslims made the journey to Mecca. As previously discussed, as early as the seventeenth century (or possibly earlier), Muslims from the Malay-Indonesian archipelago voyaged to Mecca to learn Islam, while conducting a pilgrimage and other ritual practices, in the world's most sacred place for Muslim societies.[9]

Although there is no reliable data on the exact number of Indonesians who studied in the Haramain in the past, it is obvious that, as reported by some noted scholars (e.g., Hurgronje 1970; Azra 1992), there was a large number of Muslims from the Malay-Indonesian archipelago who learned Islam in the cities of Mecca and Medina, besides performing the hajj pilgrimage. After completing their studies, some of them even chose to stay (some until their death) in Mecca, while others returned to their home in the Malay-Indonesian archipelago. There were several fundamental reasons why some Indonesians preferred to stay in Mecca rather than to return home. These reasons include (1) a lack of money and equipment to return to their homeland after spending them on the way to Mecca and on living expenses in Mecca itself, (2) the risky and uneasy journey that took months at sea to return to the Malay-Indonesian archipelago, (3) attacks by disease, (4) working with other people or their masters to pay their debts, and (5) Mecca was considered a holy and blessed place, therefore living and dying their was viewed as an honor for some Indonesian Muslims, since they believed that dying in Mecca would guarantee their body entry to paradise.

Second, unlike other countries in the Middle East, Saudi is blessed with the presence of Ka'ba, the holiest site for Muslims, and Mecca is the birthplace of Islam and Prophet Muhammad. Therefore, it is logical if many Muslims across the globe, from the African continent to South and Southeast Asia, dream of visiting Mecca. It is a dream because by studying Islam in this holy land, Muslims could also perform hajj, umra, and other religious rituals in Masjid al-Haram, where the House of God Kaaba is located, as well as visit Medina to conduct ritual practices at Masjid Nabawi and *ziyara* at Prophet Muhammad's shrine. According to hadith, conducting prayers and ritual practices in this holy mosque, unlike in other mosques, would be blessed with thousands of rewards. In brief, for many Muslims in the world, learning Islam in Mecca is a plus and gains lots of advantages: knowledge, sciences, hajj, God's rewards, and heaven. In modern Saudi Arabia, the benefits include sums of money because most, if not all, Indonesian students in the kingdom are there through full scholarships from the Saudi government that include a monthly stipend.

It is true that the nature of contemporary Indonesian students in Saudi differs from that of the past. In the past, however, most students in the Haramain were self-funded or perhaps sponsored by some elite members of Indonesian society. It is thus reasonable to state that most (perhaps all) Indonesian Muslims who learned Islam in the Haramain in the past came from middle-class or elite family that had sufficient wealth, since the journey from Indonesia to Mecca, which took some 6 months by boats, needed more preparation and equipment. However, in the modern era, most, if not all, Indonesian students are there via scholarships provided by the Kingdom of Saudi Arabia as well as some of Saudi's private institutions and generous individuals. Since the 1970s and 1980s, following the oil booms, after the founding of the Islamic University of Medina, followed by the establishment of Al-Imam Muhammad bin Saud Islamic University (Riyadh) and Umm al-Qura University (Mecca), the Saudi government began to fund or provide scholarship for foreign Islamic studies students.

At the time, the Saudi government sponsored foreign students, including those from Indonesia, to learn and pursue degrees in Islamic studies in the kingdom hoping that they would become "ambassadors" of Islamic Salafism (or "Wahhabism") in their home countries upon finishing their studies. The scholarship in Islamic studies for foreign students was also part of a Saudi-sponsored "pan-Islamism project," namely a movement promoting popular assistance to worldwide Muslims in need, including the need to educate Muslims and eradicate ignorance among them. Hegghammer (2010: 18–9) said that the "populist pan-Islamist movement, which emerged in the international atmosphere of 1970s Hijaz, developed a particularly alarmist discourse about external threats to the umma and the need for grassroots inter-Muslim assistance." Saudi Arabia was keen to promote pan-Islamism across the world, in part because it faced an external ideological threat from some extremist-Islamist groups such as the Egyptian Muslim Brotherhood that undermined the kingdom's political authority and religious practice. In this regard, providing Muslims worldwide with an Islamic education, in accordance with Saudi's Islamic Salafism, through generous scholarships for foreign students is one of the keys to safeguarding Muslims from the influence of Saudi rival religious groups such as the Egyptian Brotherhood or Iranian Shia.

Obviously, Saudi's scholarships for international students are only in the field of the Islamic sciences not in the hard sciences and engineering. The latter fields were designed specifically for Saudis. As the kingdom, following the oil boom in the 1970s, has transformed itself from a desert area into a modern nation, it needs more Saudi engineers, scientists, and skilled professionals to work in its industrial sectors and to help boost economic programs and developmental projects. Until now, the priority of scholarships in the fields of science and engineering as well as other non-Islamic studies programs (e.g., computing, banking, finance, medicine) is still for Saudi students. Since the last decade or so, however, the kingdom has begun to open up the opportunity for foreign students, mostly at the graduate level, to study and take majors in non-Islamic studies programs (the hard sciences, engineering, medicine, etc.) in Saudi's prestigious universities such as King Fahd University of Petroleum and Minerals (KFUPM), King Abdullah Science and Technology, and King Saud University, among others. This scholarship program is fully sponsored by the Saudi government. The scholarship usually covers a stipend, housing, and annual tickets from and to the students' home countries. Plus there is no need to pay tuition fees since public universities in Saudi are free.

Moreover, in contrast with today, Indonesians in the past who studied the Islamic sciences in the Haramain were not really "students" since many of them were actually well-established teachers and Islamic scholars in their own societies. As discussed earlier, many students in the Haramain were Islamic scholars and teachers (Javanese: *kiai*) who taught multiple Islamic sciences (especially Islamic law) by using classical Arabic books at Indonesia's Islamic boarding schools (pesantren). Some of them voyaged and studied in the Haramain to deepen their Islamic knowledge and to look for blessings and religious authority from noted Islamic scholars, teachers, and shaikhs in Mecca and Medina, either of Malay-Indonesian, Arab, or other (e.g., Kurdish ulama) origins.

Furthermore, while Indonesian students in the past mostly studied the Islamic sciences, in the modern era, however, they do not only study the Islamic sciences but also the "secular sciences," all of which through scholarships mainly provided by the Saudi kingdom, non government organizations, and society. Unlike in Turkey, Morocco, Sudan, and most of the Arab Middle East (except Yemen and Egypt), where Indonesian students studied at the university level, in Saudi Arabia, they study at both university and non university educational institutions (such as madrasahs and ribats). Before the founding of the Islamic University in Medina in the early 1960s, all Indonesian students learned Islam at madrasahs and informal centers of Islamic learning such as ribats (Islamic boarding schools), mosques, or houses. Al-Azhar Mosque (Cairo), Haram Mosque (Mecca), and Nabawi Mosque (Medina) have all been used for teaching Islam for centuries. Many Muslims from many parts of the world have studied Islam in these three mosques. Local shaikhs sometimes also used their houses for teaching Islam, while some generous rich individuals donated money to establish madrasahs and ribats. The tradition of Islamic learning for Indonesian students in Saudi persists today, but most students study at universities or colleges. Only a few students study Islam at madrasahs (e.g., Madrasah Shaulatiyah, Mecca) or ribats (e.g., Ribat Sayyid Alawi at Mecca).

Moreover, since the 1970s in particular, Indonesian students have learned Islamic studies at universities and colleges, most notably Umm al-Qura University (Mecca), Islamic University (Medina), Al-Imam Muhammad bin Saud Islamic University (Riyadh), Taibah University (Medina), Qassim University, Majmaah University, and King Abdul Aziz University, among others. Of these universities, the Islamic University of Medina (IUM) has been the largest host for Indonesian Muslim students pursuing multiple degrees in the Islamic sciences and disciplines such as Islamic law, hadith exegesis, *da'wa* (proselytizing), Qur'anic exegesis, and Islamic theology (*aqidah*), among others. At present, there are some 800 Indonesian students at the Islamic University of Medina, while in other universities such as Umm al-Qura University, Taibah University, and Al-Imam Muhammad bin Saud Islamic University, there are less than a hundred students. In addition to universities in Saudi Arabia, some Indonesian students also study Arabic and Islamic studies at the Jakarta-based Lembaga Ilmu Pengetahuan Islam dan Bahasa Arab (LIPIA, the Institute for Islamic and Arabic Studies, formerly Lembaga Pengajaran Bahasa Arab, or LPBA—the Institute for Arabic Teaching), a branch of the Al-Imam Muhammad bin Saud Islamic University of Riyadh. Built in 1980 by the Saudi government, LIPIA offers bachelor degrees in Islamic studies and the Arabic language. For many years, the best alumni of LIPIA have had a chance to continue their studies and pursue degrees at the Al-Imam Muhammad bin Saud Islamic University. LIPIA represents a Saudi microcosm where Salafi norms and traditions prevail. Moreover, LIPIA not only helps Saudis influence Indonesian society but it also provides a gateway to all of Southeast Asia.

It is central to note that, as depicted before, Indonesian students in Saudi do not only study the Islamic sciences but also non-Islamic sciences as well such as the hard sciences, engineering, computing, medicine, the social sciences and humanities, petroleum and minerals. These non-Islamic studies students—both at the undergraduate and graduate levels—mostly study at King Saud University (Riyadh), King Fahd University of Petroleum and Minerals (Dhahran), and King Abdullah University of Science and Technology (Thuwal, Jeddah) but also are spread out in other universities such as King Abdul Aziz University (Jeddah), King Faisal University (Al-Ihsa), Prince Sultan University (Riyadh), and Jazan University (Jazan), among others. In 2016, eight Indonesian students received scholarships from the Saudi government to study in the Faculty of Medicine, Sulayman al-Rajhi College in the city Bukairiyyah, Qassim (PPI Dunia 2016). The number of Indonesian students majoring in non-Islamic studies programs is limited (about 100), which is in sharp contrast with Islamic studies students. Their presence in Saudi is poorly understood and researched. Their backgrounds, motives, and activities also remain unexamined even though they compose an essential part of Saudi's Indonesian students.

The requirements to get scholarships in the fields of non-Islamic studies are harder to acquire than in Islamic studies, with only a few students passing a series of exams and administrative checks (GPA, placement tests, TOEFL, interviews, among others), albeit scholarship places for non-Islamic students is quite high. For example, the kingdom has provided the opportunity for 200–250 Indonesian students to receive scholarships in the fields of science and engineering, outside of Islamic education. At present, Indonesia and Saudi Arabia have agreed to cooperate in higher education and research, with a focus on petroleum and minerals. The Indonesian Minister of Research, Technology and Higher Education Muhammad Nasir said that the cooperation has been formalized through a memorandum of understanding (MoU) signed in conjunction with the visit of King Salman bin Abdulaziz to Indonesia in March 2017. Of all these universities, King Saud University hosts the largest number of Indonesian students (approximately sixty-five students in 2016), whereas King Fahd University of Petroleum and Minerals hosted some forty students in 2016 (both master's and PhD students). Other universities have roughly tens of Indonesian students.

Besides hard requirements, the low number of Indonesian students in non-Islamic studies fields might be due to the image of Saudi education in these fields as not good enough for Indonesians, compared to Australia, the United States, Japan, China, Singapore, and European countries. Indonesian students have yet to display enthusiasm for taking the opportunity of studying in Saudi Arabia, due to the belief that Saudi Arabia still lags behind in the fields of scientific research and education in non-Islamic studies. In reality, thanks to positive cooperation with the United States and European countries in developing their research and educational infrastructure, Saudi Arabia has risen into the upper echelons. In recent years, Saudi has been consistently ranked among the world's top universities and has excellent programs in scientific research, the sciences, and engineering. However, most Indonesians still understand Saudi as a center for Islamic education. Although still low in numbers, compared to Islamic studies students, trends to pursue degrees in the sciences and engineering is quite good, thanks to the efforts or roles played by the Indonesian Embassy in Saudi Arabia, the Saudi Embassy in Indonesia, and the Association of Indonesian Students in Saudi as well as alumni networks.

The third main reason for the distinctiveness of Saudi Arabia in contrast with other Middle Eastern countries is that Indonesian Muslims did not only study at Saudi institutions but also built their own Islamic schools and learning centers in Mecca. As depicted in Chapter 4, some Indonesian Islamic scholars in Mecca (e.g., Shaikh Yasin bin Isa Padang, Sayyid Muhsin al-Musawa, Kiai Abdullah Muhaimin, Janan Muhammad Tayyip, and Tengku Mukhtar, among many others) founded several Islamic schools such as Madrasah Dar al-Ulum, Madrasah Indonesia al-Makkiyah, Ma'had al-Mu'allimat al-Ahliyah, and Madrasah Ibtidaiyah li al-Banat al-Ahliyah (this school is special for female students), among others. Students in these institutions were not only Indonesian but also Malay, Thai, or even Arab. For several years, Habib Zain bin Smith also established an informal center of Islamic learning for Indonesians in Medina. Unfortunately, all of these educational institutions collapsed.

In the contemporary era, there are three Indonesian secondary schools in Saudi Arabia, namely Sekolah Indonesia Makah, Sekolah Indonesia Jeddah, and Sekolah Indonesia Riyadh, all of which follow Indonesian curricula and are run in Bahasa Indonesia. Since 2001, there is also a branch of Indonesian-based Universitas Terbuka (UT, Open University) in Riyadh. Founded in 1984, the UT is a state/public university that introduced a long-distance teaching-learning process (via online tutorials, video, media, and so forth, not through face-to-face lectures and discussions in a classroom) and is "open" (no limitation of age, lengthy semesters, dates of high school graduation, etc.). The university is primarily designed for those who work in companies, government offices, and other institutions and do not have enough time to study and pursue higher education degrees. There are hundreds of Indonesians in Saudi Arabia who are registered at this university, most notably in three faculties: Faculty of Sciences, Faculty of Economy, and Faculty of Social Sciences and Humanities (see "Universitas Terbuka UPBJJ Riyadh" n.d.).

The depiction sketched above suggests that Indonesian students in Saudi Arabia do not only focus on Islamic studies, as many people have assumed, but also on non-Islamic studies. Although for the moment, Indonesian students who study in the fields of non-Islamic sciences are still lagging behind, there is a tendency that in the upcoming years should result in the number of the latter type of students increasing, as the image and reputation of Saudi education and universities among Indonesians gradually tends to improve. It is true that Indonesian Islamic studies students are still dominant in part because of the nature and much older history of Islamic studies programs in Saudi Arabia than that of non-Islamic studies. Ever since Saudi Arabia founded the Islamic University in Medina in the early 1960s, the kingdom has become the biggest exporter of Islamic education. This development has been driven by certain domestic and global political turning points, beginning with the so-called Arab Cold War, in which socialist Egypt, under President Gamal Abd al-Nasser, and Saudi Arabia used educational institutions to battle for ideological hegemony.

At the time, President Nasser used al-Azhar University as a center for propagating Islam and his Arab-socialist vision of pan-Arabism. This, for sure, was a frontal attack on Saudi Arabia's religious and political status within the Muslim world. To counter Nasser's ideological mission and ambition of pan-Arabism and socialism, Saudi Arabia founded the Islamic University of Medina in 1961, whose stated goal was an international mission, which today occurs mostly through generous scholarships for foreign students, including Indonesians. With the oil booms in the 1970s and the 1980s, Saudi Arabia invested huge funds for scholarship programs for foreign students to study Islam in the kingdom, not only at the IUM but also at other Islamic universities within the kingdom, particularly Al-Imam Muhammad bin Saud Islamic University and Umm al-Qura University. Together these three universities became the backbone of Islamic teachings, forming the core of the Saudi religious system, and developing into the largest Salafi educational institution in the country (Kovacs 2014: 1–8). Former Indonesian Prime Minister Muhammad Natsir (1908–1993), who was appointed to one of the international advisory boards of the IUM as well as being one of the key figures in the Muslim World League, in which Saudi Arabia played a major role, had been instrumental in linking Indonesian students to study Islam at the IUM, Umm al-Qura University, and Al-Imam Muhammad bin Saud Islamic University. However, it is important to note that, whereas in the past these three universities only offered programs in Islamic studies, at present they have non-Islamic studies programs and faculties.

The nature and history of these Islamic studies differ substantially from those of non-Islamic studies programs. While programs and scholarships for foreign students to study Islam within the kingdom have been offered since the founding of the IUM in the 1960s, non-Islamic studies scholarships only began to be available for foreign students perhaps in the 2000s. Before that time, programs and scholarships in non-Islamic studies, particularly the hard sciences and engineering, were only offered to Saudi students. It is hence understandable why the number of Indonesian students in non-Islamic studies is far behind those of Islamic studies. However, with hundreds of Indonesian non-Islamic studies students (mostly at graduate levels) every year, they represent a significant minor group in the kingdom that could open our minds regarding the plurality of Indonesian students in Saudi Arabia and could play major roles in their fields upon completing their studies.

Indonesian students' backgrounds and rationales for studying in Saudi Arabia

From 2014 to 2015, I developed a questionnaire[10] for Indonesian students in Saudi Arabia—studying both Islamic studies and non-Islamic studies—all of whom had scholarships provided by either the Saudi government (as in the case of university students) or private institutions and individuals (as in the case of non university disciples) aiming at understanding their biographical sketches, socio economic backgrounds, and rationales for studying in the kingdom. The survey was conducted among Indonesian students at King Fahd University of Petroleum and Minerals (Dhahran), King Saud University (Riyadh), Al-Imam Muhammad bin Saud Islamic University (Riyadh), Islamic University (Medina), and Umm al-Qura University (Mecca). About seventy-five respondents were students from multiple disciplines. With he aim of obtaining comprehensive data and information, I selected respondents, all of whom were male students, based on some basic criteria such as age, majoring or main fields of study, regions in Indonesia where they lived, and pre-Saudi universities, schools, or any educational institutions they had previously attended. During the survey, I employed student assistants from universities where the survey was administered to help distribute the questionnaire and choose the "right respondents" based on the above criteria.

The survey question topics included: the students' academic and family backgrounds (e.g., schools or universities prior to studying in Saudi, parents' professions, income, religiosity, and literacy, etc.); the fields of study before and during their study in the kingdom; the degrees of the students' religiosity before and during their stay in Saudi Arabia (e.g., ritual practices, Qur'anic recitations, mosque visits, public sermon attendance, etc.); the students' social (or political) activity before coming to Saudi; the students' organizational affiliations; the students' ability/inability to read, write, and understand Arabic texts; the courses they studied and books they used during their studies; the admission process and their scholarship information; among others. I also drafted questions about the reasons, motives and purposes of their study in the kingdom. In this regard, as I explain below, students vary, indicating the diversity and complexity of their rationales, motivations, and objectives of studying in Saudi Arabia. I also questioned whether or not Islamic teachings, doctrines, texts, and discourses had influenced or driven the Indonesian Muslim students to study in the kingdom. Last but not least, I also questioned them about their future plans or careers after completing their studies and whether they will pursue academic or professional careers.

In addition to the survey, in 2015, I also held a focus group discussion (FGD) involving Indonesian students from multiple disciplines, some of whom had already graduated. Also, I conducted interviews and conversations with numerous Indonesian university students in the kingdom. The interviews and conversations took place between 2014 and 2016.

Based on the findings from the survey, added to the interviews and conversations, it is obvious that Indonesian university students come from varied backgrounds and have multiple motives and purposes for studying in Saudi Arabia. They also have multiple individual and institutional networks and a variety of ways for finding (and having) scholarships to study in the kingdom. The data show that most university students in Saudi come from low-income families whose parents are mostly farmers, fishermen, petty traders, middle school teachers, retired civil servants, gardeners, or even unemployed. The monthly income for the students' parents was between 1,000,000 Indonesian Rupiah (US$100) and 5,000,000 Indonesian Rupiah (US$500). Only a few students' parents had a monthly income of more than 5,000,000 Indonesian Rupiah ($US500). From this data, it is understandable why Indonesian students (at both the university and non university level) in Saudi Arabia are mostly there through scholarship programs provided by the Saudi government, universities, the private sector, or even individuals such as those who studied (or are studying) Islam in the Ribat Sayyid Alawi of Mecca, whose studies have been assisted by the generous support of the Sayyid Alawi family. The support includes lodgings and a modest monthly stipend for at least six years until the students have completed their Islamic studies courses. Part of the learning contract is that the students of the Ribat (or Rubat) Sayyid Alawi are not allowed to return home until they finish all of their Islamic/Arabic courses.

The survey findings also show that the majority of student (both Islamic studies and non-Islamic studies students) said that they came from a devout Muslim family, indicated by performing regular prayer and other Islamic ritual activities, and only a few admitted they were from a less-religious family[11] (say, a nominal Muslim family). However, interestingly, a great deal of students (more than 80 percent) recognized that their parents are not able to read, write, and understand Arabic. Some of them said that their parents can read the Qur'an but cannot write in Arabic much less understand Arabic writings. This fact, it is worth mentioning, is not only parents of non-Islamic studies students but also for Islamic studies students in the Islamic University of Medina, Umm al-Qura, and Al-Imam Muhammad bin Saud Islamic University. Indeed, although the majority of the Indonesian population are Muslim (about 87 percent of 260 million people) most of them do not read, write, or understand Arabic. Only those who have been trained in madrasahs or Islamic schools (or Islamic boarding schools) are familiar with Arabic.

How about the students' religious background? The majority of students said that before coming to Saudi Arabia they were devout Muslims, regular visitors of mosques, and active participants of Islamic sermons (*pengajian*), or even members of religious groups. Only a few said that they were "not really religious," performing only prayers (*salat*) or fasting (*puasa*) occasionally. Concerning the Arabic language issues, Islamic studies students mostly could read, write, and understand Arabic prior to coming to Saudi. This is, certainly, unsurprising because Arabic proficiency is the primary prerequisite for students who would like to study Islam that use Arabic texts as the main resources of learning or to pursue degrees in Islamic studies. But, for the non-Islamic students, they mostly knew little Arabic since they were not trained in Islamic schools and universities, albeit many of them could read the Qur'an. In addition, non-Islamic studies students study in a university where English is the language of instruction. Accordingly, at KFUPM, for instance, students need to have English skills. Indonesian graduate students (and others) who apply to this university require a high TOEFL (Test of English as a Foreign Language) or IELTS (International English Language Testing System) score.

However, interestingly, I found that there are some non-Islamic studies students (in KFUPM, Al-Imam Muhammad bin Saud Islamic University, and King Saud University) who can read, write, and understand Arabic texts well. This type of student usually had double training: secular universities and Islamic schools (madrasahs or pesantren). Abdul Latif Ashadi, for instance, a graduate student at KFUPM majoring in geosciences from Central Java (now graduated), can read and comprehend classical Arabic-Islamic texts in part because he learned Arabic and classical Islamic texts (known as *Kitab Kuning* or "Yellow Book") while studying for a bachelor of science at the Diponegoro University in Central Java. Throughout their studies in Saudi Arabia, students' religiosity tends to increase, while only a small number of students said that their religiosity did not seem to have increased significantly. Some students at KFUPM, in particular, are involved in several Qur'anic studies and are active members of Islamic centers outside the university which are organized by a group of Indonesian Muslims in the Dammam/Al Khobar area.

As for the students' academic background, there is an essential difference between those learning Islamic studies (in university or non university educational institutions) and those pursuing degrees in non-Islamic studies such as science and engineering. Obviously, students who study the Islamic sciences, either at a university (e.g., IUM, Umm al-Qura, or Prince Muhammad bin Saud Al Imam Islamic University) or at a non university educational institution (e.g., Ribat Sayyid Alawi or Madrasah Shaulatiyah), were all graduates from Islamic learning institutions (e.g., madrasahs, pesantren, ma'had, colleges, and universities) in Indonesia.

These educational institutions include, but are not limited to, Pondok Modern Gontor, Pondok Pesantren al-Anwar (Rembang, Central Java), Pondok Pesantren al-Amien Penduran (Madura), Pondok Pesantren al-Ikhlas (Bone, Sulawesi), STAIMAFA (Sekolah Tinggi Agama Islam Mathali'ul Falah in Pati, Central Java), Mah'ad Aly Arrayah (Sukabumi, West Java), Pondok Pesantren Rafah, STIT Al-Marhalah, Madrasah Aliyah al-Ikhlas, STAI al-Mawaddah (Kolaka), Madrasah Aliyah Sulamul Huda, UIN Sunan Kalijaga (Yogyakarta), UIN Alauddin (Makassar), Pondok Pesantren Al-Kautsar (Lombok), Pondok Pesantren Tebu Ireng, LIPIA (Jakarta), Universitas Al-Azhar Indonesia, UIN Malang, and SMAIT Darul Hikmah. As for non-Islamic studies students, many of whom were postgraduates (most at the master's level and some at the doctorate level), they were graduates from public/private universities whose main focus is not the study of Islamic sciences such as Universitas Indonesia, Institut Teknologi Bandung, Institut Pertanian Bogor, Universitas Diponegoro, Universitas Gadjah Mada, Universitas Wahid Hasyim, Universitas Sultan Ageng Tirtayasa, Institut Teknologi Surabaya, Universitas Negeri Yogyakarta, and Universitas Ibnu Khaldun Bogor, among others.

Furthermore, regarding social-organizational backgrounds, whereas some students were neither involved in nor members of any social organization (except for students' bodies in their universities), others were affiliated with some civic institutions in Indonesia. Some organizations that students were engaged with included Nahdlatul Ulama, Gerakan Pemuda Ansar (the youth body of Nahdlatul Ulama), Pergerakan Mahasiswa Islam Indonesia (PMII), Muhammadiyah, Ikatan Mahasiswa Muhammadiyah, Jamaah Masjid Manarul Ilmi at Surabaya Institute of Technology, Taman Pendidikan Qur'an Hidayatus Shibyan, Al Mizan (a group of Qur'anic recitation), Al-Irsyad, Kelompok Studi Pelajar Muslim Bogor, Youth Care International, Qousan Community for Training, and Lembaga Dakwah Kampus. Of all these organizations, Nahdlatul Ulama and Muhammadiyah seem to be the largest social institutions that Indonesian students are affiliated with. This tendency or characteristic looks similar to Indonesian students in Egypt, Turkey, Pakistan, and Yemen, previously depicted.

In addition to social organizations, some students are active members of a political party in Indonesia. It is true that the great majority of students stated clearly that they have no affiliation with any political party in the country, while others preferred to not declare their political affiliation. But, some students said that they are active members of (or supporters for) Indonesia's political parties, with the majority supporting the Partai Keadilan dan Kesejahteraan (Justice and Welfare Party), an Islamic political party resembling Turkey's Justice and Development Party. The other political parties mentioned were Partai Kebangkitan Bangsa, a religious-traditionalist-nationalist political party, and Gerindra, a secular nationalist party. Interestingly, the Islamic studies students at the IUM said that they did not have political links with any political party in Indonesia or did not state their political affiliation, in contrast with non-Islamic studies students. It is unclear whether or not their political parties helped them with their university admission or provided with them a channel for getting a scholarship to study in the kingdom.

There are multiple subjects that Indonesian students study. As for Islamic studies students, they study a variety of Islamic disciplines such as Islamic sharia or *fiqh* (Islamic jurisprudence), da'wa (Islamic propagation), *ushuluddin* (Islamic theology), hadith science (*'Ilm al-Hadith*), Qur'anic exegesis (*'Ilm al-Tafsir*), Arabic literature, and Arabic language, among others. Of all these fields or subfields, Islamic law seems to be the most popular one, followed by da'wa, hadith, and others. For these students, there are several favorite courses such as Arabic language, *usul al-fiqh* (Islamic legal theory), *tarikh* (history), *sirah* (i.e., the history of Islam and Prophet Muhammad), hadith, *tauhid* (doctrine of the oneness of God), Arabic grammar, Islamic culture (*tsaqafah al-Islamiyyah*), Arab cultures, and speech skills. As for non-Islamic studies students (both undergraduates and postgraduates), they study geoscience, chemical engineering, environmental science, physics, civil engineering, mechanical engineering, earth science, software, computer sciences, math, statistics, applied physics, geophysics, and sociology, among others.

How did they get information about scholarships and studying in Saudi Arabia? Students varied in explaining the sources of information for their scholarship to study in the kingdom. These included friends and colleagues, social media networks (Facebook, WhatsApp, Twitter, mailing lists, etc.), pamphlets in their previous schools, the homepages of Saudi universities, alumni networks, former teachers, family members, and organizational networks, among others. Although sources of information look similar for all students, the process of admission differs from non-Islamic studies students to Islamic studies students. For the former (i.e., students of King Saud University and King Fahd University of Petroleum and Minerals), most, if not all, students applied directly to the university through an online system by completing a form that is available on the university website. However, for the latter (i.e., students of the IUM and Al-Imam Muhammad bin Saud Islamic University), the selection process and exams began in Indonesia. Once they passed the preliminary tests, they were interviewed by authoritative relevant persons. Once they passed both exam and interview, they are recommended to study in Saudi Arabia. In the kingdom, some students could directly take courses, while others needed language adjustment (English or Arabic) for at least a year before taking classes.

It is interesting to find out that Islamic and non-Islamic studies students have common motives and objectives for learning in Saudi Arabia. Based on the survey findings, conversations, and interviews, there are several primary motives and purposes of study in Saudi Arabia as follows:

- Scholarship/studentship from Saudi Arabia
- Hajj and *umrah* (a small hajj) pilgrimages
- Easy access to Islamic historic sites in Mecca and Medina
- Ability to visit shrines of Prophet Muhammad and his esteemed companions
- An image and reputation of Saudi Arabia as a religious country and a center for learning Islam as well as the land of Islam and the birthplace of Prophet Muhammad
- Academic programs in Saudi universities are relevant for their interests and intentions
- Learning Islam from its primary sources
- Deepen their knowledge on Islam from authoritative Islamic scholars
- A home to Salafism and Sunni Islam
- Be closer to Prophet Muhammad peace be upon him
- Islamic doctrines and teachings on the compulsion, significance, and advantage of pursuing knowledge (*thalab al-ilm*) for a Muslim from birth to death.

From these data it is obvious that a mixture of secular and religious motivations has driven Indonesian students to learn various sciences and pursue knowledge in Saudi Arabia. In other words, for the students, studying in the kingdom has multiple advantages: knowledge, learning the sciences, diplomas, money (stipends), the title of hajj, rewards from God (*pahala*), *ijazah* (official recognition) and *sanad* (intellectual chains),[12] religious prestige, Islamic authority, and even heaven! As for Islamic studies disciples in Mecca and Medina, they expressed their happiness and pride for studying there because these Muslim holy cities have been sources of Islamic learning for centuries.

What makes the students—both Islamic and non-Islamic studies students—happier studying in the kingdom is the "spiritual benefit." They believed that by performing the hajj pilgrimage, conducting ritual practices in the holy mosques of Masjid Haram and Masjid Nabawi, and visiting the sanctuary of Prophet Muhammad, a Muslim would be guaranteed entry by God (Allah SWT) to paradise in the afterlife. Performing hajj has been dreamt of by the Indonesian students in the kingdom in part because this pilgrimage is a very important Islamic ritual as well as an uneasy business in Indonesia. A person who registers for the hajj has to wait ten to fifteen years (in some cases twenty years) before they can depart for Mecca. A limited quota of hajj pilgrims from Indonesia are permitted by the Saudi government, while at the same time huge number of Indonesians register for the hajj every year, which has created a long waiting list of hajj pilgrims in the country. Accordingly, studying in the kingdom means a good opportunity for the students to perform the hajj at a low cost, with simple bureaucracy, and no need for them to be on a waiting list. They also can perform umrah as many times as they want. All students whom I interviewed and conversed with had already performed hajj at least once. They have also done umrah multiple times, some of them even could not remember how many times they had performed umrah pilgrimage since they are regular visitors of Mecca.

For Indonesian Muslims, the hajj is not simply about performing a ritual practice or fulfilling the religious obligation of Islam's fifth pillar (which is the last pillar of Islam according to most Sunni scholars) but also a prestige. Having the title "Haji" (the Hajj) is a socioreligious prestige, symbolizing one's socioeconomic class in the society, and therefore could elevate the social status of the hajj in that society. In Indonesia, a Muslim who has already performed the hajj will use the title "Hajj" (Haji or Hajjah for female) in the beginning of his/her name, signifying the pride of having completed the hajj, which not every Muslim is able to do. Also, the students believe that prayers during the hajj season will be accepted by God; accordingly, they make every effort to conduct the hajj in Mecca to pray to God asking for a better life, success in future careers, a good economic condition, family safety, or even heaven.

A very common question from Indonesians to Indonesian students in Saudi Arabia is: "Have you performed hajj?" This type of question indicates the vitality of the hajj for Indonesian Muslims. Moreover, the hajj season is also a great opportunity for the students, particularly those who live in the areas of Jeddah, Mecca, and Medina, to earn some money by becoming a tour guide for Indonesian pilgrims or a substitute for Indonesian Muslims who are not able to perform the hajj directly due to critical physical conditions that hinder them from coming to Mecca. In Islam, a Muslim can pay someone to perform the hajj on his/her behalf due to some legitimate critical reason that prevents him/her from going directly to Mecca. A student at KFUPM told me that he has been paid at least 6,000 Saudi Riyal for being a hajj substitute for an Indonesian.[13]

The plurality and complexity of Indonesian students

There are indeed multiple factors, rationales, motives, and purposes for studying in Saudi Arabia; accordingly, generalizing information about Indonesian students in the kingdom (e.g., Saudi alumni are followers of intolerant, severe, and conservative Islam) will be misleading. There are also multiple groups of Indonesian students at Saudi universities and other educational institutions, ranging from traditionalist and conservative to moderate and progressive, Salafi and non-Salafi, Islamic and non-Islamic sciences students, and so forth. The plurality and complexity of the Indonesian students concerning their backgrounds, goals, networks, motivations, academic interests, and fields of study are obvious. Some important findings can be drawn here.

First, students pursuing Islamic studies in Saudi educational institutions, either in Saudi Arabia or Indonesia (e.g., LIPIA), do not always automatically become "Islamist" or "Salafi," much less "Wahhabi," as many people have erroneously understood. There are multiple and complex factors that contributed to their "Salafi-ness," "Islamist-ness," or "Wahhabi-ness." It is true that some Islamic studies students have been radicalized by religious thoughts, discourses, understandings, interpretations, teachings, and practices of some Saudi or non-Saudi Salafis. Some Salafi teachers, professors, and scholars (again, both Saudi and non-Saudi) have indeed changed and transformed the way Indonesian students think about, understand, and practice Islam and Muslim culture. Fatwas, thoughts, and opinions of some well-known Salafi ulama, although they might not teach or lecture at a university, have also influenced some Indonesian Muslim students. They are, among others, Shaikh Abd al-Aziz ibn Baz (1910–1999), Muhammad Nasiruddin al-Albani (1914–1999), Muhammad ibn al-Uthaymin (1929–2001), Saleh al-Fauzan (1933–), and Abd al-Aziz ibn Abdullah Al Ashaikh (1943–).

However, generalizing or attaching the labels of "Salafi," "Islamist," or "Wahhabi" to all Indonesian students trained at Saudi educational centers is a big mistake. There are several fundamental reasons why such a simplification is invalid. First, not all Islamic teachers and scholars in Saudi Arabia follow Salafism, Wahhabism, or even Islamism. Second, not all Indonesian students are interested in the study or following of Salafi, Wahhabi, or Islamist notions, concepts, understandings, interpretations, and practices. In fact, there are hundreds of Indonesian students pursuing degrees in non-Islamic studies. Those who study Islamic sciences also by default do not have an interest in practicing Salafi, Wahhabi, or Islamist ideas. Indonesian students who have a non-Salafi, Wahhabi, or Islamist background (e.g., students of Nahdlatul Ulama and others) would most likely tend to practice their traditional, non-puritan, and non-reformist beliefs.[14]

Third, not all Salafi-ness, Wahhabi-ness, or Islamist-ness of Indonesian students was influenced or shaped by Salafi, Wahhabi, or Islamist teachers and scholars. Saudi's Indonesian Muslim communities, friendship networks, Islamist political party cadres, and religious sermons run by Indonesian Salafi groups in Saudi Arabia have also been important factors for the shaping of Salafi-ness, Wahhabi-ness, or Islamist-ness among Indonesian students. In fact, there are a large number of Indonesian students, of both Islamic and non-Islamic studies, who join religious sermons, Qur'anic studies classes, and any religious meetings run by Indonesian Salafi groups in the kingdom. They usually invite Indonesian Salafi preachers and teachers (either from Indonesia or Saudi Arabia) to give Islamic lectures and sermons in cities where there is a great number of Indonesian inhabitants. They also provide Qur'anic and religious classes for Indonesian children whose parents are professional expatriates (lecturers or staff of universities or engineers of Saudi companies). Actually, these religious sermons, Qur'anic studies circles, and Islamic lectures have been designed for Indonesians in general not just for students. The students do not only attend Indonesian–run religious sermons, they also join religious sermons and lectures run by Saudi Salafi clerics in homes, mosques, and other places. According to some informants, there is a tendency for Indonesians who learn Islam through *majelis pengajian* (informal religious sermons) with Salafi clerics, shaikhs, or ulama to be more radical, militant, and conservative than those who study Islamic sciences through the class system with university professors.[15]

Fourth, there are a great deal of Indonesian Muslim students who have essentially already become Salafi, Wahhabi, or Islamist before their departure to Saudi Arabia since they have long been educated in Indonesia's Salafi, Wahhabi, or Islamist educational institutions such as Al-Irsyad, Pesantren Darun Najah, Pondok Modern Gontor, Pondok Pesantren Imam Bukhari, Islamic Center Bin Baz, Ma'had Al Birr, Pondok Pesantren Hidayatullah, and Pondok Pesantren Khusnul Khotimah, among others.[16] Students from these Islamic learning centers are able to continue their studies in Saudi Arabia because of networks or well established contact they (the institutions and their teachers and owners) have long built with Saudi academic institutions.

Scholarships for these students are not always provided by the Saudi government, Saudi private agencies, and Saudi individuals. Many are actually provided by Indonesian governmental institutions, Indonesian private agencies, and Indonesian individuals or the two (Saudi and Indonesia) share financing of scholarships to cover tuition, airfare tickets, stipends, and living expenses in the kingdom. Yayasan Maghfirah Bina Ummat (YMBU),[17] Jakarta, for instance, has begun to provide scholarships for talented students interested in studying Islam at the IUM. This foundation has signed an MoU with the Islamic University. Part of the agreement is that the YMBU will provide scholarship grants of SR 30,000 per year while the university will provide airfare tickets, stipends (SR 800 per month), books, and so on. Currently, there are about fifty students studying at the Islamic University under this scholarship scheme.

Upon completing their Islamic studies, they would tend to introduce, develop, and become strong advocates of multiple Islamic forms and *madhahib* (schools of thought) depending on their religious beliefs, practices, and understanding, or on what they received from their Islamic teachers and scholars. Students receive Islamic training from teachers and scholars of traditionalist Maliki, "moderate" Shafi'i, rationalist Hanafi, or reformist Hanbali madhahib, they would tend to introduce, practice, and propagate Islam in accordance with these schools of thought. Students who obtain Sufism and particular Sufi orders, would develop their Sufism and Sufi orders. Also, students who receive their Islamic training from Salafi teachers and scholars would also tend to introduce, develop, and become the strongest advocates of Islamic Salafism, puritanism, or Wahhabism in Indonesia.

Later on, the militant factions of the Salafi groups created and raised tension and conflict with the local Muslim and non-Muslim populations in many areas in the archipelago from West Java to Papua. There are at least three reasons for the tension and conflict. First, most Indonesians have practiced religious tolerance where the local populace have lived side by side in peaceful coexistence for many years, while the Salafi groups mostly practice religious intolerance and anti-pluralism, and consider that Islam should be superior to other religions. Second, most local societies embrace "nominal religion" combining religious doctrines and teachings with local traditions and cultures, while the Salafis are mostly intolerant with locals because they believe that local traditions and cultures (including customs that have been practiced by local societies for centuries) are irreligious, un-Islamic or *bid'ah* (innovative and heretical practices); thereby practicing them will desecrate or disgrace the purity of Islamic doctrine. This trend does not only happen in Islam but also in other religion, particularly Christianity which also has strong puritanical groups. Third, the Salafis mostly admire "Arab cultures" and want to export them to Indonesian societies while at the same time they bitterly oppose their own "Indonesian cultures."

Furthermore, most of the Salafi students received their academic training at the IUM, which since its inception in the early 1960s has been the vanguard of Salafism and Wahhabism (see Chapter 3), and Al Imam Muhammad bin Saud Islamic University and its branch in Jakarta (Lembaga Ilmu Pengetahuan Islam dan Bahasa Arab), are other centers for Salafism. However, it should be noted again, that it is mistaken to conclude that all alumni of these two institutions have become Salafis, radicals, and supporters of strict conservative forms of Islam. In fact, some notable alumni of these two Islamic universities have been the backbone of traditionalist, moderate, or even progressive Islam in Indonesia. How and why have alumni of the same Islamic universities turned into different expressions, practices, and understandings of Islam? I will explain these interesting dynamics in Chapter 6.

The second finding of this chapter that needs to be underlined is that there are multiple types of Salafism expressed by the Indonesian students (and alumni of Saudi universities and Islamic learning institutions, see Chapter 6), ranging from "apolitical Salafis" to "political Salafis." Some of these Salafi groups are involved in tension and conflict with one another due to having different interpretations, understandings, practices, and purposes concerning how Islam should ideally be interpreted, understood, and implemented in the society. Some Salafi groups said that Islam should be far removed from political practices, focusing only on moral, religious, and theological issues. They affirm that, for Muslims, involvement in political organizations, parties, and activities are *haram* (unlawful) under Islamic law. This is among the reason why some Indonesian Salafi students in the kingdom strongly criticize Bachtiar Nasir, chairman of the Indonesian alumni of the IUM, due to his involvement in political movements. Indeed, Saudi's Indonesian students were split in response to a series of mass marches and political protests aimed at toppling a Christian Jakarta governor, Basuki Tjahaja Purnama, as well as the Indonesian President Joko Widodo, organized by groups of militant Islamists and Salafis.

Other Salafi groups, moreover, are keen to struggle for Islam through the political sphere to realize an Islamic government or Islamic state aimed at maintaining what they call "the unity of Islamic umma." Still, other Salafi groups are devoted to purifying Islam from all local cultures and traditions which they dub un-Islamic or irreligious, which in turn disturbs the purity of the Islamic faith. Others still preserve some local cultural practices which they consider still good and beneficial for Muslim societies and that do not contradict Islamic teachings. Sometimes the students were involved in harsh debates due to small things such as whether or not a Muslim should grow a beard, whether a cloak should be below or above the ankle, whether the status of the sadah group (descendants of Prophet Muhammad) should (or should not) be venerated or given priority, whether corruption is a bad or good practice, and so forth.

It is also central to underline that each group (and individual) tended to claim to be "more Salafi" than others meaning that each claimed to be a more devout and authentic follower of early generations of Islam or *salaf al-shalih*, which is the root of the word "Salafism." Some describe themselves as, or prefer to be called, "Salafiyyah," not "Salafism" since the latter has been associated with new reformist groups, mostly following the Hanbali school, which has very strict understandings and practices of Islam. The term "salafiyyah" has long been used by members and followers of Nahdlatul Ulama (called "Nahdliyyin"). Many clerics (or kiais) of Nahdlatul Ulama name their traditional Islamic learning institutions (i.e., pesantren) "salafiyyah" (sometimes "salafiyyah Syafi'iyyah") as a sign that the pesantren follows (and is based on) intellectual traditions of early Muslim generations (aslaf) and teaches of classical Arabic Islamic texts of the Sunni school, particularly from Shafii madhhab. The contest of the Salafi discourses is obvious and ubiquitous across the country. While students and alumni of IUM or Al-Imam Muhammad bin Saud Islamic University usually follow or embrace Salafism, those of Ribat Sayyid Alawi (or Umm al-Qura University) usually become supporters of Salafiyyah. While both share a common regard for their disagreement with liberalism, pluralism, secularism, or Shiism, the followers of salafiyyah are very critical toward Wahhabism which is not always the case for those of Salafism. Some issues on which the "salafiyyah group" disagrees with the "Salafism group" includes, among others, local religious-cultural practices (e.g., *tahlilan, kenduren, adat*, etc.), the veneration of Prophet Muhammad's descendants (sadah/ashraf), and the practice of Sufism and Sufi orders.

Third, the Indonesian students in Saudi Arabia do not always study the Islamic sciences and pursue degrees in these fields. In recent decades, a large number of non-Islamic studies students from various parts of Indonesia have studied in the kingdom pursuing degrees (from BS to PhD) in multiple disciplines and focusing on various academic programs from the hard sciences and chemical engineering to geophysics and computer science. Since this group is relatively new, their role and contributions in Indonesia are not visible yet. This is, for sure, in sharp contrast with the Islamic studies group. Interestingly, although they are not Islamic studies students, some of them have been very active in various Islamic programs such as, among others, religious sermons, Islamic gatherings, and Qur'anic recitation clubs, all of which have been organized by Indonesian Muslim groups.

These groups, some of which are supported by Indonesia's Islamist political party and Salafi groupings, have conducted regular meetings in cities where many Indonesians reside. The organizers do not only invite Indonesian Salafi speakers who live in Saudi Arabia but also Salafi preachers from Indonesia. Due to becoming regular participants of these Salafi-supported Islamic meetings and sermons (*pengajan*), some non-Islamic studies students have become devout adherents of Salafism and Wahhabism which is sometimes stricter and more radical than the practices of the Islamic studies students. Other non-Islamic studies students focus on developing their research and academic interests in the "secular sciences" and are not interested in following particular religious/Islamic streams, including Salafism, although they try to be a devout Muslim by performing the hajj and umra pilgrimage, fasting during Ramadlan, and regularly praying in mosques. Some of them also wear *jalabiyah* (Arab-style robe) and grow a beard. However, they are not interested in spreading and advocating Salafi practices and ideas into Indonesian society.

Conclusion

It is now clear that Saudi's Indonesian students are incredibly diverse and complex in terms of their motives and objectives of learning, social backgrounds, fields of study, academic and research interests, religious understandings, organizational affiliations, and political orientations; therefore, generalizing them would be seriously misleading. It is true that some students, upon completing their studies, became sturdy advocates of particular forms of religious conservatism, fanaticism, Salafism, or Islamism. But, this phenomenon, it should be noted, are only "one among many," in part because there are a great deal of Indonesian students in the kingdom who do not follow strict forms of Islam. This chapter also shows that Saudi Arabia is not the only agent that has shaped the Salafi-ness of Indonesian students since many students have already become devout followers of Salafism long before their arrival in Saudi Arabia, while others were formed by Saudi's Indonesian Salafi communities. Last but not least, this chapter also indicates the growing number of Indonesian graduate students in the kingdom who learn various non-Islamic subjects such as the hard sciences, engineering, geophysics, computer science, medicine, among others, which adds to the complexity of Indonesian students in Saudi Arabia. Whatever their differences, the students seem to agree that Saudi is a "sacred geography," a fine center of Islamic learning, and a good place to work and live.

Chapter 6

SAUDI ARABIA-TRAINED INDONESIAN ISLAMIC SCHOLARS AND ACTIVISTS: CONSERVATIVE AND PROGRESSIVE

In Chapter 5 I explain the plurality and complexity of Indonesian students in Saudi Arabia. This chapter will specifically focus on the discussion of the role and contributions of alumni of Saudi's Islamic learning institutions (university/college or non university/college) in the development of Islam and Muslim cultures in Indonesia. It is common knowledge and a common understanding among Indonesian scholars, foreign specialists of Indonesian studies, and Indonesian societies in general that the alumni of Saudi Islamic universities are at the forefront of conservatism, intolerance, and radicalism. It is also a common fallacy that everyone studying in Saudi academic institutions (including their Indonesian branches) will become a religious cleric, teacher, preacher, or Islamic scholar in the future.

In fact, there are many graduates who have become government officials, policymakers, politicians, businessman, and high-ranking bureaucrats, among others. Whereas it is accurate to say that some leaders of radical and intolerant groups in the country have been trained in Saudi (or Saudi-affiliated Islamic learning institutions), generalizing Saudi alumni as conservative, intolerant, anti-pluralist, and radical is inaccurate and misleading. In reality, many graduates in the country have been the vanguard of the ideas of democracy, liberalism, secularism, moderation, tolerance, pluralism, and progressivism. Indeed, conservatism and radicalism in Indonesia have nothing to do with Saudi academic institutions. In fact, some conservative, intolerant, and radical Islamic leaders in the country graduated in Egypt, Sudan, Yemen, Morocco, Tunisia, India, Pakistan, Malaysia, or even the United States, to name a few.

Why and how do they play a different role? What factors contribute to these differing ideas and practices? How do Indonesian local societies respond to the surge of Islamic conservatism and radicalism? Focusing on both radical-conservative and moderate-progressive groups (of any profession), this chapter will examine these dynamics and the recent development of graduates in order to understand the plurality and complexity of Saudi-educated Islamic activists and scholars. This chapter, in particular, will analyze some contemporary leading figures of both camps who have been trained in either Saudi Islamic universities and schools or their branches in Indonesia such as, most notably, LIPIA (the Institute for the Study of Islamic Sciences and Arabic Language in Jakarta), a branch of

Riyadh-based Al Imam Muhammad bin Saud Islamic University; will depict their specialties; and will examine their role in Indonesian society. The aim of this chapter is to gain a wide-ranging knowledge, perspective, and understanding of the diversity of Saudi graduates in Indonesia.

It is central to underscore that the plurality and complexity of understandings, interpretations, thoughts, and practices among the graduates are not a new phenomenon in the history of Indonesian Islam. Conservative and progressive interpretations of Islam had already taken been around for centuries, and, in many cases, supporters of both camps were involved in harsh debates and tensions such as the rivalry between sharia-minded clerics versus tasawuf/Sufism-oriented masters, followers of particular *tariqa* (Sufi orders), or *adat*-oriented ulama; orthodox (*kaum putihan*) versus heterodox Muslims ("syncretic Muslims"), pro-colonial versus anti-colonial Muslims, and reformists versus traditionalists, among others (see, e.g., Azra 1992). This chapter will only focus on contemporary Muslim individuals of both groups. Furthermore, it is important to note that the degree of conservatism and extremism differs from one group to another, and, as usual, they are far from being monolithic.

This is to say that, although they share some Islamic knowledge, cultures, and practices, they differ from one another on some fundamental issues such as those concerning the loyalty to the government, Indonesian state ideology and Constitution, Jihadism, women's rights, civil rights (including non-Muslim's), citizenship, interreligious pluralism, nationalism, the implementation of *Perda Syariat* (sharia-based regional laws), public morality, Muslims' public dress code, local customs, and many others. Some conservative individuals and groups, moreover, express their difference and disagreement through intolerance, and by taking radical and violent action against other groups and individuals whom they dub un-Islamic, irreligious, or deviant, whereas others tend to avoid clashes and violence using only "verbal violence" through harsh comments and offensive *da'wa* (Islamic propagation) against opposing groups and individuals. Some groups and individuals, furthermore, only emphasize theological and religious issues, whereas others are actively engaged in sociopolitical matters, and many times they mobilize the Muslim masses to join their campaigns such as Bachtiar Nasir, chairman of the Islamic University of Medina Alumni Association, who mobilized various Muslim groups to get involved in a series of religiopolitical protests against Jakarta Christian Governor Basuki Tjahaja Purnama.

There are many contemporary conservative and radical individuals, some of whom will be highlighted here, who graduated from Saudi universities or LIPIA and who played a vital role in preaching and spreading Islam as well as radicalizing Indonesian Muslim societies. They include, but are not limited to, the following figures: Ja'far Umar Talib, Abu Nida, Muhammad Rizieq Syihab, Hidayat Nur Wahid, Yazid bin Abdul Qadir Jawas, Bachtiar Nasir, Khalid Basalamah, Firanda Andirja, Reza Basalamah, Najih Maimun Zubair, Abdullah Taslim, Abdullah Zaen, Ali Musri Semjan Putra, Abu Yahya Badrussalam, Muhamamd Arifin bin Badri, Abdullah Saleh Ali Hadrami, Muhamamd Abduh Tuasikal, Erwandi Tarmizi, Armen Halim Naro, Abu Ubaidah Yusuf, Ahmad Ridwan, Khalid

Syamhudi, Musyaffa Addiriny, Abu Zubair al-Hawaary, Abu Hudzaifah al-Atsary, Anas Burhanuddin, Ashim Musthafa, Zainal Abidin Syamsuddin, Muhammad Wasitho, Fachruddin Nu'man, and Khalid Syamhudi, among many others. Again, they vary in terms of the implementation of "Islamic Salafi-ness" in everyday life in which some are stricter, more radical, and more conservative than others.

Equally important, moreover, although not as many as in the conservative and radical group, there are numerous Saudi graduates who embrace moderate, tolerant, and progressive forms of Islam, which is in sharp contrast with the names mentioned previously. Unlike the figures listed above, this group in many ways are advocates of interfaith and intrareligious tolerance, civic pluralism, local traditions and cultures, nationalism and patriotism, citizenship culture, democracy, individual and societal rights, and women's rights and feminism, among many others. This group is also against any intolerant, anti-pluralist, extremist, and terrorist acts in society. They, furthermore, disagree with the idea of the Islamic state and the formal implementation of Perda Shariat since potentially it will bring tension and conflict to society. They are also defenders of Indonesian state ideology (*Pancasila*) and the Constitution (UUD 1945). As with the conservative and radical group, the moderate and progressive group also vary regarding their views, thoughts, interpretations, and understandings about Islam and societal issues. They include the following names: Said Aqil Siradj, Ahsin Sakho Muhammad, Ali Mustafa Ya'qub, Satria Effendi, Masyhuri Naim, Hanif Ismail, Ahmad Fahmi, Abdur Rozaq Pamekasan, Said Jauhari Jember, Muslih Abdul Karim, Asrorun Ni'am Sholeh, Muhammadun, Muhammad Cholil Nafis, Maghfur Usman Cepu, Kiai Mahfudz Lombok, Ulil Abshar-Abdalla, Abdul Adzim Irshad, Sayyid Aqil Al Munawar, Imdadun Rahmat, Ahmad Baso, Kiai Sirojan Wates, Kiai Rasyim Jogjakarta, Kiai Bakrun, and Wawan Gunawan, among many others.

Let me briefly highlight some of the individuals both radicals and conservatives and moderates and progressives.

The radicals and conservatives

There has been a great number of Saudi graduates who follow the strict practices of Salafism and who have been the backbone of conservatism or even radicalism. The term Salafism, it is worth noting, arose nearly one century after Muhammad bin Abdul Wahhab (the founder of "Wahhabism") had succeeded in exerting his influence throughout the Arabian Peninsula. At first, Salafism, pioneered by such leading figures as Jamaluddin al-Afghani (1839–1837), Muhammad Abduh (1849–1905), and Muhammad Rashid Rida (1865–1945), referred specifically to the reform movement centered in Egypt that introduced new approaches to Islam in response to the contemporary demand of modernity. Accordingly, Salafism resembled Islamic reform. This Salafism or Islamic reform was not merely a continuation of the older tradition of revitalization of Islamic faith and practices. Rather, it incorporated a new dimension, formulated to "integrate modern thought and institutions with Islam" (Rahman 1969: 222).

This reformist, modernist movement has influenced many Muslims across the world. Many Muslim organizations from the Middle East to South and Southeast Asia (including Indonesia) have been formed based on the notions of this type of Salafism. However, unlike any reformist, modernist organizations that emerged across the Muslim world, the Salafi Da'wa movement is squarely within the puritanical classic Salafi-Wahhabi tradition. Emad Eldin Shahin (1995: 463–64) said that this Salafi movement is marked by its concern with matters of creed and morality, such as strict monotheism, divine attributes, the purification of Islam from accretions, anti-Sufism, and the development of the moral integrity of the individual. To a large extent, according to Noorhaidi Hasan, an expert of Indonesia's Salafi movement studies, this type of Salafism can be conceptualized as a form of "reconstituted Wahhabism." This is, Hasan has argued, indicated by the determination of its proponents to codify and follow more systematically the thoughts formulated by both the classic Wahhabi aspirators (i.e., Ahmad bin Hanbal, Ahmad ibn Taimiyyah, and Muhammad ibn al-Qayyim al-Jauziyyah) and contemporary Wahhabi authorities (e.g., Abdul Aziz bin Abdullah bin Baz and Muhammad Nasiruddin al-Albani). In fact, it was part of the transnational Salafi society, representing the most puritanical Saudi style of Islam. It is obvious that the term Salafi itself has been used as the banner of the movement because of the pejorative connotation of the term Wahhabi among many Muslims in the world, thus making it crucial for political convenience (Hasan 2007, 2010a).

The Salafi figures highlighted here, either from radical factions or less-violent groups, are those linked to this Saudi type of Salafism. One of the notorious figures in this camp is Muhammad Rizieq Syihab (known as Habib Rizieq), the founder and head (now the "Grand Imam") of the Front Pembela Islam (FPI, the Islamic Defenders Front), one of Indonesia's infamous intolerant and radical Muslim groups. Rizieq was born in Jakarta in 1965 to Husein bin Shihab and Syarifah Sidah al-Attas, both were of mixed Betawi and Yemeni Hadrami descent. After completing his high school education, Rizieq was trained at the Saudi-funded LIPIA (the Institute for Islamic and Arabic Studies) in Jakarta. Considered by his neighbors to be a troublesome youth with a penchant for getting into fights, he was sent by his family to study at King Saud University (Riyadh), majoring in *usul al-fiqh* (Islamic legal theory) and education, in order to "pacify" and "straighten him out." Rizieq studied and completed his degree in the field of Islamic law. After finishing his studies and spending a year teaching at a high school in Saudi Arabia, he returned home and, together with his Arab fellows, established and transformed the FPI, a violent extremist organization (Fealy and White 2014: 201–02).

Founded just three months after Suharto's collapse from his throne, FPI made its first public appearance during the political turmoil and Indonesian transition of 1998 as part of the pro-Habibie Pam Swakarsa militia group established by General Wiranto (now coordinating minister for politics and security affairs) to curtail the pro-reform student movement. Soon after, the group was involved in a bloody confrontation with Ambonese gangsters in Ketapang that left fifteen dead. Since its founding in 1998, FPI has been responsible for numerous attacks on those they deem religiously, socially, or sexually deviant. Known for its motto

"Live Honorably or Die as a Martyr," FPI's initial aims were twofold: (1) to fight against the plague of drugs, pornography, gambling, and prostitution, which FPI deems as vice (*maksiat*) and "public immorality," and (2) to react toward suspected human rights transgressions against Muslims.[1]

Since its inception, Rizieq Syihab, along with FPI members and activists, often color mass media headlines for their disgraceful activities and violent acts against innocent civilians and religious groups in some major cities and small towns across the country. For the sake of, or, more precisely, the claim of, "commanding right and forbidding wrong" (*amr ma'ruf nahi munkar*), which is derived from the hallowed Qur'anic injunction (see, for instance, Sura Luqman ch. 31, v. 17), FPI, which has branches in several major cities in the country, has moved beyond their initial objectives, not only combating what they call the "vice" but also battling against Christian evangelicals and non-conformist Muslim groups they carelessly dub as deviant, sacrilegious, and liberal, and as infidels such as Ahmadiyah, Shia, Salamullah, Satariyah, al-Qiyadah, and the Liberal Islam Network, among many others. Of all of the local religious sects and beliefs, the Ahmadiyah community probably has suffered the most: its mosques razed, its offices plundered, and its followers expelled out of their homes. Survey results from various research centers and academic institutions such as, among others, the Wahid Institute, the Maarif Institute for Culture and Humanity, and Gadjah Mada University's Center for Religious and Cross-Cultural Studies have placed FPI on the top list as perpetrators of religious violence, extremism, and anti-tolerance and pluralism in post-Suharto Indonesia.

Still, while exploiting public moral anxieties to skirmish centers of vice and immorality, Rizieq Syihab and FPI have challenged prodemocracy students, anti-extremist government officials, pro-peace religious leaders, progressive scholars, human rights activists, and defenders of Muslim tolerance and religious pluralism from both state and society. Syihab's intolerant actions and FPI's brutality have indeed met with widespread criticism and peaceful resistance from various groups and individuals throughout the archipelago ranging from local ordinary villagers and townspeople to academics, grassroots activists, interfaith practitioners, prodemocracy leaders, and the country's moderate Islamic social organizations such as Nahdlatul Ulama (NU; lit. "awakening of religious scholars") and Muhammadiyah.[2] Notwithstanding the pervasive popular resistance, disparagement, and condemnation, FPI's intolerant and violent actions continue to persist.[3] Lastly, FPI sympathizers tried to commit riots in Pontianak of West Kalimantan. However, the situation for the moment is quite peaceful since the police, under the direction of General Tito Karnavian, take firm actions against FPI and Rizieq Syihab, who has recently been charged with numerous cases ranging from pornography and abasement of the Christian faith to disdain of the Indonesian state symbols.

Ja'far Umar Thalib (1961–), a descendant of a religious Yemeni-Madurese family and one of Indonesia's Salafi ideologues, is another notorious figure of Saudi-trained alumni. Born into a Hadrami (Arab) family in Malang, East Java, and raised in the puritanical atmosphere of al-Irsyad (i.e., an Indonesian reformist, modernist Muslim organization predominant among the Hadramis, see Mobini-Kesheh 1999), Ja'far Thalib was the founder of the Laskar Jihad (the Jihad Force), a Java-based jihadist group and a paramilitary wing of the FKAWJ (a Sunni communication forum) whose militia members were fiercely involved in the battleground during the Maluku (Moluccas) Christian–Muslim violence from 1999 to 2002. Unlike Rizieq Syihab and his FPI members and sympathizers, who have been involved in routine intolerant and violent actions against individuals or groups whom they considered sinful, immoral, or religiously deviant, Ja'far Thalib and his Laskar Jihad members were only engaged in what they called a "jihad movement" in the Moluccas (Al Qurtuby 2016). Since that time, many members of this jihadist group have been pacified, while others joined other organizations. Since the Laskar Jihad was dissolved by the Indonesian government in late 2002, following the Bali bombings, Ja'far Thalib returned to lead his Islamic boarding school (Pesantren Ihya al-Sunnah) in Jogjakarta.

A central figure who defined the dynamics of the Salafi movement in Indonesia, Ja'far Thalib was educated at several reformist conservative Islamic learning institutions including the al-Irsyad al-Islamiyah School (Malang, East Java), Pesantren Persis (Bangil, East Java), LIPIA (Jakarta), the Maududi Islamic Institute (Pakistan), and at a madrasah in Dammaj (Yemen), where he studied under the guidance of Shaikh Muqbil bin Hadi al-Wadi'i, Yemen's Salafi ideologue par excellence. A typical cadre of Islamism, Ja'far Thalib was an ambitious youth with a rebellious streak. When he studied at LIPIA, a Jakarta-based institute of higher learning established and directly sponsored by Saudi Arabia, Ja'far was involved in tensions and disagreements with his teachers on some fundamental issues. After falling out with a member of the teaching staff, the LIPIA director Abdul Aziz Abdullah al-Amr paved the way for him to study at the Maududi Islamic Institute in Lahore, Pakistan, in 1987, in which he joined forces with the Afghan mujahidin to defeat the Red Army of the Soviet Union. Reportedly, while Ja'far engaged in the battle in Afghanistan, he supported the radical factions of both Abdul Rasul Sayyaf (founder of Jami'at-i Islami) and Gulbuddin Hikmatyar (founder of Hizb-i Islami). However, the puritanical insights cultivated previously at al-Irsyad, Persis, and LIPIA eventually led him to join the Jama'at al-Da'wa ila al-Qur'an wa Ahl al-Hadith (the Society for Call to the Qur'an and the People of Hadith), a strict Salafi faction and Saudi Arabian "principality" led by Jamil al-Rahman. This faction had special relations with the Pakistani Ahl al-Hadith, a reformist movement founded in India in the nineteenth century that shares many similarities with Wahhabism. In brief, while Ja'far was in Afghanistan, he not only learned how to use arms and to battel against the Soviets but was exposed to Salafi-Wahhabi teachings under the auspices of Shaikh Jamil al-Rahman.

When the Afghan War ended in 1989, Ja'far returned to Indonesia and directed the al-Irsyad Islamic School in Salatiga, Central Java, before leaving for Yemen in 1991 to study with Shaikh Muqbil bin Hadi al-Wadi'i, a Salafi ideologue and scholar who was supported by the radical Islamist Islah Party. In addition to Jamil al-Rahman and Muqbil bin Hadi al-Wadi'i, Ja'far also learned Salafi teachings from Saudi prominent Islamic scholars, most notably Abdul Aziz Abdullah bin Baz and

Muhammad Nasiruddin al-Albani, when Ja'far performed the hajj (Umam 2006: 1–26). After completing his educational journeys in multiple countries, Ja'far came back to Indonesia in 1993. Having widened and deepened his knowledge of Salafi-Wahhabi, Ja'far was committed to spreading Salafi thoughts in Indonesia through da'wa and education. To accomplish his mission, accordingly, Ja'far established a pesantren, named Ihya al-Sunnah, in Jogjakarta, which is arguably Indonesia's oldest Salafi-Wahhabi Islamic boarding school. In this pesantren, Ja'far teaches Salafi-Wahhabi thoughts and introduces the works of classic and contemporary Salafi-Wahhabi scholars, including some written by his former teachers. Within this historical trajectory, it is thus understandable why he founded the Laskar Jihad to assist Muslims fighting against Christian militias in Ambon and other areas of the Moluccas.

It is important to note that Ja'far was not alone in this regard. There were several Indonesian students of Saudi universities who joined the mujahidin in the Afghan war in the 1980s. The appeal for volunteers to wage jihad in Afghanistan emerged as the first serious challenge to foreign students studying in Saudi Arabia with grants from the kingdom. As we know, at the time, Saudi, along with the United States and Pakistan, supported the Afghan mujahidin to battle against the communist Soviets. Many young Arabs, including university students, had been mobilized to engage in the combat zone to oppose the red army. They were required to prove their commitment to Islam. It is hence unsurprising that after completing their studies, many such students decided to take part in the Afghan War. The same holds true for students from Indonesia.

Hasan (2007: 89–90) notes that a dozen Indonesian students preferred not to return to Indonesia directly but to spend some time in Afghanistan to join the Afghan mujahidin in combating the Soviets. Participating in the jihad in Afghanistan turned out to be a sort of fieldwork for the students. The return of the LIPIA graduates who had completed their studies in Saudi Arabia and had undergone their baptism of fire in the Afghan War marked the birth of a new Salafi-Wahhabi generation in Indonesia. Among them are some noted names in Salafi circles such as Chamsaha Sofwan (known as Abu Nida), Ahmad Faiz Asifuddin, and Ainur Rafiq Ghufran, among others. They were sent to teach in various Islamic schools affiliated to the Dewan Dakwah Islamiyah Indonesia (DDII), one of the most prominent da'wa organizations in modern Indonesia linked to reformist Muslim groups. These schools include Pesantren al-Mukmin (Solo, Central Java), Pesantren Wataniyya Islamiyya (Kebumen, Central Java), and Pesantren al-Furqan (Gresik, East Java).

Later on, some Salafis of Saudi-trained universities were split and involved in conflicts, mainly due to different understandings and interpretations of some fundamental Salafi doctrines and ideology, distinctive focuses and purposes of the movement among them, as well as competition over the Salafi Da'wa movement's legitimate leader and authority. Some argued that submission to sharia does not require the founding of an Islamic state since it is not a priority, while others considered it an important medium for Muslims in order to consistently implement the sharia. Some believed that da'wa was the only acceptable form of politics;

thereby they refused the ideas of the *hizbiyya*, meaning participation in practical politics, which is considered to be a form of *bid'a* (unwholesome innovation) and *shirk* (polytheism) that oppose the fundamental tenets of the Islamic religion. Others, however, insisted that the hizbiyya is an integral part of the Salafi Da'wa movement. Moreover, some Saudi-trained Islamic studies graduates claimed to be more authentic Salafis who are committed to the movement's main goal of purity than other Salafi groups. Since then, clear-cut differences have been drawn between the Salafis and activists of such Islamist organizations as the Muslim Brotherhood (Ikhwanul Muslimin), Hizbut Tahrir Indonesia, and the home-grown NII (the Indonesian Islamic State), a movement which had itself emerged in the 1970s and since then has actively campaigned, clandestinely, for the founding of an Islamic state in Indonesia.

Generally speaking, the group was split into two camps: (1) da'wa-oriented Salafis who are less-engaged with (and have no interest in) political practices, focusing mainly on religious–theological–cultural issues, and (2) hizbiyya-driven Salafis who are actively involved in political activities and have a strong interest in establishing a political order in the country. The first camp, led by Ja'far Umar Thalib, included the following notable names: Usamah Faisal Mahri, Abu Munzir Zul Akmal, Ainur Rafiq Ghufron, and Agus Rudianto, among others. The second group, led by Abu Nida, included the notable names of Ahmad Faiz Asifuddin, Yusuf Usman Baisya, Muhammad Yusuf Harun, Ahmad Zawawi, and Abdul Hakim Abdat, among others. The trigger of the split, which took place in the 1990s, was what Hassan (2014: 7–10) has called "the Sururiyya issue"; named after Muhammad Surur bin Nayef Zain al-Abidin, one of the strongest critics of Saudi Arabia. Criticizing Saudi Arabia for its decision to invite American troops into the kingdom following the Gulf crisis in 1990, Muhammad Surur was condemned by prominent Saudi Salafi authorities linked to Shaikh Abdul Aziz bin Abdullah bin Baz (1910–1999) as a proponent of the takfiri doctrine,[4] developed by Egyptian Muslim Brotherhood (Ikhwanul Muslimin) thinkers such as, most notably, Sayyid Qutub (1906–1966), one of the Brotherhood's main ideologues, who was consequently expelled from the kingdom.

Ja'far Thalib and his fellows accused Abu Nida and his group as the "Sururis," a term referring not only followers of Muhammad Surur bin Nayef Zain al-Abidin but also activists, supporters, and sympathizers of the Brotherhood who utilize Salafi only as a mantle but actually believed in the takfiri doctrine (see Hassan 2007, 2010a, 2014). From this brief historical sketch, it is obvious that Ja'far Thalib and his group wanted to distance themselves from Abu Nida, Yusuf Baisya and others whom they dubbed the "betrayers" of (Saudi) Salafi doctrines due to their attachments to the doctrines of—and their links to—the Egyptian Brotherhood. Ja'far Thalib and his "followers" claimed that the "Salafi-ness" of Abu Nida and his group was only a camouflage to obscure their real political motives and objectives, namely pursuing the establishment of an Islamic state in Indonesia. Suffice to say that tensions and conflicts among the Indonesian Saudi-graduate Salafis grew from multiple factors ranging from religion to social politics.

However, it is vital to acknowledge that tensions and conflict between Ja'far Thalib and Abu Nida, along with their supporters, are not the only ones among the Saudi alumni. Due to their different ideas, opinions, thoughts, understandings, exegeses, schools, social groupings, or even political parties, these graduates have been involved in tensions and clashes with one another. Sometimes conflicts also take place due to each individual insisting on defending the ideas, opinions, or thoughts of their respected Islamic teachers (or Salafi scholars whom they follow) on particular issues. As well, it is also important to note that there are plenty of Salafi groups of Saudi graduates in the post Rizieq Syihab, Ja'far Thalib, and Abu Nida era, making Saudi-educated conservative and radical groups in Indonesia more complicated.

Due to limited space, I will only describe some notable figures outside the above circles (say, the new generation of post-Ja'far Thalib, Abu Nida, or Rizieq Shihab) who have played a vital role and made a significant contribution in the introduction and development of Salafi and Islamic discourses in the country through da'wa, education, or publications. Some of these new figures are their disciples such as Dzulqarnain M. Sanusi, who was a former student of Ja'far Thalib when he learned Islam at the Pesantren Ihya al-Sunnah in Yogyakarta. It was through Ja'far's connections that Dzulqarnain left for Yemen, in the mid-1990s, to study Islam at the Ma'had Dar al-Hadith under the mentorship of Shaikh Muqbil bin Hadi al-Wadi'i, a former teacher of Ja'far and a renowned Salafi Islamist scholar. After completing his studies in Dammaj of northern Yemen in 1999, Dzulqarnain returned to Yogyakarta to teach in the Pesantren Ihya al-Sunnah while serving on an editorial board of *Salafi* magazine. After spending a year in Yogyakarta, he returned to his native city, Makassar in South Sulawesi. There, in 2000, Dzulqarnain founded Pesantren al-Sunnah, along with alumni of Dar al-Hadith (Yemen) and the Islamic University of Medina (IUM) such as Khidhir, Mustamin, and Luqman Jamal. In 2002, they founded *al-Nashihah* magazine.

Although Dzulqarnain did not receive a formal education from a Saudi university and madrasah, since 2004, he nonetheless was able to learn Islam informally with notable Saudi ulama such as Shaikh Rabi' bin Hadi al-Madkhali, Shaikh Ahmad bin Yahya al-Najmi, Shaikh Shalih bin Abdillah Al Fauzan, and Shaikh Zaid bin Muhammad bin Hadi al-Madkhali, among others. In addition to teaching and preaching, Dzulqarnain also wrote several books, published by Pustaka al-Sunnah, including a book about jihad and terrorism in which he criticizes the work of Imam Samudra, one of the people responsible for the Bali Bombings, which legalizes terrorism and suicide bombings as part of jihad movements.[5] Like Ja'far Thalib, Duzlqarnain has been engaged in critical debates and disagreements with other Salafi groups. Dzulqarnain once reminded Muslims not to follow Salafi-linked media channels: Rodja Radio and Rodja TV.

Another noteworthy name in this new circle is Ali Musri Semjan Putra, the chairman of Sekolah Tinggi Dirasat Islamiyat Imam Syafii (STDIIS), a higher learning institution of Islamic studies in Jember, East Java. After completing his elementary and secondary education in his native West Sumatra (all Islamic schools of both madrasah and pesantren), Ali Musri continued his studies at

LIPIA and in the Faculty of Da'wa and Ushuluddin of the Islamic University of Medina (from undergraduate to doctorate, 1995–2007). Born in 1972 on the Island of Sumatra, Ali Musri has translated a selection of Arabic books authored by Salafi scholars into Bahasa Indonesia. A preacher and a columnist of several Salafi media outlets such as al-Sunnah, al-Furqan, and al-Dzakhirah, Ali Musri is very active in multiple Salafi-linked organizations and foundations such as Yayasan Darul Iman (Sumatra), Yayasan al-Najiyya (Sumatra), Yayasan Ibnul Qayyim (Makassar of Sulawesi), Yayasan al-Raudhah (Yogyakarta), and Yayasan Imam Syafii (Banyuwangi), among others.[6]

Abdullah Zaen bin Zaini Muhajjat, the director of Pesantren "Tunas Ilmu" in Purbalingga, Central Java, and a lecturer at the Sekolah Tinggi Dirasah Islamiyyah Imam Syafii, Jember, East Java,[7] is another figure who deserves to be mentioned in this camp. A graduate of Pondok Modern Darussalam Gontor, Ponorogo, East Jawa, Abdullah Zaen is an active preacher on YuFid TV, a noted Salafi television channel in Indonesia. From 2000 to 2009, Abdullah Zaen learned Islam at the IUM focusing on the study of *aqidah* (theology), *hadith*, and Dirasat Islamiyah. At IUM, Abdullah Zaen studied with some notable Islamic studies teachers including Shaikh Abdul Muhsin bin Hamad al-Abbad, Ibrahim bin Amir al-Ruhaili, Abdurrazaq bin Abdul Muhsin al-Abbad, Muhammad bin Khalifah al-Tamimi, Shalih bin Sa'ad al-Suhaimi, Shaikh Ubaid al-Jabiri, and Sulaiman bin Salimullah al-Ruhaili, among others. Abdullah Zaen has translated some works of his teachers into Bahasa Indonesia including *Khutab wa Mawaizh min Hajjah wa al-Wada'* (by Shaikh Abdurrazaq bin Abdul Muhsin al-Abbad) and *al-Takfir wa Dhawabithuh* (by Shaikh Ibrahim bin Amir al-Ruhaily). He also translated *al-Bayan al-Mufid fi mat tafaqa alaih Ulama Makkah wa Najd min Aqa'id al-Tauhid*, a compilation of thoughts of Najd and Meccan Islamic scholars on the defense of Islamic theology (*tauhid*) and the attack of shirk. In addition to translating Arabic works, Abdullah Zaen also wrote at least two books: (1) *Imam Syafii Menggugat Syirk: Pembelaan Imam Syafii dan Pengikutnya terhadap Tauhid* (Imam Shafii against Shirk: The Defense of Imam Syafii and his Followers toward Tauhid) and (2) *14 Contoh Praktek Hikmah dalam Berdakwah* (14 Examples of Wisdom Practices in Da'wa).

Erwandi Tarmizi (1974–) is another contemporary figure of Saudi-trained Salafi. After completing his studies at LIPIA, Erwandi continued his studies in the Faculty of Sharia at the Al-Imam Muhammad bin Saud Islamic University (both master's and doctorate) focusing on usul al-fiqh. Born and raised in Pekanbaru, Sumatra, Erwandi is known as a specialist in fiqh and usul al-fiqh, who has become a resource person on these topics in Salafi-related media such as Rodja Radio and Rodja TV (Bogor, West Java). In addition, he has been an adjunct lecturer in several universities such as the University of Ibn Khaldun, Institut Pertanian Bogor (a state-run agricultural university based in Bogor, West Java), and the Muhammadiyah University of Surakarta, among others. A columnist of several media outlets, Erwandi has been active in translating Arabic Islamic books into Bahasa Indonesia.[8]

Born in Lampung on Sumatra Island, Kholid Syamhudi is another figure of the most recent Salafi group. A graduate of Dar al-Hadith al-Khairiyya, Pakistan,

Kholid continued his Islamic education in the Faculty of Hadith at IUM, where he studied under the mentorship of prominent Salafi scholars such as Shaikh Rabi' bin Hadi al-Madkhali, Shaikh Abdul Muhsin al-Abbad, and Muhammad Khalifah al-Tamimi, among others. Before studying Islam in Pakistan and Saudi Arabia, Kholid studied for his undergraduate degree at Gadjah Mada University (a state-run public university in Yogyakarta) majoring in nuclear technique. A former head of Ma'had Jamilurrahman al-Salafi (Yogyakarya), he has been active in several Salafi-related organizations and educational institutions such as Ma'had Imam Bukhari, Ma'had Ibnu Abbas (Sragen), and Ma'had al-Ukhuwah (Sukoharjo). He is also a member of the editorial board of some Salafi magazines such as *al-Fata* and *al-Sunnah* (Solo), in addition to translating Arabic Islamic books into Bahasa Indonesia.[9]

The "duo Basalamah," namely Khalid Zeed Abdullah Basalamah[10] (known as Khalid Basalamah) and Syafiq Riza Hasan Basalamah (known as Syafiq Basalamah), also represent a new generation of Saudi-trained Indonesian Salafis. Although both have the same family name, indicating that the two came from Yemeni origins, Khalid and Syafiq are not relations. Having a long beard, a typical of Salafi follower, both Khalid and Syafiq Basalamah are very active Islamic preachers whose da'wa activities are conducted through various television channels focusing on Islam- and Muslim-related matters (e.g., Rodja TV, Insan TV, Wesal TV, Yufid TV, etc.), radio shows, Facebook online streaming, YouTube, or via "conventional da'wa" such as delivering religious sermons in mosques, Islamic schools, and other public places. For Indonesian Muslim society, the two Basalamah are known as "Ustad Wahabi." The term "ustad" in Indonesia does not refer to a school teacher or university professor but, more or less, resembles an Islamic preacher. Unlike other Salafis who are interested in political activism and practices, the main concerns of the two Basalamah are in the issues of theology, religion, culture, and societal morality. In other words, both Khalid Basalamah and Syafiq Basalamah are "apolitical Salafis."

As of their social-educational backgrounds and professions, they share similarities and differences. A graduate of the IUM, Khalid Basalamah, in particular, is building an Islamic center in Jakarta as a base for holding and developing Islamic and da'wa activities. Born in Makassar of Sulawesi Island in 1975, Khalid Basalamah obtained his academic training in Islamic studies not only in Medina but also in Universitas Muslim Indonesia (Sulawesi) and Universiti Tun Abdul Razak (Malaysia), for his doctorate. A firm religious believer and a devout follower of Salafism and Wahhabism, Khalid is not only a lively Islamic preacher but also active in various foundations, forums, and business activities. An active user of social media such as Facebook, Instagram, and Twitter, Khalid is chairman of the Jakarta-based Yayasan Ats Tsabat (Ats Tsabat Foundation) and the Forum for Sending an Islamic Preacher to Papua as well as the director of the Ajwad company that runs businesses from selling Gaharu wood and gold and Arab souvenirs to operating Middle Eastern-style restaurants. The company also has a publishing division that publishes Islamic books.

Unlike Khalid Basalamah, who received training from multiple academic institutions, Syafiq Basalamah gained his bachelor's degree, master's degree, and

PhD from the IUM. In addition, he was trained at Pesantren Islam al-Irsyad, Bondowoso , East Java. During his doctorate studies, he was active in attending religious sermons and lectures by Shaikh Abdul Mohsin bin Hamad al-Abbad al-Badr, Saudi's renowned Islamic scholar in Medina. Syafiq wrote a dissertation on the efforts of Islamic organizations in Indonesia to prevent the Christianization of the country. As a teacher at STDIIS in Jember, East Java, Syafiq is also an active preacher on Rodja TV and Rodja Radio, two famous channels for Indonesian Salafi groups.

The two Basalamah have similar concerns about how to purify Muslim's religious practices and thoughts in accordance with those of early Muslim generations (*salaf al-salih*); therefore both are anti-religious innovation (bid'ah) and against non-Arab local traditions and cultures since these are considered un-Islamic or irreligious, and away from the religious practices of Prophet Muhammad and the early Muslim generations. In this regard, it is unsurprising that both Khalid and Syafiq have often met with resistance from a variety of Muslim groups in Indonesia in part because their da'wa activities have often offended non-Salafi Muslims (e.g., Muslim, or *abangan*; Nahdliyin or followers of the NU; Sufis; Muslim adat or adat-oriented Muslims; nationalist Muslims, or *wong nasional*) who have practiced particular forms of Islam or have embedded local traditions and cultures into their religious practices, beliefs, and thoughts from generation to generation. Tensions and conflicts have often been aroused due to Khalid and Syafiq both attacking the theological and religious foundations of some Muslim groups in Indonesia. As a result, in some regions, the two have been prevented by local Muslims from da'wa activities.

Last but not least, I will briefly introduce Firanda Andirja Abidin (known as Ustad Firanda) in the camp of the new generation of Indonesian Salafi activists and scholars. Born in Surabaya, East Java, Firanda grew up on Papua Island, the most eastern part of the Indonesian archipelago. After completing his primary and secondary school education in Sorong, Papua Island, he studied engineering at Gadjah Mada University in Yogyakarta for a year. He then studied at the IUM, where he wrote a doctoral thesis on critiques toward Islamic textual foundations of moderate-progressive Indonesian Islamic preachers and scholars. An active Islamic preacher and a regular contributor for the Rodja Radio, Firanda teaches at the STDIIS, Jember, East Java. In addition, Firanda is also active in delivering religious sermons for Indonesian pilgrims in Masjid Nabawi, Medina. Some have said that it is through his connection with Shaikh Abdur Razzak bin Abdul Mohsin al-Abbad, his teacher at the IUM, that he can teach and give sermons (*pengajian*) in the Masjid Nabawi. Firanda has also invited Shaikh Abdur Razzak to Indonesia several times to give religious sermons or to speak on Rodja Radio.[11]

Like other radical Salafis, Firanda's da'wa activities have also met with resistance from a variety of local Muslim groups because his da'wa, in many ways, is in opposition with thoughts, beliefs, and practices of some Muslim groups in the country, especially those affiliated with the NU and other traditional and adat-based Muslims. Sensitive issues, such as the religious traditional practices of *tahlilan, manaqiban, mauludan, barzanjenan, dhiba'an,* visits to shrine, that have long been practiced by traditional and nominal Muslims in the country have become the main target of criticism of Salafi preachers such as Firanda since they consider these traditions as bid'ah, haram (unlawful), and un-Islamic. Accordingly, it is understandable if they are angry with Salafi preachers, activists, and scholars and cast-off their da'wa activities.[12]

The Salafi figures mentioned above are just a small example aiming to highlight a variety of contemporary Salafi circles and Islamic studies graduates of Saudi academic institutions that follow a strict form of Islam and therefore tend to be conservative, intolerant, and radical. However, it is worth mentioning that, as discussed in the previous paragraphs, these conservative and radical groups, including those who claim to be Salafi are not a monolithic group having similar opinions, thoughts, concerns, purposes, and agendas. In fact, this phenomenon is not unique to Indonesia. It takes place in many parts of the world. It has been a "public secret" particularly among Indonesian academic circles who have an interest in Islamic and Muslim studies that Salafi groups, more specifically, have been involved in disagreement, tension, and conflict with one another because of their dissimilar ideas, thoughts, opinions, and objectives on issues concerning how Islam should be understood, interpreted, implemented, and practiced in society, or how socio cultural-political phenomena and developments should be in line with the basic tenets of Salafi Islamic teachings. Interestingly, each Salafi group and individual, mostly graduated from Yemen or Saudi, also claims to be "more authentic and Salafi" than the others. They have accused each other of being deviant, *ahl al-bid'ah* or *mubtadi'* (doers of religious innovation), less-Salafi, and so forth. Sometimes they are involved in severe tension and harsh comments against each other because they are trying to defend their respective Islamic teachers and scholars who have been the target of criticism by other Salafi individuals and groups.

The phenomena of "intra-Salafi war" can be seen, for instance, between "Rodjaliyyun" (a term used for Salafi preachers who give religious sermons on— or support—Rodja Radio and Rodja TV) versus Dzulqarnain Muhammad Sanusi (Makassar) and Afifuddin (Gresik, East Java). Dzulqarnain and his group have also been involved in conflict with Luqman Ba'abduh (Jember, East Java) and his circle. Luqman Ba'abduh himself has been involved in harsh tension with Ali Musri, a former chairman of STDIIS, who accused Luqman of being a thief who thieved books worth 2 million Indonesian Rupiah. Again, a Salafi preacher from Malang, East Java, Agus Hasan Bashori has also been involved in a conflict with Abdurrahman al-Tamimi (Surabaya, East Java). Faisal Usamah Mahri and Ahmad Khadim from Malang have also strongly criticized Abdurrahman al-Tamimi. In Medan, Sumatra Island, pioneers of Salafism such as Ustad Indra, Usman Salih, Abu Ihsan, and Ali Nur have attacked each other due to differences of opinions and practices concerning some social–political–religious matters. Moreover, a group of Salafi preachers and scholars from Sekolah Tinggi Agama Islam (STAI) Ali Bin Abi Thalib in Surabaya, East Java, have been involved in disputes for a long time with such Salafi figures as Khalid Basalamah, Abdullah Hadrami, Agus Hasan

Bashari, and Ahmad Rofi'i, among others. Again, this is only a small example of how conservative, or even radical, religious groups are far from monolithic and united as some have assumed.

The moderates and progressives

Unlike the conservatives and radicals sketched above, the moderate and progressive groups of Saudi alumni are difficult to map, in part this is because of the limited resources available on this group. Abdul Adzim Irshad, a graduate of Umm al-Qura University, Mecca, said that there are a large number of Saudi graduates in Indonesia who have been the vanguard of inter- and intrareligious tolerance, moderation, and civic pluralism in society. However, he said, many of them live in the countryside, leading a traditional Islamic boarding school (Pondok Pesantren) in villages or suburban areas, besides being unfamiliar with the internet and social media.[13] It is true and intriguing to find out that, in contrast with contemporary Saudi-trained conservative or radical Salafis that are aware of the use of social media and the internet, most non-Salafi Saudi alumni and traditional moderate groups are unfamiliar with the internet and do not use it as a main medium to disseminate and market their ideas, understandings, and interpretations of Islam, Islamic history, Muslim practices, the Qur'an, hadith, and the like. Unlike the conservatives and radicals who aggressively use radio, television, YouTube, or Facebook live broadcast for their da'wa activities, the moderates and progressives still utilize traditional and conventional ways such as delivering religious sermons (*pengajian*) in villages, mosques, schools, offices, and other public sites with a limited audience. One of the reasons for doing this is because they want to get closer to and have a familiarity with their target audience, besides their unfamiliarity with modern technology. It is only recently that a small number of moderate figures have tried to employ social media and the internet for their religious sermons, Qur'anic recitations, Islamic book discussions, and other da'wa activities. But still, the conservatives and the radicals are far more aggressive and massive than the moderates and progressives in marketing their ideas and Islamic preaching through the internet and social media.

Apart from these shortcomings, there are indeed a substantial number of Saudi graduates who put an emphasis on the dissemination of Islamic moderation, tolerance, and pluralism and even have been the backbone of the notions of democracy, freedom, civil rights, and liberalism, some of whom will be briefly highlighted here. They include the following noted figures: Professor Dr. KH Said Aqil Siradj, Dr. KH Ahsin Sakho Muhammad, Professor Dr. KH Ali Mustafa Ya'qub, Professor Dr. Satria Effendi, Dr. KH Muhammad Masyhuri Naim, Professor Dr. Said Aqil Husin Al Munawar, KH Hanif Ismail, Dr. KH Ahmad Fahmi, KH Abdur Rozaq Pamekasan, KH Said Jauhari Jember, KH Muslih Abdul Karim, Dr. KH Asrorun Ni'am Sholeh, Muhammadun, Dr. KH Muhammad Cholil Nafis, Maghfur Usman Cepu, Kiai Mahfudz Lombok, Ulil Abshar-Abdalla, Abdul Adzim Irshad, and Imdadun Rahmat, among many others. Interestingly, many of these tolerant, pluralist graduates are members, followers, supporters, or sympathizers of the NU, which is arguably the world's largest Muslim social organization linked to the Sunni tradition with some 60 million members. It is, however, not to say that all NU leaders, activists, and followers are backers of religious tolerance and civic pluralism. In fact, some NU members were engaged in intolerant actions against religious minority groups (e.g., Shia, Ahmadi, local religious sects, etc.).

Apart from this unpleasant issue, it is indeed fascinating to find out that, as noted earlier, many of the NU's leading figures—both the early and the most recent generations—that have been the backbone of Indonesia's peace, tolerance, democracy, and pluralism, have received academic training from learning institutions in the cities of Mecca and Medina (known as Haramain), in addition to Indonesia's traditional Islamic schools (madrasahs and pondok pesantren). These distinguished NU-affiliated scholars and activists who were trained in the Haramain include Kiai Hasyim Asy'ari, Kiai Abdul Wahhab Chasbullah, Kiai Raden Asnawi, Kiai As'ad Syamsul Arifin, Kiai Raden Hambali, Kiai Ridwan Abdullah, Kiai Mas Alwi bin Abdul Azis, Kiai Khalil Masyhuri, Kiai Muhammad Zubair, Kiai Ridwan Mujahid, Kiai Abdul Wahid Hasyim, Kiai Ali Maksum, and Kiai Sahal Mahfudh, among many others. Although they studied in the Haramain, these noted Islamic scholars mostly studied with non-Wahhabi Sunni ulama and professors affiliated with Hanafi, Maliki, or Shafi'i schools of thought.

Nahdlatul Ulama boasts an expansive network that covers some 30 regions with some 339 branches, 27 international branches, 2,630 representative councils, and 37,125 subbranch representative councils across Indonesia. NU's overseas branches exist in countries from Yemen and Saudi Arabia in the Arab Middle East to Australia and the United States in the West. Nahdlatul Ulama also has some 6,830 Islamic boarding schools and 40 universities across Indonesia. It is thus unsurprising that this organization has had a strong influence ever since it was established. The current general chairman of this massive organization, namely Professor Dr. KH Said Aqil Siradj (known as Kiai Said), who will be briefly depicted below, is also a Saudi alumni. With a solid structure of central and regional boards, branch and special branch boards, and various advisory councils, Siradj sits at the top of the executive council of this increasingly powerful Sunni movement.

Born in Cirebon, West Java, in 1953, Kiai Said, a prolific Islamic scholar who has written numerous books, chapters, articles, and essays on Islam, has held this position since 2010. Previously, he served as one of the Supreme Council members in the NU's central body, namely PBNU (Pengurus Besar Nahdlatul Ulama; headquartered in Jakarta). He began his career in the NU in 1994, following the completion of his PhD from the Umm al-Qura University of Mecca. It was the late KH Abdurrahman Wahid (known as Gus Dur), the general chairman of PBNU from 1984 to 1999 and the former president of Indonesia, who endorsed him to be a member of the PBNU. Gus Dur was very familiar with Kiai Said, particularly since he studied in Saudi Arabia. At the time Gus Dur praised Kiai Said as a "walking dictionary" due to his extensive knowledge on classical Arabic Islamic texts as well as Islamic discourses and history.

Kiai Said has been active not only the NU but in numerous organizations, including the Indonesia Anti-Discrimination movement (Gerakan Anti Diskriminasi Indonesia or Gandi), the Forum for National Union and Communication (Forum Komunikasi dan Kesatuan Bangsa), and the Center for the Study of the Middle East, among others. He is also a professor at several Islamic universities in Indonesia such as Universitas Islam Negeri Syarif Hidayatullah, Universitas Islam Malang, and Institut Pendidikan Tinggi Ilmu Al-Qur'an, among others. Recently, Kiai Said founded the Said Aqil Center in Egypt, a center that focuses on the study of Islam in the Arab world. Moreover, Kiai Said has an extensive academic background in the Islamic sciences and regards education as a tool for development.

After spending his early years at three different traditional Islamic schools in Java, namely Cirebon (Madrasah Tarbiyatul Mubtadi'in, Kempek), Kediri (Pesantren Lirboyo), and Yogyakarta (Pesantren al-Munawwir Krapyak), Kiai Said continued his studies on Islam as an undergraduate at the King Abdulaziz University in Jeddah, before attending the Umm al-Qura University in Mecca for his master's degree and doctorate. He spent nearly fourteen years (1980–1994) in Saudi Arabia learning Islam and pursuing degrees in Islamic studies (particularly in the fields of theology, Islamic philosophy, comparative religion, and mysticism) from undergraduate to doctoral study. While his doctoral dissertation was about Sufi perspectives on God and nature, his master's thesis analyzed the Old Testament and Letters of St. John. Hence, it is understandable that Kiai Said is familiar with Christianity and is active in several interfaith organizations.

It is important to acknowledge that Kiai Said, a noted Indonesian Islamic scholar and cleric, is one of the celebrated figures among Saudi alumni in the moderate and progressive camp. As the leader of Indonesia's largest independent Muslim organization and one of the world's most powerful Islamic organizations, Kiai Said's role in defending Indonesian tolerance and pluralism is enormous and has been recognized by many leading figures and organizations at home and abroad. Kiai Said's role has been instrumental and widely acknowledged in the areas of Islamic education, civic pluralism, critical thinking, human right issues, feminism, interreligious dialogue, social services, moderation, and Muslim–non-Muslim relations, among others. Kiai Said is also one of the strongest defenders of the ideas of democracy, liberalism, and citizenship. Therefore, it is unsurprising that in the 2016 publication of *The 500 Most Influential Muslims* by the Jordan-based Royal Islamic Strategic Studies Center, in association with the Prince Alwaleed bin Talal Center for Muslim Christian Understanding, Georgetown University, Kiai Said ranked 20th in the world in part due to his primary role as NU's leading figure.

Let me briefly depict the NU's role in Indonesia. Notwithstanding its considerable contribution to Indonesian politics and cultures, many of the NU's religious clerics, leaders, and activists are Saudi graduates, and the organization has been poorly understood in the West. With a mainly rural membership base, the NU distinguishes itself from other Islamic organizations in Indonesia by positioning itself as a premier organization of traditional Islam, with an emphasis on education and political engagement based on Islamic principles. Since its founding in 1926, the NU has focused on social services, human rights activism, and educational reform, among many others. The NU has also made substantial charitable contributions to Indonesian society in the fields of educational development, health care, and poverty alleviation. Unlike contemporary radical Islamist groups in Indonesia, some of which have been influenced by Middle Eastern ideas while others are purely local phenomena, the NU is one of foremost Muslim associations on earth that is devoted to the spread of the Islamic message of justice, peace, and tolerance. Founded as a critical reaction to the growth of Indonesia's Salafi-Wahhabi reformist and modernist groups, which were attempting to shrink Indonesian Muslim practices of locally inspired religious traditions, cultures, and knowledge, the NU has developed a reputation as the guardian of traditions—both classical Islamic traditions of knowledge and local traditions and cultures. Accordingly, the NU has been dubbed a "traditional Islamic organization"—a label that can be easily misconstrued.

Indeed, since its inception the NU has served as one of Indonesia's leading Muslim institutions dedicated to the protection and attainment not only of traditional values and practices of Islam but also citizenship, democratic civility, intergroup conciliation, religious tolerance, and the public good. In this regard, the NU is traditional and modern, conservative and progressive alike. It is also important to note that, since its founding, NU leaders and clerics, many of whom received their academic training in Mecca and Medina, which have been centers of Islamic learning for centuries, have worked consistently to preserve the country's peace, toleration, and harmony. The founding fathers of the NU worked hand in hand with secular nationalists, both Muslims and non-Muslims, to create a public culture of citizenship and to establish a political basis for a deeply plural society in the newly established nation state of Indonesia. Embracing the inclusive state ideology of Pancasila and the Constitution (UUD 194), the NU founders challenged reformist and Islamist aspirations of establishing an Islamic state in the country—a legacy that continues today through the NU's defense of pluralism and the Constitution. Kiai Said, like his predecessors, also propagates the NU as an organization that is geared toward establishing a secular nation-state based on a body of modern and moderate Muslims, with agenda items such as anti-corruption laws and social reform measures that are deeply rooted in Islamic principles.

It is vital to understand that the NU has historically pressed Indonesian political elites and government officials to move beyond procedural democracy and to embrace a "substantial democracy" that is typified by freedom from "money politics" or *risywah siyasiyah* (vote buying), voluntary participation in elections, and the pursuit of the common public goods rather than sectarian interests. Moreover, the NU has historically advocated good governance in Indonesia, a fact which is highlighted through the NU's rivalry with Suharto's authoritarian New Order government. Under the leadership of the late Gus Dur, who was selected as the NU general chairman in 1984 and continued until 1999 before becoming the Indonesian president, the NU evolved into a religiously inspired civil society force aimed at providing a counterbalance to the power of Suharto's regime, and struggling for the achievement of global justice, democracy, citizenship, and freedom of religion. Despite Suharto's tireless efforts to weaken the political influences of the NU's ulama, Gus Dur, who was a mentor of Kiai Said, along with other anti-New Order NU leaders, continued to resist Suharto's New Order by developing unique nonviolent models of opposition and cultural protests.

Since its founding, the NU has worked together with secular and religious forces to secure religious freedom, guarantee interreligious tolerance, and to defend Indonesia's plural ethno-religious societies from violent threats posed by minority extremist groups. This commitment to religious freedom and human rights was demonstrated through Gus Dur's instruction that the NU's youth wing, Banser, send its members to churches across the country in order to protect Christian places of worship and to guarantee the safety of Christians, especially during Christmas. In fact, one of the Banser's members, Riyanto, tragically died while protecting the Eben Heizer Church in Mojokerto, East Java, from a terrorist bomb attack in 2000. Until now, under the leadership of Kiai Said, the NU continues to send thousands of Banser members to guard churches from extremist onslaughts. In a world torn by tensions and conflicts between competing ideologies, Indonesia continues to produce men and women whose nonsectarian vision remains every bit as pluralistic, tolerant, and spiritual as that of the country's founding fathers. Nahdlatul Ulama is just one of Indonesia's many Muslim groups and religious associations that are ardently devoted to extending the very fundamental teachings of Islam and the Qur'an as *rahmatan lil 'alamin*—"a source of love and compassion for all humanity" and to ensure that this message is embodied on earth.

However, the NU is currently facing several challenges. First, radical Islamic groups, such as the self-proclaimed Islamic State, have threatened the NU's promotion of moderation, toleration, and respect toward the sovereignty of the Indonesian state. Second, the NU faces strong competition from newer, conservative-leaning Islamic groups, which are attracting many of its members, particularly young university-age Muslims. Facing these challenges, the NU has decided to reinvent its theological outlook by rebranding itself as "Islam Nusantara"—Islam from the Indonesian Archipelago—which is tolerant toward local cultures and traditions while remaining faithful toward the basic tenets of Islamic teachings. As the NU leader, Kiai Said has been one of the advocates and defenders of the concept and practices of "Islam Nusantara" that promotes religious moderation, tolerance toward other faiths, and peaceful dialogue between different faiths and nations. He has also been active in promoting Islam Nusantara to other countries across the world.

Another Saudi alumni who stood for moderate and progressive ideas is the late Professor Dr. KH Ali Mustafa Ya'qub (known as Kiai Ali, 1952–2016).[14] Born in Batang, Central Java, Kiai Ali was widely known as a moderate Muslim cleric, hadith expert, and a professor of hadith sciences at the Institute for Qur'anic Studies, Jakarta. He was also the Grand Imam of Jakarta's Istiqlal Mosque, arguably the largest mosque in Southeast Asia and one of Indonesia's iconic and Islamic symbols. Kiai Ali's undergraduate studies took place at two universities: Universitas Hasyim Asy'ari (Jombang, East Java) and Al-Imam Muhammad ibn Saud Islamic University (Riyadh). After finishing his undergraduate studies, Kiai

Ali pursued a master's degree at the King Saud University (Riyadh) specializing in hadith exegesis (*Tafsir al-Hadith*) and then a doctorate in Islamic law at the Jamia Nizamia (Jami'ah Nizamiyyah), one of the oldest Islamic seminaries of higher learning for Muslims belonging to Sunnis in Hyderabad, India. Kiai Ali's studies on Islamic sciences began at several NU-affiliated Islamic boarding schools (pesantren) in Jombang, East Java (i.e., Pesantren Seblak and Pesantren Tebuireng). During his life, Kiai Ali had several strategic positions including as chairman of the Fatwa Commission at the Indonesian Council of Ulama, director of STIDA (Sekolah Tinggi Ilmu Dakwah) al-Hamidiyah (Jakarta), secretary-general of Ittihadul Mubalighin (an association of preachers in Indonesia), and a member of the Indonesian Council of Sharia, among others. In 1997, Kiai Ali founded (and directed) Pondok Pesantren Darus Sunah in Tangerang, Banten. Previously, with his family members, Kiai Ali had also founded Pondok Pesantren Darus Salam in his birthplace in Batang, Central Java.

A prolific Islamic scholar, Kiai Ali authored numerous books and popular essays. He also translated several Arabic books on Islam into Bahasa Indonesia. Some of his writings have provoked tension and criticism. Kiai Ali was the subject of controversy mainly due to his ideas and thoughts that occasionally contradicted and challenged those of the Muslim mainstream. One of his controversial ideas that raised tensions among Indonesian Muslim societies was about the hajj pilgrimage, in which he blatantly criticized Muslims who have the habit of performing the hajj or umra several times (say, a "hajj/umra addict"), while at the same time neglecting critical human problems and humanitarian issues in society such as dearth, lack of education, illiteracy, extremism, corruption, global warming. In his article published in *Gatra* magazine, titled "Haji Pengabdi Setan" (Yaqub 2006), Kiai Ali argued that there was no single verse in the Qur'an that instructs a Muslim to conduct hajj multiple times. Prophet Muhammad himself performed hajj only once in his lifetime. He also did not perform umra multiple times. This is to say that, for Kiai Ali, a Muslim who conducts the hajj several times does not follow or obey the prophet's religious practice. As for Kiai Ali, those who perform the hajj several times while ignoring humanity such as taking care of orphans and the poor resembles a "demon worshiper" or "Satan follower." Kiai Ali argued that the prophet did not perform the hajj several times in part because this ritual practice does not include what he called "ibadah muta'addiyah" (social worship—namely a practice that has a strong social dimension such as helping the poor, taking part in charitable activities, preserving nature and the environment, building educational institutions) but "ibadah qashirah" (individual worship—namely a ritual practice whose benefits are only for him/herself such as prayer, hajj pilgrimage, fasting, etc.). Accordingly, Kiai Ali argued, that when there is a conflict between "ibadah qashirah" and "ibadah muta'addiyah," the prophet chose the latter which is, in Kiai Ali's view, a sharp contrast to the practices of most contemporary Muslim societies. Following Prophet Muhammad's example and an Islamic legal maxim (i.e., *al-Muta'addiyyah afdhal min al-qashirah*), Kiai Ali also argued that "social ibadah" is much more important than "individual ibadah."

Another idea of Kiai Ali that provoked a public debate is the resemblance between the NU and Wahhabism. In an article published by *Republika* newspaper, titled "Titik-Temu Wahabi–NU" (Yaqub 2015), Kiai Ali wrote and made a list of several similarities between the NU and Wahabi, especially in some Islamic thoughts and ritual practices, which in turn provoked tensions among Muslims, particularly followers of the NU. Kiai Ali himself was an NU member and was trained at NU-linked Islamic schools in Jombang, East Java. But, since the appearance of this column, many Muslims, including Nahdliyyin (NU's followers), accused him of being Wahhabi. However, Kiai Ali refused to be associated with Wahhabism since he himself practiced some religious rituals uncommon to followers of strict Salafism-Wahhabism such as shrine visits, celebration of Prophet Muhammad's birth (*maulud*), and commemoration of one's death, among others (Wafa 2017). Historically, the establishment of the NU in 1926 was, in particular, due to its response to the Al Saud occupation of Hijaz that, according to the NU's founding fathers, potentially endangered traditional religious practices and Islamic beliefs of non-Wahhabi Sunni Muslim societies in Hijaz and other areas, including Indonesia through the hajj connection. Nahdlatul Ulama is one of the Muslim organizations that practice tariqa, Sufism, and any religious rites or ritual practices that in many ways do not meet with those of purist Salafi-Wahhabi. Accordingly, it is reasonable to assume that the founding fathers of the NU were afraid of the Wahhabi influence. In order to discuss its concerns, the NU even sent a special envoy consisting of some Mecca-trained senior clerics and ulama to meet King Abdul Aziz Al Saud (1875–1954), who warmly welcomed them and agreed upon several issues raised by the NU leaders and ulama.

Dr. KH Ahsin Sakho Muhammad (1956–) is another respected moderate figure, cleric, and scholar who was educated at the IUM and Mecca's various learning centers such as Markaz Ta'lim al-Lughah al-Arabiyyah and Masjid al-Haram, where he studied the Qur'an under the mentorship of Shaikh Abdullah al-'Arabi. After spending a year in Mecca learning the Qur'an with several ulama, Kiai Ahsin, in 1977, began his intellectual journey to Medina as an undergraduate student in the Faculty of Kulliyyat al-Qur'an wa al-Dirasat al-Islamiyyah of the Islamic University. After completing his undergraduate studies, he continued his graduate studies (master's degree and PhD) at the same university specializing in Qur'anic exegesis and science and wrote his master's and doctoral theses on issues around the Qur'an.[15] Given his solid academic background on Qur'anic studies, it is understandable why Kiai Ahsin is a well-known scholar of Qur'anic studies and Qur'anic sciences (*Ulum al-Qur'an*), and contrasts with Kiai Ali, depicted earlier, who was famous as a specialist of hadith and hadith science.

A founder and director of Pondok Pesantren Dar al-Qur'an in Cirebon of West Java, Kiai Ahsin is able to memorize whole verses of the Qur'an; thereby he obtained the title of al-Hafidh. Before studying in Saudi Arabia, Kiai Ahsin learnt Islam in Java's multiple traditional Islamic boarding schools linked with the NU, including Pesantren Lirboyo, Kediri, East Java, where he studied fiqh and Arabic grammar, and Pesantren al-Munawwir Kerapyak, Yogyakarta, where he learned and deepened his knowledge on the Qur'an and Qur'anic sciences. In addition,

Kiai Ahsin briefly studied under the guidance of such respected Islamic scholars and leading authorities in Qur'anic studies as KH Umar Abdul Manan (Solo, Central Java) and KH Muhammad Arwani Amin (Kudus, Central Java). Since his childhood, Kiai Ahsin has indeed been passionate to learn anything related to the Qur'an. Because of his expertise and thorough understanding and knowledge of the Qur'an, Kiai Ahsin has been appointed to numerous prestigious positions such as Rector of the Institute for Qur'anic Science (the Institut Ilmu Al-Qur'an) and chairman for a committee of Qur'anic translation and exegesis (into Bahasa Indonesia), formed by the Indonesian Ministry of Religious Affairs. Along with KH Syukron Makmun, Kiai Ahsin established the Institut Islam Darul Rahman in 1992. Kiai Ahsin also teaches at the Perguruan Tinggi Ilmu Al-Qur'an (PTIQ) and UIN Syarif Hidayatullah.

A chairman of the Advisory Board Council for "Nusantara Mengaji," a nationwide network for reciting the Qur'an, Kiai Ahsin became well known to the Indonesian public in particular after his defense of a man who had been bullied and criticized by groups of Muslims for reciting the Qur'an using a Javanese style. For Kiai Ahsin, reciting the Qur'an can be done in any style as long as it uses Arabic. Moreover, Kiai Ahsin, a leading authority of Islam and Qur'anic studies, argues that there are at least three fundamental characteristics of Islam that each Muslim should understand and practice, namely (1) *rahmah* (love and compassion to all creatures), (2) *tawasuth* (using the moderate or the "middle way" in solving a problem), and (3) *tasamuh* (tolerance of others). Kiai Ahsin maintains that Islam is and should become a blessing for all humanity (*rahmatan li al-alamin*) (see Sukoyo 2017).

Another leading moderate figure and a tolerant Islamic scholar that graduated from a Saudi university is Professor Dr. Said Aqil Husin Al Munawar (1954–). Born in Palembang, Sumatra, to a *sadah* (those who claim to be the progeny of Prophet Muhammad) family, Kiai Said Aqil obtained his bachelor's and master's degrees and doctorate from the IUM and Mecca's Umm al-Qura University focusing mostly in the field of Islamic law. A professor at multiple Islamic universities in Indonesia, Kiai Said Aqil was the Indonesian minister of religious affairs from 2001 to 2004, during which time he formulated several important programs, visions, and missions in dealing with interreligious harmony and cooperation on the one hand and strategies of reducing intolerance and radicalism on the other. Kiai Said Aqil is also fiercely against religious extremism and terrorism stating that Islam and any religion is and should be able to bring peace and tolerance to society (Munawar 2003).

Dr. Asrorun Ni'am Sholeh (called Kiai Ni'am) is another moderate Saudi-educated scholar. Born in Nganjuk, East Java, Kiai Ni'am is renowned as the defender of children's rights in all aspects (education, health, regulation, etc.), as he serves as chairman of Komisi Perlindungan Anak Indonesia (KPAI), an independent institution based on Undang-Undang No. 23 Tahun 2002 on Children Protection, from 2014–2017. Previously, he served as vice-chairman of this institution. He also founded and directed the Al-Nahdlah Islamic Boarding School whose main objective is to help potential students from rural areas who are not able to continue their education due to limited financial resources. Trained in both Al-Azhar University and Jakarta's branch of Al Imam Muhammad bin Saud Islamic University, Kiai Ni'am also serves as the chairman of the Sharia Committee for the World Halal Food Council. Also, Kiai Ni'am has been active in a number of Islamic organizations such as the Indonesian Council of Ulama and the NU. A prolific scholar who has written more than twenty books on particular aspects of Islam, Kiai Ni'am also teaches at the Syarif Hidayatullah State Islamic University.

Other moderate Saudi-trained Muslim scholars and activists include Ulil Abshar-Abdalla (founder of the Liberal Islam Network and a director of the Freedom Institute), Muhammad Imdadun Rahmat (a former commissioner of the National Commission on Human Rights), Dr. KH Muhammad Cholil Nafis (deputy chairman of the Fatwa Commission of the Indonesian Council of Ulama), and Ahmad Baso (author and intellectual), among others. However, due to limited space, I cannot elaborate on all of them in this chapter. It is nonetheless vital to notice that, as with the conservative camp, the progressive and moderate camp is also far away from being a monolithic group having similar interpretations, understandings, and practices on issues around Islam, Muslims, and society in general. Nevertheless, by sharing and presenting their thoughts and notions on moderate and progressive Islam, this group has significantly contributed to the growth, plurality, and complexity of Islamic discourses and practices in Indonesia.

Factors contributing to conservatism and progressivism

It is fascinating to discover that although the scholars and activists sketched above (both radical conservatives and moderate progressives) were trained in the same Saudi academic institutions, they have expressed different understandings, interpretations, and practices of Islam. What factors, then, contributed to these differences? In this regard, I underline several key factors that contributed to the shape of their distinctions such as the Islamic teachers who teach and transform knowledge to the students, the organizational backgrounds of the students, the social environment, friendship networks, Islamic training prior to departure to Saudi Arabia, the Muslim groups they follow during their studies in Saudi Arabia, and the types of scholarship. Apart from these factors, particular political, economic, sociocultural, and religious interests have made these variances even more plural, dynamic, and complicated. Due to different political expressions, for instance, they were involved in conflicts. Because of different interpretations of particular Islamic texts and discourses, they were engaged in tensions with one another.

Let me briefly highlight these points. The first major factor is the Islamic teacher, meaning that different Islamic teachers have tended to contribute to dissimilar ways of understanding, interpreting, and practicing Islam on the part of students. Indonesian Islamic studies students usually, or typically, follow their teachers' Islamic schools of thoughts, understandings, interpretations, and practices. This is to say that an Indonesian Muslim student traditionally does not only transform their teachers' ideas and thoughts but also tends to transfer the *madhhab*, teaching methods, curricula, Islamic book references, educational institutions, and everyday practices of their respected Islamic teachers. Accordingly, it is understandable that the Islamic studies graduates of Saudi academic institutions tend to build, introduce, and develop Saudi-type educational centers, along with teaching-learning processes, whether in the forms of traditional Islamic boarding schools, ma'had, madrasahs, or higher learning institutions. Some graduates have established Islamic colleges in several major cities (Jember, Malang, Surabaya, Makassar, and Medan, among others), while others have founded modern madrasahs or ma'had. Still, others have founded Islamic centers that run religious sermons, social gatherings, Qur'anic recitations, and so forth. The great majority of the graduates, however, have established Islamic boarding schools (pesantren) or Islamic centers for dakwah activities.

Saudi alumni—both past and present—in the radical conservative camp depicted earlier usually studied under well-known Salafi authorities such as Shaikh Saleh Al-Fawzan, Shaikh Hammad Al Hammad, Shaikh Muhammad ibn al-Uthaymeen, Shaikh Abdul Mohsin al-Abbad, Shaikh Muhammad Nasiruddin al-Albani, Shaikh Abdullah bin Abdulaziz bin Baz, Shaikh Abdulrahman bin Shalih al-Dahsy, and Shaikh Abdur Razak bin Abdul Mohsin al-Abbad, among many others. Books authored by these Salafi scholars, some of whom have been invited to visit Indonesia to give public lectures and religious sermons, have been translated by their students into the Indonesian language. As for the moderate group—again, past and present—they mostly studied with non-Salafi scholars such as Sayyid Alawi bin Abbas al-Maliki, Sayyid Bakri Syatha, Ahmad Zaini Dahlan, Shaikh Muhammad bin Sulaiman Hasbullah al-Makki, Ahmad Khatib Sambas, Shaikh Mahfudh Termas, Sayyid Muhammad Alawi al-Maliki, Muhammad bin Isa Padang, Imam Nawawi al-Bantani, Shaikh Muhammad Amin al-Kutbi al-Hasani, Shaikh Khalifah bin Hamd al-Nabhani al-Maliki, and Shaikh Hasan bin Muhammad bin Abbas al-Maliki, among many others. Here we can see that, unlike the radical conservative group in which their Islamic teachers were non-Indonesian, some teachers of the moderate progressive group were Indonesian Islamic scholars who resided in Mecca (see Chapter 4).

Within the Indonesian traditional Muslim cultural context, the relations between Islamic teachers and students is very unique, and in some sense special, in that a student does not only regard his/her teacher as an "intellectual teacher" per se but also as a "spiritual guru." In this regard, traditionally, a Muslim student does not only absorb science and knowledge from his/her teacher but also absorbs the guru's wisdom and spirituality. The disciple–guru relations do not end upon the completion of the student's studies but continues after graduation. The maintenance of their relationship takes pace in multiple forms such as visits to one another; translations of the teacher's work; invitations to present lectures, attendance at special family events, and delivery of religious sermons, among others. Some teachers of both camps have visited Indonesia through the connections of their former students. The alumni also play the role of an "intellectual network" and an "academic channel" to their former teacher whose roles include selecting talented students and giving them a recommendation to study in Saudi Arabia. For many years alumni such as KH Maimun Zubair of Pesantren Sarang (Lasem, Central Java) or KH M. Ihya Ulumiddin of Ma'had Nurul Haromain (Malang, East Java),[16] for instance, have been an important channel for Indonesian Muslim students who want to learn Islam in the Ma'had Sayyid Alawi in Mecca.

The second factor is the organizational background of the students. It is interesting to find out that students who have affiliations with the NU and its sister organizations (e.g., GP Ansor and PMII) tend to maintain their moderate or progressive views although they receive training from strict Salafi scholars. The fact that the moderate/progressive scholars sketched above are mostly active members of the NU signifies this tendency and strengthens this assumption. Like non-NU students, NU students usually form groups among themselves and create specific religious activities that preserve traditional ritual practices commonly practiced by NU members. However, this does not mean that only students from NU backgrounds stand for moderate and progressive points of view. This also does not mean that all NU-linked students and graduates tend to be moderate or progressive. In fact, there are some NU-affiliated alumni who follow strict forms of Islam and become supporters of intolerance fighting against religious minority groups in the country such as Shiites, Ahmadis, and followers of local religious sects. Also, there are significant numbers of non-NU moderate and progressive scholars, activists, preachers, and teachers. Moreover, the conservatives and radicals are mostly from social organizations, Muslim groups, or learning institutions that have long been the voices of conservatism, militancy, radicalism, and intolerance. My survey of Indonesian Muslim students across the kingdom (see Chapter 5) indicates that students who have previously been active in Indonesia's Salafi-linked organizations or institutions (either based at the university or outside campus) that historically and traditionally support conservatism, narrow-mindedness, fanaticism, ethnocentrism, and anti-pluralism in the society would most likely continue this tendency upon their arrival in Saudi Arabia. For this type of student, Saudi provides abundant religio–cultural resources to cultivate, radicalize, strengthen, and deepen their previous thoughts, ideas, and practices.

The third important factor is pre-Saudi academic trainings. It is also interesting to discover that pre-Saudi academic trainings have been a key ingredient that has contributed to the shape of the students' Islamic thoughts, notions, and religious practices. Students who were previously trained in Indonesia's NU-linked traditional Islamic boarding schools (pesantren), for instance, would almost certainly maintain the pesantren's religious cultures and intellectual traditions that generally respect opinions, diversity, and differences. Some of them have transformed themselves into non-Salafi strict scholars following severe traditions of Sunni schools of thoughts. Moreover, students who were formerly educated at firm, conservative Islamic schools most likely preserve these conformist religious ideas and practices in Saudi Arabia. Furthermore, students with no educational background in Islamic studies (or only with brief training on Islam) such as students of secular universities (i.e., universities focused on science and engineering, not Islamic studies) tend to follow their close cohorts' religious views, acts, and understandings. Some of them become moderate while others turn out to be conservative, following their friends' religious views.

The fourth factor is friendship networks, which also play a crucial role in forming students' understandings and notions of Islam. Sometimes becoming a conservative or moderate depends on whom you befriend. As a matter of fact, Indonesian Muslim students tend to find acquaintances and build friendship with those who have similar thoughts and ideas about what Islam is and how Islam should be practiced in society. For some students, friendship is not simply about "making a connection" with someone having a particular interest but also a marker of one's religious affiliation. In other words, whom you befriend would determine your Islamic affiliations. It is also through friendship networks, among others, that students find ways of learning Islam, Arab cultures, and socializing with other groups having similar concerns and understandings about Islam. Still, friendship networks have been used to look for an appropriate religious (Islamic) group that runs religious sermons, Qur'anic recitation, and Islamic learnings, among others. The students usually utilize Indonesian (university and non university) student associations such as Perhimpunan Pelajar Indonesia (PPI) and Perhimpunan Pelajar dan Mahasiswa Indonesia (PPMI) to seek and build networks and friendship. Some students, informed by friends, seniors, or the internet, knew of these student organizations before coming to Saudi Arabia. Members of PPI and PPMI also actively recruit new cohorts and cadres to run the organizations in the future.

The fifth factor is the social environment that students engage with during their studies in both Indonesia and Saudi Arabia. The social milieu is a cultural field that provides plentiful resources for students to learn and imagine a "proper" Islam. Being a conservative or progressive Muslim in many ways also depends on this social environment. A milieu (social, political, or religious) could change and transform one's religious understandings, thoughts, and ideas. Furthermore, the environment—whether conservative or progressive—is sometimes closely connected to a particular organization that created the environment. Hence, organizations such as the NU, for instance, tend to create a social–cultural–religious milieu that is in line with the NU's traditions and cultures and conducive for NU members (nahdliyyin) aimed at, on one hand, preserving its Islamic traditional cultural practices (e.g., holding small religious ceremonies such as maulid, *Isra' Mi'raj, barzanji* recitations, among others) and strengthening a social bond and a group solidarity among nahdliyyin, on the other. Moreover, taking the same line, a variety of Salafi puritanical groups also generate a social, cultural, educational, and religious environment that is in accordance with their cultural-religious practices. In some cases, this environment could change one's religious views from conservative to progressive or vice versa. It has been a public secret, for instance, that the noted NU leader Kiai Said Aqil Sirodj, described earlier, was transformed into a progressive cleric and scholar after his activity and involvement in the NU socioreligious settings, besides his friendship with the late Gus Dur.

Pre-Saudi Islamic training also deserves to be mentioned as one of the vital factors (sixth) that contributed to the shape of the students' religious views. Many said that it is Saudi Arabia that has formed strict conservatism, or even radicalism, in the religious views of its students and graduates. Looking closely at the phenomena of Saudi-trained Indonesian students and alumni, we find that, being a radical conservative or moderate progressive is not a simple phenomenon. In fact, in many cases, students of Islamic studies have become radical conservative or moderate progressive prior to their departure to Saudi Arabia. It is imperative to note that before studying in Saudi, all Islamic studies students receive Islamic training in Indonesia's academic institutions and learning centers that in turn shape their religious views and understandings. Radical conservative students/alumni were usually trained at Indonesia's Salafi schools, colleges, and universities, while moderate/progressive ones obtained their training on Islamic studies at multiple Islamic boarding schools, colleges, and universities in the country. This is to say that Saudi Arabia is not the only factor that has contributed to the Indonesian students' conservatism (or progressivism), albeit it is accurate to say that Saudi Arabia has played a role in deepening and radicalizing their Islamic thoughts and understandings.

Last but not least, scholarship is also an important factor in this regard. Many students whom I interviewed stated that a generous scholarship from the Saudi government and non governmental agencies has been one of the important factors for their educational travel to the kingdom. They praised to the Saudi kingdom and society highly for their generosity and support of their study, and some of them promised to "pay the debt" by conforming to the religious practices commonly performed by Saudi society. Some students even feel guilty if they do not follow the Saudi type of Islam and culture. For this type of student, "Saudi Islam" means (strict) Salafism in religious thoughts and everyday cultural practices; accordingly, following Saudi Islam means conforming to Salafi-Wahhabi ideas, understandings, traditions, and cultures. This impression is, for sure, not wholly correct, in part because Saudi as a sociocultural-religious field is far from being a monolithic group following the same pattern of religiosity, Islamic understandings, and cultural practices. The problem becomes more complicated partly because most Indonesian students, both Islamic studies and non-Islamic studies students, cannot differentiate between Islamic doctrines (and teachings) and Saudi cultures (and traditions). As a result, they tend to blend these doctrines and teachings in their everyday lives.

The depiction sketched above suggests that Saudi-educated alumni, particularly those focusing on Islamic studies, are very diverse and complex in their expressions, understandings, and interpretations of Islam, Muslim traditions, and Arab cultures. Becoming conservative or progressive (or a mixture of conservative and progressive) depends on which factor features strongest in shaping and influencing the students/graduates before, during, and after their studies in the Arabian Peninsula.

The pros and cons of Saudi alumni's role in Indonesian society

As with alumni of universities in other countries, the role of Saudi-educated graduates also generates conflict and tensions, on the one hand, and conciliation and integration in society, on the other. Some Indonesian Muslims said that the Arab and Middle East, including Saudi Arabia, represents the "true and pristine Islam"; therefore its Islamic studies graduates would bring and introduce proper notions, understandings, and practices of Islam. It is true that some Muslims tend to distinguish between Western, Middle Eastern, and non-Western/Middle Eastern graduates of Islamic studies, and consider alumni of Middle Eastern universities and Islamic learning institutions "more authoritative" and "more genuine" in the study of Islam than the others. Islamic studies alumni of Western universities, for some Muslim groups, tend to be seen as secular or liberal Muslim graduates influenced by Western notions of democracy, secularism, and liberalism that do not actually denote an "authentic" meaning of Islam. This phenomenon, for some Muslim groups, differs from graduates of Middle Eastern Islamic learning institutions whom they see as "more Islamic." In this regard, they would welcome the Middle Eastern alumni of Islamic studies.

In fact, the alumni themselves very often speak frankly and claim that they are "more Islamic" in Islamic practices and "more authoritative" in Islamic understandings than those of non-Middle Eastern universities. Fluency in Arabic and proficiency in classical Islamic texts of Middle Eastern Islamic studies graduates have attracted some Muslims of urban areas (called "Muslim kota") and new generations of Islam (youths and muallaf), in particular, who have a desire for learning and understanding a "true and authentic Islam." Moreover, the Middle Eastern Islamic studies graduates are very active in introducing and spreading Islam and conducting religious sermons across the country through multiple mediums (televisions, radios, mosques, malls, and any public spaces that can be used for Islamic preaching) that have appealed to many Muslims in the country.

This of course does mean that Islamic studies alumni of Western universities do not have expertise in the study of Islam and eloquence in comprehending classical and contemporary Arabic Islamic texts. Although they have such masterpieces, some contemporary Muslim groups tend to devalue their intellectual authority blaming them on a "Western [read: 'un-Islamic'] mouthpiece." This is an interesting phenomenon, in contrast with the previous era. During the New Order era, particularly from the 1980s onward, a celebrated Muslim intellectual and a graduate of a Western university, the late Nurcholish Madjid (Cak Nur), was an icon in Muslim societies in major cities (especially in Jakarta) that attracted many middle-class and urban Muslims. In recent years, however, this tendency has shifted with graduates of Middle Eastern universities appealing to some urban Muslim groups, particularly in major cities or towns where conservative Muslims and "new Muslim generations" usually live.

Moreover, while the Middle Eastern-trained Salafi conservatives have been quite successful in attracting some urban Muslim groups and new generations of Islam, the moderates have also succeeded in appealing to some traditional and intellectual Muslim groups not only in urban areas but also in the countryside. The latter have also attracted the academic community, particularly those of well-established Islamic universities, since many of them teach in the universities (e.g., UIN, IAIN, STAIN). Some Salafi conservative Islamic scholars also teach at higher learning institutions. However, they mostly teach at small colleges or less well known private universities. They could reach a well-established university student audience generally not by teaching courses but by means of religious sermons at university mosques sponsored by groups of university-based non campus Muslim organizations. In their da'wa movement, the Salafi conservatives mostly put an emphasis on non-academic Muslim communities as their target audience.

Despite attracting some Muslim groups, both Middle Eastern/Saudi-trained conservatives and progressives have created conflict and tension in the society. While the moderates, even though trained in the Middle East, have been accused by some Muslim groups of introducing and bringing Western ideas of pluralism, tolerance, civil rights, democracy, freedom, feminism, and many others into the society. The conservatives, by contrast, have been accused of destroying Indonesia's rich traditions, local wisdoms, and cultural practices. Some strict Salafis even undermine traditional Muslim practices, religious rites, and Muslim customs ("adat Muslim") practiced in the society for generations calling them bid'ah and un-Islamic. These judgments and accusations have in turn generated conflict and tension with local Muslim societies. As a result, some Saudi-educated Salafi conservative preachers, such as Khalid Basalamah, Firanda Andirja, and Syafiq Basalamah, among others, have been prevented by local Muslim groups in several areas in Indonesia (East Java, Central Java, Yogyakarta, and Kalimantan, among others) from delivering religious sermons.

Some local Muslim groups have accused these Salafi conservative figures of being provocateurs of anti-Indonesian Islam (or what they call "Islam Nusantara") while introducing, if not forcing, "Arab Islam" in Indonesia, whose preaching and speeches contain intolerance, hate, racism, ethnocentrism, and prejudice as well as being anti-local cultures and contra-pluralism. It should be noted, however, that anti-Arab or "Arab Islam" actions is not a new phenomenon in Indonesian history. Long before Indonesia gained its independence in 1945, such acts had already taken place. Narratives of anti-Arab and "Arab Islam," for instance, can be seen in the Javanese classical texts such as *Serat Centhini* (also known as *Suluk Tambanglaras* or *Suluk Tambanglaras-Amangraga*), one of Java's greatest works of literature (composed by the palace writers in the instruction of KGP Adipati Anom of Surakarta Court), *Serat Darmogandul*, and *Serat Gatoloco*, all of which represent past opposition against Arabs, "Indo-Arabs," Arab-influenced Indonesian Muslims (or "kaum putihan"), and "Arab Islam" in Java, while favoring Javanese local religio-cultural practices. This legacy continues today.

Furthermore, as discussed earlier, conflict and tension are not only between the elites and the masses but also among the elites (e.g., conservatives versus progressives, among conservative elites, or among conservative progressives), and among the ordinary masses of both supporters of radical conservatism and moderate progressivism. Apart from these conflicts, tensions, and disagreements, it is vital to acknowledge that Saudi-educated graduates have played a crucial role in Indonesian society, whether or not their contributions in introducing and spreading Islam generate tensions/harmony in the society is a matter of opinion and interpretation. History notes that interactions between pro-Arab Muslims and anti-Arab Muslims have been part of the Indonesian history of Islam that in turn contributed to the shape of plurality and complexity of Muslim societies in the archipelago.

Conclusion

It is thus obvious that, based on the depiction and analyses sketched above, Indonesian alumni of Saudi educational institutions, especially those who formerly received academic training in Islamic studies, are very diverse and far from being monolithic. Some graduates follow conservatism, while others embrace progressivism. The chapter shows that there are multiple factors, reasons, and arguments for their choice in conservatism or progressivism. But, this category, it should be noted, is not unchanging, meaning that they could shift from progressive to conservative, or vice versa. In fact, some who were previously advocates of conservatism later became defenders of progressivism. Others who were formerly followers of progressivism shift to become champions of conservatism.

The shift is, for sure, due to a number of socio economic-political factors. Some changed their ideas due to pragmatic choices and reasons, others because of "internal conflict" or adaptation to local societies. Still, others change their views and practices due to contact and interaction with others. Individual contact, group interaction, or social relations with others could contribute to the changing phenomena of the Saudi alumni in Indonesia. This phenomenon is a reminder of Barth's (1959) concept of a "social boundary" which is always fluid and changing.

The chapter also tells us that Saudi Arabia is not the only agent of transformation of Indonesian Muslims, particularly those who have studied in the kingdom, from strict followers of Islam to moderate and progressive Muslims, or vice versa. There are, again, lots of factors that have contributed to the conservatism and progressivism of the Saudi-trained Muslim scholars and activists. Whatever the dynamics that take place among the alumni of Saudi Islamic universities and schools, there is an indication that the future of Indonesian Islam, state, and society will be dependent upon who is the winner of the rivalry and contest between the conservatives and the progressives.

CONCLUSION

Based on the depiction and analyses described in the previous chapters, several conclusions and remarks can be drawn as follows.

Travel is not simply about the movement of body but also the movement of ideas, concepts, thoughts, and cultures in general. People travel, among other things, to meet, chat, and interact with other people. Through a series of interactions, people introduce, share, take, and give their cultural practices. This is among the reasons why travel and encounter between human individuals and societies always concern dynamics.

The contact between Arabia and Indonesia, both past and present, has also been very dynamic, altering and stimulating, involving multiple actors within state and society ranging from government officials and business groups to Islamic scholars and students. In other words, the interaction between Arabia and Indonesia does not only take place between government officials (G-to-G) but also between business communities (B-to-B) and ordinary people (P-to-P) of the two countries. The underlying idea of this work, among other things, is that the state is not the only central actor of interstate relations, as the "conventional approach" of international relations has suggested (in fact, states are considered as the dominant actors by almost all perspectives in the field of international relations, see Tayfur 1994: 113–41). As Steve Smith (1986: 13–29) has argued, the state-centric perspective is outdated as new actors have come on the scene and as new forces "have altered the nature of international relations by entangling states in a network of interdependences."

However, unlike Smith's argument that puts the emphasis on economy and economic interests as the principal forces of international relations, the case of Saudi–Indonesian relations shows that religion and religious identity (besides politics, schooling, business, and economy, for sure) have also been essential factors that drove the two countries and societies to build contact or make connections with each other. As Preuschaft (2016: 16–28) has rightly pointed out, although the religious dimension of Saudi foreign policy is not an end itself, religion does matter to Saudi foreign relations. The same argument is applied to Indonesia in which "Islamic/Muslim identity" has also been used by some groups (state and non-state actors alike) as a vehicle to make links with Saudis. However, it is imperative to note that, religion (in this case Islam) is not the first and foremost driving force behind Saudi/Indonesian foreign relations. Rather, religion, among other factors, serves as a means for Saudi/Indonesian foreign relations to further some of the major interests of the leadership of the two nations. Equally important, this book is not simply about "foreign policy" or "international relations." It is about why and how people (of Arabia and Indonesia) of multiple backgrounds and professions build contact with one another and what impacts, outcomes, or consequences result from these connections and encounters.

As explained in this book, encounters between people of the Arabian Peninsula and those of the Indonesian archipelago have taken place for centuries, long before the founding of the modern Kingdom of Saudi Arabia in 1932. Multiple push-pull factors, ranging from religion and education to business and occupation have driven people from the two regions to travel to Arabia and Indonesia and build contact with local societies of these areas.

Historically, Indonesians (generally Muslims) who traveled to Arabia—both past Hijaz and contemporary Saudi Arabia—were mostly driven by their desires to perform a pilgrimage (*hajj* or *umra*), conduct religious/ritual activities in the birthplace of Islam, learn Islamic knowledge with respected scholars (both Indonesian scholars of Mecca/Medina residents or non-Indonesian Islamic scholars of Arab, Kurdish, Thai (Pattani), Malay, or Indo-Pakistani origins), study the sciences (religious and secular sciences), pursue employment in either informal economies (e.g., drivers or housemaids) or professional jobs (engineers, technicians, or university professors), among others. Arabs/Saudis made contact with Indonesian societies, mostly for commerce, Islamic *da'wa*, lectures, leisure, or tourism. Some Saudis journey to Indonesia because they work in Indonesia-based Saudi educational institutions or business enterprises. Others travel to the archipelago due to an invitation from their associates and networks, especially alumni of Saudi universities and other learning institutions, to give a public lecture or to preach.

As the book has shown, relations between Saudi Arabia and Indonesia—both state and society alike—are highly dynamics and unpredictable, marked by a constant ebb and flow. The encounter between the two has been marked by tensions and conflicts as well as by cooperation and dialogue across these deep plural societies and overlapping cultures. Domestic, regional, or international sociopolitical developments have influenced the dynamics of Saudi–Indonesian relations. During the anti-Iranian campaign of the early 1980s (in the aftermath of the Imam Khomeini-led 1979 Iranian/Islamic Revolution), for instance, relations between the two countries had been reinforced and intensified. At the time, both Saudi and Indonesia, unlike in previous years, had strengthened their cooperation and joined forces partly because the two have shared interests and purposes to weaken the ideological-political influences of the Iranian-Shiites in their respected nations and societies. However, when there were bitter incidents such as maltreatments by Saudi landlords toward Indonesian domestic workers in the kingdom (especially housemaids) relations deteriorated. In recent years, since both countries have agreed to revise governmental policies related to "conditions of employment" in order to resolve the critical issues, relations between the two regions have improved significantly.

The post-Iranian revolution era was actually not the first time Saudi Arabia tried to build contact with Indonesia. Endeavors of the Saudi kingdom to reach and forge an alliance with the Indonesian government took place long before that period. Similarly, attempts of Indonesian societies to build communication with elite members of the Al-Saud family occurred long before the 1980s. Efforts to establish contact with the Al Saud family began in the 1920s when Ibn Saud conquered Mecca (or Hijaz). While Indonesian modernist Muslim groups were content with the "Al Saud control" over Hijaz, the traditionalist Muslims were unhappy and afraid of the political changes in the region. They feared that the new ruler would abolish Hijaz's Muslim religious practices outside the Hanbali *madhhabs* (most notably Maliki, Hanafi, and Shafi'i within the Sunni traditions). Accordingly, they sent a group of Islamic scholars and traditionalist leaders to meet and express their ideas and concerns with King Ibn Saud.

Long before the 1980s, the Kingdom of Saudi Arabia had also tried to establish connection with the Indonesian administration. In the aftermath of the Second World War, particularly in the 1950s, for instance, to counter the influence of the variety of the Arab Middle East's sociopolitical movements (e.g., the Arab Socialist movement, Arab Nationalism, and a number of brands of radical republicanism), the kingdom had built a regional and international alliance with Muslim-majority nations, including Indonesia. However, the kingdom's attempts to make contact with the Indonesian rulers only brought slight success. One of the reasons for the failure in approaching Indonesia was because the late President Sukarno of the Old Order government was a devotee of republicanism and socialism; therefore, he was unenthusiastic to join a Saudi-led campaign. This condition surely differed when Suharto's New Order government saw the post-revolution Iran in which he viewed as a hazard to his reign. Suharto feared that Iran's Shia Islamist and revolutionary political ideology would influence and "contaminate" Muslims in Indonesia. Because of this fear and suspicion, he had made every effort to diminish and eradicate Iranian influences in the country.

In general, it is correct to state that the Indonesian government, in sharp contrast with Iran, did not perceive the Saudi kingdom as a "green peril" for its political authority. In general, what Indonesians, notably in the post-Suharto era, see relating to Saudi Arabia is a cultural-religious challenge not a political danger. Accordingly, unlike Iran, Saudi Arabia at the time could easily build connections with Suharto's New Order and some factions of Indonesian Muslim groups. Like Indonesia, Saudi Arabia actually faced the challenge of Khomeini's Iran; therefore, it built a global alliance with various anti-Iranian Shia Muslim groups around the globe from Egypt to Indonesia aimed at blockading Iranian influences. Furthermore, Saudi–Indonesian relations became more productive in the 1990s when Suharto began to change his policies and political orientation, marked by building close connections—and reinforcing good relationships—with Islamic elements and urban middle-class Muslim groups. In the post-Suharto's New Order Indonesia, relations between Saudi Arabia and Indonesia have been even more fruitful, indicated by mutual productive cooperation in multiple sectors: business, economy, education, religion, culture, security and defense, and so forth.

Another important finding is that Indonesians in the past, unlike in the contemporary era, had contributed to the development of Saudi's Islamic schooling, knowledge, and scholarships via the role of notable Indonesian ulama, some of whom were residents of Haramain. It is unsurprising, therefore, if in the past, in contrast with the contemporary era, perceptions and the reputation of Indonesians in Hijaz were generally positive, considering them as a learned society. This constructive image about Indonesian society began to change from the 1980s when the government of Indonesia started "exporting" menial workers to the kingdom. Moreover, Arabia-educated Indonesian Islamic scholars in the previous centuries did not only play a constructive role in Hijaz but also made productive contributions in Indonesia by building various types of Islamic schools and religious centers; producing multiple religious forms, interpretations, and understandings; and generating a variety of sociocultural discourses and practices, which continue today.

This is to say that, views were unlike common perceptions among Indonesian societies, which tend to view Arabia as a producer of a single Muslim group having similar severe Islamic understandings, interpretations, and practices. In reality, however, such a portrayal is only a "half-truth," no longer accurate. As this book has shown, throughout the centuries, Arabia has produced diverse Islamic scholars of multiple specialties (e.g., mysticism, Islamic law, Qur'anic exegesis, hadith science, Salafism), scientists, and engineers, some of whom have been supporters of religious conservatism, fanaticism, and radicalism, while others become advocates of moderatism, progressivism, and liberalism.

Equally important, Saudi Arabia is not the only agent that produces conservatism and militancy among Indonesian Muslims. Indonesian graduates of, among others, Egyptian, Yemeni, Sudanese, Moroccan, Tunisian, Malaysian, or Indo-Pakistani Islamic educational institutions have also played an important role in introducing Islamic conservatism among Indonesian Muslim societies. Interestingly, some graduates of Western universities have also contributed to introducing, spreading, and deepening Islamist militancy, fanaticism, anti-pluralism, and intolerance, because of having particular political agendas and economic interests.

Moreover, not only foreign academic institutions but also Indonesia's local Islamic schools and organizations have contributed to the shape of radicalism, extremism, and zealotry in the country. Many Indonesian radical religious activists, groups of Muslim zealot, or members of Islamist organizations have actually been the product of the country's Islamic *madrasahs*, schools, colleges, and universities, or the fruits of regular informal religious sermons and Islamic gatherings organized by some Muslim groups and political parties. It is imperative to understand that many Indonesian students were conservative and radical long before their departure to Saudi Arabia to continue their studies.

It is also important to take note that Saudi Arabia does not only produce graduates of Islamic studies but also, since the last decade or so, have generated alumni of the hard sciences, engineering, economics and management, computer sciences, and even medicine. Although their role and contributions are still limited for the moment, which contrast with the Islamic studies alumni, these non-Islamic science graduates have added to the plurality of Saudi-educated Indonesians.

While Saudi has offered scholarship for foreign students from Muslim-majority nations to study Islamic sciences since the early founding of the Islamic University of Medina (particularly since the 1970s, following the oil boom), scholarships for studying the hard sciences and engineering and other non-Islamic studies subjects were opened for foreign students only in recent decades. Previously, the latter type of scholarship was only provided to Saudi citizens. Since the kingdom started opening scholarships in the hard sciences and engineering for non-Saudi students, some Indonesians began to apply for them. Today, as a result, Saudi's recent Indonesian students, unlike in the preceding centuries of Hijaz in which all students learned Islamic sciences, are varied particularly in terms of subjects or disciplines they study, ranging from geosciences to chemical engineering, not limited to Islamic sciences like *fiqh* (Islamic jurisprudence), *usul al-fiqh* (Islamic legal theory), *ilm al-kalam* (theology), *ulum al-qur'an* (science of the Qur'an), and so forth.

Interestingly, although they study non-Islamic sciences, have secular educational backgrounds, and came from less-religious family settings, some students have been active in religious sermons, Muslim gatherings, and Qur'anic study circles, mostly coordinated by Saudi's Indonesian Muslim student associations. Also, some of these non-Islamic studies students, due to their regular visits to non campus Salafi-type religious sermons, Qur'anic studies meetings, and Islamic centers, run by Indonesian Muslim groups in Saudi Arabia, have been radicalized and adopted austere forms of Islamic understandings, interpretations, and practices. Still, other students, especially those linked to such Muslim organizations as Nahdlatul Ulama, have been active in promoting traditional and tolerant forms of Indonesian or Nusantara Islam. Not only non-Islamic studies students, disciples of Islamic sciences, either university or non university Muslim students, are also far from being a monolithic group. As discussed in this book, multiple factors have contributed to the diversity and complexity of these students.

The future relationship between Saudi Arabia and Indonesia will be heavily dependent on the socio political-religious dynamics within the two states and societies as well as regional or international factors that directly or indirectly influence the domestic politics of both countries. Nevertheless, although occasionally the two states and societies might be involved in tensions (due to such issues as the poor treatment toward some unskilled Indonesian domestic workers or the death penalty of some Indonesian migrants in the kingdom), they most likely will not engage in direct violence and confrontation because, from a geopolitical perspective, Saudi Arabia and Indonesia are far away from each other; therefore there are no direct regional political interests between the two. They have many things in common—culturally, religiously, politically, and so forth—some of which have taken place for centuries.

Furthermore, the two countries have built mutual constructive cooperation in many sectors from the economy, culture, and education to defense and security (e.g., counterterrorism programs). All of these factors will certainly contribute to deepening productive relationships between these two Muslim-majority countries in the years to come. In the 33rd Janadriyah Festival, an annual heritage and cultural festival organized by the Saudi Ministry of the National Guard, which ran from December 21, 2018, to January 8, 2019, the Republic of Indonesia has been selected by the Kingdom of Saudi Arabia to be a special guest of honor, reflecting the special and positive connection between the two nations. Indeed, the relations between Saudi Arabia and Indonesia have now become more fruitful, positive, and constructive than before since the Kingdom has embraced and echoed "*wasatiyyah* Islam," a form of Islam that endorses and advocates moderation and tolerance as well as anti-radicalism and anti-terrorism. Interestingly, at the same time, the Indonesian government has also embraced and extoled the "*moderasi Islam*," a sort of moderate, peaceful, tolerant, and anti-radical Islam.

Certainly, the idea of "*wasatiyyah* Islam" or of the "*moderasi* Islam" will not be easy to implement in the societies since the two countries have also been populated by sizable religious conservative, intolerant, and militant groups that have often, if not always, challenged the notions of moderation, tolerance, peace, pluralism, women's empowerment, and so forth which they consider "un-Islamic Western products." The future of each country and Saudi–Indonesian relations will depend upon, among others, who wins the contest between the conservatives and the moderates. Although Saudi Arabia and Indonesia have been facing the same problems and challenges against the radicals and conservatives, the nature, characteristics, density, and history of the two countries and societies are quite dissimilar; therefore the two countries need different approaches, strategies, and tactics for fighting extremism, on one hand, and establishing moderation, on the other.

However, as long as the ruling authority, the military/security forces, and the political establishment of the two countries are controlled and governed by a moderate faction as well as there being substantial support and backing from the moderate religious factions, there is still optimism for a bright future, a moderate Saudi Arabia and Indonesia, and productive relations between the two Muslim-majority nations. But this is, off course, beyond the scope of the subject of this book. This theme, moreover, will be the subject of my next book project, titled *Struggling for Moderate Islam: Saudi Arabia and Indonesia*.

GLOSSARY

abaya A simple, loose overgarment or a robe-like dress (typically black), worn by some Muslim women in various parts of the world, especially the Arabian Peninsula and North Africa.
adat Customs, customary laws.
ahl al-bait Literally "people of the house"; family of Prophet Muhammad.
ahl al-bid'ah (*or* mubtadi') Doers of religious innovation.
ahl al-hadith (*or* as'hab al-hadith) Literally "people of Hadith" (Prophet Muhammad's sayings); specialists in Hadith; traditionalists.
ahl al-kitab Literally "People of the Book"; term used in the Qur'an for adherents of non-Islamic religions with sacred scriptures revealed by God (e.g., Jews or Christians).
ahl al-ra'y (*or* as'hab al-ra'y) Literally "people of reason"; reasoners; rationalists.
ahl al-sunnah wa al-jamaah Sunni Islamic sect of Islam; literally "family or followers of the Sunnah" (Prophet Muhammad's deeds); and the consensus of the Muslim/ulama community in Medieval Islam.
ahlaq al-karimah Good or noble morality.
akhlaq Morality.
Alawi An adjective denoting, or related to, Prophet Muhammad's nephew Ali ibn Abi Thalib. It is also a collective family name of the descendants of Prophet Muhammad living in Hadramaut, southern Yemen.
al-Jawi Literally "people of Java"; Arab term referring to people in Mecca coming from the Malay-Indonesian archipelago. This term is no longer commonly in use.
aliyyah (madrasah) Senior high school.
al-madrasah al-ahliyah Private school.
al-tahdiriyah Preparatory school.
amr ma'ruf nahi munkar Literally "commanding right forbidding wrong."
aqidah Creed, religious beliefs, theology.
asabiyya Group solidarity; group feelings. The term first was popularized by Ibn Khaldun (1332–1406), a well-known Tunis Islamic scholar, historian, and sociologist.
ashab al-Jawiyyin Malay-Indonesian students.
baig *or* bey A Turkish term for a higher official.
bait al-hikmah Literally "house of wisdom."
baraka Seeking blessings from God.
barzanji A recitation to commemorate the birth of Prophet Muhammad.
begum A female royal and aristocratic title from Central and South Asia.
berkah Blessing.
bid'a (bid'ah *or* bidat) Unwholesome or heretical religious innovation.
Bu Nyai Female Islamin scholars.
dakwah *or* da'wa Islamic propagation; outreach; proselytizing.
dar al-Hadith Literally "house of Hadith"; a school for teaching Hadith.
dar al-kufr Literally "house of infidelity"; non-Muslim lands.

dar al-Islam Literally "house of Islam"; Muslim lands.
dar al-ilm Literally "house of science."
dar al-ulum Literally "house of sciences."
dar al-kutub Literally "house of books."
dar al-qira'ah Literally "house of reading"; a school for teaching the Qur'an.
Darul Ulum Mecca's oldest Indonesian Islamic school (established in 1934).
daura A type of workshop held for a certain length of time.
falak Astronomy.
faqih (*pl.* fuqaha) Expert in Islamic jurisprudence or Islamic law.
fiqh Islamic jurisprudence, Islamic law.
fard kifaya An obligation performed by a sufficient number of Muslims.
fard 'ain An obligation performed by an individual Muslim.
fatwa (*pl.* fatawa) A non-binding Islamic legal opinion issued by a sharia or Islamic law expert. Fatwa can be issued by an individual Islamic scholar (*ulama/fuqaha*) or by an authoritative Islamic organization.
FORMIDA a forum for the Indonesian community in Jeddah, Saudi Arabia.
fuqaha Islamic jurists.
fushah Classical Arabic.
guru Teacher.
hadith Report or account of Prophet Muhammad's words transmitted through a chain of narrators.
hajah A Malay-Indonesian term for a female Muslim (*Muslimah*) who has undertaken the religious pilgrimage to Mecca (*hajj*).
haji (*Arabic*: hajj) A Malay-Indonesian term for the fifth pillar of Islam; literally "to intend a journey." It refers to an annual pilgrimage to Mecca that takes place in the month of Dzulhijjah in the Islamic/Hijri calendar. The hajj is a mandatory religious duty for an adult Muslim, who is physically and financially capable of undertaking the journey, once during his/her lifetime. In Indonesia (also Malaysia and Brunei) the term also refers to a pilgrim or a Muslim (male) who has made this pilgrimage.
halal Lawful, permitted.
halaqah Study circles.
hamala Carriers of traditions.
Hanafi maddhab An Islamic school of Islamic law in Sunni Islam founded by Abu Hanifah (d.767).
Hanbali Adherent of the Hanbali madhhab (school of Islamic law), founded by Ahmad bin Hanbal (780–855).
haram Forbidden; unlawful.
Haramain Literally "two harams"; a term referring to Mecca and Medina, Muslims' two most sacred places.
hijab A head covering worn by some Muslim women; headscarf.
Hijaz A region in the west of present-day Saudi Arabia covering Mecca and Jeddah.
hijra (*or* hijrah) Literally "to abandon," "to break ties with someone," or "to migrate" in Arabic; migration from an unsafe place, arid lands, or dangerous, poor areas to other lands or regions that are safer, securer, and prosperous for political, economic, and religious reasons; migration of Prophet Muhammad from Mecca to Medina.
hizbiyya Participation in practical politics or political practices; political activism.
ibadah (*pl.* ibadat) Worship; divine service; religious ritual practices; prescribed ritual duty.
ibtidaiyyah Elementary.

ICMI Stands for Ikatan Cendekiawan Muslim Indonesia (Association of Indonesian Muslim Intellectuals).
ijazah An official recognition and confirmation given by an Islamic teacher to students who have completed their studies.
ijma Consensus or agreement of *ulama* and *fuqaha*, basically on religious issues.
ijtihad Literally "effort"; Islamic legal term meaning "independent reasoning"; a technical term of Islamic law that depicts a process of making a legal decision by independent interpretation of the legal sources, the Qur'an and the Sunnah.
ikhlas Literally purity, sincerity, or refinement.
ilm Knowledge; science.
ilm al-kalam Scholastic theology.
imam Leader, leader of prayer; Islamic leadership position.
imama Turbans.
Indunisi An Arab/Saudi term for contemporary Indonesians.
isbal Trousers right to men's ankles.
Islamism A political ideology based on a reinvented version of Islamic law; a political reform movement within Islam advocating the reordering of government and society in accordance with laws prescribed by Islam; Islamic revival movement; social and political activism advocating that public and political life should be guided by Islamic principles.
Islamist A devout follower of Islam.
isnad Intellectual descent.
Isra' Mi'raj The two parts of a night journey that, according to Islam, the Prophet Muhammad took during a single night around the year 621. Within Islam it signifies both a physical and spiritual journey.
ittiba Innovations or change.
jalabiyya Arab-style flowing robe.
jamaah Community; members of an organization.
jami'ah University/college.
jam'iyyah Association, organization.
Jamiyyah Khairiyyah An Indonesian Islamic school and learning center for women in Mecca, founded by Siti Aminah, the wife of renown Sumatran Islamic scholar Yasin bin Isa, in honor of Khairiyyah, the wife of Mecca-based Javanese ulama Kiai Abdullah Muhaimin Lasem (b.1890).
Jawah (or the Jawis) Malay-Indonesians resident in Mecca.
jihad Exertion; struggle for the way of God.
ka'ba (*or* kabah) Cube-like building located in the Grand Mosque of Haram in Mecca.
kafir (*pl.* kafirun or kuffar) Unbeliever, infidel.
Kampung Jawah (or Kampung Jawa) Literally "Javanese Village"; a special district in Mecca, which is historically only inhabited by Muslims coming from the Malay-Indonesian archipelago who have performed the hajj pilgrimage or learnt Islam there.
kaum abangan Literally "red group"; nominal Muslims in Java/Indonesia.
kaum hitam Literally "black people."
kaum muda Literally "young group"; reformists or advocates of Islamic reform in West Sumatra.
kaum putihan Literally "white group"; orthodox Muslims.
kaum tua Literally "old group"; traditionalists; defenders of *adat* or customs in West Sumatra.
kesaktian Divine supernatural power.

KFUPM King Fahd University of Petroleum and Minerals. Located in Dhahran, Saudi Arabia.

khanqah Sufi convent.

kiai A Javanese word for a male Islamic scholar, cleric, or ulama more broadly; a guardian of a *pondok pesantren* (an Islamic boarding school in Java); someone or something that is believed by local people to have a supranatural, divine power.

kitab (*pl.* kutub) Book; in Indonesia, kitab commonly refers to an Arabic book.

kitab kuning Literally "yellow books"; books on Islam, mostly authored by classical Islamic scholars, printed on yellow paper (which is cheaper than white paper) traditionally used as teaching or learning texts by Islamic students and *kiais* of pesantren.

khuttab Lecture.

Komite Hijaz Hijaz Committee; a small group of Islamic scholars affiliated to Nahdlatul Ulama, Indonesia's largest Muslim social organization, who visited Saudi Arabia in the late 1920s to meet and give a letter of request and concerns from Nahdaltul Ulama to King Abdulaziz Ibn Abdul Rahman Al Saud (1876–1953), the founder of modern Saudi Arabia, related to sociocultural-religious issues in Saudi Arabia.

Laskar Jihad Jihad Force.

lihya Long beards (for men), typically for Salafis.

LIPIA Institute for the Study of Islamic Sciences and Arabic Language (founded in Jakarta in the early 1980s); a branch of Riyadh-based Imam Muhammad ibn Saud Islamic University.

madhhab (*pl.* madhahib) Path; direction; schools of Islamic law/legal thought. Within Sunni Islam, there are four main madhahibb (Maliki, Hanafi, Syafi'i, and Hanbali), distinguished from each other by their different methods of jurisprudential reasoning.

madrasah (*pl.* madaris) [Islamic] school.

Madrasah Ibtidaiyyah li al-Banat al-Ahliyyah An elementary school for female students in Mecca (built in 1957 by Indonesian/Sumatran Islamic scholar Yasin bin Isa al-Fadani, 1915–1990).

Madrasah Indonesia al-Makiyyah (MIM) A private school in Mecca run in Bahasa Indonesia/Bahasa Melayu (built in 1947 by Janan Muhammad Tayyip and Muhammad Nur Salim).

Madrasah Khuttab al-Banat An Indonesian school for girls in Mecca, built in 1942 by Khairiyah, the daughter of Kiai Hashim Asy'ari, founder of Nahdlatul Ulama.

ma'had Islamic learning center; informal Islamic boarding school.

majelis al-ilm An informal place for teaching and preaching Islam.

majikan Master or landlord.

makafiyat God's rewards.

maksiat Vice.

Maliki madhhab A school of Islamic school within Sunni founded by Malik ibn Annas (711–795).

manaqiban A ritual practice to commemorate previous saints by reciting their biographies.

Masjid Haram Grand Mosque of Haram in Mecca.

masjid jami' Cathedral mosque for Friday prayers.

Masjid Nabawi Nabawi Mosque in Medina.

maulid Prophet Muhammad's birth.

Mauludan (*or* barzanjenan *and* dhiba'an) A ritual practice to commemorate the life of Prophet Muhammad by reciting and chanting the biographies and stories written in some books.
muallaf New convert.
muamalah (*pl.* muamalat) Acts involving interaction and exchange among people, such as sales and sureties.
mudarris A person who teaches at a school or madrasah.
mudir Principal (of *madrasah*).
mukim (*pl.* mukimin) Settlers; foreign people living in the Arabia Peninsula.
murid Student network.
mursyid *Tariqa* master or guru.
Muslim kota Muslims from urban (city) areas.
muwahhidun Monotheists.
Nahdlatul Ulama (NU) Literally "Revival of Religious Scholars"; Indonesia's largest Muslim social organization, founded in 1926.
Nahdliyyin Members of Nahdlatul Ulama organization.
nasab (*pl.* ansab) Genealogy; lineage.
New Order The Suharto era (1966–1998) of the Indonesian government.
niqab A face veil covering all but the eyes (of women or girls).
niqash Discussions.
Old Order The Sukarno era (1945–1965) of the Indonesian government.
pahala Rewards from God.
pahlawan devisa Heroes/heroines of foreign exchanges or remittances.
Pancasila Literally "five foundations"; the Indonesian state ideology.
Pembantu Rumah Tangga (*PRT*) Domestic workers.
pengajian Indonesian term for religious sermons.
Perda Syariat Sharia-based regional laws.
pesantren (pondok pesantren) An Indonesian term for an Islamic boarding school.
puasa Fasting.
qadi (*pl.* qadis) Judge.
qibla Center.
rahmah Love and compassion to all creatures.
rahmatan li al-alamin Blessing for all humanity.
ribat Islamic boarding school; hostel; base; a small place to study Islam in an informal way; fortified Sufi retreat.
ridha Allah compliance.
rihla The pursuit of knowledge, science, and wisdom within the Islamic tradition.
risywah siyasiyah Vote buying; money politics.
riwaq Dormitory.
ruh Spirit; soul.
sadah Those who claim to be the progeny of Prophet Muhammad.
salaf (*pl.* aslaf) al-salih Pious forefathers/predecessors/ancestors; the early generation of Muslims.
salafism The salafi movement or salafist movement is a reform branch or revivalist movement within Sunni Islam that developed in Egypt in the late nineteenth century as a response to Western European imperialism. It advocates a return to the traditions of the first three generations of Muslims called *al-salaf al-salih*.
salafiyyah Islamic movement emulating the tradition of the pious forefathers.
salat Prayer.

sanad Intellectual chains.
santri Disciples of *pesantren* or *pondok pesantren* (Islamic boarding school) in Java, Indonesia.
sayyid (*pl.* sadah): Literally lord; traditional title for descendants of Prophet Muhammad.
sekolah School.
Sekolah Indonesia Makkah An Indonesian school in Mecca built in the late 1990s (officially in 2000).
Sekolah Indonesia Pancasila An Indonesian school in Saudi Arabia (built in 1963) which was later renamed Sekolah Indonesia Jeddah.
Sekolah Indonesia Riyadh An Indonesian school in Riyadh.
Shafii maddhab One of the four schools of Islamic law in Sunni Islam, founded by Muhammad Ibn Idris al-Shafii (767–820).
sharia Islamic legal codes and rules.
sharif (*pl.* ashraf) Person claiming descent from Prophet Muhammad (fem. *sharifah*).
sheikh (*pl.* shuyukh *or* mashayikh) An Arab leader; a chief of an Arab tribe or village; a leader in an Arab Muslim community; a respected title used for elderly gentlemen, religious scholars, local dignitaries, and tribesmen.
shirk Literally ascribing or establishing "partners" beside God; blasphemy; heresy; polytheism.
shura Consultation.
silsilah Descent line.
sirah Prophet Muhammad's biography.
sopir pribadi Personal driver.
STAI Sekolah Tinggi Agama Islam (Islamic College).
STAIN Sekolah Tinggi Agama Islam Negeri (State Islamic College).
Sunnah (*or* Sunna) Prophet Muhammad's actions or practices; prophetic traditions.
ta'allum The teaching and learning process.
tabaqat Generations; classes.
tabarrukan Seeking blessings from God.
Tablighi Jamaat Literally "Society for Spreading Faith"; a transnational nonpolitical Sunni Islamic missionary movement (established in 1927 and headquartered in India).
tafsir Qur'anic exegesis.
tahdiriyyah Preparation.
tahlilan A ritual practice of dhikr (remembering God) by utering multiple Arabic sentences such as "La ilaha illa Allah" (there is no god but God).
taqlid Imitation, emulation, copying.
tariqa (*pl.* turuq; *Indonesian:* tarekat) Way, path; Sufi order.
tarikh History.
tasamuh Tolerance of others.
tasawuf Islamic mysticism; Sufism.
tasawuf falsafi Philosophical Sufism.
tauhid Doctrine of the oneness of God (monotheism).
tawasuth Using the moderate or the "middle way" in solving a problem.
Tenaga Kerja Wanita Female workforce.
thalab al-ilm Journey for learning and pursuing science.
Thawab Saudi term for Arab-style flowing robes.
tsaqafah Cultures.
tsaqafah al-Islamiyyah Islamic cultures.
tsanawiyyah (madrasah) Junior high school.

UIN Universitas Islam Negeri (State Islamic University).

ulama (*sing.* 'alim) Scientists, Islamic scholars, highly educated in Islamic knowledge, sciences, and scriptures.

umma (*or* ummah) Muslim community.

umra (umrah) Literally "a visit to a populated area"; a minor/lesser pilgrimage to Mecca which is, unlike the hajj, not compulsory for a Muslim.

universitas University.

urf Customary law.

ushuluddin Islamic theology.

usul al-fiqh Islamic legal theory.

zawiya (*pl.* zawaya) Islamic religious monastery; Sufi lodges.

ziyara Visitation to shrines or sacred sites (i.e., tombs of a holy person).

wahdat al-shuhud Sufi concept of "unity of witness."

wahdat al-wujud Sufi concept of "unity of being."

wali (*pl.* auliya) Saint; pious men/women.

waqf Endowment.

wasatiyyah (wasat) Centrist.

watan Homeland.

wataniyya Citizenship.

wong alim A learned person.

wong nasional A nationalist person.

zawiya (*pl.* zawaya) Sufi lodges.

ziyara Visits to shrines and sacred sites.

Zubdat al-Asrar Sufi concept of "The Essence of Secrets."

NOTES

Introduction

1 The term "Indonesians" in this book refers to people who inhabited what is now "Indonesia" (formerly the Dutch East Indies). Since it gained independence in 1945, the country has been officially named the Republic of Indonesia.
2 In this book, I use the term "Saudi Arabia" not only for the "modern Saudi kingdom" that was built in 1932 but also for the past Arabia, especially Hijaz.
3 History notes that the migration of Indonesian women from rural areas to urban regions in the country to work as domestic servants has taken place since European colonialism. However, only since the 1970s have Indonesian women migrated overseas in large numbers to find jobs in urban households (Krisnawaty et al. 2003). More specifically, the migration of female domestic workers to Saudi Arabia began in the 1980s following the agreement between the Indonesian government (the Ministry of Labour) and the Kingdom of Saudi Arabia. With the globalization of Indonesian women's migration, migrant women's rights, morals, and protection have emerged as focal points of national public debate and national activity (Silvey 2006). As a result, the numbers of non governmental organizations (NGOs) emphasizing women's issues and migrants' rights have grown significantly since the 1990s (Robinson and Bessell 2002; Abdul Rahman 2004).
4 The holy land of Mecca is impressive by any standards. Paterson (1980: 1261) describes Mecca as follows: "it lies in a mountainous cleft that stands out from a vast wilderness of barren desert. Right in the center stands the 'Forbidden Mosque' [Masjid al-Haram], a huge marble clad building of great presence and from it the rest of the city radiates out in all directions stretching high up the surrounding rocky slopes." On the history of Mecca, see, for example, Peters (1994b) and Kister (1972).
5 Another difference between the hijra to Medina and that to Abyssinia is that while there was no pact between the King of Abyssinia and Muslims, the migration to Medina was preceded by pacts (*baiat al-harb/hijrah*)—including the treaty of war or emigration between Prophet Muhammad and the people of Medina, who swore allegiance to protect Muslims and to wage jihad against their enemies.
6 Pilgrimage to sacred places is a global phenomenon found almost universally across human cultures and traditions. Present in all known cultures, pilgrimages gained social visibility with the advent of the great religions: Islam, Hinduism, Buddhism, Judaism, Christianity, Shintoism, and many others. In many (secular or religious) societies pilgrimages are central rites, making up the diversified social and cultural scenario of the societies. In India, by prescribing certain pilgrimage sites to his followers, the Buddha turned pilgrimages into a central aspect of human experience, sanctioned by the sacred writings, although not mandatory, as is the case in Islam. Just like Christianity's relation to the Holy Land, these sites trace a map of Buddha's spiritual biography which dots the landscape of Northern India. With

Buddhism's worldwide expansion, pilgrimages to these sites have become a universal phenomenon (see, e.g., Reader 2015).
7. Tabaqat literally means "classes" or "generations." It is a label for one of the most characteristic genres of historical writing in Arabic, Persian, and Turkish—the biographical dictionary. The tabaqat collections deal with all manner of individuals (caliphs, poets, saints), but in this case it refers to collections devoted to religious scholars.

Chapter 1

1. While "the liberals" tend to portray Saudi in a negative way, "the radicals" tend to see it as a place of severe Islamic conservatism that restricts interactions with other religions and non-Muslim societies.
2. The aim of King Faisal's visit in 1970 was mainly in support of the Palestine issue. Moreover, his visit to Indonesia was as a part of official visits to Malaysia, Thailand, and Afghanistan (Altahaowi 2008).
3. See http://www.telegraph.co.uk/news/2017/03/01/1500-people-two-mercedes-benz-459tonnes-luggage-golden-escalator/ (accessed May 8, 2017).
4. Interview with Ambassador Agus Maftuh Abegebriel, Al Khobar, Saudi Arabia, on April 14, 2017. See also http://www.arabnews.com/node/1061456/saudi-arabia (accessed May 8, 2017).
5. On the five points requested by the Hijaz Committee to King Ibnu Saud, see http://www.nu.or.id/post/read/39479/komite-hijaz (accessed April 13, 2016).
6. This tradition of educational travel has continued till today. Saudi Arabia is now home to thousands of Indonesian Muslim students pursuing diverse studies from Islamic disciplines to hard sciences and engineering. In the past, a great number of Indonesian scholars taught purely Islamic sciences in madrasah, mosques, and informal centers of learning in the Haramain. However, in recent decades, some Indonesians have begun to teach "secular sciences" at universities and colleges across Saudi Arabia (see Chapter 4).
7. Not only in the Java War or the Padri War, during the Banten Revolt of 1888, there were also numerous haji ("Haji") that initiated and led the resistance including Haji Wasith, Haji Abdurrahman, Haji Akib, Haji Harist, Haji Arsyad Thawil, Haji Isma'il, and Haji Arsyad Qashir, many of whom were linked to Tariqat Qadiriyah-Naqsabandiyah (Kartodirdjo 1966).
8. In his dissertation, Snouck Hurgronje not only described the pilgrimage and its ritual in a historical perspective but also addressed the question of how and why Prophet Muhammad had incorporated this pre-Islamic, basically pagan, ritual of the pilgrimage into his new religion. He came up with the answer that this had mainly been for reasons of political expediency. How he debunks the Abrahamic legend in Islam is a telling example of his nonreligious perspective. Indeed, Hurgronje was fascinated with the study of religion as a social phenomenon.
9. On the discussion of the practice of bondage of hajj pilgrims in Hijaz in the past, see Husson (1997) and Hutson (2002), among others.
10. In the last few years, the number of Indonesian menial laborers in Saudi Arabia has decreased significantly since Jakarta stopped sending them to the kingdom.
11. See its official website at http://www.fiwa.sch.id/ (accessed November 11, 2016).

12 See the pesantren's official website at http://binbaz.or.id/ (accessed November 11, 2016).
13 In 2001, according to the International Monetary Fund *Balance of Payments Yearbook*, remittances from the US totaled US$28.4 billion; Saudi Arabia was in second place, with US$15.1 billion, followed by Germany, Belgium, and Switzerland (Ratha 2003).
14 It is unclear about the statistics of foreign workers in Saudi. Dr. Ali al-Namlah, Saudi Arabia's then long-serving minister of labor and social affairs, said that there were 7 million expatriates in the kingdom, about one-third of the total population, in 2003. He added that 5.5 million of the total number of foreigners were workers and the remainder their dependents. New statistics were disclosed in May 2004, indicating an even higher number of expatriates. According to labor minister Dr. Ghazi al-Ghosaibi, there were 8.8 million foreigners in the kingdom representing almost 50 percent of the indigenous population. The statistics department of the ministry of economy and planning reported in 2004 that non-Saudis accounted for 67 percent of the kingdom's labor force. See https://www.hrw.org/reports/2004/saudi0704/4.htm#_Toc75678056 (accessed November 12, 2016); see also http://www.arabnews.com/saudi-arabia/news/697371 (accessed November 10, 2016).
15 *Kompas*, August 23, 2009.
16 See the official website of BNP2TKI at http://www.bnp2tki.go.id/ (accessed November 10, 2016).
17 *Tempo*, October, 28, 1978.
18 Informants in Jeddah and Mecca told me that many family members of Indonesians who live in Saudi are without legal work documents because they entered the kingdom with umrah or hajj visas.
19 See http://saptco.com.sa (accessed November 12, 2016).
20 Conversations with Indonesian drivers took place multiple times in multiple places in Saudi during fieldwork or umrah and hajj pilgrimage in 2015 and 2016.
21 Unlike Indonesian migrants who are mostly in the western part of Saudi, most Filipino immigrants reside in the eastern part of the kingdom, particularly in the cities of Dammam and Al Khobar. Most Filipinos in the kingdom work in low-middle private sectors outside households such as barbershops, malls or shopping centers, restaurants, factories, and other small businesses.
22 A conversation with some Indonesian informants took place in Mecca, September 8–12, 2016.
23 *Duta Masyarakat*, April 29, 2003.
24 This impression is based on my numerous conversations with educated Saudis, including my Saudi friends and colleagues.
25 See http://www.thejakartapost.com/news/2009/09/30/saudi-arabia-eyes-special-relationship-with-ri-envoy.html (accessed November 15, 2016).
26 See http://atdikriyadh.org/index.php (accessed November 15, 2016).
27 See http://www.kingdom.com.sa/president-of-indonesia-receives-prince-alwaleed (accessed November 16, 2016).
28 See http://saudigazette.com.sa/saudi-arabia/broadening-indonesia-saudi-bilateral-relations/ (accessed November 13, 2016).
29 The deal was signed by Saudi Deputy Defense Minister Prince Salman bin Sultan Abdulaziz Al Saud and Indonesian Lt. Gen. (ret.) Sjafrie Sjamsoeddin (now, former Deputy Minister of Defence). On the reportage of joint conference on DCA, see http://www.thejakartapost.com/news/2014/01/24/saudi-arabia-ri-ink-defense-cooperation-agreement.html (accessed November 16, 2016).

30 See http://thediplomat.com/2014/01/indonesia-and-saudi-arabia-sign-defense-cooperation-agreement/ (accessed November 16, 2016).
31 See http://saudigazette.com.sa/saudi-arabia/broadening-indonesia-saudi-bilateral-relations/ (accessed November 16, 2016).
32 Based on data from Statistics Indonesia, the total non-oil and gas trade value between Indonesia and Saudi Arabia in 2011 and 2015 showed an annual positive increase of 3.89 percent. Indonesia's average non-oil and gas export value to Saudi Arabia in the period of 2011–2015 was recorded to be US$1.83 billion per year. Meanwhile, Indonesia's average non-oil and gas imports from Saudi Arabia were recorded to be US$921.23 million per year during the same period. The non-oil and gas trade balance between the two countries experienced a 29.84 percent surplus in 2015. Meanwhile, Indonesia's main exports to Saudi Arabia in 2015 were motor vehicles, palm oil, tuna, rubber and rubber products, plywood, paper and paper products, pulp, wood charcoal, and textile and textile products. See http://saudigazette.com.sa/saudi-arabia/broadening-indonesia-saudi-bilateral-relations/ (accessed November 16, 2016).
33 Responding to this commitment and considering Saudi Arabia one of the biggest potential markets for Indonesia in the Middle East, the Indonesian Trade Ministry encouraged Indonesian businesses to increase the quality of their products to meet the requirements set by the Saudi authorities and the Saudi Standards, Quality, and Metrology Organization (SASO).
34 http://www.arabnews.com/node/927996/saudi-arabia (accessed November 13, 2016).

Chapter 2

1 Islamic law or Islamic jurisprudence (*fiqh*) divides all legal acts into either *ibadat* (sing. *ibadah*) or *muamalat* (sing. *muamalah*). Ibadat are acts of ritual worship such as prayer or fasting, while muamalat are acts involving interaction and exchange among people, such as sales and sureties. The distinction is important because the principle in all matters involving ibadat is that they are not susceptible to innovations or change (*ittiba*). In muamalat, however, there is considerably more room to develop and change the law to facilitate human interaction and to promote justice. There is disagreement among Muslim jurists on whether certain legal acts, such as marriage or divorce, fall under the category of muamalat or ibadat. See "Muamalat." In *The Oxford Dictionary of Islam*, ed. John L. Esposito. *Oxford Islamic Studies Online*, http://www.oxfordislamicstudies.com/article/opr/t125/e1564 (accessed December 5, 2018).
2 The world of Minangkabau is regarded as an integral concept representing the overall system, institutions, and life of people of Minangkabau in the western part of Sumatra Island. It consists of four main domains: Agam, Limapuluh Kota, Tanah Datar, and Solok, all of which are known as Padang Darat and each of which has a *nagari* (a sort of a large village) (Graves 2009).
3 http://www.let.uu.nl/~martin.vanbruinessen/personal/publications/Wahhabi%20influences%20in%20Indonesia.htm (accessed December 10, 2018).
4 Tuanku Imam Bondjol was a formal title given to Muhamad Sahab (or Peto Syarif). "Tuanku" was a title given to high-ranking ulama (Islamic scholars) in West Sumatra who were recognized authorities in the Islamic sciences of tauhid (oneness of God), fiqh (Islamic jurisprudence), or tasawuf (mysticism) (Hadler 2008: 971–1010).

5   This Sufistic characteristics of Islam in the past, actually, is not exclusive to Minangkabau but is present in the Malay-Indonesian archipelago in general (see Johns 1993).
6   Pesantren, technically, is a place where *santri* (students of pesantren) live for a period of times (months or years depending on the santri's situation and interests) during their study in this institution. Pesantren is a total educational environment in the fullest sense. A pesantren consists of teacher-leaders (called "kiai," a Javanese term for a male Islamic scholar, cleric, or ulama more broadly. Female Islamic scholars are called "Bu Nyai." Nowadays there are many female only pesantrens run by "Bu Nyai.") and a group of pupils ranging from tens to thousands. In the past, due to difficult situations, most students were male, but now there are many pesantrens that host female students. Pesantren generally teach classical Islamic books known as "Kitab Kuning" (lit. "yellow book," books on Islam printed on yellow paper). Pesantren also played an important role in introducing and spreading teachings of Sufism and Sufi orders, in addition to Islamic law, morality (akhlaq), the Qur'anic exegesis (tafsir), Hadith, theology, and so forth (see, e.g., Dhofier 1982; Van Bruinessen 2015).
7   The word santri originally means a dedicated (male) student of a pesantren. The term presumably derives from *shastri*, a Sanskrit word for a scholar specializing in scriptures. Anthropologically speaking, however, the term "santri" does not only means "a student of pesantren" but also refers to a Muslim who takes his Islamic teachings and values seriously (e.g., praying, fasting, etc.). Besides "santri," the term "*santriwati*" is also common in use referring to a female student of pesantren.
8   *Tanah Perdikan* was a free land with certain privileges. It was linked to a religious location where the state tax and any burden was excused by the ruler. The tanah perdikan was enlarged into a special village with certain religious functions such as preserving shrines, visiting mosques, taking care of pesantren, and so on.
9   This information is based on narratives of Tobagus Mansyur, director of Pondok Dondong. See Ceprudin and Cahyono 2014.
10 Snouck Hurgronje, for instance, suggested that the Dutch rule should not pay attention so much to the hajj returnees but to the "*mukimin*" instead, namely Indonesian Muslims who lived in Mecca, who played a central role in influencing Indonesian pilgrims to fight against the colonials.
11 A regulation in force between 1825 and 1852 which aimed to discourage the hajj by prescribing the enormous sum of 110 guilders for a pilgrim passport. New restrictions in 1859 required each pilgrim to obtain a certificate from their Regent showing their financial ability to make the return journey and provide for dependents at home.

Chapter 3

1   There are several theories concerning the origin of the madrasah. Some say that the madrasah was inspired by Buddhist monasteries in Central Asia, others suggest that the creation of the madrasah was stimulated by the institutions of *Dar al-'Ilm* or *Bait al-Hikmah*. Still, some see the rise of the madrasah as the logical outgrowth of the function of the mosque, whereas others believe that the madrasah evolved from khanat (hostels) where students resided while studying with teachers (see, for instance, Leiser 1976).

2   Ottoman records in the first half of the 1880s listed only eighteen teachers working in Nabawi (or the Prophet's) Mosque, while in the Haram Mosque, around that time, there were fifty or sixty Islamic teachers who were engaged in convening regular study circles in the mosque's courtyard and colonnades (Hurgronje 1970: 199–200).
3   Not only the Nizamiyya, the contributions of Ghazali, a brilliant Sunni scholar, prolific author, and genius theologian, was also significant in the defense and advance of Sunnism in medieval Islam.
4   The expression of Mecca as a "second homeland" for (some) Indonesian Muslims, especially those from Madura, Lombok, Banten, or Minangkabau, is still valid today. When I conducted fieldwork between 2015 and 2016, and had conversations with Indonesian Muslims in Mecca, many of them still expressed their admiration of Mecca and wanted to die and be buried there due to its status as a sacred place.
5   Not only madrasahs, numerous other structures of historical importance in the neighborhood of the Great Mosque were also destroyed to make way for municipal development projects.
6   Begum, a female royal and aristocratic title from Central and South Asia, is equivalent of the title *baig* or *bey*, which in Turkish means "higher official." Begum Shaulah al-Nisa was a descendant of the pious Muslim ruler of the erstwhile kingdom of Mysore in South India, Hadrath Tipu Sultan, who fought against the hegemony of the English until his death. At the time, she visited Mecca probably for hajj. While there, she received news regarding a plan to set up an educational institution, proposed by a noted ulama Shaikh Rahmatullah al-Hindi. She then supported the proposal and donated the funds for the noble cause. It was then that Syaikh Rahmatullah attributed the school to her and named it "Madrasah Sawlatiyya," which continues to exist even to this day.
7   See the homepage of this school at: http://sekolahindonesiajeddah.sch.id/?page_id=51 (accessed November 10, 2017).
8   "Profil Sekolah Indonesia di Arab Saudi" n.d.
9   Conversations with Muhammad Noor Chanafi, a Jeddah resident, Jeddah, March 26, 2016.
10 Interview with Sinsin Rasyidin, Mecca, March 25, 2016.
11 Interview with Rasyid Sukri, a Medina resident, Medina, March 24, 2016.
12 On the short bio of Sayyid Muhammad Alawi, see al-Alawi 2007.
13 Interview with Holil Ahmad, a Mecca resident and a regular visitor of the ma'had, Mecca, March 25, 2016.

Chapter 4

1   Masjid al-Haram (the Haram Mosque) is the Grand Mosque of Mecca in western Saudi Arabia. Along with Prophet Muhammad's Mosque in Medina (Masjid Nabawi), it is one of the two holiest shrines in Islam, its spiritual center, and the focus of the hajj pilgrimage. A place of worship even before the time of the prophet, the mosque is organized around the Ka'ba, a pre-Islamic "House of God" founded by Abraham (Ibrahim) and Ishmael, toward which all Muslim prayer is directed. The present layout of the Grand Mosque evolved from a series of enlargements during the Umayyad and Abbasid periods, Ottoman refinements, and the modern Saudi kingdom.

2. According to Malay sources his full name was Abdus Samad bin Abdullah al-Jawi al-Palembani, but Arabic sources call him Sayyid Abd al-Samad bin 'Abd al-Rahman al-Jawi.
3. As with many details of his life, it is also uncertain when Ahmad Khatib Sambas died. Some said in 1872/3, others in 1878. However, it is obvious that Kiai Abdul Karim returned to Mecca, perhaps to take the master's place in the tariqa Qadiriyya wa Naqsabandiyya upon his death, in 1876.
4. For a brief bio of Kiai Abdul Karim, see Djaya 2013.
5. For more on Pesantren Suryalaya, see "Thariqah Qadiriyah Naqsyabandiyah" n.d.
6. Lasem-based prominent ulama (kiai) from the past who have influenced many generations of Muslim scholars not only in Lasem of Central Java but also across the Indonesian archipelago include Sunan Bonang, Sayyid Abdurrahman, Kiai Baidlowi bin Abdul Latif, Kiai Ma'shum Ahmad, Kiai Khalil Masyhuri, Kiai Baidlowi bin Abdul Azis, among others.
7. See Devi Anggraini Oktavika and Chairul Akhmad, "Syekh Ahmad Khatib Al-Minangkabawi, Dari Minang ke Masjidil Haram (1)." 2012.
8. Sharif (sometimes spelled "Sherif") was the title of the leader of the Sharifate of Mecca (or Hijaz) in Arabia in the past. In Arabic, the term sharif means "noble" and is also used to describe the male descendants (sharifah for female offspring) of Prophet Muhammad (known as *Ahl al-Bait*). The sharif was charged with protecting the holy cities of Mecca and Medina and their environments and ensuring the safety and security of hajj pilgrims.
9. For a brief bio of Sharif Hussein, see New World Encyclopedia contributors 2008.
10. As for Shaikh Yasin's notable Indonesian students, they included such noted figures as KH Ahmad Damhuri (Banten), KH Abdul Hamid (Jakarta), KH Maimun Zubair (Rembang), KH Ahmad Sahal Mahfudh (Pati), KH Ahmad Muhajirin (Bekasi), KH Syafii Hadzami (Jakarta), KH Ahmad Muthahar (Demak), KH Zayadi Muhajir, Tuan Guru M. Zaini Abdul-Ghani (Kalimantan), among many others. Moreover, prominent non-Indonesian students of Shaikh Yasin that later became celebrated Muslim figures in the world included, among others, Sayyid Umar bin Muhammad al-Yamani, Professor Dr. Ali Al-Shobuni, Dr. M. Hasan al-Dimasyqi, Shaikh Ismail Zain al-Yamani, Professor Dr. Ali Jum'ah, Shaikh Hasan Qathirji, Professor Dr. Umar Hashim, Shaikh Ramzi Sa'ad al-Din al-Shami, and Sayyid Muhammad Alawi al-Maliki.
11. Conversations with some Indonesian students and residents in Medina, March 14, 2016.
12. *Shirk* in Arabic literally means ascribing or the establishment of "partners" placed beside God. In Islam, it refers to the sin of practicing idolatry or polytheism, namely the deification of worship of anyone or anything other than the singular God (i.e., Allah).
13. Conversations with Rusydi Sukri, an Indonesian who has been living in Medina for twenty years, Medina, March 14, 2016.
14. See more about him in his official website at https://www.firanda.com/ (accessed December 20, 2016).
15. Conversations on several occasions with Bambang Tribursyah, Dhahran, Saudi Arabia.
16. I had several conversations with Prasetyo Edi in Dhahran, Saudi Arabia.
17. Conversations with Yose Kadrin, April 4, 2016, Dhahran, Saudi Arabia.
18. Conversations with Yose Kadrin, April 4, 2016, Dhahran, Saudi Arabia.

19 Shaikh Bin Baz, the former Grand Mufti of Saudi Arabia from 1993 until his death in 1999, according to Kepel (2004: 186) was a "figurehead for institutional" whose "immense religious erudition and his reputation for intransigence" gave him prestige among the population of Saudi Arabia and he "could reinforce the Saud family's policies through his influence with the masses of believers," and his death left the government without a comparable figure from within the Salafi clergy to "fill his shoes," not even a noted figure such as Shaikh Abd al-Aziz Al Shaikh from Shaikh Abd al-Wahhab's lineage.

Chapter 5

1 Salafis are followers of Salafism, a broad, trans-local multilayered, and multistranded social movement that encapsulates a variety of different actors, institutions, and foundations. It refers to a school or movement seeking to return to what its adherents see as the purest form of Islam, practiced by the Prophet Muhammad (PBUH) and the early Muslim generations (known as *salaf-al-salih*). In practice, it means the refusal of unwarranted innovations (*bid'ah*) brought to the religion in later years. There are some various types of salafi organizations in Indonesia, ranging from "radical-conservative" to somewhat "moderate" ones. From this point of view, "Wahhabism" is part of radial Salafi movement (Hasan 2007). Salafism, as Chaplin (2014: 218) has noted, is sustained not through any singular organizational structure, but through the lived experiences, divergences, and multiple ways in which it is "enacted" within a given locale.
2 This ideal image about Saudi is clearly expressed by Indonesian Salafi students in present-day Saudi Arabia. They expressed their views about the kingdom with me during my fieldwork in Saudi from 2015 to 2016.
3 This classification is only in general sense because in reality a great deal of followers of Muhammadiyah also learned Islam in Mecca, while those of Nahdlatul Ulama studied in Cairo.
4 Pakistan is never likely to rival countries like Egypt, Saudi, Yemen, or Turkey as a destination for Indonesian Muslim students. As at 2009 there were some 150 Indonesian students studying at a variety of institutions in Pakistan registered with the Persatuan Pelajar dan Mahasiswa Indonesia or PPMI (the Indonesian High School and University Students Association). It is worth mentioning that not all Pakistan's Indonesian students are registered with the PPMI, especially those studying at madrasah. Learning institutions where Indonesian students mostly study in Pakistan include International Islamic University, Binoria University, Abu Bakr Islamic University, Madrasah Ahl al-Hadith, as well as learning centers associated with the Jama'at al-Tabligh (Tablighi Jama'at) movement. Of all these learning institutions, the International Islamic University in Islamabad has been the largest concentration for Indonesian students (see Bubalo, Phillips, and Yasmeen 2011: 11–30).
5 The official figure for Egypt (as for 2014) is 3,500 students but the PPMI believes that the actual number is between 4,500 and 5,000.
6 Reportedly, Abdul Rahim, the son of the cofounder of Indonesian-based terrorist group Jamaah Islamiyah Abu Bakar Ba'asyir, as well as Syaifuddin Zuhri, a terrorist who blasted the Ritz-Carlton and Marriott Hotels in Jakarta in 2009 (he was killed by the Indonesian police), studied at al-Iman University.

7   See www.ppiturki.org (accessed April 3, 2017).
8   Interview with Ahmad Jauhari Umar, Saudi Arabia, April 5, 2017.
9   It is imperative to note that these educational travelers and intellectual migrants are only a small portion of Indonesians in Saudi Arabia, the largest portion, especially since the late 1970s/early 1980s, are "labor migrants." Since the 1980s there has been a new wave of Indonesian migrants in Saudi Arabia typified by in search of employment and "unskilled" jobs. The early 1980s was the period where Indonesia started to "export" menial workers and housemaids to the kingdom as a result of agreements between the two countries (Machmudi 2011).
10 Aditia Rifai (an Indonesian graduate student at King Fahd University of Petroleum and Minerals) and Zia al-Haramain (an undergraduate student at the Islamic University of Medina) assisted with the questionnaire. Rifai and Zia helped me distribute the questionnaire among Indonesian students of Saudi universities. I thank them for their assistance.
11 In Indonesia, there are several attributes, calls, or terms for a less-religious Muslim. Sometimes it is called Muslim *abangan, wong nasional* (nationalist person), or "Islam KTP" (his/her Islam is only on their ID card, not practiced in everyday life).
12 For Islamic studies students, it is important to obtain *ijazah* (an official recognition and confirmation given by an Islamic teacher to students who have completed their studies) and *sanad* (intellectual chains) from their respected teachers as a proof of their completion and expertise in the study of Islam. Islamic studies students are proud of having ijazah from their teachers.
13 Interview with Abdul Latif Ashadi, Dhahran, Saudi, May 20, 2015.
14 This conclusion is the outcome of my conversations with multiple Indonesian students, including Zia al-Haramaian and other Islamic studies students at the Islamic University of Medina, and Yusuf Mufti of King Fahd University Petroleum and Minerals, during my fieldwork between 2015 and 2016.
15 Interview with students of the Islamic University, Medina, November 2017.
16 This information is the result of conversations with a number of Indonesian students from the Islamic University and Taibah University (both in Medina), November 2017.
17 This foundation was established by Ahmad Hatta and chaired by Wildan Abdul Malik.

Chapter 6

1   The FPI founders claimed that the desire to assist Muslim victims of human rights infringements was driven by the failure of the government and democratic activists in protecting their rights, says Jajang Jahroni (2008). Up until this day the FPI has indeed accused prodemocracy elements, interfaith activists, progressive-minded scholars, and "liberal" non governmental organizations (NGOs) (including those run by Muslims), among others, of being Christian-Western-biased and anti-Islam.
2   Religious leaders from these two Muslim associations are frequently involved in the hot debates with FPI commanders over various "burning issues" from religious pluralism and minority rights to the Christmas greeting (such as the debate between Said Aqiel Siradj of the NU vs. Salim Selon or Buya Syafii Maarif of Muhammadiyah vs. Rizieq Syihab). From time to time, the NU use its youth militia wing—the Banser—to protect and blockade churches and religious minorities from the FPI

rampages in the regions of Cirebon, Yogyakarta, Semarang, Solo, and many places in East Java. In outer Java in places such as Kalimantan and Sulawesi, local governments, adat (customary law) chiefs, traditional leaders, NGO activists, and college students also challenge the FPI's anarchism and anti-pluralist acts.

3   It is thus obvious that the rise and persistence of the FPI—and other anti-pluralist and intolerant religious groups—is not simply driven by the group's founders' dissatisfaction with the country's law enforcement or as a response to the "state weakness," as some analysts have observed, but more significantly that the group's occurrence is the fruit of mutual collaboration between anti-pluralist and intolerant factions in both state (government) and society, military and civilian alike. In other words, the emergence of the FPI and similar groupings were the product of synergy between "uncivil states" and "uncivil society" (Hefner 2000, 2011). The phenomena of the FPI on the stage of Indonesian politics also mirror the recurrence of the age-old politico-religious coalitions that run society.
4   This doctrine considers that a regime is necessarily apostate if it does not follow the sharia and that violence can be used to topple such a regime and replace it with a true Islamic state.
5   See more information about Dzulqarnain at http://dzulqarnain.net/ (accessed June 22, 2017).
6   For more details about Ali Musri, see "Profil Ustadz" 2019.
7   For more information about Abdullah Zaen, see "Biografi Singkat Pengasuh Tunasilmu.com" n.d.
8   For a short bio about Erwandi Tarmizi, see Tarmizi n.d.
9   For his short bio, see "Biografi Ust. Kholid Syamhudi, LC" 2011.
10 For more information about Khalid Basalamah, see "Biografi Ustadz DR. Khalid Basalamah, MA" 2016; and his official homepage at https://www.khalidbasalamah.com (accessed July 4, 2017).
11 For a short bio of Firanda Andirja, see Andirja. n.d.
12 For an example of this sort of tension between Nahdlatul Ulama and Salafi, see "Lagi-Lagi Wahabi Numpang Nama Aswaja' STAI Ali Bin Abi Thalib', Isra' Mi'Raj Bid'ah." 2015.
13 Interview with Abdul Adzim Irshad, Saudi, June 17, 2017.
14 For a short bio of KH Ali Mustafa Yakub can be, see "Profil Khadim Ma'had" 2016. For information on Kiai Ali's work, see Prawira 2016.
15 While his MA thesis was about the history and development of Qur'anic Science, his doctoral dissertation was a commentary on a leading academic book on the Qur'an, namely *al-Taqrib wa al-Bayan fi al-Ma'rifati Shawadh al-Qur'an* (by Imam Shafrawi).
16 On his short biography, see Bapak e Muhammad 2012.

BIBLIOGRAPHY

Abaza, Mona. 1990. "Cultural Exchange and Muslim Education: Indonesian Students in Cairo." PhD Thesis, University of Bielefeld, Germany.

Abaza, Mona. 1994. *Islamic Education, Perceptions, and Exchanges: Indonesian Students in Cairo*. Paris: Archipel.

Abaza, Mona. 2007. "More on the Shifting Worlds of Islam. The Middle East and Southeast Asia: A Troubled Relationship?" *The Muslim World* 97: 419–36.

Abdillah. Masykuri. 1997. *Responses of Indonesian Muslim Intellectuals to the Concept of Democracy (1966–1993)*. Hamburg: Abera Verlag Meyer and Co.

Abdul Rahman, Noorashikin. 2004. "Shaping the Migrant Institution: The Agency of Indonesian Foreign Domestic Workers in Singapore." In Lynn Parker (ed.), *The Agency of Women in Asia*, pp. 182–98. Singapore: Marshall Cavendish.

Abdullah, Taufik. 1966. "Adat and Islam: An Examination of Conflict in Minangkabau." *Indonesia* 2: 1–24.

Aboebakar, H. 1957. *Sedjarah Hidup K.H.A. Wahid Hasjim dan Karangan Tersiar*. Jakarta: Panitia Buku Peringatan Alm. K.H.A. Wahid Hasjim.

Abouhaseira, Maher. 1998. "Education, Political Development and Stability in Saudi Arabia." PhD Thesis, University of Southern California.

Abuza, Zachary. 2002. "Al-Qaeda's Asian Web of Terror." *Time (Asia)* 160 (22): 38–40.

Abuza, Zachary. 2003. *Millitant Islam in Southeast Asia: Crucible of Terror*. Boulder, CO: Lynne Rienner.

A'la, Abd. 2008. "The Genealogy of Muslim Radicalism in Indonesia: A Study of the Roots and Characteristics of the Padri Movement." *Journal of Indonesian Islam* 2 (2): 267–99.

Al-Alawi, Ifan. "Guardians of Islamic Pluralism." Centre for Islamic Pluralism, January 8, 2007. Available online: http://www.islamicpluralism.org/about/guardians (accessed May 10, 2017).

Al-Attas, Muhammad Naquib. 1970. *The Mysticism of Hamzah Fansuri*. Kuala Lumpur: University of Malaya Press.

Al Fasi, Taqiyuddin. 1985. *Sifa al-Gharam bi Akhbari al-Balad al-Haram*. Beirut: Dar al-Kitab al-Arabi.

Al Jufri, Habib Musthofa bin Husain. 2017. "Madrasah Al Falah di Mekkah." *Majalah Mafahim* 42: 56–57.

Al-Moalimi, Abdallah Abdulrahman. 2000. *A'lam al-Makkiyyin, 832–1399 H*. 2 vols. London: Al-Furqan Islamic Heritage Foundation.

Al Qurtuby, Sumanto. 2003. *Arus Cina-Islam-Jawa: Peranan Tionghoa dalam Proses Penyebaran Islam di Jawa Abad ke-15 dan 16*. Jakarta: INTI-Inspeal.

Al Qurtuby, Sumanto. 2016. *Religious Violence and Conciliation in Indonesia*. London: Routledge.

Al Qurtuby, Sumanto. 2017. "Arabs and Indo Arabs in Indonesia: Historical Dynamics, Social Relations, and Contemporary Change." *International Journal of Asia Pacific Studies* 13 (2): 45–72.

Al Qurtuby, Sumanto and Shafi Aldamer. 2018. "Saudi-Indonesian Relations: Historical Dynamics and Contemporary Development." *Asian Perspective* 42: 121–44.

Aldamer, Shafi. 2001. "Saudi-British Relations, 1939–1953." PhD diss., University of Durham.

Altahaowi, Abdulhakeem. 2008. *Almalik Faisal wa Ilailaqat Alkharijah al-Saudiyah* [King Faisal and Saudi Foreign Relations]. Cairo: al-Dar al-Thqafiah lilnasher.

Ambary, Hasan Muarif and Jacques Dumarcay. 1990. *Kesultanan Banten*. Jakarta: Grademedia.

Andirja, Firanda. n.d. "Profil Firanda Andirja Abidin." Firanda Andirja. Available online: http://firanda-andirja.blogspot.sg/p/firanda-andirja-abidin-ustadz-firanda.html (accessed July 5, 2017).

Anggraini Oktavika, Devi and Chairul Akhmad, "Syekh Ahmad Khatib Al-Minangkabawi, Dari Minang ke Masjidil Haram (1)." *Republika*, January 16, 2012. Available online: http://www.republika.co.id/berita/dunia-islam/khazanah/12/01/16/lxvt00-syekh-ahmad-khatib-alminangkabawi-dari-minang-ke-masjidil-haram-1 (accessed June 17, 2016).

Azra, Azyumardi. 1992. "The Transmission of Islamic Reformism to Indonesia: Networks of Middle Eastern and Malay-Indonesian Ulama in the Seventeenth and Eighteenth Centuries." PhD Diss., Columbia University, New York.

Azra, Azyumardi. 2003. Review of *Islam and the Malay—Indonesian World: Transmission and Responses*, by Peter Riddell, pp. 103–06. Honolulu: University of Hawaii Press.

Azra, Azyumardi. 2004. *The Origins of Islamic Reformism in Southeast Asia: Networks of Malay-Indonesian and Middle Eastern Ulama in the Seventeenth and Eighteenth Centuries*. Honolulu: University of Hawaii Press.

Azra, Azyumardi. 2005. "Islam in Southeast Asia: Tolerance and Radicalism." Meigunyah Public Lecture, University of Melbourne.

Azra, Azyumardi. 2006. *Islam in the Indonesian World: An Account of Institutional Formation*. Bandung: Mizan.

Bapak e Muhammad. 2012. "Biografi—KH. M. Ihya' Ulumiddin." Ma'had Nurul Haromain, July 2012. Available online: http://kabarpujon.blogspot.sg/2012/07/biografi-kh-m-ihya-ulumiddin.html (accessed July 26, 2017).

Barth, Fredrik. 1959. *Political Leadership among Swat Pathans*. London: The Athlone Press.

Basri, Basri. 1997. "Indonesian Ulama in the Haramayn and the Transmission of Reformist Islam in Indonesia (1800–1900)." PhD Diss., University of Arkansas, Fayetteville.

Benda, Harry J. 1958. *The Crescent and the Rising Sun: Indonesian Islam under the Japanese Occupation 1942–1945*. The Hague: W. van Hoeve Ltd.

"Biografi Singkat Pengasuh Tunasilmu.com." n.d. Tunasilmu. Available online: https://tunasilmu.com/profil/ (accessed June 21, 2017).

"Biografi Ust. Kholid Syamhudi, LC." 2011. Direktori Pesantren, April 20, 2011. Available online: https://dirpesantren.wordpress.com/2011/04/20/biografi-ust-kholid-syamhudi-lc/ (accessed June 22, 2017).

"Biografi Ustadz DR. Khalid Basalamah, MA." 2016. Ikhwan Sunnah, November 1, 2016. Available online: http://www.ikhwansunnah.net/2016/11/biografi-ustadz-dr-khalid-basalamah-ma.html.

Boissevain, Jeremy. 1978. *Friends of Friends: Networks, Manipulators, and Coalitions*. Oxford: Blackwell Publishing.

Bowen, John R. 1991. *Sumatran Politics and Poetics: Gayo History, 1900–1989*. New Haven, CT: Yale University Press.

Braginsky, Vladimir I. 1999. "Towards the Biography of Hamzah Fansuri. When Did Hamzah Live? Data from His Poems and Early European Accounts." *Archipel* 57: 135–75.

Bubalo, A., S. Jones, and N. Nuraniyah. 2016. "Indonesian Students in Egypt and Turkey." Lowy Institute Report, Australia.

Bubalo, Anthony, Sarah Phillips, and Samina Yasmeen. 2011. *Talib or Taliban? Indonesian Students in Pakistan and Yemen*. Sydney, NSW: The Lowy Institute for International Policy.

Ceprudin and Cahyono. 2014. "Pondok Dondong, Pesantren Tertua di Jateng." eLSA, March 21, 2014. Available online: http://elsaonline.com/pondok-dondong-pesantren-tertua-di-jateng/# (accessed August 27, 2017).

Chaplin, Chris. 2014. "Imagining the Land of the Two Holy Mosques: The Social and Doctrinal Importance of Saudi Arabia in Indonesian Salafi Discourse." *Austrian Journal of Southeast Asian Studies* 7 (2): 217–36.

Chernoff, John. 1984. "The Pilgrimage to Mecca: An Excerpt from a Drummer's Testament." *Chicago Review* 34 (3): 68–94.

Christakis, Nicholas and James Fowler. 2009. *Connected: The Surprising Power of Our Social Networks and How They Shape Our Lives*. New York: Little, Brown and Company.

Clancy-Smith, Julia A. 1990. "Between Cairo and the Algerian Kabylia: The Rahmaniyya Tariqa, 1715–1800." In Dale Eickelman and James Piscatori (eds.), *Muslim Travellers: Pilgrimage, Migration, and the Role of Imagination*, pp. 200–16. Berkeley: The University of California Press.

Commins, David. 2009. *The Wahhabi Mission and Saudi Arabia*. London: I.B. Tauris.

Commins, David. 2016. *The Mission and the Kingdom: Wahabi Power behind the Saudi Throne*. London: I.B. Tauris.

Cook, Michael. 1992. "On the Origins of Wahhabism." *Journal of the Royal Asiatic Society* 2 (2): 191–202.

Darban, Adaby. 1988. "Kiai dan Politik pada Zaman Kerajaan Islam Jawa" [kiai (Islamic Cleric) and Politics during the Islamic Kingdom in Java]. *Pesantren* 5 (2): 32–38.

Das Gupta, Ashin. 1979. *Indian Merchants and the Decline of Surat, c. 1700–1750*. Wiesbaden: Harrasowitz Verlag.

DeHanas, Daniel Nilsson. 2013. "Of Hajj and Home: Roots Visits to Mecca and Bangladesh in Everyday Belonging." *Ethnicities* 13 (4): 457–74.

Delaney, Carol. 1990. "The 'Hajj': Sacred and Secular." *American Ethnologist* 17 (3): 513–30.

Delong-Bas, Natana J. 2004. *Wahhabi Islam: From Revival and Reform to Global Jihad*. Oxford: Oxford University Press.

Depnakertrans (Departemen Tenaga Kerja dan Transmigrasi). 2004. "Penempatan TKI Formal ke Luar Negeri" [Formal international Indonesian labor placements]. Available online: http://nakertrans.go.id/statistik_naker (accessed October 5, 2017).

Dhofier, Zamakhsyari. 1982. *Tradisi Pesantren: Studi tentang Pandangan Hidup Kiai*. Jakarta: LP3ES.

Diederich, Mathias. 2005. "Indonesians in Saudi Arabia: Religious and Economic Connection." In Madawi Al-Rasheed (ed.), *Transnational Connection and the Arab Gulf*, pp. 128–46. London: Routledge.

Djajadiningrat, Hoesein. 1983. *Tinjauan Kritis atas Sadjarah Banten*. Jakarta: Djambatan.

Djaya, Sulaiman. 2013. "Syekh Abdul Karim al Bantani." [Blog] suarakatak, February 8, 2013. Available online: http://suarakatak.blogspot.sg/2013/02/syekh-abdul-karim-al-bantani.html (accessed June 23, 2016).

Dobbin, Christine. 1972. "Tuanku Imam Bondjol (1772–1864)." *Indonesia* 13: 5–35.
Dobbin, Christine. 1974. "Islamic Revivalism in Minangkabau at the Turn of the Nineteenth Century." *Modern Asian Studies* 8 (3): 319–45.
Dobbin, Christine. 1977. "Economic Change in Minangkabau as a Factor in the Rise of the Padri Movement, 1784–1830." *Indonesia* 23: 1–38.
Dobbin, Christine. 1983. *Islamic Revivalism in a Changing Peasant Economy: Central Sumatra, 1784–1847*. Richmond: Curzon Press.
Douwes, Dick and Nico Kaptein. 1997. *Indonesia dan Haji* [Indonesia and Hajj]. Jakarta: INIS.
Duncan, Katie. "Turkey: Government Invests Record Amount in HE Scholarships." *The Pie News*, August 13, 2014. Available online: http://thepienews.com/news/government/turkey/ (accessed July 12, 2019).
Eickelman, Dale F. 1992. *Knowledge and Power in Morocco*. Princeton, NJ: Princeton University Press.
Eickelman, Dale F. 1997. *The Middle East and Central Asia: An Anthropological Approach*. Upper Saddle River, NJ: Prentice-Hall.
Eickelman, Dale F. and James Piscatori (eds.). 1990. *Muslim Travellers: Pilgrimage, Migration, and the Role of Imagination*. Berkeley: The University of California Press.
Elyas, Tariq and Michelle Picard. 2013. "Critiquing of Higher Education Policy in Saudi Arabia: Towards a New Neoliberalism." *Education, Business and Society* 6 (1): 31–41.
Fahmialinh. 2016. "Kh A. Muhaimin Bin Abdul Aziz Lasem." catatan fahmi ali, January 3, 2016. Available online: https://fahmialinh.wordpress.com/2016/01/03/kh-a-muhaimin-bin-abdul-aziz-lasem/ (accessed December 20, 2017).
Farquhar, Michael. 2015. "Saudi Petrodollars, Spiritual Capital and the Islamic University of Medina: A Wahhabi Missionary Project in Transnational Perspective." *International Journal of Middle East Studies* 47: 701–21.
Farquhar, Michael. 2017. *Circuits of Faith: Migration, Education and the Wahhabi Mission*. Stanford, CA: Stanford University Press.
Fathurrahman, Oman. 2003. "Tarekat Shatariyah di Dunia Melayu—Indonesia: Kajian atas Dinamika dan Perkembangannya Melalui Naskah-Naskah di Sumatra Barat." PhD Thesis, University of Indonesia, Jakarta.
Fealy, Greg and Anthony Bubalo. 2005. *Between the Local and the Global: Islamism, the Middle East and Indonesia*. Brookings: Caban Center.
Fealy, Greg and Sally White (eds.). 2014. *Expressing Islam: Religious Life and Politics in Indonesia*. Singapore: Institute of Southeast Asian Studies.
Feener, Michael R. 2011. *Muslim Legal Thought in Modern Indonesia*. Cambridge: Cambridge University Press.
Freitag, Ulrike and William G. Clarance-Smith (eds.). 1997. *Hadrami Traders, Scholars, and Statesmen in the Indian Ocean, 1750s–1960s*. Leiden: Brill.
Fussell, Paul. 1980. *Abroad: British Literary Travelling between the World Wars*. London: Oxford University Press.
Geertz, Clifford. 1976. *The Religion of Java*. Chicago: University of Chicago Press.
Gellens, Sam I. 1990. "The Search for Knowledge in Medieval Muslim Societies: A Comparative Approach." In Dale Eickelman and James Piscatori (eds.), *Muslim Travellers: Pilgrimage, Migration, and the Role of Imagination*, pp. 50–65. Berkeley: University of California Press.
Gibson, Tom. 2010. *Islamic Narrative and Authority in Southeast Asia*. London: Palgrave Macmillan.
Gold, Dore. 2003. *Hatred's Kingdom: How Saudi Arabia Supports the New Global Terrorism*. Washington, DC: Regnery Publishing, Inc.

Goldziher, Ignaz. 1889–1890. *Muhammedanische Studien*. 2 vols. Halle: Niemeyer.
Graves, Elizabeth. 2009. *The Minangkabau Response to Dutch Colonial Rule in the Nineteenth Century*. Sheffield: Equinox Publishing.
Gunaratna, Rohan. 2002. *Inside Al-Qaeda: Global Network of Terror*. Columbia, NY: Columbia University Press.
Hadler, Jeffry. 2008. "A Historiography of Violence and the Secular State in Indonesia: Tuanku Imam Bondjol and the Uses of History." *Journal of Asian Studies* 67 (3): 971–1010.
Hamka. 1981. *Sedjarah Umat Islam* [History of Muslim Society]. Jakarta: N.V. Nusantara.
Hanif, N. 2000. *Biographical Encyclopaedia of Sufi*. New Delhi: Sarup and Sons.
Hasan, Noorhaidi. 2005. "Saudi Expansion, the Salafi Campaign and Arabised Islam in Indonesia." In Madawi Al-Rasheed (ed.), *Transnational Connection and the Arab Gulf*, pp. 263–81. London: Routledge.
Hasan, Noorhaidi. 2007. "The Salafi Movement in Indonesia: Transnational Dynamics and Local Development." *Comparative Studies of South Asia, Africa and the Middle East* 27 (1): 83–94.
Hasan, Noorhaidi. 2010a. "The Failure of the Wahhabi Campaign: Transnational Islam and the Salafi Madrasa in post-9/11 Indonesia." *Southeast Asia Research* 18 (4): 675–705.
Hasan, Noorhaidi. 2010b. "From Apolitical Quietism to Jihadist Activism: 'Salafi', Political Mobilization, and Drama of Jihad in Indonesia." In Azyumardi Azra, Kees van Dijk, and Nico J. G. Kaptein (eds.), *Varieties of Religious Authority: Changes and Challenges in 20th Century Indonesian Islam*, pp. 139–56. Singapore: Institute of Southeast Asian Studies.
Hasan, Noorhaidi. 2014. "Ambivalent Doctrines and Conflicts in the Salafi Movement in Indonesia." In Roel Meijer (ed.), *Global Salafism: Islam's New Religious Movement*, pp. 1–27. London: Oxford Scholarship Online.
Hefner, Robert W. 1989. *Hindu Javanese: Tengger Tradition and Islam*. Princeton, NJ: Princeton University Press.
Hefner, Robert W. 2000. *Civil Islam: Muslims and Democratization in Indonesia*. Princeton, NJ: Princeton University Press.
Hefner, Robert W. 2011. *Shari'a Politics: Islamic Law and Society in the Modern World*. Bloomington: Indiana University Press.
Hefner, Robert W. and Muhammad Qasim Zaman. 2007. *Schooling Islam: The Culture and Politics of Modern Muslim Education*. Princeton, NJ: Princeton University Press.
Hegghammer, Thomas. 2010. *Jihad in Saudi Arabia: Violence and Pan-Islamism since 1979*. Cambridge: Cambridge University Press.
Heidhues, Mary Somers. 2000. *Southeast Asia: A Concise History*. London: Thames and Hudson.
Henderson, Joan Catherine. 2011. "Religious Tourism and Its Management: The Hajj in Saudi Arabia." *International Journal of Tourism Research* 13: 541–52.
Ho, Engseng. 2006. *The Graves of Tarim: Genealogy and Mobility across the Indian Ocean*. Berkeley: University of California Press.
HRW (Human Rights Watch). 2004. "Migrant Communities in Saudi Arabia." Available online: https://www.hrw.org/reports/2004/saudi0704/4.htm#_Toc75678056 (accessed June 12, 2017).
Hugo, Graeme. 1995. "Labour Export from Indonesia: An Overview." *ASEAN Economic Bulletin* 12 (2): 275–98.
Hugo, Graeme. 2002. "Women's International Labour Migration." In Kathryn Robinson and Sharon Bassell (eds.), *Women in Indonesia: Gender, Equity, and Development*, pp. 158–78. Singapore: ISEAS.

Hurgronje, C. Snouck. 1970. *Mekka in the Later Part of the 19th Century: Daily Life, Customs and Learning. The Moslims of the East Indian Archipelago*, trans. Johan Monahan. Leiden: Brill.

Husson, Laurence. 1997. "Les Indonésiens en Arabie Saoudite pour la foi et le travail" [Indonesians in Saudi Arabia for Worship and Work.] *Revue européenne des migrations internationales* 13 (1): 125–47.

Hutson, Alaine S. 2002. "Enslavement and Manumission in Saudi Arabia, 1926–38." *Critique: Critical Middle Eastern Studies* 11 (1): 49–70.

ICG. 2005. "Weakening Indonesia's Mujahidin Networks: Lessons from Maluku and Poso." Asia Report No. 103, October 13, 2005.

Igarashi, Daisuke. 2013. "Madrasahs, Their Shaykhs and the Civilian Founder: The Basitiyah Madrasahs in the Mamluk Era." *ORIENT* 40 (8): 79–94.

Indra, Ristapawa. 2017. "Wahhabism: Padri Movement in Minangkabau to the Islamic Defender Organization in Indonesia." *Journal of Arts, Science and Commerce* 8 2[1]: 79–91.

Irianto, Sulistiyowati. 2011. *Akses Keadilan dan Migrasi Global: Kisah Perempuan Indonesia Pekerja Domestik di Uni Emirat Arab*. Jakarta: Yayasan Pustaka Obor Indonesia.

Irsad, Abdul Adzim. 2015. *Ulama Nusantara: Kiprah Ulama Nusantara di Tanah Suci Makkah*. Malang: Unisma Press.

Jahroni, Jajang. 2008. *Defending the Majesty of Islam: Indonesia's Front Pembela Islam, 1998–2003*. Seattle, WA: University of Washington Press.

Jahroni, Jajang. 2013. "The Political Economy of Knowledge: Shari'ah and Saudi Scholarship in Indonesia." *Journal of Indonesian Islam* 7 (1): 165–86.

The Jakarta Post. 2014. "More RI students interested in Morocco, says envoy." *The Jakarta Post*, May 6, 2014. Available online: http://www.thejakartapost.com/news/2014/05/06/more-ri-students-interested-morocco-says-envoy.html. (accessed April 5, 2017).

Jalil, Abdul. 2016. "Mengaji Hadis kepada Ulama Indonesia di Mekah." Available online: http://ilmuhadis.uin-suka.ac.id/index.php/page/kolom/detail/12/mengaji-hadis-kepada-ulama-indonesia-di-mekah (accessed July 6, 2017).

Johns, Anthony H. 1961. "Sufism as a Category in Indonesian Literature and History." *Journal of Southeast Asian History* 2 (2): 10–23.

Johns, Anthony H. 1993. "Islamization in Southeast Asia: Reflections and Reconsiderations with Special Reference to the Role of Sufism." *Indonesia* 31 (1): 43–61.

Johnson, Mark. 2010. "Diasporic Dreams, Middle Class Moralities, and Migrant Domestic Workers among Muslim Filipinos in Saudi Arabia." *Asia Pacific Journal of Anthropology* 11 (3–4): 1–22.

Kartodirdjo, Sartono. 1966. *The Peasants' Revolt of Banten in 1888: Its Conditions, Course, and Sequel: A Case Study of Social Movements in Indonesia*. The Hague: Nijhoff.

Kartodirdjo, Sartono. 1979. *Protest Movements in Rural Java: A Study of Agrarian Unrest in the Nineteenth and Early Twentieth Centuries*. London: Oxford University Press.

Kawach, Nadim. 2003. "Expats Remit $76b during Saudi Five-Year Plan Period." *Gulf News*, September 5.

Kepel, Gilles. 2004. *The War for Muslim Minds: Islam and the West*. Cambridge, MA: Harvard University Press.

Kister, M. J. 1972. "Some Reports Concerning Mecca from Jahiliyya to Islam." *Journal of the Economic and Social History of the Orient* 15 (1–2): 61–93.

Kovacs, Amanda. 2014. "Saudi Arabia exporting Salafi education and radicalizing Indonesia's Muslims." GIGA Focus International, 7th Edition. Hamburg: GIGA German Institute of Global and Area Studies - Leibniz-Institut für Globale und Regionale Studien. Available online: https://nbn-resolving.org/urn:nbn:de:0168-ssoar-402325

Krisnawaty, Tati, Rusdi Tagaroa, Eko Indriati, Yohanes Budi Wibawa, Ali Muchsin, Asmaul Khusnaeni, Tety Kuswandari, Kamala Chandrakirana, Pande K. Trimayuni, and Geny Achnas. 2003. *Buruh migrant pekerja rumah tangga Indonesia (TKW–PRT): kerentanan dan inisiatif-inisiatif baru untuk perlindungan hak asasi TKW–PRT* [Indonesian Overseas Migrant Domestic Workers: Sensitivity and New Initiatives for the Protection of the Human Rights of Overseas Migrant Domestic Workers]. Jakarta: Komnas Perempuan (National Commission for Women's Human Rights).

Laffan, Michael. 2003a. *Islamic Nationhood and Colonial Indonesia: The Umma below the Winds*. London: Routledge.

Laffan, Michael. 2003b. "The Tangled Roots of Islamist Activism in Southeast Asia." *Cambridge Review of International Affairs* 16 (3): 397–414.

Laffan, Michael. 2004. "An Indonesian Community in Cairo: Continuity and Change in a Cosmopolitan Islamic Milieu." *Indonesia* 77: 1–26.

Laffan, Michael. 2011. *The Makings of Indonesian Islam*. Princeton, NJ: Princeton University Press.

"Lagi-Lagi Wahabi Numpang Nama Aswaja' STAI Ali Bin Abi Thalib', Isra' Mi'Raj Bid'ah." 2015. Arrahma News, May 3, 2015. Available online: https://arrahmahnews.com/2015/05/03/lagi-lagi-wahabi-numpang-nama-aswaja-stai-ali-bin-abi-thalib-isra-miraj-bidah/ (accessed July 5, 2017).

Leiser, Gary. 1976. "The Restoration of Sunnism in Egypt: Madrasah and Mudarrisun, 495–647/1101–1249." PhD diss., University of Pennsylvania.

Leiser, Gary. 1986. "Notes on the Madrasah in Medieval Islamic Society." *Muslim World* 76 (1): 16–23.

Lewis, Bernard. 2003. *What Went Wrong? The Clash between Islam and Modernity in the Middle East*. New York: Harper Perennial.

Lewis, Bernard. 2004. *The Crisis of Islam: Holy War and Unholy Terror*. New York: The Random House.

Lim, Merlyna. 2011. "Radical Islamism in Indonesia and Its Middle Eastern Connections." *Middle East Review of International Affairs* 15 (2): 31–41.

Lombard, Denys. 1994. *Nusa Jawa Silang Budaya*. Jakarta: Gramedia.

Low, Michael Christopher. 2008. "Empire and the Hajj: Pilgrims, Plagues, and Pan-Islam under British Surveillance, 1865–1908." *International Journal of Middle East Studies* 40: 269–90.

Lucking, Mirjam. 2014. "Making Arab's One's Own Muslim Pilgrimage Experiences in Central Java," *Internationales Asienforum* 45 (1/2): 129–52.

Machmudi, Yon. 2011. "Muslim Intellectual or Housemaids? The Saudi Perceptions of the Indonesian Domestic Workers." *Journal of Indonesian Islam* 5 (2): 225–47.

Mansur, Ziyad M. 1990. *Kitab al-Mu'jam*. Medina: Maktaba al-Ulum wa al-Hikam.

Makdisi, George. 1961. "Muslim Institution of Learning in Eleventh-Century Baghdad." *Bulletin of the School of Oriental and African Studies* 24 (1): 1–56.

Makdisi, George. 1970. "Madrasah and University in the Middle Ages." *Studia Islamica* 32: 255–64.

Masud, Muhammad Khalid. 1990. "The Obligation to Migrate: The Doctrine of Hijra in Islamic Law." In Dale Eickelman and James Piscatori (eds.), *Muslim Travellers: Pilgrimage, Migration, and the Role of Imagination*, pp. 29–49. Berkeley: University of California Press.

Matthiesen, Toby. 2014. *The Other Saudis: Shiism, Descent and Sectarianism*. Cambridge: Cambridge University Press.
Meijer, Roel. 2010. "Reform in Saudi Arabia: The Gender-Segregation Debate." *Middle East Policy* 17 (4): 80–100.
Mobini-Kesheh, Watalie. 1999. *The Hadrami Awakening: Community and Identity in the Netherlands East Indies, 1900–1942*. Ithaca, NY: Cornell Southeast Asia Publications.
Mortel, Richard T. 1997. "Madrasas in Mecca during the Medieval Period: A Descriptive Study Based on Literary Sources." *Bulletin of the School of Oriental and African Studies* 60 (2): 236–52.
Mujani, Saiful. 2003. "Muslim Democrats: Democratic Culture and Muslim Political Participation in Post-Suharto Indonesia." PhD Thesis, Ohio State University.
Munawar, Said Agil. 2003. "Kerukunan Modal Keberhasilan." *Tokoh Indonesia*, August 21, 2003. Available online: http://www.tokohindonesia.com/biografi/article/285-ensiklopedi/2243-kerukunan-modal-keberhasilan (accessed July 20, 2017).
Nafi, Basheer M. 2006. "A Teacher of Ibn 'Abd al-Wahhab: Muhammad Hayat al-Sindi and the Revival of Ashab al-Hadith's Methodology." *Islamic Law and Society* 13 (2): 208–40.
Nawab, Mohamed. 2011. "Transnational Islamism and Its Impact in Malaysia and Indonesia." *Middle East Review of International Affairs* 15 (2): 42–52.
Netton, Ian Richard (ed.). 1993. *Golden Roads: Migration, Pilgrimage, and Travel in Medieval and Modern Islam*. Richmond: Curzon.
Netton, Ian Richard. 2016. "Rihla." In P. Bearman, Th. Bianquis, C. E. Bosworth, E. van Donzel, and W. P. Heinrichs (eds.), *Encyclopaedia of Islam, 2nd Edition*. Leiden: Brill Online. http://referenceworks.brillonline.com/entries/encyclopaedia-of-islam-2/rihla-SIM_6298 (accessed December 11, 2018).
New World Encyclopedia contributors. 2008. "Hussein bin Ali, Sharif of Mecca," *New World Encyclopedia*, last updated April 2, 2008. Available online: http://www.newworldencyclopedia.org/entry/Hussein_bin_Ali,_Sharif_of_Mecca (accessed June 17, 2016).
Nilan, Pam. 2009. "The Spirit of Education in Indonesian Pesantren." *British Journal of Sociology of Education* 30 (2): 219–32.
Norman, Alex. 2004. "Spiritual Tourism: Religion and Spirituality in Contemporary Travel." BA Thesis, University of Sydney, Australia.
Ochsenwald, William. 2007. "Islam and Loyalty in the Saudi Hijaz, 1926–1939." *Die Welt des Islams* 47 (1): 7–32.
Okruhlik, Gwenn. 2002. "Networks of Dissent: Islamism and Reform in Saudi Arabia." *Current History*, January: 22–28.
Panda, Ankit. 2014. "Indonesia and Saudi Arabia Sign Defense Cooperation Agreement." *The Diplomat*, January 25. Available online: https://thediplomat.com/2014/01/indonesia-and-saudi-arabia-sign-defense-cooperation-agreement/ (accessed July 12, 2019).
Paterson, F. W. N. 1980. "Letter from … Abu Dhabi: Welfare of the Hajj." *British Medical Journal*, May 24: 1261–62.
Patrick, Neil (ed.). 2016. *Saudi Arabian Foreign Policy: Conflict and Cooperation*. London: I.B. Tauris.
Pearson, Michael N. 1994. *Pious Passengers: The Hajj in Earlier Times*. Dhaka: University Press Limited.
Peters, F. E. 1994a. *The Hajj: The Muslim Pilgrimage to Mecca and the Holy Places*. Princeton, NJ: Princeton University Press.
Peters, F. E. 1994b. *Mecca: A Literary History of the Muslim Holy Land*. Princeton, NJ: Princeton University Press.

PPI Dunia. 2016. "8 Mahasiswa Indonesia Tembus Beasiswa Kedokteran Arab Saudi." *Good News from Indonesia*, November 30, 2016. Available online: https://www.goodnewsfromindonesia.id/2016/11/30/8-mahasiswa-indonesia-tembus-beasiswa-kedokteran-arab-saudi (accessed April 6, 2017).

Prawira, Adam. 2016. "KH Ali Mustafa Yaqub, Mantan Imam Besar yang Lahirkan Banyak Karya." *Sind News*, April 28, 2016. Available online: https://nasional.sindonews.com/read/1104647/15/kh-ali-mustafa-yaqub-mantan-imam-besar-yang-lahirkan-banyak-karya-1461811132 (accessed July 18, 2017).

Preuschaft, Menno. 2016. "Islam and Identity in Foreign Policy." In Neil Patrick (ed.), *Saudi Arabian Foreign Policy: Conflict and Cooperation*, pp. 16–28. London: I.B. Tauris.

"Profil Khadim Ma'had." 2016. *Darus Sunnah*. Available online: http://darussunnah.id/profil-khadim-mahad/ (accessed July 18, 2017).

"Profil Sekolah Indonesia di Arab Saudi." n.d. Indonesian Embassy in Saudi Arabia (KBRI Saudi Arabia). Available online: http://atdikriyadh.org/page.php?7 (accessed December 15, 2017).

"Profil Ustadz." 2019. Dzikra. Available online: http://dzikra.com/profil-ustadz-ali-musri/ (accessed June 21, 2017).

Prokop, Michaela. 2003. "Saudi Arabia: The Politics of Education." *International Affairs* 79 (1): 77–89.

Rachman, Abd. 1997. "The Pesantren Architects and Their Socio-Religious Teachings (1850–1950)." PhD Diss., University of California, Los Angeles.

Rahardjo, Dawam. 1985. *Pergulatan Dunia Pesantren*. Jakarta: LP3ES.

Rahman, Fazlur. 1969. *Islam*. Chicago: Chicago University Press.

Rakhmat, Muhammad Zulfikar. 2016. "Morocco: Indonesia's Long-Time Best Friend." *The Diplomat*, June 24, 2016. Available online: http://thediplomat.com/2016/06/morocco-indonesias-long-time-best-friend/ (accessed April 5, 2017).

Raphaeli, Nimrod. 2005. "Demands for Reforms in Saudi Arabia." *Middle Eastern Studies* 41 (4): 517–32.

Ratha, Dilip. 2003. "Workers' Remittances: An Important and Stable Source of External Development Finance." *Global Development Finance*, April 23, 2003. Available online: https://ssrn.com/abstract=3201568 (accessed July 12, 2019).

Reader, Ian. 2015. *Pilgrimage: A Very Short Introduction*. London: Oxford University Press.

Reid, Anthony. 1967. "Nineteenth Pan-Islam in Indonesia and Malaysia." *Journal of Asian Studies* 26 (2): 267–83.

Ricklefs, Merle C. 1993. *A History of Modern Indonesia c. 1300*. London: Macmillan.

Ricklefs, Merle C. 2007. *Polarizing Javanese Society: Islamic and Other Visions (1830–1930)*. Honolulu: University of Hawaii Press.

Riddell, Peter. 2001. *Islam and the Malay–Indonesian World: Transmission and Responses*. Honolulu: University of Hawaii Press.

Robinson, Kathryn and Sharon Bessell (eds.). 2002. *Women in Indonesia: Gender, Equity and Development*. Singapore: Institute of Southeast Asian Studies Press.

Roff, William R. 1970. "Indonesian and Malay Students in Cairo in the 1920s." *Indonesia* 9: 73–87.

Roff, William R. 1982 "Sanitation and Security: The Imperial Powers and the Nineteenth Century Hajj." *Arabian Studies* 6: 143–60.

Roy, Olivier. 1996. *The Failure of Political Islam*. Cambridge, MA: Harvard University Press.

Roy, Olivier. 2004. *Globalized Islam: The Search for a New Ummah*. New York: Columbia University Press.

Said, Edward W. 1983. *The World, the Text, and the Critic*. Cambridge, MA: Harvard University Press.
Saudi Ministry of Education. 1978. *Educational Policy in the Kingdom of Saudi Arabia*. Riyadh: Ministry of Education.
Schrieke, B. J. O. 1973. *Pergolakan Agama di Sumatra Barat: Satu Sumbangan Bibliografi*. Jakarta: Bharatara.
Schwartz, Stephen. 2003. *The Two Faces of Islam: Saudi Fundamentalism and Its Role in Terrorism*. New York: Anchor Books.
Scott, Margaret. 2016. "Indonesia: The Saudis Are Coming." *The New York Times*, October 27. Available online: http://www.nybooks.com/articles/2016/10/27/indonesia-the-saudis-are-coming/ (accessed July 5, 2017).
Shahin, Emad Ekdin. 1995. "Salafiyah." In John Esposito (ed.), *The Oxford Encyclopedia of the Modern Islamic World*, vol. 3, pp. 463–69. Oxford: Oxford University Press.
Shalabi, Ahmed. 1954. *History of Muslim Education*. Lebanon: Dar al-Kashaf.
Shellabear, William G. 1933. "A Malay Treatise on Popular Sufi Practices." In William G. Shellabear, Edwin Elliott Calverley, Elbert C. Lane, Ruth S. Mackensen, and Duncan Black Macdonald, *The MacDonald Presentation Volume*, pp. 351–70. Princeton, NJ: Princeton University Press.
Silvey, Rachel. 2004a. "Transnational Domestication: State Power and Indonesian Migrant Women in Saudi Arabia." *Political Geography* 23: 245–64.
Silvey, Rachel. 2004b. "Transnational Migration and the Gender Politics of Scale: Indonesian Domestic Workers in Saudi Arabia." *Singapore Journal of Tropical Geography* 25 (2): 141–55.
Silvey, Rachel. 2006. "Consuming Transnational Family: Indonesian Domestic Migrant Workers to Saudi Arabia." *Global Networks* 6 (1): 23–40.
Silvey, Rachel. 2007. "Mobilizing Piety: Gendered Morality and Indonesian-Saudi Transnational Migration." *Mobilities* 2 (2): 219–29.
Sirozi, Muhammad. 2005. "The Intellectual Roots of Islamic Radicalism in Indonesia." *Muslim World* 95: 81–120.
Smith, Larry and Abdulrahman Abouammoh (eds.). 2013. *Higher Education in Saudi Arabia: Achievements, Challenges and Opportunities*. Heidelberg: Springer.
Smith, Steve. 1986. "Theories of Foreign Policy: A Historical Overview." *Review of International Studies* 12: 13–29.
Spencer, Robert. 2004. *The Myth of Islamic Tolerance: How Islamic Law Treats Non-Muslims*. Amherst, NY: Prometheus Books.
Steenbrink, Karel A. 1974. "Pesantren, Madrasah, Sekolah." PhD Thesis, Radboud University, Nijmegen.
Steenbrink, Karel A. 1993. *Dutch Colonialism and Indonesian Islam: Contacts and Conflicts*. Amsterdam: Rodopy.
Sukoyo, Yeremia. 2017. "Ini yang Diungkapkan KH Ahsin di Hadapan Raja Salman." Berita Satu, March 4, 2017. Available online: http://www.beritasatu.com/nasional/417539-ini-yang-diungkapkan-kh-ahsin-di-hadapan-raja-salman.html (accessed July 19, 2017).
Sunyoto, Agus. 2015. *Atlas Wali Songo*. Yogyakarta: Pustaka Ilman.
Tagliacozzo, Eric. 2010. "Trans-Regional Indonesia over One Thousand Years: The Art of the Long View." *Indonesia* 90: 1–13.
Tagliacozzo, Eric. 2014. "Southeast Asia's Middle East: Shifting Geographies of Islam and Trade across the Indian Ocean." *Comparative Studies of South Asia, Africa and the Middle East* 34 (3): 565–73.

Tangban, O. E. 1991. "The Hajj and the Nigerian Economy, 1960–1981." *Journal of Religion in Africa* 21 (3): 241–55.

Tapper, Nancy. 1990. "Ziyaret: Gender, Movement, and Exchange in a Turkish Community." In Dale Eickelman and James Piscatori (eds.), *Muslim Travellers: Pilgrimage, Migration, and the Role of Imagination*, pp. 236–55. Berkeley: University of California Press.

Tarmizi, Erwandi. n.d. "Me: Edwardi Tarmizi." Available online: http://erwanditarmizi.com/about/ (accessed June 21, 2017).

Tayfur, M. Fatih. 1994. "Main Approaches to the Study of Foreign Policy: A Review." *METU Studies in Development* 21 (1): 113–41.

"Thariqah Qadiriyah Naqsyabandiyah." Selamet Datang di Pondek Pesantren Suryalaya. Available online: http://www.suryalaya.org/tqn1.html (accessed June 23, 2016).

Torrance, Arthur. 1930. "The Joys and Sorrows of the Mecca Pilgrims." *Current History* (July): 707–11.

Touati, Houari. 2010. *Islam and Travel in the Middle Ages*. Chicago, IL: University of Chicago Press.

Ulum, Amirul. 2015. *Ulama-Ulama Aswaja Nusantara yang Berpengaruh di Negeri Hijaz*. Yogyakarta: Pustaka Musi.

Umam, Saiful. 2006. "Radical Muslims in Indonesia: The Case of Ja'far Umar Thalib and the Laskar Jihad." *Explorations in Southeast Asian Studies* 6 (1): 1–26.

Umam, Saiful. 2013. "God's Mercy is Not Limited to Arabic Speakers: Reading Intellectual Biography of Muhammad Salih Darat and His Pegon Islamic Text." *Studia Islamika* 20 (2): 275–324.

"Universitas Terbuka UPBJJ Riyadh." n.d. KBRI. Available online: http://atdikriyadh.org/page.php?13 (accessed April 6, 2017).

Van Bruinessen, Martin. 1995. "Muslims of the Dutch East Indies and the Caliphate Question." *Studia Islamika* 2 (3): 115–40.

Van Bruinessen, Martin. 1998. "Biographies of Southeast Asian Ulama." In Marc Gaborieau, Nicole Grandin, Pierre Labrousse, and Alexandre Popovic (eds.), *Dictionnaire Biographique des Savants et Grandes Figures du Monde Musulman Peripherique, du XIXe siècle a nos jours*, pp. 1–42. Paris: CNRS-EHESS.

Van Bruinessen, Martin. 2002. "Wahhabi Influences in Indonesia, Real and Imagined." A summary of the paper presented at the *Journée d'Etudes du CEIFR (EHESS-CNRS) et MSH sur le Wahhabisme*. Ecole des Hautes Etudes en Sciences Sociales / Maison des Sciences de l'Homme, Paris, June 10.

Van Bruinessen, Martin. 2015. *Kitab Kuning, Pesantren, dan Tarekat*. Yogyakarta: Gading Publishing.

Van Doorn-Harder, Nelly and Kees de Jong. 2001. "The Pilgrimage to Tembayat: the Tradition and Revival in Indonesian Islam." *Muslim World* 91: 325–53.

Van Niel, Robert. 1960. *The Emergence of Modern Indonesian Elite*. Chicago: Quadrangle Books.

Voll, John. 1975. "Muhammad Hayya al-Sindi and Muhammad ibn Abd al-Wahhab: An Analysis of an Intellectual Group in Eighteenth-Century Medina." *Bulletin of the School of Oriental and African Studies* 38 (1): 32–39.

Von den Mehden, Fred R. 1993. *Two Worlds of Islam: Interactions between Southeast Asia and the Middle East*. Gainesville: University Press of Florida.

Vredenbregt, Jacob. 1962. "The Haddj: Some of Its Features and Functions in Indonesia." *Bijdragen tot de Taal-, Land- en Volkenkunde* 118: 91–154.

Wafa, Muhammad Ali. 2017. "Haul Prof. KH Ali Mustafa Yaqub: Menepis Tuduhan Wahabi." *Majalah Nabawi*, April 15, 2017. Available online: https://majalahnabawi.com/haul-prof-kh-ali-mustafa-yaqub-menepis-tuduhan-wahabi/ (accessed July 18, 2017).

Wahib, Ahmad Bunyan. 2006. "Salafi Da'wa Movement after the Dissolution of Laskar Jihad." Unpublished paper.

Wahid, Din. 2014. "Nurturing the Salafi Manhaj: A Study of Salafi Pesantren in Contemporary Indonesia." PhD Thesis, Universiteit Utrecht.

Watt, Montgomery. 1971. "Hidjra." In *The Encyclopaedia of Islam*, III, 2nd edition, pp. 366–67. Leiden: Brill.

Wha, Min Byung. 1991. "Baraka, as Motif and Motive, in the Rihla of Ibn Battuta, 1304–1369." PhD Thesis, The University of Utah.

Witkam, Jan Just. 2007. "Introduction." In C. Snouck Hurgronje (ed.), *Mekka in the Latter Part of the 19th Century*, xiii–xxi. Leiden: Brill.

Woodward, Mark. 1989. *Islam in Java: Normative Piety and Mysticism in the Sultanate of Yogyakarta*. Tucson: University of Arizona Press; Association for Asian Studies.

Woodward, Mark. 2010. *Java, Indonesia and Islam*. Dordrecht: Springer.

Yaqub, Ali Mustafa. 2006. "Haji Pengabdi Setan." *Gatra*, January 16, 2006. Available online: http://arsip.gatra.com/2006-01-26/artikel.php?id=91593 (accessed July 17, 2017).

Yaqub, Ali Mustafa. 2015. "Titik Temu Wahabi-NU." *Republika*, February 13, 2015. Available online: http://www.republika.co.id/berita/koran/opini-koran/15/02/13/njp7g851-titik-temu-wahabinu (accessed July 18, 2017).

Yunus, H. Mahmud. 1979. *Sejarah Pendidikan Islam di Indonesia*. Jakarta: Penerbit Mutiara.

Zakaria, Hafiz and Mohd Afandi Salleh. 2011. "From Makkah to Bukit Kamang?: The Moderate versus Radical Reforms in West Sumatra (ca. 1784–1819)." *International Journal of Humanities and Social Science* 1 (14): 195–203.

INDEX

Abah Anom, (Ajengan Ahmad Shahibul Wafa Tajul Arifin) 118
Abah Sepuh (Muhammad, Ajengan Abdullah Mubarak bin Nur) 118
Abaza, Mona 5, 14–16, 29, 32–3, 57
Abbas, Sayyid 135
Abd al-Aziz ibn Abdullah Al Ashaikh 156
Abd al-Jabbar, Shaikh Umar
  books and publications 123
Abd al-Nasser, Gamal 149
Abdat, Abdul Hakim 168
Abdillah. Masykuri 84
Abduh, Muhammad 70, 163
Abdul Latif bin Ibrahim Al, al-Shaikh 107
Abdul Aziz Abdullah bin Baz 164, 166, 168
Abdul Aziz Al Saud (King) 180
Abdul Aziz bin Ibn Saud (King) 31
Abdul Aziz ibn Abdul Rahman Al Saud (Ibn Saud) 53, 77, 106, 134, 180
Abdul Ghani bin Shubuh 122
Abdullah, Abbas 124
Abdullah al-Amr, Abdul Aziz 166
Abdullah al-Shami, Shaikh Ahmad 127
Abdullah Basalamah, Khalid Zeed 171
Abdullah bin Al Hasan, al-Kuhaji 96
Abdullah bin Hasan al-Jawi 116
Abdullah Zaen bin Zaini Muhajjat 170
Abdul Qadir bin Abdurrahman al-Fatani 119
Abdul Wahab, Shaikh Muhammad 64
Abdurrahman, Mas 122
Abdurrazaq bin Abdul Muhsin al-Abbad 170
Abdus Satar bin Abdul Wahhab al-Shadiqi Shaikh, al-Makki 122
Abdush Shamad bin Abdulrahman 122
Abegebriel, Agus Maftuh 26, 45
Aboebakar, H. 97
Abouammoh, Abdulrahman 105
Abouhaseira, Maher 107
abu khamsin (i.e., goods for SR 50) 44
Abuza, Zachary 1
Aceh War 70
adat 59, 61–63, 65, 72–3, 125, 159, 162, 172, 188
Addiriny, Musyaffa 163
Afifuddin 173
Afif Abdullah bin Muhammad, al-Arsufi 94
Agung Hanyokrokusumo, Sultan 66
ahl al-bid'ah (*or* mubtadi') 173
ahl al-hadith (*or* as'hab al-hadith) 15, 166
ahl al-ra'y (*or* as'hab al-ra'y) 15
ahlaq al-karimah 95
Ahmad, Abdullah 124
Ahmad bin Yusuf Shaikh, al-Qisti 118–19
Ahmad bin Hanbal 80, 164
Ahmad bin Idris 53
Ahmad, Haji 117
Ahmad, ibn Taimiyya 75, 164
Ahmadiyah 165
Ahmad Khatib, Sambas, Shaikh 68, 115, 117–18, 122, 134, 183
Ahmad Zaini Dahlan, Shaikh, *Fath al-Mutafakkirin*) 119
akhlaq 123
A'la, Abd 58, 60, 63, 65, 107
al-Adeni, Abdul-Rahman 141–2
al-Afghani, Jamal al-Din 70
al-Ahgaf University 141–2
al-Albani, Muhammad Nasiruddin 156, 164, 167, 183
al-'Arabi, Shaikh Abdullah 180
al-Atsary, Abu Hudzaifah 163
Al-Attas, Muhammad Naquib 55, 164
al-Attas, Syarifah Sidah 164
Alawi, Sayyid Muhammad 23–4, 68, 95, 101–3, 109, 120, 128–9, 135, 146, 151–2, 159, 183–4
al-Azhar Mosque 139–40, 146
Al-Azhar University of Cairo 91, 94–5, 98–9, 102, 128, 135, 137, 139–40, 149, 182

al-Baijuri, Ibrahim Shaikh 122
al-Banggali, Abdul Khaliq 95
al-Banjari, Abdul Karim 99
al-Banjari, Ali bin Abdullah 115
al-Banjari, Muhammad Arshad 56–7, 93, 113–14, 116
   Sabil al-Muhtadin 57
al-Banjari, Muhammad Nafis 56, 113
   Tuhfat al-Nafis 57
al-Banna, Hassan 79
al-Bantani, Abdul Karim 115, 122
al-Bantani, Arsyad Thawil 122
al-Banyumasi, Ahmad Nakhrawi 115
al-Barzanji, Ja'far
   Maulid 119
al-Batawi, Abdurrahman 113, 116
al-Batawi, Junaid 115
al-Baweani, Asy'ari 122
al-Baweani, Muhammad Zainuddin 115
al-Bimawi, Abdul Ghani 115, 127
al-Bugisi, Abdul Wahhab 113, 116
al-Daghistani, Shaikh Abdul Hamid al-Shirwani 119
al-Dahlawi, Abdul Sattar 122
al-Damanhuri, Abdul Mun'im 116
Aldamer, Shafi 26–8
al-Dimyathi, Ahmad Shaikh 122
al-Din, Burhan 63
al-Din al-Albani, Muhammad Nasir Shaikh 75, 82
al-Dzakhirah 170
al-Fadani, Abdullah Dardum 115
al-Falimbani, Abdus Shamad 93
al-Fansuri, Hamzah 55–6, 113
Al Fasi, Taqiyuddin 94
al-Fattani, Daud 114, 116
al-Fauzan, Saleh 156
Al-Fawzan, Shaikh Saleh 183
al-Furqan 167, 170
al-Gawhar 140
al-Ghazali 57
Al-Ghumari, Sayyid Abdul Aziz 128
al-Hajuri, Shaikh Yahya 141–2
al-Hamid II, Abd 33
al-Hamidiyah 179
Al Hammad, Shaikh Hammad 183
al-Hasan Ali Nadwi, Abu 107
al-Hawaary, Abu Zubair 163

Ali, Khatib 124
Ali, Sayyid Muhsin bin 119
Ali, Shaikh Muhammad 119
Ali al-Banjari 127
Ali Bin Abi Thalib 173
Ali bin Ibrahim al-Namlah 38
Ali Hadrami, Abdullah Saleh 162
Al Imam Muhammad bin Saud Islamic University 80, 82–3, 145–52, 154, 158–9, 162, 170, 182
al-Iman University (Sana'a) 141
Ali Musri Semjan Putra 162, 169–70, 173
Ali Mustafa Ya'qub 163, 178
Ali Nur 173
Ali Rinaldi 131
Al-Irshad 73, 79, 137, 153, 157
Al-Irsyad al-Islamiyah 166
Ali Shariati 80
aliyyah (madrasah) 3, 5, 14, 17–18, 22–4, 31, 35–7, 50, 54–5, 66, 71, 80–1, 86, 88–9, 90–104, 110, 112, 118, 120, 129–30, 135, 140, 166, 169
al-Jabiri, Shaikh Ubaid 170
al-Jamiah al- Amrikiyyah al-Maftuhah 140
al-Jauziyya, Ibn al-Qayyim 82
al-Jawi, Marzuki 116
al-Jawziyya, Muhammad ibn Qayyim 75
al-Jubeir, Adel 46
Al Jufri, Habib Musthofa bin Husain 95
al-Jugjawi, Muhammad Baqir 127
al-Jukjawi, Baqir bin Muhammad Nur 115, 120
al-Kadiri, Dahlan Hasan 98
al-Khalidi, Muhammad Nur Salim 99
Alkhateeb, Shaikh Abdulhameed 124
Alkhatib, Abdulmalik 124
al-Khatib, Muhib al-Din 82
Al Khayyat, Abdulrahman Mohammed Amen 45
al-Kurani, Shaikh Ibrahim 56–7, 63
al-Kurdi, Shaikh Saleh 124
al-Kutbi al-Hasani, Shaikh Muhammad Amin 183
All Islam Congress 73
al-Madkhali, Shaikh Rabi 141
al-madrasah al-ahliyah 99
al-Mahrusi, Shaikh Umar Hamdan 127

al-Maimani, Shaikh Sa'dullah 127
al-Makassari, Muhammad Yusuf 55–7, 56, 93
  Zubdat al-Asrar or "The Essence of Secrets") 57
al-Makki, Ahmad al-Nakhrawi Shaikh 122
al-Makki, Muhammad Ali bin Hussein Shaikh 119
al-Malik al-Kamil, Ayyubid Sultan 90
al-Mandili, Abdul Qadir 116
al-Mandili, Abdul Qodir bin Abdul Muttolib 115
al-Mandili, Zubair Ahmad 98–9
Al Masyyath, Hasan Shaik 95
al-Minangkabawi, Akhmad Khatib 115
al-Minangkabawi, Ismail al-Khalidiyah 115
Al Mizan 153
Al-Moalimi, Abdallah Abdulrahman 18, 123
al-Mulk, Nizam 71
Al Munawar, Professor Dr. Said Aqil Husin 163, 174
al-Musawa, Sayyid Muhsin 128, 148
  al-Nafhatu al-Tsaniyah Syarh Tuhfatu al-Tsaniyah 120
  al-Rihlah al-'Aliyyahila Diyar al-Hadramiyya 120
  Wa Madkhalu al-Wushul ila 'Ilm al-Ushul 120
Al-Nahdlah Islamic Boarding School 181
Al-Nasiriyah 101
al-Nisa, Begum Shaulah 95–6
al-Palembani, Abdus Samad 116–18
al-Palimbani, Abd al-Samad 56–7, 113
al-Palimbani, Sayyid Muhsin bin Ali al-Hasani 115
al-Qiyadah 165
al-Qudsi, Abdul Hamid 122
Al Qurtuby, Sumanto 26–7, 69, 114, 120, 131, 166
al-Rafiq Pasha, Sharif 'Awn 124
al-Rahman, Shaikh Jamil 166
al-Raniri, Nur al-Din 55–6, 113–14
  al-Sirat al-Mustaqim 56
  Bustan al-Salatin (The Garden of Kings) 56
al- Rasuli, Sulaiman 124
al- Sarbini, Shaikh Muhammad 127

al-Sariaki, Jinan Muhammad Thayyib 116
Al Saud family 124
al- Shinqithi, Shaikh Habibullah 127
al-Sindi, Muhammad Hayya 53, 113–14
al-Sinkili, Abd al-Ra'uf 55–6, 63, 113
  Mir'at al-Tullab 56
  tafsir (Qur'anic exegesis) 56
  Tarjuman al-Mustafid 56
al-Sinkili, Abdurrouf 113
al-Sofwa 83
al-Sumatrani, Shams al-Din 55–6, 113–14
al-Sumbawi, Muhammad Zainuddin 127
al-Sumbawi, Shaikh Umar 118
al-Sunnah 83, 170–1
al-Syami, Shaik Umar 68–9
al-tahdiriyah 98
al-Tambusi, Abu Bakar bin Syihabuddin 116
al-Tamimi, Abdurrahman 173
al- Tamimi, Muhammad Khalifah 171
al-Turath al-Islami 83
al-Utaybi, Juhayman 81
Alwaleed, bin Talal (prince) 45–6
al-Zawawi, Muhammad Shalih 68, 119
al- Zindani, Abd al-Majid 141
Ambary, Hasan Muarif 118
Aminah, Nyai 129
Aminah, Siti 100
amr ma'ruf nahi munkar (commanding right) 84, 165
Amrullah, Abdul Karim 124
Andirja, Firanda 131, 162, 172, 188
anti-colonialism 21, 69–74
anti-Dutch movements 72
anti-Iranian campaign 28
anti-Iran Islamist groups 80
anti-Sufism 74
anti-*ziyara* 74
Anton Satria Prabuwono 131–2
aqidah 76, 102, 123, 125, 131, 146, 170
Arab Cold War 149
Arab-Hadramis 17
Arab–Israeli war 37, 77
Arab Muslims
  anti- and pro 188–9
  cultural practice 73–4
  traders 30
  preachers 138

Arab Socialist movement 28
Arab Socialist Nationalism 77
Arab ulama 124, 128
Arief, Haji Muhammad (of Sumanik) 58, 64
arkan al-Islam 70
Armen Halim Naro 162
ashab al-Jawiyyin 57
Ashadi, Abdul Latif 152
Ash'arism 67, 91
Asifuddin, Ahmad Faiz 167–8
Asma' bint Abu Bakar 123
Asrorun Ni'am Sholeh 163, 174, 181
Association of Indonesian Muslim Intellectuals (Ikatan Cendekiawan Muslim Indonesia, or ICMI) 84, 98, 101
Asy'ari, Hashim Shaikh 120
Asy'ari bin Abdurrahman al-Baweani 115
Ataturk, Mustafa Kemal 79
Atmojo, Raden 98
At-Turots (Yayasan Majelis al-Turots al-Islami) 82
Aziz, Abdul 94
Azra, Azyumardi 6, 16, 29, 53, 55–8, 60, 63–4, 112–14, 112–17, 113, 116–17, 144, 162

Bab al-Fattah 94
Bab al-Salam 94
Bab al-Umrah 94
Ba-Basil, Muhammad Sa'id 126–7
Badrussalam, Abu Yahya 162
Bafadhal, Saleh Shaikh 119
Bafaqih Ba'lawi, Shaikh Ahmad 68
Baisya, Yusuf 168
Bait al-Hikmah 91
Bajunaid, Umar Shaikh 119
Bali Blast 2002 47
Bambang Trigunarsyah 131
Banjar, Arshad bin Abdus Samad Shaikh 121
Banten, Abdul Qadir 116
Banten, Imam Nawawi 67–9, 102, 116, 120–7, 134–5, 183
  death 123
  multiple religious titles 122
  Tafsir al-Munir 123
  works 123

Banten, Shaik Abd al-Karim 69, 134
Banten Revolt 70
Banyumas, Ahmad Nahrawi 126
baraka 15
Barth, Fredrik 189
barzanji 185
Basalamah, Khalid 83, 162, 171, 173, 188
Basalamah, Reza 162
Basalamah, Syafiq 171, 188
Bashari, Agus Hasan 173–4
Baso, Ahmad 163, 182
Basri, Basri 6, 112, 126
Basyuni, Maftuh 42
bayt al-hikma or *dar a-'ilm* (libraries) 90
Benda, Harry J. 60, 69, 71
Berita Nahdlatul Ulama 97
berkah 49
bid'a (bid'ah or bidat) 75, 158, 168, 188
Bima, Shaik Abd al-Ghani 68, 122
Boissevain, Jeremy 20
Bonang, Sunan 120
Bowen, John R. 16
Braginsky, Vladimir I. 55
Bubalo, Anthony 79, 138–9, 141–2
Bukhari, Imam 127, 157, 171
Burhanuddin, Anas 163
Busail, Ba 125
Buyids 91

Caliph 140
Cepu, Maghfur Usman 163, 174
Chaplin, Chris 74, 85, 137
Chernoff, John 9
Christakis, Nicholas 20
Clancy-Smith, Julia A. 11
College of Sharia in Mecca 88
Commins, David 64
Committee of Islamic Charity 81
Cook, Michael 75

Daghastani, Abdul Hamid Shaikh 122
Daghistani, Abdulkarim 125
Dahlan, Shaikh Zaini 56, 93, 96, 119, 121, 124, 127
dakwah or da'wa 4, 7, 16, 21, 31, 36, 74–6, 79, 81, 84, 146, 153, 162, 164, 166–8, 171–4, 179, 183, 188
Dar al-Hadith 90, 141, 169–70
Dar al-Hadith al-Khairiyya 170

dar al-hadith (school for teaching hadith) 90, 141, 169–70
Dar al-'Ilm 88, 91
dar al-Islam 9
dar al-kufr 9
dar al-kutub 88
dar al-Mustafa 141
dar al-qira'ah (school for teaching the Qur'an) 90
dar al-Zahra 141
Darban, Adaby 66
Darul Ulum 22, 93–100, 104, 110, 118–19, 120, 128–9, 135, 139, 148
  learning divisions 98
Das Gupta, Ashin 29
daura 74
Dawud bin Abdullah 119
Defense Cooperation Agreement (DCA) 47
DeHanas, Daniel Nilsson 8
de Jong, Kees 10
Delaney, Carol 8–9
Delong-Bas, Natana J. 18, 64
Depnakertrans 39
Dewan Dakwah Islamiyah Indonesia (DDII) 4, 21–3, 31, 79–81, 167
Dhofier, Zamakhsyari 65, 89
Diederich, Mathias 34–5, 41
Dihan, Daud Shaikh 96
Dimyati, Sayyid Ahmad 68
Diponegoro University 152
Djajadiningrat, Hoesein 69
Dobbin, Christine 58–60, 64, 73, 125
Douwes, Dick 8–9, 30
Dumarcay, Jacques 118
Duncan, Katie 143
Dunia, PPI 140, 142, 147, 185
Dutch East Indies (VOC) 61, 65, 70–4

Effendi, Satria 163, 174
Egyptian Nasserism 76
Eickelman, Dale 4–5, 10–14, 136
Elyas, Tariq 109
ex-Laskar Jihad or Jihad Forces 83–4

Fadlilah, Farid 131
Fahad, Malik 94
fahmialinh 100, 129
Faisal, bin Abdul Aziz Al Saud, (King) 26, 77
Fakhruddin, Kemas 113

falak 118, 128
Fansuri, Hamzah 114
faqih (*pl.* fuqaha) 68, 113, 128
Farquhar, Michael 18, 75, 77, 87, 107, 131, 134
Fathurrahman, Oman 63
Fatimid Dynasty (Daulah Fatimiyya) 91
Fealy, Greg 79, 138, 164
Feener, Michael R. 53
fiqh 56–8, 61, 68, 80, 88, 90, 102, 108, 119, 123, 126–8, 134, 153, 164, 170, 180, 195
FORMIDA (Forum for Indonesian community in Jeddah) 101
Fouad Abdulhameed bin Ahmad Alkhateeb 124
Fowler, James 20
Freitag, Ulrike 29
fushah 128
Fussell, Paul 14

Gadjah Mada University 171–2
Geertz, Clifford 59
Gellens, Sam I. 13–14
General Tito Karnavian 165
General Wiranto 164
Georgetown University 176
Gerakan Pemuda Ansar 153
Ghaznavid Empire 91
Ghazni, Mahmud 91
Ghufran, Ainur Rafiq 167–8
Gibson, Tom 56–7
Gold, Dore 1
Goldziher, Ignaz 15, 91
Grand Mosque of Mecca
  seizure of 81
Graves, Elizabeth 10, 125
Gulacir, Tubagus Ismail 118
Gulen, Fethullah 143
Gunaratna, Rohan 1
guru 34, 54, 56, 63, 66, 117, 183
Gus Dur 175, 177–8, 185

Habibullah bin Maya'aba, al-Shinqithi 96
Habib Zain bin Smith 102, 148
hadith 13–16, 22, 36–7, 56, 90, 96, 98, 102, 108, 116, 121, 123, 126–30, 138, 141, 146, 153, 166, 169–71, 174, 178–180
Hadiwijaya, Sultan 120

Hadler, Jeffry 59, 62, 73
Hadramaut 141–2
Hadrami, Abdullah 173
Hadrami sojourners 29–30
haji (*Arabic:* hajj) 12, 32, 58, 63–4, 70, 117, 124, 155, 179
hajj pilgrimage. *See also* rihla
   Dutch views 35
   Indonesian pilgrims 31–4, 39
   Malay 34
   motivations 10–12
   new Saudi regulation 40
   as social status 50
   travel theories 7–10, 13, 17
halal 132, 182
halaqah 5, 22–3, 35, 94, 101, 112, 123
Halaqa Masjid Haram 94
halqa 74
hamala 15
Hamid al-Makki, Shaikh Abdullah 127
Hamka 62, 124
Hanafi maddhab 24, 31, 90, 95, 105, 128, 134, 157, 175, 193
Hanbali 24, 27, 31, 55, 76, 80, 90, 105, 122, 128, 133–5, 157, 159, 193
Hanif, N 56, 163, 174
haram (sinful) 10, 44, 133, 136, 158, 173
Haramain 6, 17–18, 31, 44, 49–50, 53–8, 63, 66–7, 70, 111, 113–22, 128–9, 134–6, 144, 146, 175, 194
Harimau Nan Salapan (the "Eight Lions") 64
Harun, Muhammad Yusuf 168
Hasan, Ahmad 73
Hasan bin Muhammad, al-Mashshath 96
Hasan, Noorhaidi 7, 28, 31, 74–5, 78–9, 164, 167
Hasanuddin, Maulana Sultan 118
Hasbullah, Shaikh 122
Hasyim, Khairiyah 129
Hefner, Robert W. 28, 59, 66, 78–9, 84–5, 138
Hegghammer, Thomas 18, 77, 81, 145
Heidhues, Mary Somers 55
Henderson, Joan Catherine 8
hijab 7, 9
Hijaz 2, 5, 15–18, 20, 23, 25, 27, 29–30, 31–35, 43–4, 53–4, 60, 66, 67–70, 71–2, 86–9, 91–5, 100–6, 109, 110, 111, 113–14, 119, 122, 123–4, 128–9, 133–6, 138–9, 143, 145, 180, 192–5

hijra (*or* hijrah) 7–13
Hikmatyar, Gulbuddin 166
hitam (black) 59
hizbiyya 75, 168
Hizbut Tahrir Indonesia 168
Ho, Engseng 29, 141
Hugo, Graeme 39, 42
Hurgronje, C. Snouck 32–4, 53–4, 70–2, 92–3, 121, 144
Husein bin Shihab 164
Husin Al Munawar, Dr. Said Aqil 174, 181

Ibadah (*pl.* ibadat) 50, 57, 179
Ibn al-Arabi 56
   wahdat al-wujud (unity of being) 55–6
ibn Ali, Imam Hasan 102
ibn Ali Tusi, Abu Ali Hasan (Nizam al-Mulk) 90
Ibn Hajar 123, 127
ibn Hanbal, Ahmad 75
Ibrahim bin Abullah Al Suwaiyel 46
Ibrahim bin Amir al-Ruhaili 170
Ibrahim bin Hasan al-Kurani 53
ICMI 84, 101, 130
IELTS (International English Language Testing System) 152
Igarashi, Daisuke 92
Ihsan, Abu 173
Ihya al-Sunnah 83, 166–7, 169
ijazah 154
ijtihad 76
Ikatan Mahasiswa Muhammadiyah 153
ikhlas 136, 152
Ikhwanul Muslimin 73, 168
ilm 14
ilm al-kalam 195
Ilyas, Muhammad 100
imam 102, 121, 122, 124
Imam Muhammad bin Saud Islamic University 103, 109
Indonesian Communist Party 78
Indonesian Council of Ulama 83
Indonesian government/Republic of Indonesia
   independence 76
   New Order 28, 38, 57, 78–81, 84, 177–8, 187, 193
   Old Order 28, 38, 57, 78–80, 84, 177–8, 187, 193

revolutionary government 78
state ideology 84
Indonesian Islam and society 53–86
  contemporary education, publication, and foundation 81–3
  Haramain-trained Indonesian Islamic scholars 54–8
  modern neo-Salafism 74–81
  Padri movement, West Sumatra 58–65
  pan-Islamism and anti-colonialism 69–74
  pesantren tradition, Java 65–9
  Sufi gurus 54–8
  Suharto's fall for neo-Salafis 83–5
  Sunni-Shafi'ite madhhab 65–9
Indonesian Muslim Students, or PPI 139–40, 142, 146–7, 150, 156–7, 184–5
  backgrounds and rationales for studying in Saudi Arabia 150–5
  dispute with Shaulatiyah teachers 97
  institutions of learning and education for 93–6
  Islamic boarding schools 23–4
  journey of to Arabia 16–18
  learning and education institutions 93–6
  Middle East, educational institutions 138–43
  new generation 24
  non-Indonesian educational institutions 101–4, 101–9
  past and present 143–9
  plurality and complexity 156–60
  scholarships for 36, 48
Indonesian Muslim teachers in Arabia 111–12
  past and present, comparison 111–13
Indonesian relations 25–51
  bilateral ties 4, 26–31
  changing mutual images and perceptions 43–5
  contemporary developments 45–9
  hajj pilgrimage 31–7
  historical dynamics 25
  intellectualism 5, 31–7
  labor migration 37–43
  migration, workforce, and employment 37–42

  national interests, modern developments 45–9
  pilgrimage and learning in the past 31–7
  Saudi foreign policy 29
  skilled and professional workers 43–5
Indonesian schools
  decline, causes of 104–9
  reasons for decline 104–9
  Saudi's role 96–101
Indonesian societies
  Haramain-trained Islamic scholars 55, 57–8
  Islamic intellectual life 53
  "raja-centric" 63
  Saudi alumni's role 186–9
Indra, Ristapawa 58, 173
Indunisi 43
Institut Pendidikan Tinggi Ilmu Al-Qur'an 153, 176
Institut Pertanian Bogor 152, 170
Institut Teknologi Bandung 152
Institut Teknologi Surabaya 152
International Crisis Group (ICG) 82
International Islamic Relief Organization 81
Iranian/Islamic Revolution 81, 106
Iranian revolution 80
Iranian Shia revolution 28
Iranian Shiism 76
Irianto, Sulistiyowati 42
Irsad, Abdul Adzim 99
Irshad, Abdul Adzim 163, 174
isbal 7, 74
Iskandar Thani, Sultan of Kesultanan 56
Islam
  contemporary studies 11–12
  heterodox and orthodox 56
  main pillars 17, 111
  patriarchal Arab culture 100
  rihla tradition 5–7, 13–16
  sharia-based mysticism 63–4
Islamic Center Bin Baz 157
Islamic Defenders Front 83–4
Islamic law, doctrine of hijra 11. *See also specific laws*
Islamic modernism 57, 112
Islamic reformism 54, 105, 112–14, 125
Islamic Republic of Iran 80

Islamic scholars, teachers, and scientists In Saudi Arabia
   Ahmad Khatib Minangkabau (1860–1916) 123–6
   contemporary personalities 129–133
   four leading scholars from the past 121
   in Mecca in the past 112–21
   Muhammad Mahfud Termas (1868–1920) 126–8
   Muhammad Yasin Padang (1916–1990) 128–9
   Nawawi Banten (1813–1897) 121–3
   Saudi, earliest influences 54–8
   social changes and intellectual travel 133–6
Islamic Umma Union 83–4
Islamic University of Medina (IUM) 77, 80, 82–3, 98, 103, 106–7, 134, 146, 169
Islamism 4, 21, 33, 65, 69–74, 76–7, 84–6, 145, 156, 160, 166
Islamist 21–2, 27–8, 31, 47, 62, 70, 73, 76, 78–85, 107–8, 135, 145, 156–7, 160, 166, 168–9, 177, 193–4
Ismaili Shia Imam Abu Tamim Maad al-Muizz li Dinillah 140
isnad 11

Jaho, Muhammad Jamil 124
Jahroni, Jajang 82
Jakarta-based Yayasan Ats Tsabat 171
jalabiyya 7, 9, 74, 76, 133
Jalaluddin, Muhammad Tahir 123
Jalil, Abdul 130
jamaah 153
Jamaah Masjid Manarul Ilmi 153
Jama'at al-Da'wa ila al-Qur'an wa Ahl al-Hadith 166
Jamal, Maher 47
Jamaluddin al-Afghani 163
Jambek, Muhammad Jamil 124
jami'ah 103, 106, 179
Jamiah al-Azhar 140
Jamiat al-'Uloom al-Shari'a 141
Jamil al-Rahman 166
Jam'iyyah Khairiyah 100, 129
Java War 70
Jawah (or the Jawis) 34, 70, 71–2, 93, 122
"Jawi ulama" 43–5, 119–20

Jazan University 147
Jibrin, Abd Allah ibn 82
jihad 34, 62, 70–1, 83–4, 117–18, 166–7, 169
Johns, Anthony H. 55
Johnson, Mark 1
Jones, S. 139
Jum'an bin Ma'mun, al-Tangerangi 122
Junaid Shaikh, al-Batawi 121–2

ka'ba 44
Ka'ba and Hajar Aswad (the "Black Stone") 44
Kairanavi, Maulana Rahmatullah 95
Kampung Jawah (or Kampung Jawa) 17, 34, 93, 122, 126
Kaptein, Nico 8–9, 30
Karim, Muslih Abdul 163, 174
Karim Amrullah, Haji Abdul Malik 124
Kartodirdjo, Sartono 70, 118
kaum abangan 59
kaum hitam 59
kaum muda 73
kaum putih 59
kaum putihan 31, 59, 162, 188
Kawach, Nadim 37
Kediri 176, 180
Kelompok Studi Pelajar Muslim Bogor 153
Kemas Muhammad bin Ahmad 113
kesaktian 69
KFUPM (King Fahd University of Petroleum and Minerals) 131–3, 132–3, 152, 155
Khadim, Ahmad 173
Khalwatiya order 11
khanqah 90
khanqah (Sufi convent) 90
Khatib, Ahmad 124–6, 134
Khatib Hanbali, Shaikh Muhammad 122
Khatib Minangkabau, Shaikh Ahmad 126
Khomeini, Ayatollah 28, 77, 80, 192
khuttab 18, 94, 100, 129
kiai (Islamic scholars) 32, 66–9, 100–1, 113–18, 120–4, 126–7, 130, 134–5, 146, 148, 163, 174–185
Kiai Abdul Hamid bin Muhammad Ali al-Qudsi 115
Kiai Abdullah 126
Kiai Abdul Fadhol Senori Tuban 68

Kiai Abdul Manan Dipomenggolo 96, 126
Kiai Abdullah Abbas Cirebon 68
Kiai Abdullah Mubarak Suralaya 68
Kiai Abdullah Muhaimin bin Abdul Aziz bin Baidlowi al-Lasemi 120–1
Kiai Abdullah Termas 68–9
Kiai Abdu Karim 117–18
Kiai Abdul Wahhab Chasbullah 31, 127, 175
Kiai Abdurrahman 118
Kiai Abdurrahman Wahid 127, 175
Kiai Abdur Rozaq, Pamekasan 163, 174
Kiai Ahmad, Dahlan 113, 124
Kiai Ahmad Damanhuri Arman Banten 129–30
Kiai (KH), Dr. Ahmad Fahmi 130–1, 163, 174
Kiai Ahmad Rifai Kalisak 68, 113
Kiai Ahmad Mutamakkin 113–14
Kiai Ahmad Thalhah 117
Kiai Ahsin Sakho Muhammad 163, 174, 180
Kiai (KH) Ali Mustafa Ya'qub 174, 178
Kiai Aqib 118
Kiai Arshad Qashir 118
Kiai Arshad Thawil 118
Kiai As'ad Syamsul Arifin Situbondo 68, 175
Kiai Asnawi Caringin-Banten 118
Kiai (KH). Asrorun Ni'am Sholeh 174, 181
Kiai Asy'ari, Muhammad Hasyim 113
Kiai Baidhawi bin Abdul Aziz 113
Kiai Bakrun 163
Kiai Bisri Shansuri Denanyar 68, 127
Kiai Bisri Mustafa Rembang 68
  Tafsir Al-Ibriz 68
Kiai Dimyathi 126
Kiai Faqih Maskumambang 113
Kiai Fuad Abdul Wahhab 101
Kiai Hasbullah, 120
Kiai (KH) Hanif Ismail 163, 174
Kiai Harris 118
Kiai Hasbullah, Ahmad 117
Kiai (KH) Hasyim, Asy'ari 67, 100, 122, 129, 175
Kiai Husein Palembang 130
Kiai Ihsan Muhammad Dahlan Kediri 68
Kiai Khalil Bangkalan 67, 69, 113, 117–18, 122

Kiai, Maimun, Zubair 103, 127–8, 184
KiaiMahfudz, Lombok 163, 174
Kiai Manaf Abd al-Karim Lirboyo, 68
Kiai Mas Alwi bin Abdul Azis 175
Kiai Ma'shum bin Ahmad 113
Kiai Mas Mansur 124
Kiai (KH) M. Ihya Ulumiddin of Ma'had Nurul Haromain 184
Kasan Besari 126
Kiai Marzuki Tanara-Serang 118
Kiai, Muhaimin, Abdullah 96, 98, 148
Kiai (KH) Muhammad Arwani Amin 181
Kiai (KH) Muhammad Cholil Nafis 163, 174, 182
Kiai Muhammad, Darwis 124
Kiai Muhammad Masyhuri Naim 163, 174
Kiai Muhammad Zubair 175
Kiai Mukhtar Palembang 130
Kiai (KH) Muslih Abdul Karim 174
Kiai Muslih Mranggen 68
Kiai Ni'am 181–2
Kiai Raden Asnawi 175
Kiai Raden Hambali 175
Kiai Rasyim Jogjakarta 163
Kiai Ridwan Abdullah 175
Kiai Ridwan Mujahid 113, 175
Kiai Sadzili Kaloran-Serang 118
Kiai Sahal Banten 122
Kiai Said Aqil Siradj 174–5, 185
Kiai Said Jauhari Jember 163, 174
Kiai Saleh Darat Semarang 68–9, 113
  Islamic texts in Arab Pegon 68
Kiai Sirojan Wates 163
Kiai Syafii Pijoro Negoro bin Kiai Guru Muhammad Sulaiman Singonegoro 66
Kiai Syukron Makmun 181
Kiai Thalhah bin Talabuddin of Cirebon 116, 118
Kiai Tubagus Ismail 118
Kiai Umar Abdul Manan 181
Kiai Umar bin Harun 120
Kiai Wahab Chasbullah Tambakberas 68, 113, 120, 127, 175
Kiai Wasith 118
Kiai Yasin Barhamin 130
Kiai Yusuf Purwakarta 122
Kiai Zubair Sarang 135

King Abdul Aziz University 132, 146–7
King Abdullah University of Sciences and
    Technology 83, 104, 108, 145, 147
    Tatweer Project" 109
Kingdom Holding Company (KHC) 45
King Fahd University of Petroleum and
    Minerals (KFUPM) 83, 104, 145,
    147, 150, 152, 154–5
King of Hijaz 124
King Saud University 83, 88, 104, 145, 147,
    150, 152, 154, 164, 179
kitab kuning 152
kitab (*pl.* kutub) 152
Komisi Perlindungan Anak Indonesia
    (KPAI) 181
Komite Hijaz 31
Kulliyyat al-Qur'an wa al-Dirasat al-
    Islamiyyah 180
Kutbi, Sayyid Amin 95

Laffan, Michael 32, 53, 57, 65, 71, 117–18,
    123, 125, 139
Lajnah al-Khairiyya 83
langgar 66
Lasem, Muhammad Maksum 127
Laskar Jihad 166–7
Laskar Jihad 83–4, 166–7
learning institutions, Arabian peninsula
    88–93
Leiser, Gary 90, 92
Lembaga Dakwah Kampus 153
Lembaga Ilmu Pengetahuan Islam dan
    Bahasa Arab (LIPIA) 146–7, 156,
    158, 161–2, 164, 166–7, 170
Lembaga Pengajaran Bahasa Arab, or
    LPBA 146
Lewis, Bernard 1
lihya 7, 74
Lim, Merlyna 28
Lindh, John Walker 141
LIPIA (Lembaga Ilmu Pengetahuan Islam
    dan Bahasa Arab) 21, 36, 48, 80–3,
    146–7, 152, 156, 161–2, 164, 166–7,
    170
Lombard, Denys 16
Lombok, Muhammad Amin 118
Lopa, Baharuddin 101
Low, Michael Christopher 33
Lucking, Mirjam 8

Machmudi, Yon 39, 42–5, 122
madhhab 27
madhhab (*pl.* madhahib) 27, 31, 65, 82,
    90, 105, 133–5, 141, 159, 183
Madrasah al-Arsufi 94
Madrasah al-Bashithiyah 95
Madrasah al-Falah 95, 101
Madrasah Aliyah al-Ikhlas 152
Madrasah Aliyah Sulamul Huda 152
Madrasah al-Sanjariyah 95
Madrasah al-Sulaimaniyah 95
Madrasah al-Usrufiyah 95
Madrasah Ibtidaiyah li al-Banat al-
    Ahliyah 99–100, 129, 148
Madrasah Indonesia al-Makiyyah (MIM)
    99–100, 104, 148
Madrasah Khuttab al-Banat 18, 100, 129
Madrasah of Abu Ali Abi Zakariyya 94
Madrasah of al-Malik al-Mansur 95
Madrasah of al-Nihawandi 94
Madrasah of Amir al-Zanjili 94
Madrasah of Amir Fakhruddin al-Shalah
    95
Madrasah of Ibn al-Haddad al-Mahdawi
    94–5
Madrasah of Muzaffar al-Din 94
madrasah (*pl.* madaris) 3, 5, 14, 17–18,
    22–4, 31, 35–6, 37, 50, 54–5, 66, 71,
    80, 81, 86, 88–9, 90–104, 110, 112,
    118–120, 128–30, 135, 139–40, 146,
    148, 152, 166, 169, 176
    use of the term 90
Madrasah Shaulatiyah 93–8, 101, 130,
    146, 152
Madrasah Tab al-Zaman al-Habashiyya
    94–5
ma'had 23, 24, 80, 89, 94, 99, 101–3, 109,
    128–9, 148, 157, 169, 171, 184
Ma'had Al Birr 157
Ma'had al-Mu'allimat al-Ahliyah 99, 129,
    148
Ma'had al-Ukhuwah 171
Mah'ad Aly Arrayah 152
Ma'had Dar al-Hadith 169
Ma'had/Halaqah al-Haram 101
Ma'had Ibnu Abbas 171
Ma'had Imam Bukhari 171
Ma'had Jamilurrahman al-Salafi 171
Ma'had Shaikh Ismail 101

Mahmud bin Abdulrahman Zuhdi 96
Mahmud bin Kanaan, al-Palembani 122
Mahmud bin Kinnan Shaikh, Palembang 121
Mahri, Faisal Usamah 173
majelis al-ilm 102, 104, 130
Majelis al-Nadar 88
Majid, Abdul 98
Majlis al-'Ilm 88
Majmaah University 146
makafiyat 15
Makdisi, George 89–91
maksiat 165
Maksum, Hasan 124
Malik, Muhamamd Abdul 116
Maliki 24, 31, 90, 102, 105, 128, 134, 135, 157, 175, 193
Mamduh, Mahmud Said Shaikh 98
Mamluk Dynasty 92
manaqiban 173
Mangkuto, Datuk Rangkayo 123
Mansur, Ziyad M. 15
Mansuri, Ahmad 98
Markaz Ta'lim al-Lughah al-Arabiyyah 180
Marsudi, Retno 46
Masjid Abdullah bin Muhsin al-Attas 102
Masjid al-Haram 7–8, 31, 92–6, 101–2, 111, 122, 133, 135, 139, 144, 180. *See also* Mosque Haram
masjid jami' 89
Masjid Jami' al-Mahdi 89
Masjid Jami' al-Mansur 89
Masjid Jami' al-Qasr 89
Masjid Nabawi 89, 92–4, 101–2, 111, 115, 133, 135, 144, 155, 172
Masjumi 73, 76, 78
Masud, Muhammad Khalid. 9, 11
Masyarakat Indonesia di Mesir 140
Masyumi 21, 31
Mataram, Muhammad Siddik 118
Maududi, Abu A'la 107
maulid 61, 119, 185
Mauludan (*or* barzanjenan *and* dhiba'an) 173
Mbah Shambu (Sayyid Abdurrahman) 120
Mecca. *See also* Hajj pilgrimage; Masjid Al-Haram
    second Wahhabi conquest 61
    Wahhabi movement 64

Mecca's Shafi'i mufti 127
Meijer, Roel 18
Michael Laffan 139
Minangkabau, Shaikh Ahmad Khatib 116, 121, 123–6, 134
Miskin, Haji (of Luhak Agam) 58, 63–4
Mobini-Kesheh, Watalie 166
Mohammed V University 143
Mohsin al-Abbad, Shaikh Abdul 183
monotheism 74
Mortel, Richard T. 90, 94
Mosque Haram 39, 92–3, 102–3, 105
muallaf 187
muamalah (*pl.* muamalat) 201
mudarris 90
mudir 98
Mufid TV 83
Mufti Muhammad bin Ibrahim, al-Shaikh 107
Muhamamd Arifin bin Badri 162
Muhammad bin Abdul Karim al-Salman 93
Muhammad bin Abdul Karim, al-Sammani 116
Muhammad bin Idris al-Shafii 80
Muhammad bin Sulaiman, al-Kurdi 93, 116
Muhammad, Prophet 14–15, 17, 31, 36, 49, 60–1, 68, 71, 74–5, 94, 102, 108–9, 123, 130, 144, 153–5, 159, 172, 179–81
Muhammad, Sayyid 127–8, 135
Muhammad al-Kurani, Abu Tahir 53
Muhammad bin Abdul Wahhab 163
Muhammad bin Isa Padang 183
Muhammad bin Khalifah al-Tamimi 170
Muhammad bin Muhammad al-Jawi 116
Muhammad bin Nayef (Prince) 47
Muhammad bin Umar al-Sumbawi 115, 118–19
Muhammad ibn al-Qayyim al-Jauziyyah 164
Muhammad ibn al-Uthaymin 82, 156
Muhammad Ismail bin Abdul Rahim 117
Muhammadiyah 73, 124, 137, 139, 153, 165, 170
Muhammadiyah University of Surakarta 170
Muhammad Mahfud bin Abdullah al-Turmusi Termas, Kiai Mahfud

(Termas, Kiai Mahfudz) 67, 69, 102, 116, 121, 126–8, 135, 183
Muhammad Mukhtar bin 'Atharid al-Bughuri 115, 120
Muhammad Nawawi bin Umar al-Bantani 53, 115
Muhammad, Prophet 144, 153–5, 159, 172, 179, 181
Muhammad Surur bin Nayef Zain al-Abidin 168
Muhammad Uhid bin Idris al-Bughuri 115
Muhammadun 163, 174
Muhammad Yasin bin Muhammad Isa al-Fadani 96–100, 104, 115, 128
Muhammad Zainuddin
 Siraj al-Huda 119
Muharram policy 40
Muhsin al-Abbad, Shaikh Abdul 171
Muhsin bin Ali al-Musawa 96
Mujani, Saiful 84
Mukhtar bin Utsman, Makhdum 96
Mukhtar, Tengku 98
mukim (*pl.* mukimin) 33–5, 43, 71
Munawar, Said Agil 163, 174, 181
Mungka, Shaikh Muhammad Sa'ad 125
Muqbil bin Hadi al-Wadi'i 166, 169
murid 63, 117
mursyid 117
Muslim Brotherhood of Egypt (Ikhwanul Muslimin 79
Muslims
 imagined communities 12
 Indonesians to Arabia 16–18
 learning centers 4–5, 15, 17–18
 trade routes in Indian Ocean 16
 travel, purpose of 7–18
Muslim World League (the Rabita) 79–80
Musthafa, Ashim 163
Mu'tazilism 91

Nafi, Basheer M. 18, 75
Nagari, Abdul Latif Khatib 123
Nahdlatul Ulama (NU) 27, 30, 65, 67, 73–4, 80, 97, 100–1, 113, 120, 124, 127, 130, 137, 139, 153, 156, 159, 165, 175, 178, 180, 195
Nahdliyyin 159, 180, 185
Najdi occupation of Hijaz in 1803 60

Najmuddin, Umar bin Fahd 94
Naqshabandiya 11, 54, 56, 62–3, 126, 134
Nasir, Bachtiar 158, 162
Nasser, Gamal Abdel 76–7, 106, 149
National Coalition of Anti-Shia Movement 84
Natsir, Muhammad 31, 73, 79, 149
Nawab, Mohamed 28, 73, 80
neo-Salafism 74–81
 primary concerns 75
Netherland East Indies Company (VOC) 33
Netton, Ian Richard 13, 15
New Order 28, 38, 57, 78–80, 84, 177–8, 187, 193
Nida, Abu 162, 167–9
Nilan, Pam 65
niqab 7, 74
niqash 94
Nizamiyya of Baghdad 90–1
non-Hadrami Arabs 30
Noorhaidi Hasan 164
Nu'man, Fachruddin 163
Nurcholish Madjid 187
Nurcu (Jamaat al-Nur) 143
Nur Ismail, Muhammad 124

Ochsenwald, William 75
Ogush Turk Sunni Muslim kingdom 90
Oki Muraza 131–2
Okruhlik, Gwenn 107
Old Order government 28, 78–9, 193
orang/kaum hitam (black people) 59
orang/kaum putih (white people) 59
Organizations of Islamic Cooperation (OIC) 45, 79–80
Osama bin Laden 141
Ottoman empire 33–4, 69–71, 77, 79, 93–5, 105, 133, 209 n.2

Pacific Countries Social and Economic Solidarity Association (PASIAD) 143
Padri movement 58–62, 64–5, 125
 origin of the term Padri 58–9
 "Wahhabi-centered thesis" 62, 64
Padri War 62, 70
pahala 105, 132, 154
pahlawan devisa 42

Pahlavi, Shah Muhammad Reza 81
Pajang Sultanate 120
Pamijahan, Abdul Muhyi Waliyullah 113
Pancasila 84–5, 100, 163, 177
Panda, Ankit 47
Pandegelang, Tubagus Falak 118
Pan-Islamism 21, 33, 65, 69–74, 77, 86, 145
Panji Sidarjo, Abdul Muhit 127
Partai Keadilan dan Kesejahteraan 153
Partai Kebangkitan Bangsa 153
Partai Komunis Indonesia 73
Partai Nasionalis Indonesia 73
Pasha, Sharif Ali Abdullah 124
Patrick, Neil 29
Pearson, Michael N. 30
Pelajar Islam Indonesia 140
Pembantu Rumah Tangga (PRT) 40
Pemerintahan Revolusioner Republik Indonesia (PRRI) 78
pengajian 3, 151, 157, 172, 174
Perak, Yakub Shaikh 97
Perang Padri 125
Perda Shariat 162–3
Perda Syariat 85
Pergerakan Mahasiswa Islam Indonesia (PMII) 153, 184
Perguruan Tinggi Ilmu Al-Qur'an (PTIQ) 181
Perhimpunan Pelajar Indonesia (PPI) 140, 142, 147, 185
Perkumpulan Kemerdekaan Indonesia 34
Persatuan Islam (Islamic Union) 73, 137, 79
Persatuan Pelajar dan Mahasiswa Indonesia, or PPMI 140, 185
Persatuan Tarbiyah Islamiyah (Perti) 137
Pesantren al-Furqan 167
Pesantren al-Mukmin 167
Pesantren al-Munawwir Kerapyak 180
Pesantren Darun Najah 103, 157
Pesantren Fitra Al Alam Al Islamy (FIWA) 36–7
Pesantren Gontor 103
Pesantren Ihya al-Sunnah 166, 169
Pesantren Islam al-Irsyad 172
Pesantren Lirboyo 176, 180
pesantren (pondok pesantren) 4, 7, 17, 31, 36–7, 65–9, 80, 83, 86, 89–90, 94, 103, 113, 117–18, 120, 123, 126–8, 146, 152, 157, 159, 166–7, 169–70, 174–6, 179–80, 183–4
Pesantren Tebuireng 127, 179
pesantren tradition (Java) 65–9
　　takhassus 66
　　*tanah perdikan*8 66
Pesantren Wataniyya Islamiyya 167
Peters, F. E. 9
Phillips, Sarah 141–2
Piscatori, James 5, 10–14, 136
Pondok Modern Gontor 152, 157
Pondok Pesantren al-Amien Penduran 152
Pondok Pesantren al-Anwar 152
Pondok Pesantren al-Ikhlas 152
Pondok Pesantren Al-Kautsar (Lombok) 152, 163, 174
Pondok Pesantren Dar al-Qur'an 180
Pondok Pesantren Darus Sunah 179
Pondok Pesantren Hidayatullah 157
Pondok Pesantren Imam Bukhari 157
Pondok Pesantren Islamic Center Bin Baz 37, 83
Pondok Pesantren Khusnul Khotimah 157
Pondok Pesantren Rafah 152
Pondok Pesantren Tebu Ireng 152
Pontang, Shaikh Abu Bakar 118
Pontianak, Usman bin Shihabuddin 115
Prasetyo Edi 131–2
Preuschaft, Menno 29, 191
Princess Nora University 133
Prince Sultan University 147
Prokop, Michaela 106–7
puasa 151
Purnama, Basuki Tjahaja 159, 162
Pustaka al-Sunnah 169
Putu Danu Raharja 131

Qadhi Yahya Aman al-Makki 127
qadi (*pl.* qadis) 69, 102
Qadiriya 11, 134
Qadiriyyah-Naqshabandiyyah 54, 117–18, 134
Qassim University 146
qibla 67
Qishashiyya 119
Qobrine, Sidi Muhammad Bou 11
Qousan Community for Training 153
Queensland University of Technology 131

Qur'an 3, 13–16, 23, 31, 37, 42
Qushshashi, Shaikh Ahmad 56
Qutub, Sayyid 168

Rabitat al-'Alam al-Islami (Rabita-Muslim World League) 77–8
Rachman, Abd 6, 66–8, 67, 89, 112
  "The Pesantren Architects and Their Socio-Religious Teachings (1850–1950)." 66
Raden Ronggowarsito 126
Raffles, Sir Thomas Stamford
  The History of Java 33
Rahim, Muhammad Isma'il bin Abdul 117
rahmah 44, 181
Rahman, Fazlur 53, 58, 64, 68, 116, 142, 163, 166, 181
Rahman, Haji Abdur (of Piobang) 58, 64
Rahmat, Imdadun 163, 174, 180
Rahmat, Muhammad Imdadun 182
Rahmat Allah Kairawi (1818–1890) 71
rahmatan li al-alamin 181
Rahmatullah bin Khalil al-Utsmani al-Hindi 95–6
Ra'is Shuriyah 130
Rakhmat, Muhammad Zulfikar 143
Raphaeli, Nimrod 18
Rashid Rida, Muhammad 163
Rasul, Haji 124
Ratha, Dilip 37
Raudlatul Munadzirin 120
Razak, Shaikh Abdur 131
Reid, Anthony 59, 62, 64, 69, 72
ribat 5, 22–3, 35, 87, 89–90, 93–4, 101–3, 110, 146, 151–2, 159
Ribat Abdurrahman bin Hasan al-Jufri (Ribat al-Jufri) 101
Ribat Sayyid Alawi 146, 151–2, 159
Ricklefs, Merle C. 16, 59, 63, 125
Riddell, Peter 53
ridha 15, 136
Ridwan, Ahmad 162
rihla 1–2, 5–7, 7, 10, 12–17, 14, 57, 112
  and learning tradition in Islam 13–16
  scholarship shortcomings on 5–7
rihla 'ilmiyyah 57
risywah siyasiyah 177
riwaq system 94
Rizieq Syihab 162, 164–6, 169

Rodja TV 83
Roff, William R. 57
Rofi'i, Ahmad 174
Rowah, Abdul Fattah 115
Roy, Oliver 76, 140
Rub al-Tarim 141
Rubat al- Aidrous 141
Rubat al-Batah 141
Rubat al-Idreesy 141
Rubath al-Jufri 108
Rubat Tarim 141
Rubat Yahia 141
Rudianto, Agus 168
ruh 101

SABIC 43
sadah 30, 69, 159, 181
Sa'id al-Hadrami, Shaik Muhammad 68
Salafi da'wa (Islamic propagation) movement 74, 76
  neo-fundamentalism 76
Salafism 4, 7, 18, 20, 22, 25, 27, 36, 74–80, 82–3, 86, 103, 106–7, 109, 112, 130–1, 145, 154, 156, 158–60, 163–4, 171, 173, 180, 186, 194
  -Wahhabism 75, 77–9, 82–5, 103, 106
"Salafis" or "Hanbalites" 75. *see also* Wahhabism
salafiyyah 37, 159
salaf (*pl.* aslaf) al-salih 16, 37, 60, 75, 133, 159, 172
Salamullah 165
salat 151
Saleh, Khairul 131–2
Saleh, Muhammad 124
Salim, Agus 124
Salleh, Mohd Afandi 58, 60
Salman, bin Abdulazi Al Saud (King) 25–6, 46, 147
Samudera, Pasai 16
sanad 128, 154
santri 59, 65–6, 68, 120
Sanusi, Dzulqarnain M. 169, 173
SAPTCO 41
Sarang, Zubair Shaikh 102
Sarekat Dagang Islam 73
Sarekat Islam 73
Satariyah 165

Saudi Arabia. *See also specific Indonesian entries*
  "educational policy" 108
  Indonesian schools 96–101
  learning institutions in the past 88–93
Saudi Arabia-trained Indonesian Islamic scholars
  conservatism and progressivism 182–6
  moderates and progressives 174–82
  radicals and conservatives 163–74
  Saudi alumni's role 186–9
Saudi Aramco 26, 43
Saudi ulama 141, 169
Saulatiyya Madrasah 71
SAUNESA (Saudi Arabia–Indonesia) 45
Sayyaf, Abdul Rasul 166
Sayyid Abu Bakr bin Sayyid Muhammad Shata 68
Sayyid Alawi bin Abbas al-Maliki 68, 120, 183
Sayyid Alawi family 151
Sayyid Ali bin Ali, al-Habsyi 122
Sayyid Hamid bin Alawi al-Kaff Banjarmasin 129
Sayyid Hussein bin Muhammad bin Hussein al-Habshi 127
Sayyid Muhammad Amin bin Ahmad Ridwan al-Madani 127
sayyid (*pl.* sadah) 23–4, 30, 68, 95–6, 98, 101–3, 109, 115–22, 127–9, 135, 146, 148, 151–2, 159, 163, 168, 183–4
Schrieke, B. J. O. 61
Second World War 17, 34–5, 77, 111, 193
sekolah 22, 83, 100–1, 110, 131, 148, 152, 169–70, 173, 179
Sekolah Indonesia Jeddah (SIJ) 100–1, 148
Sekolah Indonesia Makkah (SIM) 101, 110, 131, 148
Sekolah Indonesia Pancasila 100
Sekolah Indonesia Riyadh 100–1, 131, 148
Sekolah Tinggi Agama Islam (STAI) 152, 173
Sekolah Tinggi Agama Islam Ali bin Abi Thalib 83
Sekolah Tinggi Dirasat Islamiyat Imam Syafii (STDIIS) 83, 169–70, 172–3
Selim I, Sultan 133
Seljuq Dynasty 90–1

Shadhiliyya 11, 134
Shafii maddhab 31, 54, 56, 67–8, 80, 90, 96, 119, 124, 127, 130, 134, 159, 170
  Islamic law 54
Shafiite or Shafi`i *fiqh* 80
Shahin, Emad Eldin 164
Shaik Ahmad bin Sayyid Abd al-Rahman al-Nahrawi 68
Shaikh Abdul Aziz bin Abdullah bin Baz 75, 82, 131, 168, 170, 172, 183
Shaikh Abdul Mohsin bin Hamad al-Abbad al-Badr 170, 172
Shaikh Abdulrahman bin Shalih al-Dahsy 183
Shaikh Abdur Razak bin Abdul Muhsin al-Abbad 131, 172, 183
Shaikh Abu Bakar bin Muhammad al-Shatha 126
Shaikh Ahmad bin Yahya al-Najmi 169
Shaikh Bin Baz 135
Shaikh Dahlan, Ahmad Zaini 68, 122, 183
Shaikh Hasan bin Muhammad bin Abbas al-Maliki 183
Shaikh Ibrahim bin Amir al-Ruhaily 170
Shaikh Khalifah bin Hamd al-Nabhani al-Maliki 183
Shaikh Mahmud bin Uqid Padang 128
Shaikh Muhammad bin Sulaiman Hasbullah al-Makki 124, 183
Shaikh Muhammad ibn Abd al-Wahhab 75–6, 82
Shaikh Muhammad ibn al-Uthaymeen 183
Shaikh Muqbil bin Hadi al-Wadi'i 141, 166, 169
Shaikh Rabi' bin Hadi al-Madkhali 169, 171
Shaikh Shalih bin Abdillah Al Fauzan 169
Shaikh Zaid bin Muhammad bin Hadi al-Madkhali 169
Shaikh Zubair bin Ahmad al-Filfilani 96, 120
Shalih bin Sa'ad al-Suhaimi 170
Shamaniyya 134
sharia 63–5, 84–5, 88, 107, 153, 162, 167, 170, 179, 182
Sharif Husein bin Ali Pasha 124
sharif (*pl.* ashraf) 30, 69, 93, 124, 159
Shatariyyah 54, 56, 62–3

Shatta, Abu Shaikh 120
Shihabuddin bin Abdullah, Muhammad 113
sheikh (*pl.* shuyukh *or* mashayikh) 128
Shiism 91
shirk 10, 75, 168, 170
Shuaib bin Abdulkarim al-Maghribi 125
Siddiq bin Umar Khan 116
silsilah 118
Silvey, Rachel 6, 39–40, 42
sirah 102, 153
sirah (Prophet Muhammad's biography) 102
Sirhindi, Ahmad 56
SMAIT Darul Hikmah 152
Smith, Larry 105
Smith, Steve 191
Sofwan, Chamsaha 167
sopir pribadi 41
Soviet–Afghan War 82
Spencer, Robert 1
STAI al-Mawaddah 152
STAIMAFA (Sekolah Tinggi Agama Islam Mathali'ul Falah in Pati) 152
STAIN 187
Steenbrink, Karel A. 59, 94
STIT Al- Marhalah 152
Subki, Imam 127
Sufi master or a *tarekat* guru 54–5, 63
Sufism 10–11, 16, 34, 112
    in Java and Sumatra 55
    orders 54
    tarekats 63
    tasawuf falsafi 55
Suharto
    collapse of 84–5
Sukaraja, Muhammad Ilyas 116
Sukarno 28, 31, 76, 78, 193
Sukoyo, Yeremia 181
Sulaiman bin Salimullah al-Ruhaili 170
Sulayman al-Rajhi College 147
Sumanto Al Qurtuby 131
Sumatran Islam 58
Sumbawa, Umar Shaikh 119
Sunbulawi, Shaikh Yusuf 68
sunna 15–16
    revival of 75
Sunnah (*or* Sunna) 166–7, 169–71
Sunni Islam university 140

Sunniism 67
Sunni-Shafi'i 142
Sunni-Shafi'ite schools 65–6
Sunyoto, Agus 120
Surabaya 83
Surat Keterangan Jalaluddin 59
surau (traditional Islamic learning) 63–4
Suryalaya, Ajengan Abdullah Mubarak 118
Syafii, Imam 170
Syamhudi, Khalid 163, 170
Syamsuddin, Zainal Abidin 163
Syarif Hidayatullah State Islamic University 182
Syatha, Sayyid Bakri 183
Syatha, Shaikh Abu Bakar 124
Syatha, Shaikh Usman 124

ta'allum 15
tabarrukan 15
Tablighi Jamaat 16
tafsir 56, 68, 90, 102, 108, 123, 153, 179
Tagliacozzo, Eric 29
tahlilan 159, 173
Taibah University 130, 146
Taimiyya, Ibn 2, 76
Talib, Ja'far Umar 162–9
Taman Pendidikan Al-Quran (TPQ) 101
Taman Pendidikan Qur'an Hidayatus Shibyan 153
Tamrin Banjar, Shaikh Muhammad Husni 129
Tangban, O. E. 8
Tapper, Nancy 11
Taqiyuddin Muhammad bin Ahmad al-Fasi 94
taqlid 61, 76
tarekat 67
tarikh 153
tariqa (*pl.* turuq; *Indonesian:* tarekat) 11, 34, 61, 66, 70, 89, 108, 117–19, 125, 134, 162, 180
Tarmizi, Erwandi 162, 170
tasamuh 181
tasawuf 55, 89, 117, 119, 162
tasawuf falsafi 55
Taslim, Abdullah 162
tauhid 36, 58, 68, 75–6, 135, 153, 170
tawasuth 181

Tayfur, M. Fatih 191
Tayyip, Janan Muhamamd 99, 148
Tenaga Kerja Wanita 40
Tengku Mukhtar 148
thalab al-ilm 2, 14, 92, 136, 154
Thariqat Naqsabandiyah al-Khalidiyah 125
Thawab 7
Tobagus Mansyur 66
TOEFL (Test of English as a Foreign Language) 147, 152
Torrance, Arthur 8–9
Touati, Houari 5, 15
traditionalism 105, 112, 114
tsanawiyyah (madrasah) 3, 5, 14, 17–18, 22–4, 31, 35–6, 37, 50, 54–5, 66, 71, 80, 81, 86, 88–9, 90–104, 110, 112, 118–120, 128–30, 135, 139–40, 146, 148, 152, 166, 169, 176
tsaqafah al-Islamiyyah 153
Tuanku Imam Bondjol 62, 125, 207 n.4
Tuanku Nan Tuo 64
tuanku shaikhs 64
Tuasikal, Muhamamd Abduh 162
turbans *(imamah)* 74

Uhid Bogor, Shaikh Abdullah 128
UIN 152, 181, 187
UIN Alauddin 152
UIN Malang 152
UIN Sunan Kalijaga 152
UIN Syarif Hidayatullah 181
ulama (*sing.* 'alim) 6, 10, 18, 23–4, 27, 30–1, 37, 44–5, 53–7, 59, 61, 65–70, 72–4, 76, 80, 83, 86, 89–90, 93, 95–108, 113–146, 153, 156–7, 159, 162, 165, 169–70, 175, 178–80, 182, 194–5
Ulil Abshar-Abdalla 163, 174, 182
Ulum, Amirul 120–4, 128–9
Umam, Saiful 68, 167
Umar bin Harun, Rembang 122
Umar, Muhammad 119
Umar, Muhammad Thaib 124
Umar, Setiyadi 131
Umm al-Qura University 80, 88, 102–3, 109, 135, 145–6, 149–50, 174–6, 181
umma (*or* ummah) 83–4, 145, 159

umra (umrah) 7–8, 11–13, 12, 23, 29, 30, 34–5, 39, 42, 51, 92, 104–5, 130–1, 135, 144, 154–5, 160, 179, 192
Undang-Undang Dasar [UUD] 84
United Islamic Cultural Center of Indonesia (UICCI) 143
universitas 148, 152, 171, 176, 178
Universitas Gadjah Mada 152
Universitas Ibnu Khaldun Bogor 152
Universitas Islam Malang 176
Universitas Islam Negeri Syarif Hidayatullah 176
Universitas Muslim Indonesia 171
Universitas Negeri Yogyakarta 152
Universitas Sultan Ageng Tirtayasa 152
Universitas Terbuka 148
Universitas Wahid Hasyim 152
Universiti Tun Abdul Razak 171
University of Ibn Khaldun 170
University of Khartoum 143
University of Sidi Mohammed Ben Abdellah 143
Usamah Faisal Mahri 168
ushuluddin 153, 170
Usman bin Affan, Caliph 95
Usman Pontianak (al-Sarawaki Usman bin Shihabuddin al-Funtiyani)
    Taj al-Arus 119
    Tanwir al-Qulub 119
Usman Salih 173
Ustadah Soraya 130–1
Ustad Firanda 131
Ustad Indra 173
usul al-fiqh 126–8, 153, 164, 170, 195

Van Bruinessen, Martin 30, 56, 60–1, 65, 69, 71, 81, 85, 94–5, 117–19, 127–8
Van Doorn-Harder, Nelly 10
Van Niel, Robert 69, 71
Veth, P. J. 59–62
Voll, John 18, 75
Vredenbregt, Jacob 30

Wafa, Muhammad Ali 118, 180
Wahdah Islamiyah 82
Wahda Islamiyya 83
wahdat al-shuhud 56
wahdat al-wujud 55–6

Wahhabism 18, 20, 25, 33, 58–62, 64,
    75–80, 82–3, 86, 106–7, 109, 131,
    145, 156, 158–60, 163–4, 166, 171,
    180. see also Padri movement. *see
    also* Salafism
Wahib, Ahmad Bunyan 74
Wahid, Din 65, 80, 127, 152, 162, 165, 175
Wahid, Hidayat Nur 162
Wahid, KH Abdurrahman 127, 175
waqf 94, 104
wasatiyyah (wasat) 196
Washliyah 137
Wasitho, Muhammad 163
wataniyya 167
Watt, Montgomery 9
Wawan Gunawan 163
Wha, Min Byung 15
Whilst Ahmad Khatib 124
White, Sally 164
Widodo, Joko 26, 45–6, 159
Witkam, Jan Just 32
wong alim 113
wong nasional 172
wong santri 59
Woodward, Mark 138, 166
World Assembly of Muslim Youth 81
World Council of Mosques 81
World Muslim Congress 77

Yamenia University 141
Yaqub, Ali Mustafa 179
Yasin, Shaikh Muhammad 128, 135
Yasin bin Isa Padang, Shaikh 96, 102, 108,
    116–17, 121, 148
Yasmeen, Samina 141–2

Yayasan al-Najiyya 170
Yayasan al-Raudhah 170
Yayasan Darul Iman 170
Yayasan Ibnul Qayyim 170
Yayasan Imam Syafii 170
Yayasan Maghfirah Bina Ummat (YMBU)
    157
Yazid bin Abdul Qadir Jawas 162
Yemen's Salafi 141–2, 166
Yogyakarta 152, 169, 170–2, 176, 180,
    188
Yose Kadrin 131–2
Youth Care International 153
YPIA (Yayasan Pendidikan Islam al-
    Atsari) 82
Yunus, H. Mahmud 94
Yusuf, Abu Ubaidah 162
Yusuf al-Makassari, Shaik 55–6, 70, 93,
    113–14
Yusuf bin Arshad, al-Banjari 122

Zaen, Abdullah 162, 170
Zain, Muhammad 124
Zainuddin, Muhammad
    Minhaj al-Salam 119
Zainuddin Abdul Basith ibn Khalil 92
Zainuddin bin Badawi 122
Zakaria, Hafiz 58, 121
Zawawi, Ahmad 168
zawiya (*pl.* zawaya) 89
ziyara 7, 10–13, 11–13, 61, 74, 144
Zubair, Najih Maimun 162
Zubair bin Ahmad 96
Zubdat al-Asrar 57
Zul Akmal, Abu Munzir 168

www.ingramcontent.com/pod-product-compliance
Lightning Source LLC
Chambersburg PA
CBHW050325020526
44117CB00031B/1797